SAM
RAYBURN

ALSO BY ALFRED STEINBERG

THE BOSSES
SAM JOHNSON'S BOY: *A Close-up of the President from Texas*
THE FIRST TEN: *The Founding Presidents and Their Administrations*
THE MAN FROM MISSOURI: *The Life and Times of Harry S. Truman*
MRS. R: *The Life of Eleanor Roosevelt*
MY NAME IS TOM CONNALLY (with Senator Tom Connally)

"Lives to Remember" series
Richard Byrd
Dwight Eisenhower
Herbert Hoover
Douglas MacArthur
James Madison
John Adams
John Marshall
Eleanor Roosevelt
Harry Truman
Daniel Webster
Woodrow Wilson
The Kennedy Brothers

SAM RAYBURN

A Biography

ALFRED STEINBERG

HAWTHORN BOOKS, INC.
PUBLISHERS/*New York*

SAM RAYBURN

Library of Congress Catalog Card Number: 74-3604
ISBN: 0-8015-5210-9

First printing, May 1975
Second printing, July 1975

For
James Neyland,
a fine editor and Rayburn Texan

History is many times unjust and nearly as many times a lying sycophantic dream of some fellow who knew only from hearsay.

—Letter Sam Rayburn
to W. A. Thomas,
January 10, 1919

I would rather link my name indelibly with the living pulsing history of my country and not be forgotten than to have anything else
on earth.

—Letter Sam Rayburn
to W. A. Thomas
February 19, 1922

Contents

CONTENTS

Preface

I can see him now—the short, stocky, bald man scurrying through the Speaker's lobby in the United States Capitol at one minute to noon. His mouth set sternly, his expressive brown eyes filled with frontier reserve, he rushes toward the doors leading into the big chamber beyond. Congressmen along the way vie to greet him and they show pride when he nods almost imperceptibly in their direction.

Now he is inside the noisy hall and is climbing the stairs to his special place on top of the rostrum. Then his gavel crashes like a thunder clap, and the House of Representatives gets down to business.

Who was Sam Rayburn?

He was Speaker of the House longer than anyone else, and he was by far the greatest. He took so direct a role in the tempestuous public affairs of his nation and for so many decades that he symbolized the continuing, skilled hand at the helm, safeguarding the future. People gained security in the fact that day in and day out, year after year, Mr. Sam was in charge in the House wielding his gavel wisely and authoritatively. For this reason, within his own lifetime he became an American institution.

No other person came close to pushing as much worthwhile legislation through Congress as Sam Rayburn. Only after he died in November 1961 could the actual degree of his importance be measured by the legislative vacuum that followed.

At his work, Rayburn was always the professional, doing his best without a thought to time or distractions. "I love this House," he was fond of saying. He was teacher, tyrant, referee, and father to his changing brood of 434 congressmen. Behind the thick walls of the Capitol, on an average day he talked business with a hundred or more. He held uncounted private conversations with committee chairmen handling legislation and met with entire committees to impress his views on them. Individual congressmen shuttled in and out of his office for his explanations, appeals, promises, advice, and notably apt philosophy.

On the House floor, through his knowledge of the rules, deft timing, a last-minute short speech from the heart when he considered it necessary, but principally from the enormous respect members had for him, he saved many an administration's hide. Yet though he helped Presidents because of the national need, no chief executive ever found him subservient, for he bore his independence as his birthright. "I didn't serve *under* eight Presidents," he said fiercely. "I served *with* eight."

Chiefly because of his Southern origin, Sam Rayburn was robbed of becoming Vice President in 1940 and again in 1944, when he was the most logical candidate to run with Franklin Roosevelt. Of course, had he been on the ticket in 1944, he would have become President. Deprived of his ultimate ambition, Rayburn could have become embittered and made a shambles of presidential administrations that came and went in his time. Instead, starting in 1940 when he moved up from majority leader to Speaker, he was responsible for whatever legislative records Presidents claimed for the next twenty-one years.

Rayburn's story is really the saga of American history in the first six decades of the twentieth century. The two are remarkably entwined. When he won election to the Texas house at the age of twenty-four, it was in the horse and buggy year of 1906. He helped usher in the new age by writing his state's first law to regulate automobile traffic. Thirty-seven years later he helped get a secret appropriation through Congress to build the atomic bomb and bring in the nuclear age; and fifteen years after that he promoted appropriations to push the United States full-blown into the space age.

In between, he was the creative author of innumerable basic laws. They ranged from the Woodrow Wilson era's regulation of railroad securities issuance and the World War I G.I. Act to Franklin Roosevelt's New Deal regulation of the stock market, holding companies, and radio communication, and the establishment of the rural electrification program.

Through it all, Rayburn remained a rare breed—the incorruptible politician amidst the multitude with only lip-service morals. He had contempt for trickery, told no lies, made no threats, gave no false promises. He would not even let anyone buy him a meal. "I am not for sale," he said warningly. At his death he left no savings, stocks or bonds, only farm and ranch lands he had purchased decades earlier when prices were rock-bottom.

In the final appraisal, Rayburn belongs to the tiny, select company of politicians whose careers meet the high standard devised by Henri Bergson—those who "act as men of thought, think as men of action."

Acknowledgments

Much of the material for this book came from talks with political colleagues of Sam Rayburn, a list far too long to detail. Included among those interviewed were presidents, vice presidents, cabinet members, presidential aides, senators, representatives, committee staff employees, Texas politicians, and Mr. Rayburn.

In addition to the politicians who conversed about Rayburn, I should like to acknowledge my great debt to the excellent Sam Rayburn Library at Bonham, Texas. My friend, H. G. Dulaney, the director, always unearthed the missing link I was hunting for in the Speaker's life somewhere in his storehouse of letters, speeches, scrapbooks, audio tapes, films and newspaper files. Also, for their help, I want to thank Mrs. Loyce Rayburn, widow of Rayburn's brother Tom, and Mrs. Lena Cole of the library's staff, and Dr. John R. Jameson of the Texas Historical Commission, who gave me a closeup view of the preserved Rayburn lifestyle at his home.

There is also the large contribution of shared memories from Alla Clary, who worked for Rayburn for forty-two years, and from Lewis Deschler, parliamentarian of the House for almost half a century.

SAM
RAYBURN

1

The Land of Hardship

There was little excitement in the log cabin in the red-hill area of east Tennessee when Martha Waller Rayburn gave birth to a son on January 6, 1882. For Samuel Taliaferro Rayburn, as the infant was named, was already the eighth child and fifth son of a family grubbing out a bleak existence on forty acres of rocky soil near Lenoir on Clinch Creek.

"My parents, especially in the early years, were faced with all the real hardships of farm laborers," Sam Rayburn later reminisced. But hardship was nothing new among the Rayburns, who had migrated from England to Virginia. Sam's grandfather, John Rayburn, had been orphaned as a lad and was taken along to east Tennessee by an uncle who moved there. John Rayburn in turn died when his son, William Marion Rayburn, was six months old, leaving a widow with five children. [1]

Caught up by the need to help keep the family alive, William Marion Rayburn never saw the inside of a schoolroom, and he grew to manhood unable to sign his name. He was twenty in 1861 when Tennessee seceded from the Union, and though his family owned no slaves and was opposed to secession, he joined the Confederate cavalry. For a time he served under Nathan Bedford Forrest, formerly the largest slave trader in the Memphis area, [2] but now an emerging brilliant tactician on the battlefield. Rayburn's good soldiership brought him a captain's commission, but he could not accept it because his illiteracy would keep him from handling the necessary paperwork and map-reading.

After the fighting ended in the spring of 1865, Rayburn set out for home, only to have his horse stolen from him in Knoxville by a gang of neighborhood marauders. This made it necessary for him to trudge the last forty miles home and plunge wearily into the task of rebuilding a farm that had been fair game for thieving guerrillas during the war.

Three years afterward, when he was twenty-eight, he married Martha Clementine Waller, a twenty-one-year-old local girl, and they moved into a mud-chinked log cabin he built in Clinch Valley south of Oak Ridge. Almost a century later Sam Rayburn paid homage to his Waller ancestry by speaking at the marker dedication ceremony for his great-great-grandfather, Colonel George Waller, at Martinsburg, Virginia, on May 6, 1951. [3] Just the opposite of early-day Rayburns, the Waller line was filled wiith outstanding public figures. There was a Waller with William the Conqueror in 1066 when he conquered England; another, Edmund Waller, was poet laureate of England during the reign of Charles II; and Colonel George Waller, a Virginia plantation squire, fought in the Revolution and was present at Cornwallis' surrender to George Washington at Yorktown. Two generations later John Waller, a grandson of the colonel and a justice of the peace in Roane County, Tennessee, married Katherine Pickle, and Sam Rayburn's mother was the eleventh of their thirteen children.

Children came fast on the forty-acre farm, beginning with John Franklin, born in 1869, a year after Martha Waller married William Marion Rayburn. Then came Charles, Katy, Lucinda, twins—Jim and Will—Medibel, followed by Sam. "My mother's sister married a man named Sam Taliaferro in Roane County and my father and mother named me for him," Sam explained his name later. [4]

After Sam there were three more: Dick and Tom, who were born in Tennessee, and finally Abner, the eleventh child, who was born in Texas in 1891 when his mother was forty-four. They lived crowded into "a little old straight up and down house with no porch, just two rooms and a lean-to," said Mose Waller, Sam's cousin. [5]

The hard-pressed father of this large brood depended for his cash crop on the corn he raised, and he set aside precious land to produce the family's food. An extra treat came from the small orchard of "leather-coat" apples near the log house. As soon as they could pick weeds and pull out stones, the children were put into the fields to work, and between seasons they attended a one-room school at Wallerton, a country place named after the Waller clan.

Sam Rayburn's memories of his early years on the Clinch Valley farm were meager. The green fields turned blue in the distance, there were wagon rides to Kingston, the county seat, for supplies, and there were eager rushes for a good view of tooting steamboats with their "ruffle-like funnels" plying the Clinch. He also remembered that he would wash himself in "an old wash pan" and use "an old sack towel" to dry himself. His father had to climb hundreds of feet up a steep hill to bring each bucket of water to the farm.

But he had few other conscious recollections of his life in Tennessee because the Rayburns moved to Texas in 1887 when he was only five years old. The corn farm was not paying its way for the large family, and when Waller and Dickey relatives in Fannin County, northeast Texas, wrote to tell that living was comfortable just south of the Red River, the Rayburns decided to move. Sam's father sold the farm, made a last visit to the Macedonian Primitive Baptist Church he had helped build, hauled his wife and ten children by wagon to Lenoir City and set off on a 1,200-mile whistle-stop trip on the Southern and the Texas and Pacific Railroads.

Looking out the coach window, little Sam later said he saw people "on their trek west, all their earthly belongings heaped on covered wagons, men in plainsmen's outfits with wide-brimmed hats and guns on their shoulders, leading the oxen." [6]

When the Rayburns reached Dodd City, Texas, their kinfolk took them in. But that first day, tired as he was from the long trip, William Marion Rayburn was already anxious to have his own place. A hurried survey of the area led to his purchase of an available forty-acre cotton farm complete with a small frame house in the Flag Springs neighborhood, a few miles south of the small town of Windom. "It was in the black land and rolling sandy loam belt of Texas," said Sam.

Keeping only a few dollars to tide him over, Rayburn made a six hundred-dollar down payment and agreed to pay off the $1,062 balance at 10 percent interest. Just twenty-five miles north of the farm, across the Red River, was the vast Indian Territory that the native Americans called Oklahoma, a land that the United States would "buy" two years later in 1889.

That first year in Texas was miserable. The winter was freezing cold, the summer a broiler, and then came floods and the boll weevil to ruin all the cotton except a measly two and a half bales. Yet the Rayburns somehow survived and kept the farm. In fact, two new additions moved into the crowded little house. Matt Rayburn, as Sam's mother was called, gave birth to Abner, her eleventh and final child, and Uncle Jim Rayburn showed up from Tennessee and was welcomed into a household that already had thirteen members.

Only through overwork, child labor and a willingness to accept harsh living conditions did the Rayburns go on. No one could shirk chores or back-tiring field work, and often children did grown-up tasks. For instance, Sam was only a boy when he began hauling cotton to the gin at Honey Grove. "I've hauled cotton down the road when the mud was so deep it came to the wagon hubs," he once said. [7]

Even with the means for survival, living conditions in rural Texas were grim. There was no electricity or inside plumbing. Wood stoves had to be fed large amounts of timber, water hauled by the bucket from the pump, food stored in damp storm cellars and reading done by the light of flickering kerosene lamps. And there was loneliness for the outside world despite the everpresence of large numbers of brothers and sisters. "Many a time when I was a child and lived way out in the country," Sam later admitted to David Cohn, writing for the *Atlantic Monthly*, "I'd sit on the fence and wish to God that somebody would ride by on a horse or drive by in a buggy—just anybody to relieve my loneliness."[8]

By 1890 the northeastern part of Texas was caught up in the Populist fever of militant agrarianism that swept over the prairie states and the South. In 1880, when money fell into short supply and the market prices of most crops dropped to less than half their previous level, restless farmers had formed the Populist Party to combat Eastern "bloodhounds of money." Populist periodicals and speakers charged that the rich paid no taxes, futures markets were gambling dens, high tariffs on manu-factured goods a way to deprive farm families of such products, and high railroad freight rates on agricultural commodities a weapon to depress market prices.[9]

However, all this ferment passed the Rayburn farm without much notice, even though the family subscribed to the weekly *Louisville Courier-Journal.* For as Sam Rayburn once observed:

> Father's political activity started and ended with the War Between the States. His interest in politics was casual and in-consistent. He did like to talk, however, about the great political issues of his time, frequently about General Lee, and occasionally about Lincoln and Grant. . . His [Robert E. Lee's] framed picture occupied the prominent part of our living room. Aside from Lee, no other American public figure at-tracted his attention. Consequently, my interest in politics arose from elements outside the family environment.[10]

Besides the Civil War, Sam's father had a deep interest in the Bible and prided himself on knowing its contents. One time little Sam argued with him over a Biblical story. The Great Book was produced for corroboration, and the elder Rayburn insisted that the incorrect party should eat his next several meals standing up. Sam lost. "I never argued the Bible after that," he said.[11]

In the Rayburn home, the "Hard-Shell" Baptist strictures of the parents and a matriarchal ruling structure dominated the family's existence. Parents did not openly express love or kiss their children, and their religious code forbade frivolity in the household. "Mother was the stronger of the team," said Sam. "Father was a quiet and modest man who never talked loudly, never had an argument, and never laid a hand on us children. We used to call Father 'Easy Boss,' and we were completely relaxed with him. With Mother, it was different. I think she spanked me more often than I deserved." [12]

Mrs. Rayburn, whom Sam remembered as a woman who "read everything printed," was intent on providing her boys and girls with an education. Sam's father, who had overcome his illiteracy after the Civil War, was equally inclined, and when Sam was eight in 1890 he started school at Burnett, almost two miles west of the farm. This was a typical four-months-a-year, one-room school with several long benches instead of desks and with a teacher whose chief concern besides instructing youngsters was maintaining iron discipline over her one hundred charges. After a time Flag Springs built its own school and Sam transferred there, along with Tom and Dick and his sister Medibel (Meddy).

At that time, the stress in learning was on the rote rather than on the thinking method, and this meant memorizing *McGuffey's Readers*, spelling books and arithmetic tables. One teacher remembered Sam as a "wiry little fellow" who fidgeted constantly. He had to hold him tightly on his lap to teach him to read. Others remembered him as a lad who excelled in spelling bees and always had his homework done. Being thrust into the lively school mix did a great deal to curb Sam's loneliness, and fellow pupils said he joined them in rabbit hunting, jumping into swimming holes and playing baseball when all his farm chores were done.

Sam was not even into his teens when he was introduced to his life's chief passion. This was politics. The introducer was Joseph Weldon Bailey, a handsome, strapping, pushy young man, recently transplanted to Texas. [13] Bailey was born in Mississippi where he acquired a grade school education and a law practice. After serving as a presidential elector in 1884 on the Democratic ticket of Grover Cleveland and Thomas Hendricks, he moved to Gainesville, Texas, the following year.

In 1890, at the age of twenty-seven, he ran in the Democratic primary for the U.S. House of Representatives from the congressional district that included Fannin County where the Rayburns lived. Bailey's opponent was the sitting congressman, Silas Hare, who had fought in the Mexican War and the Civil War and had been chief justice of the New Mexico Territory. Once the campaign started, word spread like a cotton gin fire that Bailey was something special to see and hear, spouting Populism and Texasism in a golden voice, unlike his drab, dull opponent thirty-five years his senior. Reform had grown fashionable in Texas at that time, and Bailey's pitch was similar to that of popular gubernatorial candidate Jim

Hogg, who was pushing hard for state regulation of utilities, railroads, and large corporations.

The word about Bailey even reached the farming community of Flag Springs and into the Rayburn household. The elder Rayburn evinced little interest, but his wife was excited by the political newcomer, and there was much rejoicing when Bailey whipped Hare in the Democratic primary.

It was in 1894 that Congressman Joe Bailey came to Bonham, the county seat of Fannin County, to speak at the covered tent "tabernacle" of the Evangelical Church. When the older Rayburn boys heard about it, they begged their father to let them go. All received permission except Sam because of his youth. He was told to spend the day hitching up the team of horses and hauling wood to the house. Throughout that long Friday the twelve-year-old boy sobbed bitterly while he delivered the logs, and he did not stop until his brothers returned home with the news that Bailey was to give another speech at Bonham the next day.

Sam was up early on Saturday, completing his many chores so that his father would find no excuse to keep him from going to Bonham. This time "Easy Boss" relented; Sam washed his feet under the pump, climbed aboard a mule and set out on the eleven-mile trip. Along the way a heavy rain developed and the road grew almost impassable, but he continued and reached the town.

"I didn't go into that tabernacle," he said.

> I'd never been to Bonham since we bought the farm, and I was scared of all the rich townfolks in their store-bought clothes. But I found a flap in the canvas, and I stuck there like glue while old Joe Bailey made his speech. He went on for two solid hours, and I scarcely drew a breath the whole time. I can still feel the water dripping down my neck. I slipped around to the entrance again when he was through, saw him come out, and ran after him five or six blocks until he got on a streetcar. Then I went home, wondering whether I'd ever be as big a man as Joe Bailey. [14]

That night, while drying his clothes before the fire, he regaled his brothers and sisters with stories about his experiences at Bonham. With a prophecy born of youthful excitement, he predicted that one day he would also become a congressman like Bailey. "This Adonis of a man with a massive brain captured my imagination and became my model," he later said. [15] For a long time afterward the younger Rayburns would sneak close to the barn to hear Sam making political speeches to the cows and hens.

At the turn of the century, few rural youths from large, poor families went to college. In the Rayburn family, Frank (John Franklin) had hoped to become a doctor since his childhood. Finally in 1894, by scrimping and saving, his parents had enough money to pay his way back to Tennessee where he enrolled in the Tennessee Medical College at Knoxville.

Then came lean years with meager cash crops. But despite this situation, when Sam became eighteen in 1900, he made up his mind to go beyond the country school he had attended. He was convinced that, if he did not, he would never realize his goal of going to Washington, and that he would spend his life as a tenant farmer.

He knew he had many assets. He was strong, healthy, confident and eager, and he believed he would somehow find work at college that would pay his tuition and expenses. His mother wanted him to go to college, but the decision was up to his father.

Some time in the past, when he was chagrined that he had no money, his father had told him, "Sam, the only thing I can give you is character." Sam brought up the question of college now when the two were in the cotton field one summer day. He told his father that the school he had in mind was the Mayo Normal School at Commerce, chosen because it was only fourteen miles from home. "I'm not asking you to send me, Paw," he said, when his father made no immediate reply. "I'm asking you to let me go."

"You have my blessing," his father replied. [16]

After the Mayo Normal School accepted him and the day came for him to leave home, Sam had no suitcase to hold his belongings. This necessitated tying up his bundle of rolled clothes with a rope. Farewells were made, and his father drove him by buggy south to Ladonia where he bought a ticket for Sam on the St. Louis and San Francisco. The two, who had no small talk in their makeup, stood around in silence until the train appeared in the station. Sam was about to board when his father suddenly handed him twenty-five dollars. "God knows how he saved it," Sam said later. "He never had any extra money. We earned just enough to live. It broke me up, him handing me that $25. I often wondered what he did without, what sacrifice he and my mother made." [17]

The conductor called out, "All aboard!" and Sam's usually unemotional father grasped his hand and shook it with strong affection. "Sam, be a man!" he told his son, words that returned to Sam's mind at times of crises throughout his life.

The Mayo Normal School, or East Texas Normal College as it was formally called, turned out to be a small, poorly funded school under the inspired leadership of its founder, a short, moustached man named William Leonidas Mayo. It consisted of a handful of buildings on a bleak ten-acre piece of land. But its physical appearance was no indication of its value to the citizens of the area. For Mayo's goal was to produce good teachers for northeast Texas, and his motto for his eleven-year-old college was: "Ceaseless Industry, Fearless Investigation, and Unfettered Thought." [18]

Mayo also gave the school its reputation for helping deserving students attend, no matter how little money they had. "Come one, come all," he beckoned the young people of that area. Tuition was four dollars a month and the dormitory fee for room and board was an additional eight dollars. [19] At this rate Sam could last only two months, but Mayo did not see this as a serious problem when he spoke to the young man. He promptly hired him as the school's bell ringer at five dollars a month and helped him get a job sweeping a public school near the campus to meet the three-dollar-a-month wash bill. In addition, Sam collected another three dollars a month from a local farmer for milking his cows twice daily. When all this failed to meet his total expenses, Mayo told him he could pay the balance later.

The bell-ringing was a far more demanding task than it appeared to be on the surface. Classes lasted forty-five minutes, and Sam had to race from wherever he was on the campus, climb the tower and clang the hand-made 85-pound bell to denote the end of a class. Then exactly five minutes later he was supposed to ring the bell again as the signal to begin the next class, and then he had to run to his own classroom. This process had to be repeated all day.

It was his determination never to miss his bell-ringing that made him a lifelong stickler for promptness. Years later when he found he was going to be late to deliver a speech, he snapped at an assistant who was driving with him there, "I loathe being late. And I hate people who are late." [20]

The day started with morning chapel. Mayo, a licensed Methodist preacher, would take a line from the Bible and spin a sermon around it. Along the way he would shoot out epigrammatic shafts at his listeners, such as "Not whence you came, but whither you are going"; "Not failure but low aim is a crime"; and "It's a disgrace to be remembered for the clothes you wore." Said Sam, "He made a student feel like a criminal if he didn't work to his utmost capacity." [21]

As if his various jobs were not burdensome, Sam also carried an extra load of subjects because he intended to graduate early. Colleges in those years generally had no elective courses and all students were forced to take the same curriculum. Sam's chief interest was history, but he could not concentrate on this subject because he had to take mathematics, chemistry, and physics as well. Mrs. Mayo, a mother of eight children, headed the music department, and she made no effort to teach him to read notes once she found out he was tone-deaf. On the other hand, her husband, who taught several subjects, encouraged Sam to get into every classroom discussion. "You stand up and tell us what you understand about this lesson," he would say. What exasperated him at times about the young man was his "dogged convictions," which he held to like a bulldog. [22]

Even his extra load of classes and outside jobs failed to occupy all his waking hours, despite the seriousness with which he carried out any assignment or task. Classmates remembered him as a fleet outfielder and as a leader of the Oratorical Association and the Philomathean Literary Society on the campus. Since his discovery of Joe Bailey he knew how important the art of public speaking was for the political ambitions he harbored. So, even though he was only a freshman, he was disappointed when he was the runner-up in the Society's speaking contest in 1901. But there was some consolation when E. K. Frieze, a barber in Commerce, told him, "Sam, keep that up and you'll land in Congress some day." [23]

There was also time for the girls, for Sam was a lady's man when he had extra cash to spare. One time he and another young man borrowed a surrey to take two girls for a ride. Out in the countryside the girls insisted that they just had to have some peaches from a certain orchard. When the boys obliged, the angry farmer sicked his dogs on them. Sam lost the seat of his pants in his losing race for the fence.

At the end of Sam's first year at Mayo Normal, he found himself in a financial hole, making it impossible for him to remain in school. Professor Mayo considered his circumstances and agreed that he drop out for a year and work. Mayo suggested that he take the next examination for a teacher's certificate on the grounds that he had already passed enough school subjects to qualify. The written examination proved fairly simple, and Sam had no trouble getting his teacher's certificate. Mayo then helped place him at the one-room school in Greenwood, a town of 250 persons three miles east of Commerce in Hopkins County.

As a schoolmaster, nineteen-year-old Sam Rayburn took his work seriously. Nevertheless, he was a great favorite of the children and their parents. His food expenses were small because he was frequently invited to their homes for dinner. At many houses the special meal for the visiting teacher turned out to be "Hopkins County stew," a dish that made his mouth water. It was concocted by bringing lard to a boil in a large iron pot. Then chicken, pork, bacon and fatback were browned in the lard. Next water, seasoning, turnips, potatoes, corn, onions and tomatoes were added, and the full pot was stirred for six hours or more before delicious Hopkins County stew emerged.

Sam was back at Mayo Normal in September 1902, determined to graduate with his class the following summer, even though he had been away a year. Once more he took on a heavy courseload and several part-time jobs, and he rounded out his weeks with the baseball team, the debating society and teasing the girls.

When the year ended and graduation approached, he had mounting concern about showing up at the ceremony. "I had only one suit," he said, "and it was frayed at the elbows." But he overcame his embarrassment. Professor Mayo shook his hand as he awarded him his Bachelor of Science diploma at the graduation exercises at which nine other young men and four young women were also honored. A feeling of elation at his accomplishment was absent, for as he put it, "I was mighty worn out."

2

Speaker of the State House

In later years Sam Rayburn saw his teacher's certificate and his B.S. degree as the turning points of his life. "I came within a gnat's heel of remaining a tenant farmer," he once said, assessing their meaning.

But at the time, his graduation brought no profound changes. Faced with the need to pay his old tuition bills at Mayo and support himself currently, he became a teacher again. Dial, a tiny community not far from Windom, needed a teacher, and Sam accepted the low-paying job. He stayed at Dial two years, and in 1905 he moved on to the two-teacher school at nearby Lannius.

At both places he had a way with his pupils that made them idolize him. They vied to get him to stay overnight in their homes and spoke with pride of this accomplishment. On a clear day he was prone to organize a hike through the woods, pointing out nature's features. He might stop to build a bonfire and tell stories to the children from the history books or biographies he had read. He brought tears to their eyes when he told them about Colonel James Fannin, for whom their county was named: In the fight for independence from Mexico, Fannin had been forced to surrender in 1836, and treacherous Santa Anna, the Mexican dictator, had violated his agreement and massacred all 351 men, including Fannin, at Goliad.

Sam's pupils suffered further over Robert E. Lee, Sam Houston and James Butler Bonham, for whom the county seat was named: Jim Bonham from Alabama, the messenger of the Texas freedom fighters, had perished at the Alamo along with Davy Crockett, Jim Bowie and Barrett Travis.

Teachers in that area kept an ample supply of bois d'arc switches on hand and spent the day hitting unruly pupils. Bois-d'arc, pronounced "bow-dark" locally, was a type of tree whose wood was highly prized for bows by Western Indians. But Sam rarely struck a pupil. Sometimes in the fall he and his class went 'possum hunting. "We didn't catch many 'possums," Rayburn reminisced with his Lannius pupils fifty years later, "but we did have lots of good exercise in the outdoors as we tramped through the bottoms all around here." [1]

When he taught at Dial, he roomed with H. B. Savage, who was just starting his practice as a country doctor. Years later he reminded Savage of the fun they had had "sitting up till 12 o'clock talking about everything and nothing, never getting sleepy or tired and enjoying every minute of it." [2] When he moved on to Lannius, he commuted from his parents' farm.

During his growing-up years, Rayburn had not discarded his secret political ambitions and he had excitedly followed the progress of his hero, Joseph Weldon Bailey. Elected to the U.S. House of Representatives in 1890, Joe Bailey had climbed the political ladder in a hurry, thanks to his fine appearance, speaking ability, and shrewd success over his colleagues in satisfying his insatiable thirst for power. Politicians from the largest cities and states bowed to the views of this young man from Gainesville, with a population of only 6,500, and long-serving congressmen acted as inferiors to a man half their age and with little formal education. When William Jennings Bryan prepared for his race for President in 1896, Sam saw nothing unusual in the fact that the "Great Commoner" considered it necessary to meet with Bailey in Dallas and court him. [3] Just beginning his fourth two-year term in the House in 1897 and only thirty-four years old, Bailey would have been Speaker in McKinley's first term had the Democrats controlled the lower chamber. Instead, he had to be satisfied with being minority leader, and as Claude Bowers, the historian who watched him at this post, said, "He dominated the Democratic minority like an overseer . . . and carried himself a conqueror." [4]

It was also thrilling to young Sam to read Bailey's speeches and confirming accounts of his talent as a spellbinder. When the Spanish-American War broke out in 1898, Bailey's orations on patriotism were sufficient to send thousands of Texas youths streaming toward San Antonio where Colonel Leonard Wood and Lieutenant Colonel Theodore Roosevelt were taking on men for their Rough Riders. Unfortunately, the elder Rayburn told sixteen-year-old Sam and his older brothers that his own four years of service to the Confederacy were enough for the whole family. As for Bailey's speaking technique, newspapers lauded him as the best in Congress. One man who heard him there wrote: "His speeches were phrased in the best English, though he was prone to draw on his imagination for history to make his point. His voice was melodious and when he finished his peroration, his tones lingered in the chamber like the echo of chimes in a cathedral."[5]

Sam suffered a minor crisis over Bailey during his first year at Mayo. Bailey had decided to move to the U.S. Senate in 1901, and since the Seventeenth Amendment, which required the direct election of senators, was still far in the future, he needed the approval of the Texas legislature. Evidence was produced to show that Bailey was on the payroll of the Waters-Pierce Oil Company, a subsidiary of Standard Oil, and a fight developed over his fitness to become a senator.

Unwilling to believe the evidence against his hero, Sam Rayburn accepted Bailey's description of himself as "the tallest and cleanest Democrat in the Party." And Bailey seemed to vindicate Rayburn's faith in him when the Texas legislature elected him to the Senate.

But Bailey had accomplished this by stacking the legislative investigating committee with his friends and by threatening other legislators. One young member whom he threatened was Tom Connally, later a U.S. senator. "You've got to denounce those men who attacked me," Bailey ordered. When he refused, said Connally, "Bailey became furious; he banged on the table; he shook his big fist in my face; and he gave off a barnful of upbraiding sarcasm."[6]

In 1906, only six years after he stood in the cotton field with his father and asked permission to go to college, Rayburn decided that the time had come to join Joe Bailey in politics by running for the Texas House, even though he had had no political experience and was only twenty-four years old. This was not as preposterous as it appeared on the surface, for it was not unusual at that time for men of his age to serve in the state legislature. Some who did so considered it a basic training ground for higher office. Others viewed their service as an important way to increase their law practices or business opportunities. In Rayburn's case, it was different. He confided to a friend: "I'm going to get myself elected to the state legislature. I'm going to spend about three terms there, and then I want to be elected Speaker. After that, I'm going to run for Congress and be elected."[7]

This seemingly farfetched plan got under way when he told the school authorities at Lannius to hire another teacher for the 1906–07 year. Then in the late spring of 1906 he went to Bonham, the county seat, to file for the Texas House seat with the court clerk; and when Sam Gardner, a young man from nearby Honey Grove, also decided he wanted to go to Austin, the capital, the campaign began.

The advantages were on Rayburn's side from the start, with his large family and the parents of his pupils working tirelessly in his behalf. His brother Charles had died in 1901, but his remaining nine brothers and sisters, including Frank, the oldest, who was now a doctor, talked to everyone they knew about voting for him. Matt Rayburn, his prim, little, gray-haired mother, and William Marion Rayburn, his bearded, bent-shouldered father, never missed an opportunity to remind neighbors that their Sam had tended to their crops and cows without pay when they had been sick.

The principal campaigning, however, was done by the candidate himself. Old-timers remembered Sam Rayburn wearing a black wool hat and a black suit and traveling about the House district on a small pony. Rayburn was short and husky, standing five feet six inches and weighing about 175 pounds. His eyes were brown and soft, his dark brown hair had begun to recede, and the expression on his full face was both thoughtful and reserved. All that spring and into early summer, he was at every picnic, passing out cards that carried a plea for support and making sure he looked everyone in the eye. When called on to speak, he always mentioned that he favored local option on the liquor issue and that he liked Senator Bailey. His position on these two points generally met with approval. In Bonham, the largest town in Fannin County, with a population of five thousand, it was not necessary to promise economic aid. For the devastation from the Panic of 1893 had given way to the prosperity of 1899, when Bonham was the center for shipping tens of thousands of mules to South Africa during the Boer War. The Panic of 1907, which would again damage local business, was still a year away.

He also rode his pony to every farm in the district to meet the rural voters, for about 80 percent of Fannin County was rural. Lacking any small talk, he conversed knowingly about farm problems, a subject bound to gain him votes because of the kinship it developed. He made it a point to ask each farmer for the name of the next family so he could call the people by name at his next stop.

Toward the end of their campaigning, the two vying Sams traveled together by buggy and took turns addressing whatever crowd assembled to hear them. When Sam Gardner took ill and had to go to bed for three days, Sam Rayburn refused to take advantage of this situation. He stayed with Gardner until he was well enough to take to the hustings again.

Texas Democratic primaries, tantamount to election, were held on a Saturday in July, and the count was made at the beginning of the following week. Word finally came from the county courthouse at Bonham to the anxious Rayburn family at Flag Springs that their Sam had defeated Gardner by 163 votes. The political career that would continue without interruption until the close of 1961 had begun.

Early in January 1907, when Sam left home for Austin, his mother prepared a large breakfast, including piles of cornbread, and gave him a food box to sustain him on the long train trip to the capital. This was the first time he was traveling more than one hundred miles from home, and she packed several jars of cotton-bloom honey to sustain his well-being in his long stay away from Flag Springs. "I always eat some of this pure honey once a day—to which I attribute part of my extra-fine health," Sam was still proclaiming thirty years later.

It was a proud moment when he took his oath of office, promised to uphold the Constitution and swore, as the law required, that he had never engaged in a duel. The Thirtieth Texas Legislature consisted of 133 men. (Women were barred from voting or holding office.) Over the years the normal makeup found all members except one to be Democrats, and this single Republican was generally a black member from Colorado County in southeast Texas. A legislator's pay was a measly five dollars a day during the first sixty days of each session and two dollars a day after that. Moreover, the legislature met only during the odd-numbered years, with the result that the average annual salary for a Texas lawmaker came to two hundred dollars.

Because of this pittance, many members eagerly accepted standard-of-living gifts from lobbyists in the form of free hotel lodging, meals and liquor, prostitutes, parties at the night spots along Congress Avenue and railroad passes. Others, like Sam Rayburn, refused presents from the milling lobbyists and were forced to husband every penny like misers. Rayburn and R. Bouna Ridgway, a member of the Texas House and his roommate, paid thirty dollars a month for board and room. [8] Ridgway told about the time Rayburn was going into an Austin drug store. He met another representative and said he would buy him a soft drink. When he reached in his pocket, he found he had only a nickel, so he pretended he had lost his thirst and let the other man order. "I don't know what I'd have done if he'd ordered a dime drink," Rayburn told Ridgway afterward. [9]

It was ironic that the exploding issue that confronted the Texas legislature immediately after the secretary of state swore Rayburn and his fellow members into office was the fate of his hero, Senator Joseph Bailey. [10] The senator's wealth had increased tremendously in recent years, and now that his term was ending and he wanted a second six-year stay in the Senate, his relationship with Standard Oil and the railroads fell under home-state legislative scrutiny. Never one to be on the defensive, the husky aggressive Bailey returned to Austin to browbeat the legislature. As he bluntly put it, he intended "to drive into the Gulf of Mexico the peanut politician who would replace me with someone who would rattle around in my seat like a mustard seed in a gourd!"

On opposite sides of the Bailey issue were Sam Rayburn and his new friend, Sam Johnson, a representative from the Hill Country, who would the next year become the father of a baby boy named Lyndon Baines Johnson. Sam Johnson saw Bailey as a chiseling crook who used politics to enrich himself, while Sam Rayburn clung to the image of Bailey that had been frozen in his mind when he was twelve. In the final vote, Johnson was in the tiny minority of seven members who wanted to return Bailey to civilian life.

Afterward, Bailey came looking for Rayburn, thanked him for his help, and told him he was now one of his lieutenants. This was a compliment and also a warning that once a man was for Bailey he was always for Bailey and was expected to defend him from then on. In return, Bailey would keep him informed of his doings and intentions toward his enemies. In a typical letter, he wrote Rayburn later from Washington that he wanted to return to Texas to "smite" his foes "hip and thigh." [11] He also sent a picture of himself to Sam's parents and told them, "I feel confident enough in your friendship to know you will cheerfully give a place [to it] in your home." [12]

In his first term in the Texas House, Rayburn did little talking, but he seldom missed a debate or an opportunity to learn more about parliamentary and backstage operations. In a quiet way he also authored two basic bills that became law. The first guaranteed deposits in state banks and was a forerunner of the Federal Deposit Insurance Corporation (FDIC) in Franklin Roosevelt's New Deal almost thirty years later. The other bill was the first to regulate automobile traffic. The Rayburn-Ridgway bill set a maximum speed limit of eight miles per hour in cities, made it mandatory for cars to carry a bell and a light and declared that horses and carriages had the right of way at street corners. [13]

In addition, while other members were carousing at the Bismarck Saloon, Rayburn put in his free time studying law books. The law school of the University of Texas was only ten blocks from the capitol down Brazos Street, and Rayburn enrolled as a full-time student in 1907. His picture appeared in the University's yearbook for 1908, [14] even though he was only in the special three-months' intensive law review program. But this short study proved sufficient, for he took the state bar examination in

1908 and passed, joining the law firm of Steger and Thurmond in Bonham as a partner.

So by the time he began campaigning for a second term in 1908, Rayburn had a legislative record, a paying career and political confidence. During the campaign a friend who was running for prosecuting attorney told him that he had a problem. He wanted to work for Rayburn, but he needed the support of Rayburn's opponent. "Go ahead and vote for him," Sam assured him. "I'm going to lick him anyway."

Rayburn found the atmosphere of the Texas House far different in his second term (the Thirty-first Legislature) from what it had been in the first. In the Thirtieth Legislature, once the Bailey matter was settled, an air of fun and good fellowship existed. For instance, one member, who was a preacher, had introduced a bill to make adultery a felony. This would have put those members who freeloaded on Austin lobbyists in prison. A way out of this dilemma was found. By prearrangement every member in turn stood up and proposed an amendment to exempt his district from the minister's bill.

In the Thirty-first Legislature, however, grimness set in when a large faction of members wanted to censure the Speaker, A. M. Kennedy, charging him with paying out money for furniture and wages without regard to House rules. Rayburn, quick to fight injustice, recognized the effort as an attempt by the governor to get even with Kennedy for proposing to investigate the prison system and the way schoolbooks were selected by the state board.

As a result of his outrage, he led the fight to save the Speaker. But the anti-Kennedy Democrats were in the majority and the Speaker was forced to resign. Rayburn made no enemies by his strong defense of Kennedy, and, in fact, his roommate Ridgway found sixty-seven House members who were willing to sign a petition pledge to back Sam as Kennedy's successor. Sam was astounded at having such support, for it constituted a bare majority, sufficient to make him Speaker. But before he could openly announce his candidacy, Tom Love of Dallas, Speaker in the Thirtieth Legislature, ran about frenziedly and induced several members to unpledge themselves. This led Rayburn to drop out of the race and the post went to John Marshall, who came from Grayson County, which adjoined Fannin County. [15]

With the measure of prominence that had come to him in the Kennedy fight, Rayburn also earned a reputation as the House's workhorse. He was chairman of two committees and an active member of four others. As a new lawyer, he was a hardworking member of the Committee on

19

Constitutional Amendments, and, as a former teacher, a promoter of school reform on the Committee on Education. His other assignments were as chairman of the Committee on Banks and Banking and of the Committee on Common Carriers, and as a member of the Committee on Private Corporations and the Free Conference Committee. This last committee had the task of ironing out differences between House and Senate versions of a bill.

By 1910, he was already stamped by his energy and youthful maturity. Members liked him and so did the employees in the capitol. One man wrote him in 1957, reminding Rayburn that almost a half century earlier he had been an eleven-year-old page in the Texas House. Once, overcome by homesickness, he wrote, "I let out a loud cry on the floor of the House, and you came to me, led me to an anteroom and quieted me with kind words as a father would his own son." [16]

Then there were the black porters who asked Rayburn to present a chafing dish to former Speaker Kennedy. In doing so, Rayburn made a comment that was extremely daring in rabidly anti-Negro Texas. "I wish to say that they are the ones not so fortunate as we are," he said. "But man's soul is not to be charged to the color of his skin. Though his skin be brown or black it is possible that it holds a soul as pure and spotless as any man's." [17]

During the Thirty-first Legislature, newspapers began mentioning Rayburn regularly and his mother's pride swelled. "Dear Sam my precious boy," she wrote him. "We are proud . . . that you are always present and on the side that we think is right." She also wrote him after he told her that he owed everything to his father's farewell to him when he left for Mayo Normal: "Sam, be a man!" She said, "It was a feast to your Pa when you wrote that you remembered his last words. We hope you will ever remember them and abide by them and we believe you will." [18] Besides letters he had a further touch with home because he had brought his youngest brother, Abner, to Austin to work as a House page.

The tradition of Fannin County was to limit its members in the Texas legislature to two terms. However, in the early summer of 1910 when the Dallas and Houston papers reported that Sam Rayburn was a strong candidate for House Speaker in the next legislature, voters in the county ignored the unwritten rule and gave him a third term.

At the outset of the jockeying about among would-be Speakers, Rayburn had three chief rivals. One was Jefferson Davis Cox, who was backed by Oscar Colquitt, the plump little governor-elect; another was Clarence E. Gilmore, supported enthusiastically by retiring Governor Tom Campbell and the Anti-Saloon League; and the third was Luther Nickels, whose power backing was vague. As for Rayburn, he had the acknowledged support of former Speaker Kennedy, and he hoped for the blessing of his hero, Senator Joseph Bailey. But Bailey was playing a waiting game.

The race quickly narrowed when Nickels dropped out and pledged his support to Rayburn, though what this meant in terms of votes was a question mark on Sam's tally sheet. Weeks before D-Day on January 10, 1911, when the 133 members of the House were to elect their Speaker, beer poured freely at the Bismarck Saloon in Austin for early arrivals at the capital, as the Cox, Gilmore, and Rayburn committees went to work on members. Cigars, backslapping and promises also became the order of the day for members who wandered into the headquarters of the candidates at the Avenue Hotel.

Astute political reporters saw the race as narrowing further to Rayburn and Gilmore. Opinion was that Cox might possibly win only if the other two deadlocked and failed to win the necessary 67 votes in the early balloting.

When Cox's dozen most loyal friends insisted they would stick with him to the end no matter what, Senator Bailey decided it was time to speak. He sent a message to the Cox diehards to cave in. Cox also received word from Washington to withdraw from the race. He did this, though he refused to ask his supporters to back either Rayburn or Gilmore. But political observers viewed Cox's retirement as a boon to Rayburn.

The fateful day of January 10, 1911, came, and just after the noon hour Secretary of State W. B. Townsend, using a heavy oak rail as his gavel, crashed it on a table top and the proceedings got under way. As was customary, first came an hour of nominating speeches and last-minute efforts to gain the votes of the unannounced. Gilmoreites busily pleaded that Rayburn was too young at twenty-nine to become Speaker.

Next on the agenda clerks passed around two big gray Texas hats and members dropped their ballots into them. Tellers then counted the votes. Rayburn got the first vote, Gilmore the second and third. At the 60 mark the two were tied. Then Gilmore went ahead and it was tied again at 50 apiece. When the vote reached 131 and Rayburn had the magic number of 67, said the *Austin Daily Express*, "the House went mad." [19] A magnanimous Gilmore stood up and asked that Rayburn's election be made unanimous.

However, a minute later, Gilmore popped up again to demand a recount because of skulduggery in the vote. The final totals had been 71 to 65, 3 more than the House's membership of 133. Either 3 members had voted twice or else lobbyists who enjoyed the run of the chamber had cast them.

After the screaming and name-calling ended, the secretary of state ordered a new election. One of the big western hats was ordered set upside down on a table up front in full view of everyone. Then each member had to walk to it as his name was called and show the single piece of paper he dropped into it. This time Rayburn won, 70 to 63. [20]

He suffered no anticlimax because he had been forced to go through the voting ordeal twice. In fact, when his victory was announced and he realized that part of his prophecy of five years before had now come true, he did something extremely uncharacteristic. Said J. Lee Aston, a member from Sherman, "Sam jumped up and gave a cotton patch yell and sat down real quick—like he was ashamed of hisself."

The winner was then escorted to the rostrum for his oath of office. His mood was now different, and the House *Journal* reported that he spoke with "a huskiness in his voice" as he worked members into a maudlin condition in his acceptance speech. "Up there in Fannin County," his voice quivered, "there is an old man already past his three-score, and there by his side sits an old woman at whose feet I would now delight to worship. For them, I also thank you."

Tears poured and there was much nose blowing. A short time later the day's session ended with enthusiastic cheers and reverberating "Rah-rah-rah—Rayburn!" yells for the youngest Speaker in Texas' history.

Rayburn came to the Speakership after close observation of three previous Speakers, who had more or less wallowed in indecision regarding the powers and duties of their office. So at the start he appointed a special committee to determine the "duties and rights of the Speaker." As a result, for the first time since the legislature had started functioning more than seventy years earlier, the perimeters of the Speaker's position were defined, and there was little cause for the bitter fights for power that had erupted between legislators and Speakers in bygone sessions.

Rayburn brought a highly personal approach to his job as Speaker. He had the gavel, the right to name committee members and chairmen, and control over the House's activities, yet he never flaunted his power. His contemporaries found him a young man who never put on airs. The "high-falutin brand" of Samuel Taliaferro Rayburn, as he dubbed his given name, had long since been reduced to a casual "Sam Rayburn." He was approachable not only by members but by any House employee as well. Although his facial expression was generally serious even in repose, he liked to joke when joking was in order. "I may be accused at times of being baldheaded, but no man can accuse me of being a sorehead," he said in a speech to the House. As a rule, he was not a man who made enemies, even though in the heat of a political battle he showed a strong temper that could flash like lightning. "I have never hated any man," he once declared, "but I have been temporarily provoked with several."

Among those who provoked him while he served as Speaker were former Governor Tom Campbell and the incumbent Governor Oscar Colquitt. He lashed at Campbell for leading a band of lobbyists against needed reforms, and he hit at Colquitt for making shoddy political appointments and for vetoing an appropriation for public school improvements. "Tom Campbell is the least thing to be considered in legislation," he told reporters. [21]

At the time, the political focus in Texas was still on political and economic reforms, as it had been since the liberal administration of Governor Jim Hogg in the early 1890s. Rayburn agreed with this approach, and as Speaker he promoted bills that would regulate utilities, deposit state money in banks in order to realize interest, limit the working hours of women and establish pure-food standards.

Observers agreed that Rayburn did well in a session marked with serious fights between the legislature and the governor, and the House and Senate. "I served during the most turbulent session that body has held since the days of El J. Davis. It was a time to try men," said Rayburn. [22]

As Speaker, he played the political game in a highly partisan manner. On his patronage power, he said, "I saw that all my friends got the good appointments and that those who voted against me for Speaker got none. The man in politics who is not faithful to his friends isn't worthy to be the scavenger of the smallest town in Texas." When a legislator asked him to appoint a woman as House clerk, Rayburn turned her down because she had badmouthed his friend Kennedy. "If you don't appoint her, I'll get up a petition signed by a majority," the man threatened.

"Ben, I don't give a damn if every member signs your petition. I still won't appoint her," Rayburn said. The petition idea was dropped. [23]

At the end of the session members chipped in to buy Sam a gold watch, cufflinks and luggage. Reporters said 125 members threw their hats in the air and cheered him. He was praised for his "zeal, energy and fidelity," and there was widespread agreement that he was a natural Speaker. But as Rayburn admitted years later, he had really got through the session "by God, by desperation and by ignorance."

3

To Congress

Just after Sam Rayburn's term as Speaker of the Texas House began, he became involved in a campaign to go to Congress. Lucky circumstances in the form of a suddenly available congressional seat and an excess of competitors helped make his dream come true.

In 1900, when Joseph Weldon Bailey gave up his House seat to go to the U.S. Senate, a transplanted Georgian named Choice Boswell Randell won Bailey's seat in the House of Representatives. Five times in a row after that Randell was easily reelected, and he was considered to be "embalmed" in the House because he probably could have held that office as long as he desired it. But Choice Boswell Randell was not content to stay in the House, and when Senator Bailey said early in 1911 that he would not run for a third term, Randell quickly spoke up for his Senate seat in the Democratic primary set for Saturday, July 27, 1912.

Randell's decision was good news to Rayburn and several other aspiring politicians in his congressional district. Glancing over his possible opposition, Rayburn from the beginning concluded that State Senator B. B. Sturgeon, with a Teddy Roosevelt moustache, who was from neighboring Lamar County to the east of Fannin County, might keep him from realizing his ambition. Sturgeon, in turn, considered Rayburn his chief stumbling block, though he declared publicly that one of his "smallest worries was the ambition of Speaker Rayburn."[1] As a result, each man in the heat of expected rivalry set out to diminish the other's standing.

When Sturgeon pushed a bill through the state Senate to tax pool tables one hundred dollars each, Speaker Rayburn tossed it out of the House and sent a message back to the Senate that all tax bills had to originate in the House. Sturgeon quickly tried to offset Rayburn's publicity by raging in the Senate and to reporters that the Speaker "would not know the

Constitution if he met it on the road!" But Rayburn came out ahead when House members won a good deal of newspaper attention by introducing a resolution proclaiming that the Speaker "has, by the process of legal reasoning, transformed a Sturgeon into a Flounder."[2]

While this pushing and shoving went on, the question arose whether the two would be contenders at all. The U.S. Congress had approved a congressional reapportionment bill that gave Texas two additional seats in the House beyond its existing sixteen places, and a Texas legislative committee undertook the job of rearranging the territory of the state's congressional districts. Speaker Rayburn named the House members of this committee and his influence was felt. When the new lines were drawn, Lamar County, where Sturgeon lived, had been moved out of the Fourth Congressional District, which still included Fannin County. Lamar was put into the First District. So the contest between Rayburn and Sturgeon could not take place. [3] Rayburn's friends in the Texas House had shown their partisanship in the coming election when they said during the gold watch ceremony that they hoped it would "keep good time in Washington."[4]

But even now that he was rid of Sturgeon, who many political observers believed would have defeated him, it did not appear that Rayburn would go to Congress by default. Seven other Democrats paid their filing fees—including State Senator Tom Perkins of McKinney, who was a known vote-getter, and District Judge Ben Jones of Sherman, highly esteemed in the area. What made the race even more uncertain for Sam was that other candidates had followings in his home county, where he knew he would have to collect much of his vote.

Rayburn opened his campaign at Windom, only a few miles from his parents' farm at Flag Springs. All businesses closed for the occasion, and his mother sat tall as the master of ceremonies introduced her son with a flowery speech. When he had been a boy, Sam recalled in his talk, "the people of Windom thought those of Flag Springs to be fundamentally different from themselves in nature because Flag Springs was three miles away."[5] But now the town's entire three hundred citizens turned out to claim the Flag Springs lad as one of their own.

To cover the five counties of the Fourth District, Rayburn bought a Model-T Ford. Few of the roads were paved and many were thick and gummy mud long after a rain. But the automobile had become the symbol of a serious campaigner by 1912, and a politician without one lost prestige. Rayburn also had a volunteer campaign committee, because one man on his own could not manage the mechanics of a campaign and put himself on five-county display at the same time.

Rayburn's campaign committee was a home-area affair that included Ed Steger, his law partner, Sherwood Spotts, editor of the *Bonham Daily Favorite*, and J. B. Goober, the presiding elder of the Methodist Church. At the outset, Rayburn established the rule that he would personally steer clear of soliciting or handling campaign contributions. His committee was to handle all money and make certain that contributors understood they would not get special treatment if he won.

While he traveled about in his car to shake hands and make speeches, his campaign committee went far beyond raising campaign funds and tacking posters to trees. They organized several motorcades of tin lizzies decorated with Rayburn streamers, and these caravans fanned out with horns honking to invade the towns and cities in the district. In every town the car occupants jumped out and rushed to spread the good word about their man to those in stores and on the streets.

As for their candidate, he was doing what was considered a dangerous pastime for a campaigner. Unable to talk in generalities, he was speaking frankly about his beliefs. He insisted that labor should have the right to organize, that there should be an income and an inheritance tax, that the electoral college be abolished and the President chosen by popular vote without regard to state boundaries. Like all of his Democratic opponents, he also stood for tariffs "for revenue only," the cry of farmers for decades.

As the campaign progressed, Rayburn seemed to be in the lead according to his competitors because their attacks began to center on him. A charge repeated over and over again was that he was not his own man but only a politician in the pay of the railroads. This slander infuriated Rayburn, and he made a reply when he realized how damaging it could be.

"Never in my life have I represented a public service corporation," he said in a speech. "When I became a member of the law firm of Steger, Thurmond and Rayburn, Messrs. Thurmond and Steger were representing the Santa Fe Railroad Company, receiving pay monthly. When the first check came after I entered the firm, Mr. Thurmond brought to my desk one-third of the amount of the check, explaining what it was for.

"I said to him that I was a member of the Legislature, representing the people of Fannin County, and that my experience had taught me that men who represent people should be as far removed as possible from concerns whose interests he was liable to be called on to legislate concerning, and that on that ground I would not accept a dollar of the railroad's money, though I was legally entitled to it. I never did take a dollar of it. I have been guided by this principle in all my dealings." [6]

In the homestretch of the campaign when the miserably hot July days came, courthouse politicians in the five counties were of the opinion that the race had become nip and tuck among Rayburn, State Senator Perkins and Judge Jones. Some thought that a dark horse named Gibson might overtake all three front-runners.

Rayburn made his last major speech in the district courtroom at Bonham on July 15, 1912. All stores closed at 2 P.M., and the courtroom and galleries were crowded when he spoke. "When I was a schoolboy," he said immodestly, "I made up my mind that I was going to live to be worthy of your support and run for Congress when I was thirty years old. In this good year of 1912 I have reached that age and I am running for Congress. I believe I have lived to be worthy of your support."

As for his political philosophy, he said, "I am a Democrat. I believe that the principles advocated and adhered to by the Party since its birth are the same fundamental principles upon which our Republic was founded: A government of the people, by the people, and for the people, where every man, rich or poor, should stand equal before the law and government with the exemplification of 'equal rights to all and special privileges to none.' "

With a look of humility on his face he told the crowd, "I will not deny that there are men in the District better qualified than I to go to Congress." Amid the consternation that spread in the hall, he took on a puckish expression and added, "But these men are not in the race." A roar of approval went up. [7]

In the week before Saturday, July 27, the Rayburn family campaigned up and down the roads leading from their farm. Neighbors were urged to be sure to go to the polls. The *Bonham Daily Favorite* urged readers not to be complacent about their Sam. "The more work his friends do, the larger his majority will be." Then when the fateful primary day came, Rayburn's campaign committee put its program into effect to bring Rayburn supporters to the polling precincts.

All day long this effort continued, and when the polls finally closed the time of tension and doubt began. But eventually Chairman Clendenin of the district's Democratic committee had all the votes counted, and as he saw it, the election had been a squeaker. The vote was as follows:

Rayburn	4,983
Perkins	4,493
Jones	4,365
Gibson	3,790
Wells	1,961
Morrison	798
Erwin	656
Lovelace	290

With only 23.3 percent of the 21,336 votes cast and a margin of just 490 votes over State Senator Tom Perkins, Sam Rayburn's national political career had begun. But he wanted a unified party behind him instead of smoldering factions. "For the men who were opponents of mine in the race," he said after the primary, "I have nothing but the very kindest feelings."

There was still the general election formality to go through in November. This time his vote was 13,900, while Obenchain, the Socialist candidate got 1,340 and Barlow, the Republican candidate, 240. [8]

"It's a 'fur piece' from Flag Springs to Washington," Sam said, realizing the distance he had traveled in his thirty short years.

4

A Young Congressman

The first session of the Sixty-Third Congress was not scheduled to begin until April 7, 1913, but Sam Rayburn wanted to get to Washington early.

First of all, he wanted to have his living arrangements settled before his term began. Then he had heard that the good committee assignments were parceled out early to freshmen members, and latecomers took only what was left.

But most of all, he wanted to be on hand to watch the inauguration of Woodrow Wilson on March 4 because it would be a day of rejoicing and redemption for Democrats. As President, Wilson would be only the second Democrat to be elected to that office since 1856 when James Buchanan defeated John Fremont, the nominee of the new Republican Party. Grover Cleveland had been the other Democrat.

For the first time in his life, Rayburn would have no financial worries, because the salary of a congressman was seventy-five hundred dollars a year, a substantial sum at that time. He bought a new suit and shoes, and his mother packed jars of cotton bloom honey and a variety of other foodstuffs to sustain her son on his two-night, one-day-long railroad trip from the nearby town of Bells to the nation's capital. But the trip was not lonely, because Rayburn was bringing with him a young man named Hal Horton from Greenville to be his secretary. Horton had been a classmate of his at the University of Texas Law School. In addition, at the Denison stop of the Katy Line (Missouri-Kansas-Texas Railroad), Hatton W. Sumners, a newly elected congressman from Dallas, climbed aboard, and he and Sam became fast friends. Formerly the prosecuting attorney of Dallas County, Hatty Sumners was a country boy at heart like Sam, and their kinship was firmly established when they discovered they were both born in Tennessee. On hearing that Sam had gone to Mayo Normal School, Sumners detailed his visit there in 1911. While he had been delivering a lecture to the student body, three of the college buildings had burned to the ground.

When the train pulled into Washington's Union Station, Rayburn hastily concluded a minor flirtation with a pretty girl, and then he and Sumners had to decide where to live. There were several boarding houses in the area, but Sam had made up his mind to live in a hotel where he could have more freedom and independence. Many congressmen stayed at the high-priced Congress Hall Hotel across the street from the Capitol, while others put up at the cheaper Driscoll Hotel. Sumners, who was to earn a reputation as one of the stingiest persons on the "Hill," suggested that they catch the streetcar to the Driscoll and rent rooms there. [1] Later, they moved to the still lower-priced Cochran Hotel at Fourteenth and K Streets Northwest, two miles from the Capitol, which offered meals as part of the rent.

To a young, rural, new member of Congress with a second-rate formal education, Woodrow Wilson had to be considered with awe. Before coming to Washington, Rayburn bought Wilson's four-volume *History of the American People* and read them with reverence. The possessor of a Ph.D., author of several learned books, a former professor, college president, and governor of New Jersey, to Rayburn President-elect Wilson seemed to raise the standard of politics to an all-time high.

Little wonder, then, that on March 4 Rayburn and Sumners were in the huge crowd of three hundred thousand persons in front of the Capitol to thrill at Wilson's inaugural address. It was one of the shortest on record, only fifteen hundred words, and in it Wilson expressed the views that Rayburn had been groping toward in his mind. "My fellow citizens," Wilson called out in his magnificent speaking voice, "there has been a change of government. It means much more than the mere success of the Party. We have been refreshed by a new insight into our lives. That life is incomparably great in its material apects, great also in its moral force.

"But evil has come with good. With riches has come inexcusable waste. The great government we loved has too often been made use of for private and selfish purposes, and those who used it have forgotten the people. There has been something crude and heartless and unfeeling in our haste to succeed and be great. We have come now to the sober second thought. We have made up our minds to square every process of our national life again with the standards we so proudly set at the beginning. . . . Men's hearts wait upon us; men's lives hang in the balance; men's hopes call upon us to say what we will do."

Following the stirring speech came the five-hour inauguration parade, and Rayburn and Sumners were able to come in from the cold, windy day to watch it. On coming to Washington, Rayburn had looked up Martin Littleton, a one-term Tammany Congressman, representing Oyster Bay, New York, who was returning home once Wilson took office. Littleton's father and William Marion Rayburn had been good friends and neighbors back in Tennessee and, in fact, Martin Littleton had also known the elder Rayburn because he was eleven when he left Clinch Valley in 1881, a year before Sam's birth. [2] Hatty Sumners also found he had something in common with Littleton, who had served from 1893 to 1896 as prosecuting attorney of Dallas County, Texas, before moving to New York. Just to watch the inauguration, Littleton had kept his suite in the Willard Hotel on Pennsylvania Avenue, and it was from his windows that Sam and Hatty saw their first giant political parade. Its orderliness was in sharp contrast to the previous day's parade by the women's suffrage movement where spectators jeered and fought with the five thousand lady marchers along Pennsylvania Avenue, necessitating action by the U.S. Cavalry to rescue the suffragettes. [3]

A month-long wait followed between the inauguration and April 7 when Rayburn and Sumners walked into the House Chamber for the opening of the congressional session. This gave them ample time to wander about town to see the sights and meet early-arriving congressmen. Washington's population was estimated at 350,000 in 1913, with a small nucleus of well-to-do old settlers who had contempt for members of Congress yet invited them to parties and their wives to afternoon calls. Within the confines of political Washington, a congressman's wife was expected to pay a call in person on the wives of all members of the House and Senate and Cabinet members, staying ten minutes at each place and leaving her calling card.

About a third of the population was black and this segment worked at menial jobs and lived by the thousands in shacks and alley dwellings. The city had almost no manufacturing or financial business and resembled many a sleepy Southern town. The automobile, the taxicab and the streetcar had come to Washington, but cabinet members were still commuting between home and office by government-issue horse and carriage.

In the last two years of the preceding Republican administration of President William Howard Taft, the Democrats had won control of the House and installed Champ (James Beauchamp) Clark of Missouri as Speaker. Now in the Sixty-third Congress the Democrats had 290 members of the House's total of 435, and Champ Clark was quickly reelected Speaker on opening day. As his first order of business, Clark ordered each state delegation to come in turn to the well of the Chamber beneath his dais to be sworn in. There were forty-eight states when Rayburn took his oath, for Arizona and New Mexico had entered the Union in 1912.

One opening-day function of the House was the formal approval of committee assignments. Former Speaker Joseph "Uncle Joe" Cannon, a small, skinny Republican from Illinois, who had been in charge of the House for four Congresses preceding Champ Clark, had named both Republican and Democratic members of all committees and their chairmen, too, until the "revolution" of March 1910. Uncle Joe's dictatorship had extended also to determining what bills would be considered by the House, whether they could be amended, the length of debate on them and which ones would be approved. But in March 1910, George W. Norris, a progressive Republican from Nebraska, had introduced a resolution to overthrow "Cannonism." For three days and two nights a debating fight had gone on until Cannon finally conceded that Norris' resolution was in order and a vote would be taken on it. [4]

When the tally showed 192 for the resolution and 155 against, Cannon suffered a stunning defeat. The House Ways and Means Committee, which handled tax and tariff legislation, took over the Speaker's authority to name members of all other committees. In addition, the Speaker was removed from membership and control of the Rules Committee, which was the traffic manager of legislation in the House.

Rayburn and Sumners found when they came to Washington that John Nance Garner from Uvalde, Texas, who was a member of the Ways and Means Committee, controlled all committee assignments of Texas congressmen. Randell, Rayburn's predecessor, had been on Ways and Means, and his departure had created the opening for Garner.

Garner, with a few years of schooling, had read enough Blackstone to open a law office in 1890 at the age of twenty-two. As a member of the Texas House in 1901, he had carved out a congressional district for himself in the reapportionment act of that year. He had also picked up his nickname of "Cactus Jack" that year when he put up a hard fight in the legislature to have the cactus named the state flower instead of the bluebonnet, or "buffalo clover," as it was generally known. [5]

Cactus Jack Garner came to Washington in 1902 when the bosses of the broiling, cracked clay, mesquite country of south Texas decided he could represent them in the new district he had created. This was an area where Mexican-Americans were kept as illiterate peons at a near-starvation level and without the benefits of the U.S. Constitution. These bosses, by paying the poll tax for them, owned a sufficient number of votes to be a potent force in any statewide election. And by having their own congressmen in Washington, they could get the federal government to satisfy some of their needs. Garner understood this when he wrote to one political boss after being sworn in, "If you want a post office or some other public building on Padre Island, I'll be glad to get it for you." [6] Later on he showed his true Confederate feelings on pork-barrel bills when he said: "Every time one of those Yankees gets a ham, I'm going to do my best to get a hog."

The bosses did not expect too much from Garner in Congress because of his appearance. One declared: "That feller Garner was the worst-looking thing I ever saw." He was a scrawny, short man with a skinned nose and a face that resembled an owl. His hair was never combed, his clothes were unpressed and he seldom shaved. As for his speaking voice, it was high-pitched and carried only a short distance.

In his first eight years in the House, Garner did not utter a single word in debate. Yet other members recognized him as a comer. As he bluntly put it: "The only way to get anywhere in Congress is to stay there and let seniority take its course." [7]

But Cactus Jack's growing power was based on more than seniority. By landing a place on the Ways and Means Committee, he held authority over his fellow Democrats from Texas and had a say on revenue bills as well. Moreover, in addition to this, he possessed a friendly relaxed personality, great shrewdness about people, a keen understanding of the mechanics of House politics and an ability to be in the midst of the decision-makers at the right time. Even Uncle Joe Cannon had considered him a protégé, despite the fact that they belonged to different parties. Garner was a regular in the after-hours poker games that the leadership adopted as its sport, and he turned his office into a cozy liquor club where members congregated in the afternoon to "strike a blow for liberty," as they called their convivial drinking sessions.

From his perch on the Ways and Means Committee, Garner decided that Sam Rayburn should be assigned to the Interstate and Foreign Commerce Committee and Hatty Sumners to three unimportant committees—Public Buildings, Census, and Mileage.

On the surface, the Commerce Committee appeared to be a minor one. But it kept extremely busy with the large number of government activities with which it dealt. On the fall of Cannonism, the committee's chairman, James R. Mann, a quaint-bearded Republican from Illinois, had scrambled for extra committee authority and ended up with an outsize share that included all forms of interstate transportation and commerce, public utilities, insurance, stocks, public health, the Coast Guard and the Panama Canal. [8] But Mann had not been able to hold on to his top seat for long, because the Democrats took charge of the House in 1911, and the Ways and Means Committee named William C. Adamson of Georgia to succeed him.

Besides impressing Garner, Rayburn impressed Chairman Adamson, who adopted him as his protégé almost at sight. "Judge" Adamson, as he wanted to be called even though his only service on the bench had been as a local judge of Carrollton, Georgia, a town of fifteen hundred persons, created a problem with his favoritism toward Rayburn. For another freshman member considered himself far more deserving. He was Alben W. Barkley of Kentucky, a young man with a large head and an organ voice, who had brought his father to Washington to work as a doorkeeper at the House Chamber. [9] Barkley's name had been entered as a committee member before Rayburn's. This meant that he was higher on the committee's seniority totem pole than Rayburn, who could not hope to become chairman in time if Barkley were still a member.

One of Sam Rayburn's attributes was his understanding that a framework to his day gave him the time to do his job and a sense of inner peace. Almost from his first day in the House, he was already settled into a routine. He was up every morning at seven after nine hours of sleep, did setting-up exercises and dressed. The long, square-cut Prince Albert coats were still in style, but they did not look good on short men, and Rayburn chose instead the snug, dark short jacket and trousers and light vest. He ate a large breakfast at the hotel, took the streetcar to the Hill, and more or less trotted a few times around the racetrack walk between the Capitol and the Library of Congress before going indoors to the smoky political atmosphere. The age of the average House member was so much greater than his that even though he was thirty he felt extremely young. Sixteen years later he said in a speech, "When I came to Congress, little more than a boy . . ." [10]

Until 1908, members of the House had no offices and did their office work either at home or in committee rooms in the Capitol. But that year many members acquired personal offices when the House Office Building opened across Independence Avenue from the Capitol. In 1912, when Arizona and New Mexico joined the Union, and a reapportionment act raised the number of House members from 391 to 435, a fifth floor was added to the H. O. B. But it was unfinished when Rayburn arrived the following year, and he found an available room in the decrepit, old Maltby Building in the Senate area of Capitol Hill, a sort of "enemy territory" to House members. He was luckier than dozens of other House members who still had mail sent to their apartments. The married ones in this predicament often had wives who were angry because their apartments were cluttered with mailbags and file cabinets. [11]

Rayburn did not have to languish for long at the Maltby's closet-sized room 41, because Cactus Jack Garner invited him to occupy a desk in his own crowded one-room office that he shared with his wife Ettie, who was also his secretary, until Sam could acquire his own room in the H. O. B. This was fortunate for Rayburn because Garner, with his fatherly approach toward him, invited him to join the select company who trooped to his office to "strike a blow for liberty." After a time, the fifth floor was finished and Rayburn was assigned to room 543 and Hatty Sumners to 542 in what became known as "the attic." Each got the usual half dozen spittoons that came with that office to be put alongside each desk, waiting sofa and chair.

Rayburn started his day by reading the mail from his district of two hundred thousand people. He seldom received more than ten letters a day, and these were chiefly requests for farmers' bulletins and seed. Until 1924, congressmen had appropriations to enable them to send garden and flower seeds free to constituents. He also had occasional mail from worried parents whose son or daughter was coming to Washington to work for the government. In a typical instance, Alla Clary would be arriving on the Baltimore and Ohio at a certain time to take a job at the War Department. He went to Union Station to meet her, waited three hours, and missed her. Later he took her to dinner and treated her to oysters on the half shell, on which she almost gagged. Then he gave her a ride in the new coupe he had purchased, and as they passed the large Chevy Chase Country Club he announced, "When I get married, I want a house that big."

She asked why, and he replied, "For all my children." [12]

Early in the morning, Rayburn also read the *Congressional Record* for the previous day, talked to occasional visitors and worked on bills he wanted to introduce. By ten, he was on his way to one of the subcommittees of the Commerce Committee to which Adamson had assigned him, which was holding a hearing. Here the witnesses who testified were from government agencies and private businesses, and the sessions were usually sparring matches. The committee was not limited to considering legislation that authorized new government functions. Instead, at that time it controlled the budgets as well as the operations of the agencies it covered, and government officials were regularly before it pleading for money. In the 1920s, this money-doling function was shifted to the exclusive jurisdiction of the Appropriations Committee.

At noon, Rayburn went to the House Chamber to listen to debate and watch the parliamentary maneuvering of the experts. The Sixty-third

Congress was far from a dull one because Woodrow Wilson had a program to get through the legislative branch.

It started with a rush the day after Rayburn was sworn in, and the hectic pace continued that first year through the miserably hot summer, the December cold, and far into 1914. Wilson began the action on April 8, 1913, when he broke a tradition begun by Thomas Jefferson in 1801. Jefferson, with a high, squeaky voice, had decided to send his State of the Union Message and other addresses to Congress instead of appearing in person as his two predecessors had. Succeeding Presidents had continued the Jefferson practice, but now came Wilson to return to the old way.

His appearance was a huge success, with Rayburn and the other Democratic members cheering wildly throughout his ten-minute speech on legislative proposals to put his "New Freedom" program into effect. He had come, he said, to prove "that the President of the United States was a person, a human being trying to cooperate with other human beings in a common cause, not a mere department of the government sending messages from an isolated 'island of power.' "[13] Following the speech, Rayburn joined the long line to shake his hand in the Speaker's office, across the corridor from the House Chamber.

Not long afterward, when Adamson had to go to the White House to discuss his committee's activities with Wilson, he took Rayburn with him. Adamson was from Carrollton, Georgia, and Wilson had spent his youth in Augusta where his father had been a Presbyterian minister. The conversation was filled with reminiscences of the Peach State, including Wilson's awesome memory of himself "standing, when a lad for a moment by General Lee's side and looking up into his face."

This should have made Rayburn a blind Wilson worshipper for life. But years later he recalled: "Mr. Wilson was a very cold, frigid individual. I always thought he had the Presbyterian fervor to do a great job for humanity en masse, but he gave me the impression he wasn't too much interested in individuals. He had heavy glasses and he looked at you through rather large gray eyes. Wilson had the longest face, from lock down to chin, that I have ever seen, what you would call a horse face. But he was not an unhandsome man."[14]

After the House finished its day's business, Rayburn spent his spare time in a variety of ways. "I liked to browse through the second-hand bookstores in Washington," he said. He tended to buy biographies and histories. "But I always felt guilty if I had a book in my library that I hadn't read. I got into the habit of writing 'S. R.' on the bottom of page 99 in every book that I read."[15] His visits to the Library of Congress had revealed that each of its books had a perforated "L.C." at the bottom of page 99.

He also played baseball on occasion, though he did not excel in the game the way his brother Tom did. Tom was a star pitcher in the Texas-Oklahoma Professional League. When House Democrats played Republicans for charity in June 1913, Sam pitched for the Democrats, and one reporter referred to him as "a ball-tosser of renown."[16]

There was time also for the pretty young ladies of Washington. He and Hatty Sumners, who was also a bachelor, made a foursome with a steady change of girls, though Hatty was always searching for the cheapest entertainment and thought it sprightly conversation to tell about the latest practical joke Sam had played on him. On occasion, their social life made the papers back home. For instance, the *Farmersville* (Tex.) *Times* of May 5, 1913, carried this story from Washington:

> Representative Sam Rayburn and Representative Hatton Sumners, the two bachelor members of whom the Texas delegation is very proud, bachelor Congressmen being at a right good premium, were among the guests at a box party given by Senator Ollie James and Mrs. James in honor of their house guest, Miss Nancy O'Donahough, of Philadelphia.

Although many congressmen enjoyed freeloading around the Washington cocktail-party circuit, Rayburn tried it only once. Evelyn Walsh McLean, owner of the Hope Diamond, invited him to one right after he arrived in the capital. "I never felt she knew," he said, "or cared, whether I was there or not. So I stopped going."[17]

Once he moved from the Driscoll to the Cochran Hotel, Rayburn found a stimulating "school of political science" going on every evening in a part of the lobby. More than a dozen House and Senate members lived at the Cochran, and after dinner they congregated in the lobby to play dominoes and talk. These discussions included an exchange of intelligence on the day's activities in their committees and on the floors of both houses. There were also heated arguments on legislation and on the operations of various government departments, and advice was freely passed on to Sam from the older men in the lobby.

Cordell Hull of Tennessee, ten years his senior and a veteran of the Spanish-American War and three terms in the House, was among the first to befriend him at the Cochran. Hull had first come to the House by virtue of winning the Democratic primary by only fifteen votes. Although he later became a Secretary of State, at the time Rayburn knew him at the Cochran his concentration was not on foreign affairs but on taxes and tariffs. The tall, thin, slow-moving Hull, whose lisp made him a poor speaker, had a strong contempt for congressmen who limited their job to catering to constituents back home; and he impressed on Rayburn that a congressman had a broader duty toward the nation than merely sending "garden seeds, agricultural bulletins and yearbooks" to voters in his district. Rayburn found a most compelling reason for admiring the Tennesseean: In Hull's opinion, Joe Bailey "had a legal mind scarcely second to that of anyone else in our history." [18]

Others in the Cochran lobby to whom Rayburn felt drawn were Ebenezer Hill of Connecticut, a House member, and Senator James P. Clarke of Arkansas, the Senate's president pro tempore. Hill was considered the best informed man in the Capitol on trade and tariff questions. He always carried a little black notebook crammed with statistics, and in floor debate, said Hull, "he would draw out his little book and recite some of its contents, thereby almost invariably administering a knockout blow to his competitors." [19]

The post of president pro tempore was one of the few provided for by name in the Constitution, and though its holder's function was primarily that of presiding over the Senate when the Vice President was absent, the office was considered a great honor reserved for the longest-serving senators. Highly regarded James Clarke was elected president pro tem in 1913, even though he had served only ten years in the upper chamber. So when a man with Clarke's prestige wanted Rayburn to sit with him at dinner and spent much time talking to him in the Cochran lobby about politics and life, Rayburn felt he was getting a special education.

It was Clarke's conclusion that a congressman was not worth his pay if he did not lead his constituents. A man who determined the position of the majority or the influential back home on an issue and then bovinely voted accordingly was a waste of time, Clarke advised. He also told Rayburn that people were wrong to hide their true emotions. "A man should express his love to his family and friends," he said. His words made a deep impression on Rayburn, who had been brought up by parents to whom any show of sentiment toward young children was a sign of weakness.

So it appeared that Sam had a full, rich life, working where he had always wanted to work and associating with stimulating people. Yet he bared his soul in a letter to his former roomate at Dial, Dr. H. B. Savage, a few years later. "Dear Savage," he wrote,

> This is a lonesome, dark day here. You wouldn't think it is, but a fellow gets lonesomer here, I think, than any other place almost. It [Washington] is a selfish, sour-bellied place, every fellow trying for fame, perhaps I should say

notoriety . . . and are ready at all times to use the other fellow as a prize-pole [a lever] for it.

[But] it is my life, my whole life and I could not live without it, and I really believe I will here, as I did in the Texas legislature, rise to a place where my voice will be somewhat potential in the affairs of the nation. But sometimes it becomes a cheerless fight, and a fellow is almost ready to exclaim, "What's the use?"[20]

5

Rayburn and Wilson

Sam Rayburn's great feeling of loneliness in Washington did not affect his legislative work. In fact, he played a surprisingly important role in his freshman term.

With Wilson in office, the triple thrusts of his New Freedom were in the areas of making tariff cuts, shifting the control of bank credit from the private to the public sector and passing stringent anti-trust legislation.

Rayburn was not on the Ways and Means Committee, which set about to undo the steep import duty increases in the Republican old guard's Payne-Aldrich Tariff Act of 1909. But he had campaigned for a tariff based on revenue and not on the protection against competition for high-profit Northern industries. So he attended most of the committee's hearings chaired by Oscar W. Underwood of Alabama, an extremely conservative man who had been a rival to Wilson for the presidential nomination the year before.

Listening to the lobbyists swarming to Underwood's committee to testify against reductions was an eye-opener for Rayburn. They also roamed throughout the House Office Building in such large numbers trying to influence members that President Wilson condemned them publicly and naively demanded that they leave town.

But that was not the end of the strange doings Rayburn observed. Once the Underwood Tariff Bill left Ways and Means and went to the House floor, its guidance through the Lower Chamber fell to Underwood, who was also the majority leader. While his bill cut many import duties, it carefully retained high rates for items produced in the districts of influential members. For instance, Underwood, who came from Birmingham, did not permit any chopping of tariffs on iron and steel. Garner was another. He was outspoken in his opposition to all protective tariffs except on mohair, which came from the large number of Angora goats in his district. And so it went. By the time all the concessions were made to the various members of the House and Senate, the grand total of amendments to the original bill reached a count of 676.

During his first month in Congress, young Rayburn had listened in silence to the hearings and debate on the tariff question. He knew it was a House tradition for members to be seen and not heard in their first term. But he felt he had to make his views known on this subject that was so important to him, and he decided to be an exception to the tradition. Cordell Hull had also delivered his maiden speech shortly after coming to the House in 1907; and he cautioned Sam to prepare it well because his colleagues would "judge his ability on the basis of it, and the impression he created might determine whether they would listen to his subsequent addresses." [1]

Sam Rayburn's speech, delivered on May 6, 1913, less than a month after he was sworn in, started out in a windy way, highly uncharacteristic of the laconic man that he was. The first sentence, which was an atrocious 126 words long, lumbered as follows:

> Mr. Chairman, as a new member of this great body, I, of course, feel that I should have regard to some extent for the long-established custom of this House, which in a measure demands that discussions of questions shall be left in the main to the more mature members from the standpoint of service, but on the other hand, I feel that as a representative and commissioned spokesman of more than 200,000 citizens of the Fourth Congressional District of Texas I should be allowed to break in a measure whatever of this custom remains, and exercise my constitutional right to speak my sentiments on this floor and refuse to be relegated to the lockjawed ostracism to some extent typical of the dead past.

After that sorry beginning, he settled down to an able discussion of the tariff issue, his view of the political parties and his credo as a congressman. He referred to Wilson as "clean and matchless," Underwood as "stainless, able and peerless," and described the Republican minority in the House as divided into two factions—"one being what little remains of that great party of Lincoln and McKinley and the other the dumb, driven blind followers of the 'Terrible Teddy.' " The Republicans' promotion of "prohibitive" tariffs he saw as their "eternal solicitation for the American manufacturer to take that small rich class under its protective wing, but unwilling at all times to heed the great chorus of sad cries ever coming from the large yet poor class, the American consumer."

At the close came his credo:

> I came to this body a few weeks ago with childlike enthusiasm and confidence. It has always been my ambition since childhood to live such a life that one day my fellow citizens would call me to membership in this popular branch of the greatest lawmaking body in the world. Out of their confidence and partiality they have done this. It is now my sole purpose here to enact such wise and just laws that our common country will by virtue of these laws be a happier and more prosperous country. I have always dreamed of a country which I should believe this should and will be, and that is one in which the citizenship is an educated and patriotic people, not swayed by passion and prejudice, and a country that shall know no East, no West, no North, no South, but inhabited by a people liberty loving, patriotic, happy and prosperous, with its lawmakers having no other purpose than to write such just laws as shall in the years to come be of service to human kind yet unborn. [2]

The response of his listeners after he finished was like that normally reserved for the House's outstanding orators. The *Congressional Record* contained the word "(Applause)," but Adolph Sabath, a Democrat from Illinois, said that the cheering was long and loud and that only the hard pounding of the gavel brought it to a close. [3]

Not one of the large Eastern metropolitan papers gave a line of space to Rayburn's maiden speech. But the home editors picked it up. A favorable editorial in the *Sherman* (Tex.) *Sentinel* said: "Go to it, Sammie, we're wid you. . . . Get you some more adjectives and stay with them." The jeering view of the *Texas Republic* on May 17 was: "That speech should be good for two post offices placed at the bestowal of the Honorable Sam in the Fourth Congressional District, and Woody should see that he gets the two appointments. Parrot-like performances are worthy of some reward." [4]

Less than two weeks after his tariff speech, Rayburn became more directly involved in American trade policy. The Panama Canal, over which the House Commerce Committee held legislative jurisdiction, had been started in Theodore Roosevelt's administration and was about a year away from its scheduled opening to cargo vessels. Chairman Adamson asked Sam to go to Panama with a group of a dozen junketeering congressmen and their wives, inspect progress, talk to Panamanian and

American diplomatic officials and sound them out about Roosevelt's decision that American ships engaged in coastal trade be free of the Canal's tolls.

Although Sam was on official business, he insisted on paying his own passage, on what turned out to be the only trip abroad he took in his long career. In a letter of May 25, 1913, to "Dear Homefolks" back in Texas, he sounded like a young son and brother assuring his family he was all right and bragging about the important persons he was seeing. "We arrived here safely this morning," he wrote. "I did not get sea-sick although we were on the water 7 days and 8 nights." He went on to say that he was going to call on "the President of Panama and the American legation."[5]

On his return to Washington, he testified before his committee against the existing law that would permit toll-free passage of American vessels through the Canal. Then Wilson came to Congress in person to ask that the law be repealed. When the Commerce Committee reported such a bill out favorably, Adamson asked Rayburn to hold a news conference—his first—and explain the details and ramifications to reporters.

It was also in the spring of 1913 that Rayburn began what was an astounding adventure for a freshman congressman. During the 1890s, Governor Jim Hogg had pushed a law through the Texas legislature giving the Texas Railroad Commission authority to approve or reject the issuance by a state railroad of new stock or bonds.[6] A study of Commerce Committee and Interstate Commerce Commission documents convinced Rayburn that there should be a similar law applicable to interstate railroads. For the large lines were issuing billions of dollars worth of stock that had no backing in company assets. This was watered stock, pure and simple, with much of the money from its sale going into the pockets of railroad executives. Eventually the market quotations for the railroad stock would drop drastically, so the whole affair would amount to a gift by the public to the railroad corporations. A study that Rayburn read of the New Haven Railroad revealed that J. P. Morgan, the banker who controlled it, was using the proceeds from the sale of watered stock to buy other Eastern railroads.

To handle the national problem, Rayburn wrote a Railroad Stock and Bond Bill giving the ICC authority to bar railroads from issuing stocks and bonds without its approval. He was sitting in his office one morning shortly after he dropped the bill in the hopper, when Louis D. Brandeis, widely regarded as the country's best legal brain, walked in. Brandeis said he was coordinating all anti-trust legislation for Wilson, and the administration wanted to make Rayburn's bill an essential part of its three-pronged program for 1914. Besides the Rayburn bill, there would be the Clayton Anti-Trust Bill—named for Henry Clayton, chairman of the House Judiciary Committee—and the Covington Trade Commission Bill to be introduced by Congressman James H. Covington of Maryland.

Rayburn was flabbergasted: first, that his bill was to be a vital part of Wilson's New Freedom and second, that Brandeis would be working with him to perfect his bill. [7]

He had long known of Brandeis' activities. Brandeis was born in Kentucky before the Civil War and had made a fortune as the leading corporation lawyer of his time. Then in the 1890s he had become interested in reforms and handled economic and social reform cases before the Supreme Court for nothing. One of these was his successful action defending Oregon's ten-hour-maximum workday for women. Brandeis had also set up a system of nonprofit life insurance through the savings banks of Massachusetts, served as Senate committee counsel to investigate the Department of Interior's disregard of conservation regulations and had made the study of the New Haven Railroad that Rayburn had read. Along the route of his hectic existence, Brandeis had also become the leading opponent of swollen corporations and holding companies, and he preached extensively on the "curse of bigness," showing proof that the bigger a corporation became the more its rate of efficiency declined. Moving into politics, he had helped form the National Progressive Republican League in 1910 with eight senators, sixteen House members and six governors. They called themselves insurgents and made a futile effort to promote Senator Robert LaFollette of Wisconsin for President. Teddy Roosevelt, who had hoped to gain their support, disdainfully described an insurgent as "a Progressive who is exceeding the speed limit." [8] Brandeis eventually supported Wilson, was almost named Attorney General but became instead his adviser on much of his New Freedom.

Brandeis and Rayburn, this famous Harvard lawyer and this young man from rural Texas and Mayo Normal School, became fast friends as they hammered out revisions in Rayburn's original bill. Brandeis was writing a book in 1913 entitled *Other People's Money, and How the Bankers Use It*. One of his cardinal points was that there should be no interlocking directorates. But Rayburn impressed on him that worthwhile exceptions probably existed and that the ICC should have power to decide this point in the case of the railroads.

As he later expressed his reasoning for this provision to the House when his bill came under consideration, Rayburn said: "Take a small town and let a few men there organize a bank. Perhaps there will be half a dozen men in the town who are able to organize the bank. After a while they will want to build a flour mill, or a cotton mill, and if you prevent the interlocking directorates and leave no discretion you are likely to do a serious injustice not only to the men who own the stock in the corporation but to the public." [9]

At the beginning of 1914, when Wilson came to Congress and asked for his anti-trust program, committee hearings got under way in earnest on the three bills. Besides the hearing on his own legislation, Rayburn ran the subcommittee handling the Trade Commission Bill. The latter would establish the Federal Trade Commission with the authority to investigate and end unfair trade practices by issuing cease and desist orders. The FTC would also have power to require annual financial reports from corporations. The third bill, or the Clayton Anti-Trust Bill, listed a number of illegal practices in restraint of trade involving corporate combinations, such as price-fixing and insiders' contracts. In addition, the Clayton Bill exempted labor unions from anti-trust suits.

Strong opposition appeared against all three bills, but the Commerce and Judiciary Committees reported them out favorably to the House. Adamson singled out Rayburn's bill for long praise when it left his committee, [10] and when floor debate began on June 2, he described Rayburn as "a young member but old in wisdom and accomplishment."

Rayburn led off the debate on his bill that evening with an hour of explanation. When opponents tried to gang up on him, Cactus Jack Garner with his harsh tongue and agile mind joined Sam in fending off the attacks. At the end of the debate when Rayburn finished his remarks the *Congressional Record* reporter added, "(Loud Applause.)"

The vote on all three bills was set for the same day. But before it came, Brandeis had qualms that the conservative Supreme Court would declare Rayburn's bill unconstitutional. So Rayburn divided his bill into two sections in order to save part of it if the Supreme Court did as Brandeis feared, and he changed the title from the Railroad Stock and Bond Bill to the Railroad Capitalization Bill. [11]

When the three bills were voted on, Rayburn's bill had the largest support, winning by 325 to 12. Surprisingly, Garner was among the 12, making the false claim that Rayburn's bill would end the Hogg Act in Texas.

Rayburn's phenomenal legislative success won quick recognition. A letter of June 9 from the White House read:

My Dear Mr. Rayburn:

We have all looked on with admiration and genuine appreciation as your stock and bond bill has been put through the

45

House. It seems to me you deserve a great deal of praise for your part in the matter and I want to make my humble contribution to the congratulations which I am sure you must be receiving.

Cordially and sincerely yours,

Woodrow Wilson. [12]

Equally welcome was a letter from his mother on June 16, in which she fairly burst with pride. "I think it should go down in history as the greatest bill that was ever introduced by any man of your age and his first session in Congress. I feel so proud and thankful that I have raised a boy that can and will do things that will be an honor to his self and his people. . . . I think the way your bill went through and the letter Wilson wrote you was the greatest boon that a man could have bestowed upon him." [13]

In the midst of his great joy at having achieved the seemingly impossible for a freshman member, Rayburn suffered an enormous personal tragedy. Hal "Spec" Horton, his secretary, had left him in 1914 for a better-paying job in the executive branch, and to replace him Sam planned to bring Abner from the farm the following winter and put him through law school while he worked in his office. [14] Abner, a tall, thin young man with a sensitive expression and a forceful personality, was nine years Sam's junior and was more like a son to him than a brother. In a frank letter to his parents about his relationship to Ab, Sam said: "No one ever doubted for a moment that he was my favorite . . . and I gave him all the love I had from the time he was a small boy. You know I am of such a nature that I cannot believe many folks have a very tender devotion for me, and when I find one who I know has they can have my all." He went on to say that he knew Ab "loved me better than anyone on earth save you two." [15]

Busy in Washington in early June with his bill and the Federal Trade Commission measure, he paid little attention to the Democratic primary coming up on July 25. For a time he thought he would have no opponent because, as the *Denison Herald* pointed out, it was "the time-honored Democratic custom of rewarding a faithful friend with a second term." [16]

But former State Senator Tom Perkins, editor of the *McKinney Courier-Gazette*, decided to give Sam a second race, after having lost to him in 1912 by only 490 votes. Even so, Sam did not intend to come home and campaign. He hoped to rely instead on Ab and the rest of his family and a volunteer committee of friends to do what campaigning for him they thought necessary. His chief contribution to his own campaign was to agree to the distribution of a business card that carried the appeal

"Your support and influence will be appreciated" on one side and the Wilson letter to him on the back. [17]

Although by the end of the month campaign helpers urged him to come home because of the crowds Perkins was attracting, he did not return until early July, and then for another reason. Ab had become ill. His brother Frank, the doctor, had diagnosed his trouble as typhoid fever and was deeply worried about him. The campaign became secondary while Sam sat alongside Ab's bed, torn with distress as his little brother faded.

In the meantime, Perkins stepped up his campaign, attacking Rayburn in several speeches a day. Reluctantly, Sam left Abner to deliver a few speeches and then returned to his side. Finally Abner died shortly before the primary, and Sam's grief overwhelmed him.

It was at this point that Perkins struck the hardest. He spread a circular throughout the five counties that spuriously included Sam's name among a list of congressmen who had opposed Prohibition legislation. He also charged Sam with being antilabor and insisted that although Sam had said he was not bothering to campaign against him all his brothers had been busily campaigning.

There was no time to lose. A reply was necessary, and Sam pulled himself from his stupor long enough to write an answering circular that his friends distributed. It was dated July 23, and it said, "As I returned from his [Abner's] grave this base circular [Perkins's] was handed to me . . . ." [18] Several labor unions of the district also issued their own circular, answering the charge that Sam was antilabor.

Sam carried all five counties on July 25, and he won over Perkins by 9,146 votes. But it would be an election he would always remember because of the grief connected with it.

After the election, Rayburn returned to Washington, intent on taking his mind off his heartache by plunging into the task of helping to get his Railroad Capitalization Bill through the Senate. He was expecting no trouble because of the ease with which the bill had passed the House. But now he suffered further sorrow.

Brandeis, the superintellectual who could analyze a subject from more angles than a protractor, was no longer in favor of Rayburn's bill, despite his own work on it. Brandeis' new view, as expressed to members of the Senate Commerce Committee, was that if the ICC had to give prior approval to the issuance of railroad securities, the public would be gulled into believing that the stock had the backing of the U.S. government. This outlandish conclusion by Brandeis was accepted by Senator LaFollette and his Progressive friends, and opposition to Rayburn's bill spread to the potent group of Southern Democratic states' righters, who saw it as a federal encroachment. [19]

When Brandeis discussed his objection to Rayburn's bill with Wilson, the President agreed and offered a further objection of his own. War had broken out in Europe in August, and this was no time to antagonize the railroads who would be carrying supplies for American allies to the East Coast ports.

So early in September, Wilson told the Senate to quit its consideration of Rayburn's bill. As a consequence, only the Clayton Anti-Trust and Federal Trade Commission Bills became law. To head off any further consideration of Rayburn's bill, Wilson declared in November 1914, "The reconstruction legislation which for the last two decades the opinion of the country has demanded has now been enacted."

The reaction of Brandeis to Wilson's door closing on further anti-trust legislation was to label the new laws as only a weak start to restore competition. As he put it, the big trusts were still untouched. Then he settled down and was given a seat on the Supreme Court in 1916.

Rayburn's reaction was more direct. Early in 1915, he reintroduced the Railroad Stock and Bond Bill, and he decided to talk to Wilson in hopes of changing his mind. But by 1915, it had become difficult to get an appointment with the President, for Wilson had come to the conclusion that "interviews and consultations lead to nothing except the gratification of those who see me."

Rayburn was persistent, however, and Wilson finally relented. At their meeting in the Oval Office, he listened to Rayburn's argument that the bill was essential. Although he praised it, he refused to give it his public backing on the ground that the war had engulfed Europe and it was a poor time to have a domestic war with the railroad bosses. It would be best, he said, if Rayburn held up all action on his bill in the Commerce Committee.

"I'm sorry, I can't go along with you, Mr. President," he said angrily, picking up his hat and stalking from the room without saying goodby. [20]

Later the entire matter became academic because the House Rules Committee refused to send it to the floor for debate and a vote.

6

Wartime Congressman

After Sam Rayburn's legislative baptism of fire in his first term, he felt like an old hand at Capitol Hill politics by the time his second term began in 1915. He had shown creative skill in bill writing, forceful cross-examination ability at committee hearings and primitive aptitude in give-and-take debate on the House floor. As a result, he had standing among the older members that went far beyond what his thirty-two years of age and two years of congressional service should have given him.

Besides the Cochran lobby "school of political science" crowd, Cactus Jack Garner, and Judge Adamson, his committee chairman, one of his new friends was fifty-seven-year-old Carter Glass of Virginia, who liked the young Texan so much that he gave him a prize bull for the Rayburn farm. Glass, a five-feet four-inch ninety-five-pounder, was the angry, fighting chairman of the Banking and Currency Committee who was instrumental in getting the Federal Reserve Bill through the House in 1913. This basic cornerstone of Wilson's New Freedom established a twelve-region Federal Reserve Bank system to lend money to private national banks and wrest control of the flow and contraction of the nation's capital and credit from the domination of a few Wall Street bankers.

Glass was an unreconstructed rebel who spoke sadly but proudly about living only twenty-five miles from the scene of Lee's surrender at Appomattox when he was seven years old. He had played a huge role in disfranchising Virginia's half million Negroes in 1901 by establishing a poll tax and an "Understanding Clause" as part of the Virginia Constitution. The Understanding Clause gave election clerks the right to disqualify persons (Negroes) from voting, even if they had paid their poll tax, on the ground that they lacked a satisfactory understanding of the American Constitution.

Rayburn admired Glass' aggressive debating quality, an approach he adopted for himself. In this regard, Carter Glass was not the least bit hampered by the fact that he spoke only from the extreme right corner of his mouth. "Carter Glass is the only man I ever saw who can whisper in his own ear," Woodrow Wilson once remarked. [1]

His immediate, apt response and sharp tongue were the envy of Rayburn. Once, when a youth Glass had recommended for the Naval Academy was rejected because of poor teeth, Glass bellowed, "Goddammit! Does he have to bite the enemy?"

Glass was a fierce champion of low federal budgets, and he had only praise for Rayburn when the young Texan argued vehemently on the House floor one afternoon against a proposed appropriation of fourteen thousand dollars to increase the Patent Office's personnel. Glass' emotional concern about catastrophic government waste and the eventual ruin of the country was hardly in keeping with the facts. The entire spending by the federal government from 1789 through 1916 was only a trifling $27 billion, [2] or an average of about $200 million a year, equivalent to a single moonshot of the 1960s and '70s. Wilson's first hectic year in office saw a federal income and outgo of merely $725 million. [3]

But if Sam Rayburn had begun to consider himself a worthy member of Congress, Speaker Champ (James Beauchamp) Clark was on hand to knock him off his small pedestal. In all his time in Congress, Clark never had a piece of legislation to his credit, his intellect was sluggish and his outlook was strictly that of a rural Missourian. Yet as Speaker, he called newer members in individually to point out their shortcomings. Recent additions to the House were thrilled by the prospect of a face-to-face meeting with a man so far above them, and Rayburn was no exception.

Clark, a tall, heavy man whose appearance, manner, and voice were remindful of a high-quality Shakespearian actor, had come to Congress in 1893, had risen to Speaker in 1911, and had been the front-runner for the Democratic presidential nomination in 1912. Contending with him for that honor, Woodrow Wilson had tried to put him down as "a sort of elephantine smart aleck." The "Ol' Hound Dawg," as Clark's admirers nicknamed him because of his campaign song "Ya Gotta Quit Kickin' My Dawg Around," had won a majority of the delegates at the Baltimore convention on the tenth ballot and eight subsequent ones. But he needed a two-thirds vote and fell to Wilson on the forty-sixth ballot after William Jennings Bryan had turned his support away from Clark because he was backed by New York's Tammany and the Roger Sullivan machine in Chicago. As a result, Clark's melancholic dislike of Wilson and Bryan never abated after that.

Some of the newer members who had a private meeting with Clark spoke about it afterward; others kept silent. Ambitious Tom Connally of Texas reported that the Speaker warned him: "Connally, a new Congressman must begin at the foot of the class and spell up. It doesn't matter what your reputation was before you came to Congress. The House has a way of sizing up a man rather quickly, and once you are sized up almost nothing you do after that will change the first impression. The way to get ahead in the House is to stand for something and to know what it is you stand for." [4]

When Rayburn's turn came, Champ Clark told him abruptly that he showed possibilities of amounting to something in the House if he ever overcame his woeful educational background. What Rayburn lacked, he said, was a sense of relationship between the activities of the current Congress and the country's past history. His strong suggestion was that Rayburn do some heavy reading in American history with emphasis on presidential biographies. Among the Presidents he told Rayburn to study were George Washington, John Adams and his son John Quincy Adams, Thomas Jefferson, Andrew Jackson, James Polk and William McKinley. For good measure, he advised him also to read the two-volume *Thirty Years' View* by former Senator Thomas Hart Benton of Missouri. [5]

Decades later, Rayburn called Clark's lecture "some of the best advice anyone ever gave me." But at the time he was chagrined by Clark's condescension and foolishly confessed it to Joe Bailey, who was in Washington doing some lobbying. After Abner died, Bailey paid a visit of condolence to Sam's parents, and he managed to put Sam down as much as Champ Clark had. "You don't have to be with him [Bailey] but a few minutes until you find out that he knows nearly everything," the thrilled Mrs. Rayburn wrote her son. "He certainly speaks in the highest terms of you. . . . He said there were great things in the future for you if you would study. He always puts that in, but he said you were studying."

Sam started his second term heavily in debt. In fact, he did not go home for the holiday season at the end of 1914. "Well, Sam, Xmas came and went and a very sad one for me," his mother wrote him. "When they began coming in I would miss Ab so much, I felt like that when you all got here and him absent knowing that he never could be here anymore I felt it would almost be more than I could bear. . . . However, when the message came that you would not be here it nearly broke my heart." [6]

The debts included the unpaid bill for Abner's funeral, almost two thousand dollars for his short campaign against Tom Perkins in the 1914 primary, plus a three-thousand-dollar mortgage for another farm and mounting bills for a new house on that farm. The 40-acre place south of

Windom had been sold for three thousand dollars and the proceeds used for the cash down payment on a 120-acre farm about two miles west of Bonham. The new house, which would have a dozen rooms, was not expected to be finished until after Easter in 1915, and until then Sam's parents, his sister Lucinda, and his brother Tom—who were the only members of the family still at home—lived in a house Sam rented for them on West Fifth Street in Bonham. [7]

Yet even with his worrisome debts, Sam insisted on adding still more because of the personal sacrifices Lucinda was making, keeping a devoted eye on his parents and running the household. A pretty girl with a stately bearing, she had never married despite opportunities. "My darling Lou," he wrote his forty-year-old sister on February 7, 1915, "you truly deserve everything that is good. You are such a dear sweet sister to us all. . . . When spring comes I want you to get all the nice clothes you want and will pay all your bills. I hope from now on to give you everything you desire and I want you to be absolutely free about things." [8]

At that time congressmen got an allotment above their salaries for office help or to meet personal expenses. Rayburn did his own secretarial work for a while and spent this $125 a month to pay some of his bills. But it became more than a burden to hunt and peck replies to some of the mail he received. These were the nasty letters from several members of a large influential family in Greenville, in Hunt County, who were to send him carping letters month after month and year after year. In describing them one time to his brother-in-law, W. A. Thomas, Sam called them "the old haters at Greenville." [9]

His experiment at being both a congressman and a secretary lasted only a few months, and he hired a young man from his district to handle the office duties. Before coming to Washington, young O. L. Couch ingratiated himself with Rayburn's mother by telling her that no one in the entire world prepared pigs' feet the way she did. This prompted Mrs. Rayburn to write her son, "Tell him [Couch] everytime I cook hogs feet I think of him and wish he had one." [10]

Sam Rayburn's concern with his debts did not interfere with his work in Washington. He was fast becoming known as the "railroad legislator." In 1915, he tackled the problems of shippers whose goods were damaged during transportation by the railroads. It was common practice of most lines to write into the bill of lading that they were not responsible for damage en route. In some instances the courts ruled that this provision did not abrogate the shipper's right to sue. But since goods might be transferred through a half dozen or more lines before reaching the destination, he had to prove the place of damage. Rayburn's amendment to a bill made the initial carrier responsible and provided for full liability for the item in question.

In 1916, when a railroad strike loomed because of long workdays and poor labor conditions, continued shipments of war supplies to England and France were threatened. Wilson appealed to the four Railroad Brotherhoods and the railroad boards to settle their differences. When management refused, he asked Congress for legislation. What emerged was called the Adamson Act, which imposed an eight-hour day for railroad workers and a 20 percent boost in hourly pay. But in fairness to Rayburn's activities in committee and in the House Chamber, the bill could have been named for him. He also helped speed up the legislative action so that it beat the strike deadline by a single day.

It was the Adamson Act that grew into the chief domestic issue in the presidential race that fall between Wilson and Associate Justice Charles Evans Hughes, his Republican opponent. First, Hughes seemed to gain mileage by charging that Wilson had submitted to coercion by the brotherhoods. But Wilson effectively squelched him in a later speech, in which he said that the eight-hour day should be granted not only to railroad employees but to all workers. "A man does better work within eight hours than he does within a more extended day, and the whole theory of it . . . is that his efficiency is increased, his spirit in his work is improved and the whole physical and more vigor of the man is added to." [11]

Wilson's shadow also fell across Rayburn's Democratic primary in 1916, despite the President's repeated public declarations that he would not involve his office in primaries. Rayburn's opponent was Andrew Randell, son of Choice Randell, his predecessor in Congress who had run unsuccessfully for the Senate in 1912. Young Randell had been a student of the President at Princeton.

Randell started his campaign for the July primary in March, while the crush of legislative work kept Rayburn in Washington through June. The young man with the cultured accent hit at Rayburn relentlessly for having voted for an eight-hour day instead of a shorter day for government employees and for opposing the federal child labor law.

When Sam returned home for the final weeks before the primary, Randell's campaign manager, John Marshall, who had been Speaker of the Texas House after Speaker Kennedy had been ousted, challenged him to meet Randell in a long series of debates around the district. Rayburn's political sense told him this would only serve Randell and he refused.

Instead, he listened to his volunteer campaign groups throughout the district who advised him of the need to go from community to community and answer Randell's charges. On the issue of the Borland Bill on the federal employee workday, he also had to offset the statement from Samuel Gompers, head of the American Federation of Labor, that Randell was quoting: "The 8-hour day imperils the health of government employees," was Gompers' tearful cry.

Sam's reply to Randell and Mr. Gompers went over big. "I worked 14 to 16 hours a day in the hot sun on a Fannin County farm, and I voted to make these white-handed, bay-windowed gentry work at least eight hours a day under an electric fan, and sitting on easy cushioned seats." In a variation on this theme, he depicted himself hoeing cotton from morning to sunset and added, "I don't think it imperiled my health."[12]

On his vote against the child labor bill in the House that year, Rayburn had far more explaining to do. First, he tried the statistical and states' rights approach, pointing out that forty-four states already had such laws on the books and that he had been a strong supporter of the Texas law. When this did not seem to satisfy many listeners, he pointed out that the legislation barred interstate shipment of any product on which a child of fifteen and under had worked. This would keep almost all Texas cotton at home, he said, unless farm parents excused their children from helping in the fields. From the sarcastic laughs, Sam knew he had made his point.

But his successsful rebuttal of Randell's campaign issues did not cause his opponent to quit. In fact, only a week before the July 22 primary, Randell appeared to have placed Rayburn's entire campaign in jeopardy by dropping his Wilson bombshell. This was a widely spread letter from Wilson to him, dated July 11, in which the President came out slyly for Randell while vowing his neutrality. Referring to his own letter of two years earlier in which he had praised Rayburn's railroad stock and bond bill, Wilson wrote his student:

My Dear Mr. Randell:

I learn that certain things I have from time to time said in praise of the work of Mr. Rayburn in the House have been interpreted to mean that I was opposed to your nomination. It is hardly necessary to assure you that this was an unjustifiable construction. I do not feel at liberty to express a preference in any Congressional fight and would certainly take no such position when a friend like yourself was involved.

Cordially and sincerely yours,
Woodrow Wilson[13]

Rayburn recognized the potency of this letter and he stepped up his own campaign. When he won a third term by 4,500 votes, he considered himself lucky.

Among the many letters of congratulations was one from Joe Bailey to Sam's parents. Again the former senator showed himself the master of the left-handed compliment when he told them: "If he [Sam] will apply himself with diligence to the study of public questions, he will soon become one of the foremost men in Congress." [14]

Abner's death in 1914 had made Sam conscious that his parents were getting on in years. By the time he moved them into the new house on the Bonham farm in 1915, his father was seventy-five and his mother sixty-nine. He was concerned when he learned that his father was doing the corn harvesting like some of their young neighbors and that his mother would not give up her daily visits to the barn for the milking chore no matter how deep the snow or how blistering hot the day. It worried him when she wrote she "went right on through all the blizzards and snow, never missed wading to the lot to milk," and it pained him when she told him about working in unseasonable heat: "I just wilted like you had thrown hot water on a green weed."

When Sam came home to campaign in 1916, William Marion Rayburn no longer worked. He sat on the front porch behind the three stately white columns and rocked from morning to night. [15] His spade beard had turned white and scraggly and he lost weight steadily. Finally he died on October 16, a week before his seventy-sixth birthday, and the passing of the man whose life had climaxed during the War Between the States depressed Sam for a long time.

Eventually it was the excitement of politics and the realization that he was advancing in the House that stirred him from his anguish. By the time he was sworn in for his third term in 1917, his numerical advancement on the Commerce Committee's seniority escalator was significant. Only four years earlier he had stood twelfth in line among the committee's fourteen Democrats. Now he stood sixth from the top. [16] But more than this, he had become the committee's workhorse. On almost every matter before the committee, Chairman Adamson was relying on him to handle the hearings and the backstage details of bill writing.

Rayburn also felt he was moving ahead because of the rising Texas mystique in Washington. Although John Garner was only the fifth-ranking member of the Ways and Means Committee, he had become a key voice there and in the House generally. This was not because of his forceful personality but because he astutely brought the Texas delegation together frequently for lunch and meetings to discuss issues and positions on bills before the House. As a result, the eighteen Texans almost always voted together as a unit and had a great deal of bargaining power with sponsors of legislation. [17]

The Texas mystique was also present in the government departments, where three Cabinet members and the President's principal adviser on foreign affairs were from the Lone Star State. The Postmaster General was Albert Burleson, the Secretary of Agriculture was David F. Huston and the Attorney General was Thomas W. Gregory.

All three opened doors in their departments to requests from Rayburn and the other Texas congressmen for clerical jobs for their constituents and for handling problems for the folks back home. The chief patronage plum for House members was the naming of local postmasters in their congressional districts. This was almost lost when Wilson came into office and was unaware of this practice. When he decided that the crossroads postmasters should be chosen on merit, Burleson stalked into his Oval Office determined to resign if he could not straighten him out.

"Mr. President, these little offices don't amount to anything," he told Wilson.

> It matters little who is postmaster of Paducah, Kentucky. But these little offices mean a lot to members of Congress. If it goes out that Representative So-and-so has been turned down by the President on a little old postmastership, it means that the Congressman will have bitter trouble at home. . . . As your Postmaster General, I'm going to make 56,000 appointments. I'll see to it that honest and capable men are in every office. But I will consult with the men on the Hill. I have been here a long time—since 1899. I know these Congressmen. They are mostly good men. But if they are turned down, they will hate you and not vote for anything you want.

Wilson agreed to continue the custom.

Rayburn found that the postmastership patronage was not an unmixed blessing. One time Burleson told him that the term of the postmaster at Denison was expiring and that he should name his successor. The *Denison Herald* reported soon afterward that Rayburn had come to town and was "the most popular man in the city." [18] He was surrounded wherever he went by crowds of men who wanted the job. When he finally selected one, he found he had made a friend but also dozens of enemies in the process.

William Jennings Bryan, the Democrats' three-time loser for President, was Wilson's first Secretary of State, and Rayburn was among the Texans deriding him and boosting the mysterious Colonel Edward M. House, who hailed from Houston and was sent on mission after mission to Europe by Wilson.

Besides his duties at State, Bryan served as Wilson's lobbyist on the Hill for his New Freedom legislation. Rayburn was in awe when he first saw this familiar face buttonholing members in the Democratic cloakroom and the Speaker's lobby for their support of the Federal Reserve Bill. The hawk nose, moon face, fringe of frizzed hair and the generous mouth that showed every tooth when he spoke were exactly as in photographs Rayburn had seen of him since he was a teenager.

Tiny Carter Glass, at a crucial point, admitted that the bill was stalled in his committee with little likelihood that it would get out. Yet when Bryan, who had served two terms in the House, was able to get action in the Currency Committee by talking to "a couple of Democrats," [19] Glass was angry. Nor did his temper decline when the bill seemed dead later in the Rules Committee and Bryan won its release after a talk with his "old friend," Congressman Robert L. Henry of Waco, who was the great-great-great-grandson of Patrick Henry. Glass, who fumed to Rayburn and others that Bryan should stay downtown where he belonged, had supported him at the Democratic National Convention in 1896 where Bryan had made his famous "cross of gold" speech. When a parade for Bryan began, said Glass, he had pounced on a big fellow in the Virginia delegation to wrest the state standard from him and march for Bryan. After a fierce struggle over the standard, the two men were separated and Glass discovered that his opponent was also a Bryan man.

In the early decades of the twentieth century, the Secretaries of State, War and the Navy had their offices in a rococo-style building that had been built by President Grant just to the west of the White House. Rayburn rode the streetcar to the State, War and Navy Building only twice to see Bryan. Yet he was quick to agree with Joe Bailey's opinion of the pacifist Secretary of State that "Bryan was so anxious to speak that he started talking before he got to the bottom of a question." [20]

As for Colonel Edward House, there was an air of Texas immenseness to Rayburn in this wispy Texan's audacity. (He had suggested to Sir Edward Grey, the British foreign minister in the spring of 1914, that the two join the German kaiser at the Kiel yacht regatta to reach a firm understanding on pledges to maintain peace.) The little colonel, who insisted on this honorary military label after a Texas governor awarded it to him, had met Wilson in New York before the 1912 campaign and boasted falsely that he controlled the Texas delegation at the forthcoming Baltimore convention. Once the convention was over and Wilson won the nomination, House bragged that he controlled the Texas vote in the November election.

When Texas backed Wilson, House was off and running to European heads of state for the President, despite the fact that he was undercutting Secretary of State Bryan. House had little education, yet he convinced Wilson he was an outstanding intellectual. An acquaintance once described the colonel as "a great little man who can be silent in several languages. He is one of the few men with practically no chin who were considered forceful." An accurate judgment of the reason Wilson was so impressed with him was uttered by a contemporary: "House had a habit of finding out what was on the President's mind and then suggesting that very thing to him. This made the President think they were of one mind and extraordinarily one in their views and outlook." Another official called him "the greatest 'yes' man in history."[21]

Despite Colonel House's peace mission early in 1914, a Serbian youth assassinated Austrian Archduke Francis Ferdinand and his wife at Sarajevo in Bosnia on June 28, 1914, and provided the excuse for European antagonists to begin World War I with its eventual slaughter of 8,500,000 soldiers and the wounding of 21 million others.

At first Wilson issued a proclamation of American neutrality. His pressure on Congress for domestic legislation eased, as Rayburn found out in the case of his Railroad Stock and Bond Bill. What he did not know was that Wilson was following his own book, *Constitutional Government in the United States.* As the President told a writer, chapter three of the book "showed that in times of peace when domestic problems are uppermost, Congress comes to the front, but when foreign affairs intrude the people look to the President. His foreign policy must then be his own."[22]

Early in 1915, Wilson again ignored Bryan and sent House to Europe as his "personal representative" to make another try for peace. House, who was strictly an Anglophile, spent a month in England despite urgent cables from Wilson that he hurry to Germany before the war expanded further. What followed was a "war of notes" between Wilson and the Imperial German Government after a U-boat sank a British munitions-carrying liner, the *Lusitania,* with a loss of 112 American lives; the resignation of William Jennings Bryan who wanted strict notes sent equally to Britain as well as Germany; Wilson's successful reelection in 1916 using the slogan: "He Kept Us Out Of War"; and finally in April

1917, after Germany resumed submarine warfare against neutral shipping, his decision to ask Congress for a declaration of war against Germany.

Sam Rayburn was in the jam-packed House Chamber the night of April 2, rain beating down on the glass roof, when Wilson came to deliver his war message. Four days later the House voted 373 to 50 to enter the conflict, with Majority Leader Claude Kitchin of North Carolina leading the fight against Wilson. Then came the heated verbal battle over Wilson's demand for a conscripted army, with Speaker Champ Clark giving full vent to his hatred of Wilson in his losing fight against the draft.

Once the war was on, two members of the Texas delegation—Tom Connally and Marvin Jones—joined the army. But Rayburn, with no military experience and now thirty-five years old, stuck to the daily task, along with the mass of congressmen, to provide Wilson with dictatorial powers. These included authority to fix prices; control production; put industry on a profitable cost-plus basis; take over mines, factories, railroads, steamship lines; propagandize the nation; and throttle the Bill of Rights with the Espionage Act of 1917 (which authorized jailing anyone who interfered with the military mobilization) and the Sedition Act of 1918 ("which in effect made any criticism of the Wilson Administration illegal.") [23]

Besides voting almost on a straight-line basis for the administration, Rayburn made his own special contribution to the war effort through his committee. Chairman Adamson left the Congress in December 1917 for the security of a lifetime appointment on the Board of United States General Appraisers (later renamed the U.S. Customs Court); but his successor, Congressman Thetus Wilrette Sims from Tennessee, gave Rayburn a similar free hand.

From the young man from Texas came legislation and floor leadership involving servicemen's insurance, compensation, and vocational rehabilitation, pensions for disabled veterans, war widows' and orphans' hospitalization; low-interest postwar loans for servicemen; and protection of railroads against sabotage, a priority system to give war supplies the right-of-way over nonwar goods on railroads and government operation of the railroads during the war.

Rayburn's most creative effort involved his War Risk Insurance Bill under which the government insured American doughboys up to ten thousand dollars if they made "the supreme sacrifice." This legislation became the basis of the vast World War II GI insurance program. In 1917, when Rayburn began looking into the subject, he found that most insurance companies would not insure soldiers and those doing so charged an exorbitant premium of fifty-eight dollars per one thousand annually, according to actuarians studying the probability of soldier-death-in-action.

Rayburn's bill set the premium at eight dollars per one thousand, and even before his measure reached the House floor the insurance companies were crying, "Socialism!" Congressmen serving the companies tried to turn Rayburn's explanation of the bill in the House Chamber into a fiasco by asking him repeatedly to yield for a question. After several such interruptions, Sims and other members of his committee asked Rayburn to refuse to yield further. But Rayburn saw the advantage of letting his opponents discredit themselves in the eyes of most members by their obvious tactic, and he continued patiently to let them interrupt him. When he finally finished his presentation, he was treated to loud applause and the bill passed. [24]

The thorniest railroad problem Rayburn handled came when the administration requested authority to take over the lines during the war. The government's claim was that by organizing the railroads into a single system under a Railroad Administration soldiers, workers, and supplies could be moved more efficiently. Rayburn doubted this claim. He also cast a dubious eye at A.F. of L. President Sam Gompers, the heads of the railroad brotherhoods and William McAdoo, Wilson's son-in-law and Treasury Secretary, who was slated to become the R. A.'s boss, because they favored continued government operation in the postwar period.

Nevertheless, he handled the floor debate for the administration in February 1918, explaining the complexities involved in compensating the lines during the takeover and the question of how the thousands of rate differentials for freight and fares would be made. [25] His point of departure from the administration came over his provision for setting a time when the lines would be returned to private operation.

"I oppose an indefinite tenure," he argued. As he painted a horror picture, this condition would keep 1.7 million railroad workers as government employees and give the President a mass political force to retain his office in an election. But he lost on this point, and the question was postponed until after the war.

When the war started, Wilson was intensely fearful of the spread of disunity through speeches by the likes of Socialist leader Eugene V. Debs and Senator Robert LaFollette and through frightening acts of sabotage by the German minority. For this reason he induced Congress to pass the Espionage Act of 1917 and the Sedition Act of 1918. Although Sam Rayburn was a personal friend of Congressman Meyer London of New York, [26] who was a Socialist and labor strike leader, he was swept up by

Wilson's fervor to abridge First Amendment rights. For he had no reason to doubt the truth of Woodrow Wilson's remarks in his Flag Day address in 1917 when he charged: "The military masters of Germany denied us the right to be neutral. They filled our unsuspecting communities with vicious spies and conspirators. They sought by violence to destroy our industries and arrest our commerce."

With the madness authorized by the President, Postmaster General Burleson lost his interest in providing House members with post office patronage and found a far more absorbing one—having mail opened and read and barring from delivery materials he ruled were advocating "treason, insurrection and disobedience of U.S. laws." Attorney General Tom Gregory also found a new appetite like his Texan compatriot Burleson. Gregory in his early days had prosecuted for the state of Texas the Waters-Pierce Oil Company affiliate of Standard Oil with which Joe Bailey was secretly associated. In the first Wilson years he was ardently in pursuit of business trusts. Now he led an army in making wholesale raids without warrants in which property was stolen or destroyed, thousands of people beaten, and fifteen hundred arrested. When Eugene Debs made an antiwar speech, he was arrested, tried, and sentenced to ten years in the federal penitentiary. A young lady, not yet of age, got twenty years for expressing her opinions. And through it all, Wilson, busy in his effort to "make the world safe for democracy," offered not a single objection.

When Gregory left the administration after the Armistice, A. Mitchell Palmer, the new Attorney General, expanded "the war on Reds." He sent thousands of agents from the Justice Department to incite seditious talk and meetings, make arrests, subject victims to third-degree inquisitions and torture, and deport noncitizens. [27] Socialist Victor Berger, elected to the House from Wisconsin, was denied his seat because of his opposition to U.S. entrance into the war. Indicted on this score afterward by a federal grand jury, he was sentenced to twenty years in prison by Federal Judge Kenesaw Mountain Landis.

With such official sanction, it was little wonder that the anti-Red campaign blew like a hurricane wind across the nation. Any member of Congress who stood in its path was in grave danger of losing his seat. In the Senate, Warren G. Harding of Ohio called for putting radicals "against the wall." In the House, member after member craved time from the Speaker to express his Americanism, and Rayburn was no exception. "I believe in an America for Americans," he spoke his piece. "The anarchist and the Bolshevist shall go."

The Texas legislature had passed a state Sedition Act, making a person liable to a twenty-five-year prison sentence for expressing a disloyal opinion. This was a popular law in Rayburn's congressional district, and there were resounding cheers at the Armistice Day ceremonies at the courthouse square in Bonham for him when he said that the United States should "close the immigration gates and open up the emigration gates to deport a lot of European trash we have accumulated."

It was fortunate for him politically that he said what he did. For in 1918 he had his easiest reelection victory—about a five-to-one margin, and in 1920 he won by three to one. As the *Denison Herald* claimed about its favorite congressmen in an editorial report to its readers in November 1920: "Sam Rayburn is one of the biggest men in Congress, and if there were more like him there would be less occasion for criticism of that body."

7

Republican Doldrums

As a partisan, ambitious politician, Sam Rayburn's timetable for advancement called for continuing Democratic administrations and Congresses as the backboard needed to show off his wares. But the fabric had already begun to unravel in 1917. In the House that year, the Democrats held a precarious margin of only a few seats over the Republicans, and the presence of seven members of neither major party spelled trouble. Had Champ Clark not bought off several Republicans, including blind, greedy Tom Schall of Minnesota, whom he promised a coveted seat on the Rules Committee, he would have lost his presiding perch on the rostrum.

But two years later Rayburn found himself on the minority side, where he was to languish during the next twelve years. Wilson had made the election of a Democratic Congress in 1918 a test of the popularity of his leadership and his "Fourteen-Point" postwar international plan, which included his League of Nations. [1] While he issued broadsides and appeals on his own, he also dispatched influential members of his administrations to do some campaigning in the field. Among these was Herbert Hoover, the Food Administrator, who was sent to New Hampshire to help elect a Democratic senator and representative. [2]

The country, however, was eager to forget about the war once the Germans and Austrians asked for peace early in October of 1918, and the leadership of the House and Senate and committee control went to the Republicans on November 5. Champ Clark, assessing the Democratic debacle, called it "the greatest slaughter of the innocents since Herod."

For the first time since Rayburn came to the House Clark was not the Speaker. Instead, on the rostrum in place of the big, robust Democrat sat Frederick H. Gillett, a Republican from Massachusetts, a man with narrow political interests and limited physical energy. Gillett claimed one time that on a train trip with his pal, Senator Warren Harding, the two had climbed off at every station stop to kick a football to each other. [3] But the editor of the *Boston Transcript*, who knew Gillett well, said that he never exerted himself and did not drink coffee in the morning "for fear it would keep him awake all day." [4]

While the 1918 congressional elections gave the chairmanship of the House Commerce Committee to a Republican, John J. Esch of Wisconsin, they also boosted Sam Rayburn's status on the minority side of the committee. Only three Democrats now outranked him in seniority, and since none of them was noted for his industry Esch turned to Rayburn as the real Democratic spokesman on the committee.

Esch's big problem was what to do with the railroads now that the war was over. The Railroad Brotherhoods were pushing hard to have Congress approve the Plumb Plan, which called for government owner- ship of the railroads and Brotherhood leadership on the board of directors. William McAdoo, Director General of Railroads, talked to his father-in-law, the President, before and after his voyages to the Paris Peace Conference early in 1919 to give the government a test of its ability to operate the railroads in peacetime. The American Federation of Labor's Sam Gompers called for a five-year extension of the existing management by the government.

But the railroad industry was not the only one whose future ownership lay under consideration. The packing industry had also come "crying" to the federal government to operate it; then the telephone and telegraph industries had "started screaming" to be taken over. On the question of the new communications development called "wireless" or radio, a similar situation was developing, with Herbert Hoover championing government ownership of radio broadcasting facilities and Assistant Secretary of the Navy Franklin D. Roosevelt opposing it. [5]

In a letter to his brother-in-law on January 10, 1919, Rayburn wrote of his intention to move fast and hard into this issue with a speech "opposing continued government operation of the railroads . . . and government ownership of telephone and telegraph" systems. [6] The speech on January 30 was his opening effort to keep the government free from owning and operating businesses. "Instead of the established way of curing evils in industry by legislating to correct these evils," he said, "from many quarters the only suggestion that comes is for the government to take over, own and operate the industry. And every time some sick and tot- tering makeshift of the industry gets into deep waters it comes running to the government, crying, 'Take me over.' "

Instead of taking up the flag for private ownership in all the industries involved, Rayburn concentrated on making the railroad industry the test case, because its initial "desperate begging" had started the trend. The fight was bitter, especially with the labor leaders. He answered their arguments with countering evidence that showed rail service had deteriorated under wartime government control and the operation, moreover, had required a subsidy from taxpayers of $1 million a day. "If we had government ownership of railroads," he added, "there would be political logrolling by members of Congress and influential organizations to get new roads built." He foresaw a situation similar to the ever-increasing pork barrel for rivers and harbor projects.

Rayburn's bill to return the railroads to private ownership and operation went down to defeat in the House vote, despite the support of his chairman, John Esch, and the approval of Senator Albert S. Cummins of Iowa, the chairman of the Senate Commerce Committee. The view of President Wilson now was of vital importance if the vote was to be overturned.

While this battle was going on, Wilson paid little attention to it, for he was concentrating first on writing the Versailles treaty with its Covenant of the League of Nations, and second on winning its approval from the U.S. Senate. Faced with a malignant opposition led by Senator Henry Cabot Lodge, chairman of the Senate Foreign Relations Committee, he started out that September on a ten-thousand-mile speaking appeal to the American people to help him get his treaty through the Senate.

The enormous strain finally brought on a stroke, and at the beginning of October he lay upstairs in the White House with his left arm and leg paralyzed and his facial features twisted. In this sad condition, he suffered through the Senate's defeat of his treaty on November 19, 1919.

While he remained a bedridden invalid, as if by an afterthought he settled the vital railroad issue. On Christmas Eve, he issued a proclamation ordering the lines returned to private ownership by March 1, 1920. [7] This decision still required congressional action, but the bursting of the dam made it inevitable.

It came in the form of the Esch-Cummins Bill, or what later was called the Transportation Act of 1920. Senator Cummins, a Teddy Roosevelt trustbuster, surprised Rayburn by his insertion of a provision to encourage the merger of existing railroads under ICC supervision. Esch also surprised Rayburn by agreeing to another provision giving railroad workers the right to be represented by unions of their choice. Where Rayburn differed with both Esch and Cummins was in their desire to give the industry large sums of money to reconvert its lines from government control. Over his opposition, they put through a subsidy of $600 million during the first six months with a possible addition of $650 million more later.

In the end, Rayburn voted for the legislation after Esch incorporated his Railroad Stock and Bond Bill of 1914 in the final measure signed by Wilson. This barred railroads from issuing securities without ICC approval. So belatedly, his big bill as a freshman congressman was finally enacted into law.

By the time the 1920 election-campaign season hove into view, it was fairly obvious to Rayburn that he was going to be in the minority party again in the next Congress. There was public revulsion against the pathetic cripple who was still in the White House while the new bigger-than-life figure in foreign affairs was Senator Lodge, the same little man with the gray spade beard and spats who had manufactured the list of shortcomings in Wilson's peace treaty the year before that had helped bring on his physical collapse.

The short postwar period had so far shown a country beset with strikes, skyrocketing unemployment, race riots, anti-Bolshevik hysteria, enlarging crime, inflation, depressed farm prices and general disillusionment. It was in this setting that the Democratic National Committee first became aware of Rayburn and asked him to campaign for the national ticket in Ohio, the home state of the opposing presidential candidates, Warren Harding and Governor James M. Cox. This was Rayburn's initial political excursion into Northern territory, and he was well received by Democratic audiences though he drew little newspaper notice.

Rayburn was witness to the macabre scene at the Capitol at the start of the Harding administration. He had won reelection easily, but many Democrats, including Champ Clark and Cordell Hull, had been overwhelmed by the Republican landslide. Even worse, Clark, the symbol of House Democrats, had died on March 2, 1921, and the flag over the Capitol was remindfully depressed to half mast while Harding stood on the inauguration stand and called for a return to "normalcy."

Rayburn early understood that "normalcy" meant a return to high tariffs, tax breaks for the rich, subsidies for business, isolationism in foreign affairs and general government inaction on other matters. Harding had already spread the word that he believed that the initiative on legislation should come from Congress and not from the executive branch. [8] Moreover, when he told his first Congress, "America should put its house in order," his "do-nothing" explanation seemed to be in line with the philosophy expressed the previous year by his Vice President, Calvin Coolidge. As governor of Massachusetts, Coolidge had told the state legislature in 1920: "It is a time to conserve, to retrench, rather than to reform. The greatest benefit you can confer is the speedy making of necessary appropriations, adjustment of some details and adjournment." [9]

Having served in Congress only during the purposeful, driving years of Woodrow Wilson, Rayburn was bewildered initially by the informality and geniality of Harding's White House. The air of emergency was lifted from the Executive Mansion the few times he had occasion to observe it. Not only was it a simple matter for him and other congressmen to land an appointment in the Oval office, but anyone decently clothed could walk into the first floor of the White House during the day and look around. In addition, between 12:30 P.M. and Harding's lunchtime, the President held a daily reception and shook hands with all callers. [10] And instead of moral rectitude flowing from the White House, cloakroom-lounging congressmen gossiped about Harding's bootlegger, who delivered his liquor despite the Eighteenth Amendment, and they bragged about invitations to poker games Harding held two evenings a week in his upstairs quarters.

It was in the midst of this strange political atmosphere that Rayburn made a major advance in the House's Democratic hierarchy. When the Sixty-seventh Congress convened on April 11, his Democratic colleagues honored him by electing him Chairman of the Democratic Caucus. He wrote proudly to his sister Meddie, "It was a big surprise to me that the big fellows should get together and agree on me, but on the other hand it was not entirely a shock as I had stayed here to watch developments during the vacation." How much of this honor was the result of his own politicking he explained in this fashion: "We must meet things worth while more than half way—they do not come to us." [11]

Despite the fact that Republicans outnumbered Democrats in the House by almost three to one, he had no intention of falling back in cowed silence as did so many Democrats. From the start of the Harding regime, he was a highly partisan, truculent Democrat, ready to mix with Republicans whether provoked or not. "For eight years you have criticized, you have sneered, you have stood in the middle of the road trying to impede progress," he lashed out at his Republican brethren in 1921. "You have become a party of obstruction, not construction. You have hungered for power and office. Now you have both. . . . Under your leadership I pity you. I am distressed for the country." [12]

For the record, Rayburn's major legislative effort in that Congress appeared to be the introduction of nine bills to donate captured Confederate cannons to nine towns in his district. But this was just the cosmetic show. Republicans knew him as the Democrats' angry man with the blistering tongue. He scathingly attacked the so-called "scientific"

Fordney-McCumber Tariff Bill that raised import duties to their highest level in history, needled Republican members "to resist the lash of their masters [lobbyists for industry]." He denounced them for voting large, easy loans for railroads and for franking out bales of speeches filled with false sympathy for veterans in order to get their vote. "I do not walk in here about once every twelve months to read a sloppy speech about the soldier in order to mail it out," he rode them. [13]

On the other hand, liberals of both parties, who had considered him an ally, now found him suddenly conservative on various issues. For instance, he led the opposition in 1921 against a federal-state matching-funds arrangement for road construction, calling it an incursion violating states' rights.

In committee, too, he was a hard-hitting man on the dais. Herbert Hoover, in Rayburn's eyes the renegade who had deserted Woodrow Wilson to become a Republican, was now Harding's Secretary of Commerce and had to appear regularly before the House Commerce Committee to explain his department's activities and ask for new powers.

Part of the committee's power had been eliminated by law, or the exchanges might have been harsher. The Budget and Accounting Act of 1921 had set up a Bureau of the Budget in the Treasury Department to coordinate the entire Federal Budget and a General Accounting Office (GAO) as an arm of Congress to ferret out waste and fraud by the departments in spending their appropriations. Before this milestone law was put on the books, Herbert Hoover would have prepared the Commerce Department's budget on his own and gone to the Commerce Committee for its approval. Now his budget was prepared by the Budget Bureau, and the Appropriations Committees of the House and Senate had total jurisdiction over its consideration. This still left Rayburn's committee with the power to authorize new programs for Hoover's department and keep close watch on its operations, but the money string was gone. It also left the aggressive Hoover with the opportunity to encroach on other departments and usurp their functions.

Besides Hoover's department, the House Commerce Committee had its tentacles on other agencies. John Esch, the chairman of the committee, had lost his primary race in 1920 to another Republican, and Harding had found a place for him on the Interstate Commerce Commission. As an old friend, Esch lent a ready ear to Rayburn's suggestions.

Another agency was the newly established Veterans' Bureau (VB), one of whose duties was to administer Rayburn's War Risk Insurance Act. Rayburn tangled quickly with the Republicans, who wanted the VB decentralized. In Rayburn's view, decentralization would make it more inefficient in processing veterans' claims and more difficult to eliminate once it completed its work for World War I servicemen. He lost in the vote but history proved him correct on both scores.

Rayburn might have imagined he had good rapport with Charles R. Forbes, the VB administrator, but in reality he had none. Forbes, a.w.o.l. for four years from the army in his youth, later handled the construction of the Pearl Harbor naval base for Wilson, earned a Congressional Medal of Honor in World War I, and managed to become a member of Harding's inner coterie of poker and drinking pals. Forbes became so close to the President that one time Harding took a walk with him on the South Lawn of the White House and sobbingly wailed that he had led an empty life. [14] Rayburn never found anything amiss at the Veterans' Bureau, but after rumors spread that Forbes was milking its half-billion-dollar annual appropriation, a Senate investigation estimated his personal steal at $200 million, and a court later sent him to jail.

Rayburn was also involved with the operations of the Alien Property Custodian, whose administrator had served with him in the House. He was Thomas W. Miller, a founder of the American Legion and director of the Republican National Committee. The Alien Property Custodian was in charge of determining the fate of tens of thousands of enemy-owned industrial properties and pieces of real estate seized by the U.S. government during the war. Included were thirty-one thousand active bank trusts. Rayburn proposed legislation to return the property quickly, but a Republican bill to delay the return passed. Miller was later found to be the recipient of bribes and served thirteen months in jail.

To a man of Rayburn's straitlaced moral rectitude and belief in the "goodness" of Presidents, an administration honeycombed with crooks was a preposterous consideration. On the other hand, he had no rosy illusions that Harding's plans for the nation would improve the quality of life. In Rayburn's district and throughout the nation's farm belts, the administration's severe contraction of the money supply to fight inflation had brought a sharp drop in farm prices and a steep rise in farm bankruptcies; and in the cities large-scale unemployment and labor unrest. Rayburn's prediction in the House was that the Republicans would be properly punished in 1922 after "an outraged people have time to get to the ballot box."

As things turned out, the "outraged people" were also in Sam Rayburn's congressional district, and his Democratic primary contest in July 1922 was a harrowing cliff-hanger.

In February he had smugly written his sister Kate that he was thinking of running for the Senate that year. Ailing Senator Charles A. Culberson, in the Senate twenty-four years, was up again for another six-year term, and Sam's friends wanted him to announce for the old man's seat. "A race every two years gets pretty irksome," Sam confided to Kate about his situation as a member of the House. [15]

But after weighing various factors, he decided against making a try for the Senate. First, as he told her, his real ambition was to "rise in the House," and now that he was Chairman of the Democratic Caucus he felt he was on his way. But there were far more compelling reasons for not running for the Senate. In a statewide contest, Joe Bailey would prove to be a heavy sandbag on his back. He was no longer a Bailey admirer, but he could not say this publicly without making it sound bad, even though a general revulsion had developed against the former senator.

Bailey had run unsuccessfully for governor in 1920, and his chances of ever winning any office again, said Sam, "were as dead as hell." [16] But "just as long as Bailey is everlastingly coming to the front as a candidate that long will it be practically impossible for me to become the state figure I have reason to expect to become," he wrote Kate's husband. It was his curse, he noted, that of "all those in Texas who followed Bailey's flag, I am the only one who today holds an office." Every move Bailey made reminded the Bailey-hating press that Rayburn was the only Baileyite in a public position. "I am truly the last of the Mohicans," he complained. Yet at the same time that the anti-Bailey papers were flogging him along with his one-time hero the Bailey papers were giving Rayburn no publicity, Sam wrote, because "they were afraid that somebody might think they thought there was more than one man of brains."

Besides the Bailey handicap, there was yet another reason to avoid a statewide contest in 1922. The Ku Klux Klan, organized during the Reconstruction after the Civil War, had been reborn in 1915 and spread like wildfire throughout the Southern Populist strongholds, as well as in the North. With their fiery crosses burning across Texas in 1922, racial and religious hating Ku Kluxers holding county and local offices and Hiram Evans, a Texas citizen serving as Imperial Wizard for the entire country, an opponent of the KKK like Sam Rayburn would have been swamped in a Senate Democratic primary. Evans, who personally directed the flogging of sixty-two persons and branded an "uppity" Texas bellhop with acid, had even gained respectability when he visited the White House with the Ku Klux sculptor Gutzon Borglum for a chat with President Harding. [17]

The wisdom of Rayburn's decision was revealed by the ease with which Earle B. Mayfield, the Klan's candidate, won the Senate primary. For the hooded white Protestant bigots who could not read the KKK voting instructions, Mayfield wore an American flag in his lapel so they could recognize him as the Klan's choice. Later an effort to deny him a Senate seat because of his affiliation failed after a Senate investigation. [18]

To cement his sixth term in the House, Sam Rayburn had considered returning home in February 1922 to mend fences and deliver a rash of speeches before many of his previous supporters who strayed "became too much set in their ways." Such lighthearted comments to his sister Kate and others were absent when he finally began campaigning later that spring, for he knew he was in serious trouble.

His opponent was Ed Westbrook, a former chairman of the Texas Senate Finance Committee. He was from Hunt County below Fannin where "the old haters at Greenville" lived, the people who regularly poured complaining, condemning letters into his Washington office. Rayburn had easily defeated Westbrook in 1920, but the Westbrook running again this year was a far more formidable foe because of his powerful backing.

What Westbrook now had was a large campaign treasury and a hardworking army out to retire Rayburn from Congress. Arrayed against Rayburn were the KKK, the Farmer-Labor Union, the A.F. of L., the Railroad Brotherhoods and the railroad shopmen, and railroad management. For the purpose at hand, this strange conglomeration was united, and he recognized the immensity of the upward struggle that lay before him.

Broadsides from the farmers' association labeled him "the enemy of the farmer," and claimed he had worked in Congress for the low farm prices that were a part of Treasury Secretary Andrew Mellon's "wringing out" deflationary policy. In his speeches, Rayburn tried to undo this false charge, pointing out that he had no savings despite his congressional salary and lived off his farm's earnings. "Would it be to my interest for farming products to be low?" he asked in pained injury. And why should he be considered an enemy of the farmer when he hurried home every year after Congress adjourned to pick cotton "beause I need the money." [19] How much good his admission did him could not be determined from the sun-wrinkled faces of his audiences.

From the labor end, Sam Gompers had threatened action against congressmen who did not vote to extend federal operation of the railroads, and Sam Rayburn was enemy number one. Rayburn's remarks in the exchange on Capitol Hill had infuriated the A.F. of L. leader, especially one to Congress advising members not to be "scared by the threat of Mr. Gompers who represents less than 5 percent of the people."

To voters of the Fourth District, the A.F. of L. called Rayburn "the workingman's enemy," and pointed out that he had voted against the child labor law and the three-dollar-a-day minimum wage bill, plus voting for the "long" eight-hour day for government employees instead of retaining the seven-hour day with its two-hour lunchtime break. Rayburn offered explanations for all his votes and denied he was the enemy of labor, pointing out his strong support of the law exempting labor unions from prosecution under the Sherman Anti-Trust Act.

But all his explaining fell on deaf ears in Denison, a railroad division post with a substantial number of men employed in its shops and roundhouses. Here the Rayburn opposition gained momentum when the Railroad Labor Board ordered a 12½ percent cut in wages. Almost a half million railroad shopmen across the country, including the Denison force, went out on strike in protest on July 1, 1922, and in the heat of their anger the local leaders in Denison turned on Rayburn, who had nothing to do with their controversy.

Arm in arm in the anti-Rayburn forces were the railroad companies. While still demanding that their employees accept the wage cut, they were ignoring the ruling that they themselves reduce rates 10 percent. Yet on one issue they were agreed—Sam Rayburn had to go. Their reasons: the Rayburn stock and bond legislation and his leadership for the measure to make the railroads responsible for the full value of the damages to goods they carried.

Going into the homestretch of the campaign, Rayburn was struck with pessimism. Campaign workers asked him to attack Westbrook personally. But the most he would do was to chide him for approving higher state appropriations when he was in the state Senate than when Rayburn was Speaker of the Texas House. As the campaign neared its end, Rayburn seemed a sure loser when he told a crowd, "There are some people, that the higher I get, the more bitterly they fight me. Some fellow tells a man I'm easy to beat and he gets in the race."

The polling precincts closed on a hot Saturday night in July. A few hours before midnight, Rayburn paced the floor alongside one of his men who was copying down the total tallies from the district's precinct boxes. Places that had always voted for him were now on the Westbrook side of the ledger. "I've lost this race," he muttered glumly.

But he was too pessimistic. After the lead seesawed back and forth between him and Westbrook, the last ballot was finally counted and Rayburn was in front by the slim margin of 1,254 votes. He was saved by his home county, which had given him a 1,018-vote margin. So at the age of forty he was grudgingly returned to Congress for his sixth term.

The Democratic party in general had a far easier time than Rayburn in the 1922 elections. Considered dead and bankrupt after its 1920 debacle, the party rebounded only two years later as a national protest against the economic panic of 1921-22, the new high tariff law and the growing scandals within the Harding administration. The Harding landslide of only two years earlier was eroded so drastically that the Democrats gained seventy-five seats in the House. Harding, in a discouraged mid-term mood, wrote an adviser, "Frankly, being President is rather an unattractive business unless one relishes the exercise of power. That is a thing which has never greatly appealed to me."

Although Rayburn and the other House members of the Sixty-eighth Congress were elected in 1922, that Congress did not meet until December 1923, some four months after Harding's death in August. When it met, its biggest battle was over the election of a Speaker.

In 1921, Frederick Gillett, the Republican, had defeated Claude Kitchen, the Democrat, by a vote of 297 to 122. But in 1923 the party division was so narrow that nominal Republicans from the Wisconsin LaFollette camp were in a position to hand the Speakership to either major party. Kitchen was now dead, and Cactus Jack Garner, ranking Democrat on the Ways and Means Committee, fought Finis J. Garrett of Tennessee in the Democratic caucus for the right to oppose Gillett. Before Garner got into the contest, Rayburn had committed himself to Garrett, and for a time after the Democratic caucus Garner was "cool" to Sam, whose vote he assumed would be his automatically no matter what his prior promise. [20]

The rivalry between Gillett and Garrett for Speaker was unique in the twentieth century. The voting lasted three days and went to nine ballots, with Garrett ahead on four counts and tied with Gillett on two others. But Henry Cooper of Wisconsin was also on the ballot, and when he finally threw his seventeen votes to Gillett on the ninth go-around, Gillett won his third term as Speaker. [21]

Calvin Coolidge, the lemony-faced Puritan, was now enthroned in the White House and he had the opportunity to put his political and economic beliefs into practice. His political credo was the simple one that the government was best that governed least while his economic philosophy held that "the business of the American people is business."

Congress showed its general agreement with both beliefs. In three of its annual sessions while he was President, it adjourned after only three months; its other sessions averaged six months in length. If the Congress stirred itself as it did to pass farm price subsidies or approval of a government-owned Tennessee River electric power system there was always a Coolidge veto waiting in the wings. While Coolidge's passive role found an applauding press, Congress in contrast underwent continual lambasting. Typical was the comment of the *St. Louis Globe-Democrat*, which rasped, "The people are sick and tired of Congressional inefficiency and turmoil, they are sick of the lack of cohesion and purpose."

With the seemingly unhaltable business prosperity that developed in the Coolidge years, White House complacency and congressional innocuousness went droning on, to the great discouragement of a creative legislator like Rayburn. "We have got so many regulatory laws already," said Coolidge, "that I feel we would be better off if we did not have any more. The greatest duty of government is not to embark on any new ventures. It does not follow that because abuses exist that it is the concern of the Federal Government to attempt their reform." [22]

Once in justifying his do-nothing philosophy, Coolidge remarked: "If you see ten troubles coming down the road, you can be sure nine will run into the ditch before they reach you." [23] On the congressional front, the appalling amount of nit-picking to pass the time disgusted even some of the nit-pickers. Congressman Joseph W. Martin, Jr., of Massachusetts, later to be Rayburn's closest Republican friend, reported that the Foreign Affairs Committee on which he served spent a week arguing about a $20,000 appropriation for an international poultry show in Tulsa. [24]

As a Democrat, and one sitting far below the salt, Rayburn's personal relationship with Republican President Calvin Coolidge was insignificant. One thing he found out was that Coolidge's reputation for silence was spurious. "He was supposed to be so busy studying great questions that he couldn't look up and talk," said Rayburn. A story passing around the House cloakrooms claimed that "when Coolidge opened his mouth a moth flew out." But as Rayburn recalled later, "I visited with him in his office a few times, and then I had breakfast at the White House with him twice, and he talked enough." [25]

At one breakfast, the President, who had only four professional assistants and thirty-six clerks to help him run the Executive Office, showed his contempt for protocol. "I remember we went into the breakfast room," said Rayburn.

> There was a man named Ike Hoover, who was a kind of major-domo around the White House. This fellow Hoover, who was trying to get everyone in the right seat, was stirring around among us, saying, "Good morning, good morning." And there seemed to be still a lot of confusion in the Red Room when the

President arrived. He saw the complication and he blurted out, "Sit down anyplace gentlemen. Eating is just as good in one place as another."

He talked plenty at breakfast. And he fed the dog at the table—had a nice-looking dog sitting behind his chair, and reached back and gave him something every now and then.

Spinning through yarns to Rayburn seated next to him, Coolidge complained of his ceremonial duties. "We had one of these receptions here last night," he told Rayburn, "and I had to stand there and say, 'Howdy-do, Howdy-do,' two thousand times and it didn't do my throat a bit of good." There was one thing Coolidge said, Rayburn remembered, "that should be read by every politician over and over again. Somebody was kidding him about his silence and he said, 'Well, I found out early in life that you didn't have to explain something you hadn't said.'"

Rayburn went to his first Democratic National Convention in 1924. Later in life he would boss these clambakes, but in 1924 he was a silent witness in Madison Square Garden to the ramshackly donnybrook put on by his party to choose its presidential nominee. The prime contest was between former Treasury Secretary William McAdoo, the darling of the KKK, and Governor Alfred E. Smith of New York.

The Texas delegation was committed to McAdoo because Al Smith was the "wet" candidate, but this did not stop Rayburn from being friendly toward Franklin D. Roosevelt, who was the hit of the convention with his speech nominating Smith. This was the first time Rayburn had seen Roosevelt, though they had conversed in Washington in the Wilson years when handsome, thirty-one-year-old Roosevelt had been Assistant Secretary of the Navy. This occurred when Rayburn phoned Navy Secretary Josephus Daniels and was transferred to Roosevelt because Daniels was out of the office. "That's the nicest man I've talked to in Washington since I've been here," was Rayburn's odd remark after the call. [26] Since the Wilson administration, Roosevelt had been the Democratic vice-presidential nominee in the 1920 political disaster.

Stricken with crippling polio in August 1921, Roosevelt had come out on crutches to the Madison Square Garden podium to champion Al Smith and dub him the "Happy Warrior." A *New York Herald-Tribune* reporter said that the applause for Roosevelt was so great at the conclusion that he was "the one man whose name would stampede the convention were it put in nomination." Will Rogers, writing for *The New York Times* about the man who would one day work closely with Rayburn, said that when

Roosevelt "did get to the end and named Al, you would have thought somebody had thrown a wildcat in your face."

But Roosevelt was not a candidate, and when a stalemate ran through 102 ballots, the convention nominated John W. Davis, a Wall Street lawyer, on the following ballot. This guaranteed the election of Calvin Coolidge, for local Democrats in many places considered Davis so great a liability in their own contests that they asked him not to campaign in their states. So Coolidge had four more years of what became known as the "Roaring Twenties," an era of gangsterism, wholesale violation of the Eighteenth Amendment, and an insane speculation in stocks and real estate.

The national situation in 1924 had no influence in Texas politics. Rayburn's opponent in the primary was M. M. Morrison, who had been one of his numerous rivals in his first contest in 1912. Rayburn's campaign managers sent him word that Morrison was a pushover. So he returned home to make only a few speeches before election day, and he won by nine thousand votes.

The year 1926 was an even better political career year for Rayburn. On the political front, no opponent challenged him in the Democratic primary, the first time in his eight tries for the House that he enjoyed this pleasure.

Joe Bailey was still around, but no one cared any longer that Sam Rayburn had once been associated with him. In a letter to his sister Kate, Sam wrote that he had seen Bailey. "When he is animated as he always is when he talks, he is something of the old Bailey, but in repose he is saggy and sad looking—He is a mighty old man for 63."[27]

What added sparkle to Rayburn's victory in 1926 was that Alben Barkley, who stood above him in seniority on the Commerce Committee, beat a sitting Republican senator and moved to the Senate. This made Rayburn the top Democrat on the committee and put him in line to become chairman if the Democrats ever regained control of the House.

8

A Clutch at Happiness

Because of the short sessions of the Coolidge Congresses, Sam Rayburn was able to spend much time at home each year working as a farmer. As soon as Congress adjourned he would climb aboard the train for the thirty-six hour ride back to Texas. Occasionally he stopped off en route in Tennessee to visit his old uncles and cousins and invite them to Texas. The first time he visited the place where he was born his mother asked him to bring one of her kin, Harriett Pickel, home to Bonham with him. In case her relative was shy, Sam was to "tell her that I am still the same old Matt that I was in Tenn. living in a log house." [1]

His home ties did not diminish with passing time. Once when he could not leave Washington he phoned his mother that he couldn't wait to get home and have her fix him "a bowl of crummin'." This was corn bread crumbled in cold milk. From the time he first went to Congress, he urged his mother to visit the capital and see him in action. But she came only once, in 1919, and while she was there, she wrote home to her children Tom and Lou about her thrillling experiences. She had heard Sam speak in the House, and he had introduced her to several congressmen, and Mrs. Garner "invited us out to a 3 o'clock lunch this evening."

Thanks to his congressional salary, he paid off his campaign debts, and the 120-acre farm was expanded to 250 acres. The big white house near U.S. Highway 82 was filled with antiques and, as a concession to Sam, nineteen rocking chairs. Brother Tom, whose career as a professional baseball player was over, managed the farm, though Sam had a big say when he was home. The fields produced oats, corn, and cotton, while the chief cash "crop" came from the milk produced from the Rayburn Jersey dairy herd. Most of the milk went to a Bonham cheese factory. King of the herd of twenty registered cattle was a powerful bull named White Sox. "This potent sire is not unlike some ugly men who have very beautiful daughters," Sam Rayburn once spoke admiringly of White Sox's show-quality female calves. [2]

Martha Rayburn passed her eightieth birthday in August 1926. She no longer milked cows, canned fruits and vegetables or cooked for the family get-togethers over the Christmas season. Yet there seemed to be a continuing permanence about her relationship with Sam, praising him for his work in Congress, reading his "To My Darling Mother" letters to Tom and Lou, awaiting eagerly his return home from Washington each year, and preparing a box lunch for his long train ride back to the capital.

Despite her advanced years, she remained a matriarch to her clan, said Alla Clary, Rayburn's secretary. "And when she spoke, they still stepped."

But shortly after her birthday, she began looking worn and rapidly grew frail. By the end of the year she was seriously ill. And on February 21, 1927, six months before her eighty-first birthday, she died.

Forty-five years old at the time of her death, Sam had been his mother's boy until the end. True, he had known several girls over the years, but he had never proposed to any of them, and friends said that he felt none compared with his mother. Now in his belated loneliness he began to consider marriage seriously.

One of his closest friends in Washington was Marvin Jones, a member of the Texas congressional delegation. They had met back in 1907 at the University of Texas, and this friendship was resumed when Marvin was elected to Congress ten years later. There was another member of the Texas delegation named Jeff: McLemore, who was always good for a laugh because he put a colon after his first name and wrote himself up in the *Congressional Directory* as having been born on a farm "in a storm" and "had but little schooling, because of his aversion to teachers."

Jeff: McLemore lost his primary in 1918 because he had voted against the declaration of war the previous year. Sam and Marvin, who was also a bachelor, had been to his large apartment at the Washington Hotel, across the street from the Treasury Department, and when Jeff: left town they took over his lease. This brought Marvin into warm association with the Rayburn clan in Bonham and Sam into contact with the Jones family.

At the time Marvin and Sam lived together, Marvin had an eighteen-year-old sister named Metze, and despite the fact that he was twice her age at thirty-six, Sam started writing letters to her. [3] This correspondence continued almost a decade, though he did not have sufficient nerve to propose either in letters or when he saw her.

But in 1927 when Metze Jones was an attractive and single young woman of twenty-seven and Sam's mother was gone, he courted her ardently.

His progress was swift. A Mississippi newspaper ran a picture of the engaged couple, and to a friend Sam wrote about the speed with which he acquired a wife. "I was in a great hurry to get married . . . because I wanted to get it over before she changed her mind."

They were married on October 15, 1927, at a Methodist Church in Valley View, Texas, south of Gainesville where she lived. Sam had a new car and a membership in the American Automobile Association, and they drove to Washington on their honeymoon, taking pictures of each other along the way with their large folding Kodak camera. They stopped to see the log cabin house where he had started life, and here the only mishap took place, according to Sam's cousin, Mose Waller, who owned the farm.

"Sam brought his wife here to see where he was born," said Mose. "I took them down to the old place, and she got stuck in cockleburs and Spanish needles and th'owed a fit. I mean a bad one."[4]

Once they reached Washington, Sam wrote his sister Lou on a restful Sunday:

> As I wired you we are located at 1616-16th St. We are at present in the apartment of Finis Garrett in the same building until the party occupying the one we will have vacates Nov. 1. Then it will have to be redecorated and floors gone over. We hope to get into it by the end of the week.
>
> Our whole trip was fine. The weather every day we were out was exactly like the day we were married—and has been so since we reached here. I wrote you from Johnson City about the trip through Tennessee and the kin.
>
> The trip through Virginia was like driving through wonderfully colored woods with fine roads. We saw some fine old country homes but not as many as I have thought would be on the way. We spent the night at Natural Bridge Hotel. The Natural Bridge is the most gorgeous natural thing I have ever seen. No picture of it at all does the highness and grandeur of it justice. We saw it from the creek that flows under it at night, under artificial light and then in the morning by day light.
>
> We came on then through very historic Virginia. I saw a marker at the roadside and stopped to see what it was, and it said "on the small knoll back of here was born Sam Houston." On to Lexington the greatest, to me, of all. Here is located Washington & Lee University. Also V.M.I.
>
> We saw the tomb of Stonewall Jackson on to the chapel of Washington & Lee. In the chapel built while Gen. Lee was Pres.—is the recumbent statue of Lee by Valentine—said to be

the best of its kind in the world. Gen. Lee, his father, wife, some of his sons are buried in this chapel. His office was in the basement of the chapel still preserved as nearly as possible like he left it. It was too sacred and inspiring for description. Then on still through beautiful and historic country to Washington.

All in all it was a wonderful and almost perfect trip.

Above all right now I would like to have a letter from home. If the mail sack full of books and documents that I packed and addressed before I left there has been sent it has not reached here. I need it badly as some unanswered correspondence was in it, also other things that I need badly in the office.

Let me hear from you regularly, as you must know how anxious I am to keep in close touch with things there.

Metze has felt fine ever since we left Texas, and eats and sleeps as well as anybody.

Tell Tom and Will to write me also.

Metze says say anything sweet to you from her.

Your devoted brother,
Sam'[5]

Sam showed her off to all his friends on the Hill, the dark-haired, young woman as tall as he. Alla Clary, his secretary since 1919, pronounced her "a very beautiful woman."[6]

Sam's friends noticed that Metze spent far more time with her brother Marvin than with her husband. At Christmas, Sam and Metze were invited to a party given by House Commerce Committee Chairman James Parker of New York. When Sam took a drink, the report was that she "ate him out." Metze was rabid against alcohol. Later Sam said, "It was the driest Christmas I ever spent."

On January 7, 1928, after less than three months of marriage, Metze Rayburn went to Texas, ostensibly for a visit. The ladies in the Texas delegation kept asking Sam when she was returning, and though he expected her back, she had not given him a date.

Then came calamity. She sent him word that she had taken a job at Neiman-Marcus in Dallas and wanted a divorce.

Shortly after that Sam moved into a room at the Hamilton Hotel at Fourteenth and K streets Northwest. His marriage was over.

Washington friends wondered what might possibly have happened to end the marriage within three months. When he would not discuss it with them, the false story spread that he and Marvin Jones had participated in a double wedding ceremony in Valley View, with Sam marrying Jones' sister and Marvin marrying a friend of Metze; that the two girls had run away from their husbands in the middle of the night because they drank steadily. [7]

Conjecture regarding the seemingly happy newlyweds took several routes: Their age difference was too great; she did not like the political life; their temperaments clashed. Some guessed that the trouble was that he was really "wed to the House of Representatives and Miss Lou, his sister," [8] for whose welfare he felt personally responsible because, in order to look after her parents, she had never married.

The effect of the breakup was devastating to Rayburn, according to one friend. "At the time it almost wrecked him." In a daze he asked a hometown attorney, S. F. Leslie, who had run for county attorney when he ran for the Texas House, to handle the divorce for him. Unable to talk to others about his troubles with Metze, he spoke to Leslie "about his marriage many times." But Leslie would not relate what he said beyond a legalese "I filed suit for Mr. Rayburn and met Marvin [her brother] and her friends and got a settlement of it and got the divorce without any publicity or talk about it." [9]

Rayburn never seriously considered marriage again. It faded into his past so deeply that those who knew him in the years ahead were unaware he had ever been married. Judge Leslie recalled that in one election an opponent spread the story "but half the people didn't believe it." Not until almost thirty years later when a hotel in Tennessee changed hands did his marriage surface. The 1927 register contained an entry that read: "Sam Rayburn and Bride."

But Rayburn did not forget Metze. She later married an Amarillo insurance man named Jeff Neely and became the mother of two children. When her daughter contracted polio, said Alla Clary, "Mr. Rayburn arranged to have her go for treatment to Franklin Roosevelt's Warm Springs Foundation in Georgia."

With the failure of his marriage, Sam Rayburn was once more entirely a member of his original family. His mother's words became important to him, and he took to carrying her last letter in the briefcase that traveled with him between Bonham and Washington. This compulsion went on for several years until he lost the letter.

9

Committee Chairman

Shortly after the collapse of his marriage, friends in Rayburn's congressional district tried to talk him into running for the Senate seat held by Earle Mayfield. As the KKK's choice six years earlier, Mayfield had won in 1922 with little difficulty. But now with the Klan's bullying power on the wane, Mayfield's seat seemed ready for the taking in the July 28, 1928, Democratic primary.

But the enthusiasm of his friends had little effect on Rayburn's own determination of his chances. In the first place, he had no statewide organization. This meant he would have to conduct a tireless, personal campaign over a state extending 800 miles from east to west and 700 miles from north to south, comparable to a stretch from the Atlantic coast into Indiana and from Maine to Virginia. With Texas two-thirds rural and radios not yet in common household use, a man without any organizational backing would be confronted with a test of his stamina perhaps beyond the breaking point. Moreover, without wealthy backers to finance the undertaking, the costs could be astronomical.

So when Congressman Tom Connally, who wanted to run against Mayfield, approached Sam Rayburn and told him he would defer to him if he wanted to take on the Senate race, "Sam let me know that he preferred staying in the House and becoming Speaker eventually," said Connally. [1]

Still another consideration helping Rayburn determine his course was his hope that his 1926 uncontested House race would be repeated in 1928 and beyond. But this hope evaporated when three other Fourth District residents also paid their filing fees. So once again Rayburn had to withdraw part of his savings from the bank and wander about the district delivering self-praising speeches at every crossroad before he won his ninth term in the House with a vote that was five thousand more than the total of his opponents.

Once his own primary was safely out of the way, Rayburn felt party-bound to take part in the 1928 presidential contest between Al Smith and Herbert Hoover. The Republicans had held their convention first, and Herbert Hoover's nomination amused many national politicians who knew that Coolidge disliked him. Passed around the Capitol in the spring of 1928 was the remark Coolidge had made about Hoover to another Cabinet member: "That man has offered me unsolicited advice for six years—all of it bad!"

The Democrats had held their national convention in Houston two weeks after the Republicans met in Kansas City, and Sam Rayburn had gone there with a badly divided Texas delegation. The division was based entirely on the support or opposition to the candidacy of New York Governor Alfred E. Smith, the front-runner, who was both a Catholic and an ardent "wet."

When the convention nominated Smith on the first ballot, several members of the Texas delegation stormed out. Later, under Rayburn's old foes, former Texas House Speaker Thomas B. Love and Governor Oscar Colquitt, they announced their support of Hoover. "In my travels," Joe Bailey once said, "I have seen in the galleries of the Old World seventeen different portraits of Judas Iscariot, and every one looked like Tom Love." [2] Arrayed against these "Hoovercrats," as the renegade Democrats were called, were the loyal Democrats, including Rayburn, Garner, Tom Connally, Hatton Sumners and Marvin Jones, Rayburn's brother-in-law.

As the fall campaign of 1928 got under way, Rayburn crisscrossed eastern Texas, trying to stem the tidal wave of the Hoovercrats. Once a Populist area, then a KKK stronghold, this part of Texas had only recently cooled off when the Al Smith nomination inflamed it anew with religious bigotry. This, coupled with Smith's call for the repeal of the Eighteenth Amendment, made east Texas' political atmosphere poisonous.

At Breckinridge, west of Dallas, Rayburn scoffed at Tom Love's charge that if Smith were elected "America will be ruled by Catholics and the Pope, and the public school system will be endangered." [3] At another speaking stop where there was a coolness toward Smith for being too friendly toward Negroes, Rayburn stunned the crowd with a statement that Hoover had integrated the rest rooms in the Commerce Department. On the charge that Smith would tolerate corruptness, he condemned Hoover for being in Harding's cabinet and keeping silent "then and later on Teapot Dome. If he didn't know about it, he hasn't got sense enough to be President because everybody in Washington knew it."

A popular weapon of the Hoovercrats was the use of preachers to engulf their church members with tirades against Catholics. This forced Rayburn for the first time in his public career to assail and ridicule men of the cloth. "I understand," he told one audience, "that tomorrow night a New York *dee-vine* is going to come here to attack Governor Smith in this auditorium. He is the man who made the attack on Governor Smith in his pulpit when he knew that Governor Smith could not go to the same place and answer him."

When all else seemed to fail in his speeches for Smith, Rayburn called on the strong anti-Yankee-Republican feeling in Texas as a weapon against Hoover: "As long as I honor the memory of the Confederate dead, and revere the gallant devotion of my Confederate father to our Southland, I will never vote for electors of a Party which sent the carpetbagger and the scalawag to the prostrate South with saber and sword." [4]

His sharp political sense told him from the start that Catholic Al Smith from the streets of New York with his derby and cigar and Fulton Fish Market English and his opposition to Prohibition had little chance to win Texas. This was borne out when Texas gave her electoral votes to a Republican presidential nominee for the first time in history.

When the House convened in April 1929, a change of vital importance to Rayburn's career occurred. Finis Garrett, House minority leader since 1923, had run unsuccessfully for the U.S. Senate from Tennessee in 1928. Garrett had lent his apartment to Sam and Metze when the newlyweds came to Washington. Shortly before his term ended, Coolidge gave Garrett an appointment to the U.S. Court of Customs and Patent Appeals, a sinecure for defeated congressmen, and the race was on in the House for a new minority leader.

Rayburn had long since returned to Cactus Jack Garner's good graces, and he plunged into the task of rounding up support for Garner in the Democratic caucus. Garner won handily in the caucus, though with the Democrats so heavily outnumbered by the Republicans in the House, he lost the important fight in the Chamber for Speaker to Republican Nicholas Longworth by a vote of 254 to 143.

By House rules the minority leader acquired a suite in the Capitol, and Garner rewarded Rayburn by making him a member of his inner circle at his new office along with Fred Vinson of Kentucky, John McDuffie of Alabama, Tut Milligan of Missouri, Lindsay Warren of North Carolina and John Carew of New York. One congressman, pleased with Rayburn's rising status, inserted into the *Congressional Record* the first magazine article written about him. Though Dr. Walter Splawn, the author and former president of the University of Texas, titled the article "Rayburn of Texas," it was a dry, dull piece written chiefly on the work of the House Commerce Committee. [5] After his long service as a member of the Texas Railroad Commission, Splawn had been brought by Rayburn to Washington as an expert on railroads to advise the Commerce Committee.

The contrast between Rayburn and Garner was great. While Rayburn was oriented toward issues, Garner's interests lay far more in political maneuvering. Cactus Jack was not a man who represented specific positions on basic national and international matters. Instead he was a pragmatic, logrolling, pork-barreler with archconservative stands on his own pocketbook interests, such as wool tariffs and the use of Mexican labor.

During the 1920s, while the nation had gone on a get-rich-quick spree, poor-boy Garner had found plenty of time away from the short Coolidge-years Congresses to engage in a similar activity. From a man living on his seventy-five-hundred-dollars-a-year congressional salary, he moved forward to own two banks, the mortgages on most of the homes in and around the dusty cow town of Uvalde and a twenty-three-thousand-acre ranch that contained the largest herd of goats on the face of the earth. As a large user of cheap Mexican labor, he gave a House committee in 1926 the benefit of his views on immigrants from below the border. "They do not cause any trouble unless they stay a long time and become Americanized," he said. "They are a very docile people. They can be imposed on. The sheriff can go out and make them do anything. That is the way they are." [6]

As a member of Garner's inner circle, Rayburn was frequently invited to the afternoon stag get-togethers in a second-floor committee room commandeered by Speaker Nicholas Longworth, elected boss of the House in 1925 when Gillett moved to the Senate. Longworth was best known as the "old" husband of "young" Alice Roosevelt, daughter of Theodore Roosevelt. Nick, as he was called by intimates, was a charming, bright man who had never sponsored a significant bill since he came to the House in 1903.

Nick Longworth's normal expression was one of boredom, and he was seldom serious, except about music. One year, when the House was ready to adjourn, he had a piano hauled into the Chamber. He played for the members and teamed up with Democratic Congressman Clifton Woodrum of Virginia, who sang, "Carry Me Back to Old Virginia" to wild applause from the membership. [7] Sometimes Longworth brought his Stradivarius to his bipartisan hideaway, which John McDuffie of Alabama dubbed his "Board of Education," and he entertained his guests when they were not playing poker, drinking rye, and telling stories. He and the others knew it was foolhardy to play poker with Garner, because the Texan was an expert at bluffing as well as a human calculating machine when it came to determining the odds of getting certain cards. This was no problem for Sam because he never played cards. Sometimes Longworth left early to go on dates with his secretary, Lucille McArthur, the widow of an Oregon congressman. [8] But most times the gang walked over to the old Congress Hotel for further drinking and talking. A second House Office Building was later built on the site of the hotel and it was named the Longworth Building.

Since the Republican advent to power in 1920, Rayburn had had a long association with Herbert Hoover, because as Harding's and Coolidge's Secretary of Commerce Hoover had to frequently appear before the House Commerce Committee. Whenever he had come to testify, he was always surrounded by fawning underlings who called him "Chief," lit his pipe, and made him comfortable. Unable to slap backs or joke with committee members, he solemnly droned through seemingly endless statistics on the economy. One man said of him: "He looks as though a rose would wilt if you put it in his hand." [9] Essentially he was a shy man who was terrified when delivering a speech and frightened by large, noisy crowds. At the same time he yearned to be recognized as an exceptional leader.

Long before Hoover became President, Rayburn knew him as a propagandist for Harding's "normalcy" and the Coolidge dictum that "large profits make large payrolls." This belief in letting the economy alone and curtailing government social action was reaffirmed during his campaign against Al Smith when he advocated what he called "rugged individualism," or individual self-reliance. This was of a piece with Coolidge's point of view, which he expressed when Rayburn and others were pressing him to approve a bill for government purchase of agricultural surpluses to alleviate the farm depression in the mid-twenties. "Farmers have never made much money. I don't know that we can do much about it," said Silent Cal, who vetoed this bill twice. "Ponderously futile," he labeled the legislation. [10]

The pouring rain that provided a gloomy setting for Hoover's inauguration was an omen of the new administration's coming troubles. There were circumstances that would soon doom it, but there were also personality and philosophic deficiencies to hasten its collapse.

The "Great Engineer" and the "Great Humanitarian," as Hoover was called for his success in feeding starving women and children during and after World War I, proved to be no "Great Politician." "He was better on the team than captain," Rayburn said generously years later in analyzing the difference between the record of Hoover the cabinet member and Hoover the President. [11]

As Chief Executive, he lacked the art of compromise, an ability to judge motives and an appreciation of Congress' role in the legislative process. Both the Senate and House had a substantial number of farm-bloc Republican insurgents, or La Follette Progressives and latter-day Teddy Roosevelt Bull Moosers. Instead of meeting and working with them, Hoover considered them his enemy. In addition, he played a vacillating game with Old Guard, or conservative, congressional leaders. Longworth came back from a White House conference to tell his after-hours "Board of Education" of the President's attempts to dominate him. The opposite happened to House Majority Leader Bertram H. Snell, a short, bald, round man who manufactured cheese in New York. Snell went to the White House because Hoover wanted to handle New York State patronage appointments entirely by himself. When Snell returned to the bipartisan club he announced, "I have met the President and he is ours."

Sam Rayburn's arguments with the Hoover administration came early and were the result of the President's political blunders. Hoover could have started his administration off with nine quiet months, time to get adjusted and on top of his job because Congress was not scheduled to meet until December 1929. But he listened to Senator William E. Borah of Idaho, who insisted that he combat the farm depression by calling an immediate special session of Congress to increase tariffs on farm products imports. Hoover complied, and congressmen flooded back to Washington for a session beginning on April 15.

In his message to Congress, Hoover asked for agricultural tariffs plus a "flexible tariff" provision that would authorize the Tariff Commission to adjust other rates up or down as it determined. But the Republican Congress ignored his flexible tariff idea and immediately launched into an orgy of increased import duties across the board. Before long the original bill had a nightmarish 1,253 amendments tacked to it, most of them based on the philosophy of Senator Joseph Grundy of Pennsylvania, who said that the big contributors to the Republican Party "should be compensated for it by high tariffs."[12]

Rayburn worked himself into a hoarse rage over the Smoot-Hawley Bill, as this high tariff mess was called. Despite its support by every farm organization because of its agricultural tariffs, he denounced it as "infamous, unconscionable and unprecedented." But the bill passed and Hoover signed it.

Rayburn also tangled with Hoover on the subject of railroads. The Transportation Act of 1920, on which Rayburn had worked, had proposed that the ICC consolidate the hundred or so lines into about twenty systems. On his own, President Hoover met privately with some railroad presidents and announced agreement on a plan to consolidate all lines east of the Mississippi and north of the Mason-Dixon line into four systems.

Before it could go into effect, however, it needed congressional approval. Rayburn led the fight against it in the House, branding the plan as one that would make the weaker lines easy financial prey to the big four and bring about the closing of necessary but unprofitable branch lines. A further casualty would be the smaller railroad towns, whose populations would be ruined once the railroad operations were closed down.

Behind the scenes, he worked closely with Senator James Couzens of Michigan, the chairman of the Senate Commerce Committee, to fight the Hoover plan. Couzens, a member of the Republican insurgents, needed no urging, for he hated the President. Liberal oriented by background, he had been a checker in a coal yard when he lent Henry Ford twenty-five hundred dollars to get his automobile manufacturing company started. The stock he got in return for this small investment brought him $29 million when Ford bought it back sixteen years later.

In time, Hoover realized he could not win railroad consolidation from the Rayburn-Couzens forces. His wrath aroused, he called his opponents "an obstructionist group comprising the Radical Bloc" whose real purpose was "to keep the railroads demoralized in the hope of government operation." [13]

With a farm depression already saddling the nation, Rayburn was hardly surprised when the stock market crashed on Tuesday, October 29, 1929, because of his agrarian view that agriculture was the lifeblood of the country. But the sudden collapse of the business prosperity was the last event contemplated by the administration and academic economists.

Before leaving the White House, Coolidge had assured his countrymen that the economy was "absolutely sound" and he called stocks "cheap at current prices." Hoover's contribution to this line of thought was his comment that "we shall soon with the help of God be in sight of the day when poverty shall be banished from the nation." He also said, "The slogan of progress is changing from the full dinner pail, to the full garage." Even after Black Tuesday struck the New York Stock Exchange, Secretary of the Treasury Andrew Mellon announced, "Business is fundamentally sound."

Amid a scene of failing banks, plummeting farm prices, lengthening lines of unemployed men, bankrupt business, plus a devastating drought, came the 1930 congressional elections. Rayburn was especially optimistic that under the depressing economic conditions he would have an uncontested Democratic primary for his tenth term. But two rivals challenged him and once more he had to use part of his congressional salary to campaign.

Despite an opportunity to "throw the rascals out," a numbed electorate returned a pencil-thin Republican majority to the next Congress in the November 1930 general elections. The Republican margin in both the House and Senate was only two members. But this Seventy-second Congress did not hold its first session until thirteen months after the election, and by the time it convened on December 7, 1931, the appalling number of fourteen members had died in the interim, including Nick Longworth. Republican fatalities exceeded the Democrats' and this put the Democrats in the majority in the House for the first time since 1916.

There was great excitement among the House Democrats when it dawned on them that by a quirk of fate they would control the Speaker, the House's patronage working apparatus, and all committees. Garner was elected Speaker by a vote of 218, as against 208 for Bert Snell, the Republican leader; and 5 for George Schneider, a Progressive Republican, who was also vice president of the International Brotherhood of Paper-Makers labor union. And with Garner's victory, part of Sam Rayburn's political dream was realized: He was now the chairman of the Commerce Committee.

10

In the Kingmaking Business

Sam Rayburn had little time to enjoy himself in his new role as Commerce Committee chairman. First of all, the grimness of the economic collapse had cast a pall over Congress as well as the country. Then there was the ambition of John Nance Garner. After Cactus Jack gained his coveted seat on the rostrum of the House Chamber, he put himself into an excellent position to contest other Democrats for the presidential nomination in 1932, and the person he chose to manage his campaign for the big prize was Rayburn.

When the economy buckled after the stock market crash late in 1929, Rayburn's view on how to combat it was the traditional approach throughout American history. In the panics of 1837, 1873, 1893, 1907, 1913 and 1921, government policy had been to retrench, issue optimistic statements and hope that conditions would somehow grow better. This was no different in 1929 with President Hoover proclaiming after the opening economic earthquake, "The fundamental business of the country is on a sound and prosperous basis"; and Treasury Secretary Andrew Mellon, a small, shy man who was one of the three or four richest Americans, advising him: "Liquidate labor, liquidate stocks, liquidate farms, liquidate real estate. Leave the situation alone and it will correct itself. It will purge the rottenness out of our system. Enterprising people will pick up the wrecks from less enterprising people." [1]

As a "cut the Federal budget and don't interfere with the private economy" man, Rayburn made no friends on the Hill when he voted against a bill to increase the salary of congressmen from seventy-five hundred dollars a year to ten thousand dollars. In fact, he lost a few when he proposed a cutback in salary to $5,000 and a slash in the budget for congressional clerks. Nor did he make friends in the Treasury Department, groping for revenue, when he helped lead the fight against raising first class postage from its two-cent level to three cents and to kill a wanted stamp tax on bank checks and legal documents. [2]

When Hoover's initial expression of confidence in the economy failed to halt the decline, he disregarded Mellon's advice and brought railroad, utility, and industrial executives to the White House and asked them to expand their construction programs instead of abandoning them. But they disregarded his pleas. He also called farm leaders to the White House to tell them that the Federal Farm Board would lend money to needy farmers and purchase part of the surplus crop, and he appealed to banks and insurance companies not to seize farms for mortgage defaults. But the drought ruined crops in 1930, and the banks and insurance companies ignored him.

Yet for a time in 1930 conditions seemed to improve. "We are not through the difficulties of our situation, but I am convinced that we have passed the worst and with continued effort we shall rapidly recover," he assured the U.S. Chamber of Commerce in May. However, by the beginning of 1931 unemployment exceeded 6 million, and personal savings were swiftly being exhausted.

Hoover now faced the problem whether to have the federal government provide direct relief for the needy or continue to call on local governments and private charities to do the job. He chose the latter, and again he seemed prophetic when another upturn came that spring. At the start of April 1931, more than one hundred cities ended their relief programs on the ground that they were no longer necessary. But when Austria's largest bank failed in May and the Bank of England defaulted on payments late that summer, a new, immense downward plunge occurred in Western Europe and the United States, and the unemployment total passed the 10 million mark in the forty-eight states.

Late in 1931, Hoover told a conference of thirty-two congressional leaders, "For the first time in history the Federal Government must intervene directly to support private business." Rayburn was now in agreement with Tom Connally, who had transferred from the House to the Senate, that it was not relief for business that was needed. Instead, "millions of workers and farmers were in dire need of immediate help if they were not to starve and lose their farms," said Connally. [3]

Hoover's chief proposal in his "aid to business plan" was his request to Congress in December 1931 to establish the Reconstruction Finance Corporation (RFC). The RFC would have a capital of $500 million and authority to borrow $2 billion more from the Treasury to lend money to insurance companies, banks, railroads, exporters and to industrial firms to modernize their plants. In addition, Hoover's proposal would extend credit to state and local governments for public works projects, such as slum clearance.

It was about this time that Garner wanted his campaign for the presidential nomination to swing into high gear. As Sam Rayburn assessed his chances for winning two-thirds of the convention's delegates in the short time span ahead, much depended on his competition and his ability to make himself easily identifiable to the American public.

It was apparent to Rayburn that Governor Franklin Delano Roosevelt of New York, successfully administering the largest state, was the front-running candidate. His name was appearing frequently as a speaker on national issues, though he carefully spoke only generalities, and he had an astute organization led by bald, glad-handed, name-rememberer James A. Farley, the New York boxing commissioner, and little, wizened Louis M. Howe, a reporter who had worked for Roosevelt for twenty years. Rayburn was also aware that Roosevelt was personally working on members of Congress by stopping off on trips between Albany and Warm Springs, Georgia, at a hotel near the Capitol for conferences with influential senators and representatives. [4]

In a letter to a Dallas friend named T. W. Davidson in January 1932, Rayburn confessed that Roosevelt looked like the winner. "I have believed for some time," he wrote, "that Franklin D. Roosevelt will in all probability be nominated at the Democratic Convention at Chicago." He went on to say that "there is a nationwide movement having for its purpose the stopping of Roosevelt. Our attitude should be that we will not fight any candidate, but if neither of those most prominently spoken of now is satisfactory to the Convention, then we offer a man everybody can and should get together on." [5]

In another letter that same month, Garner's campaign manager thought that Roosevelt "has appealed to the popular imagination of the American people as no other man does at this particular time. "However," Rayburn threw in a more optimistic prediction, "within the next two months there will be developments that will show us all, I think, a clear road whether it leads to Roosevelt or another direction." [6]

Rayburn's view of the other presidential hopefuls placed them far below, yet they had importance if Roosevelt were to be stopped. Besides Garner, the chief candidate was Al Smith with Tammany support plus the backing of John J. Raskob, the director of General Motors who had always been a registered Republican before his selection as chairman of the Democratic National Committee. Also in Smith's camp were Boss Frank Hague of Jersey City, Mayor Tony Cermak of Chicago, and Governor Joseph Ely of Massachusetts. Other panting hopefuls were

Governor Albert Ritchie of Maryland; eccentric Governor "Alfalfa Bill" Murray of Oklahoma; wispy Newton D. Baker, formerly Woodrow Wilson's Secretary of War; Melvin Traylor, a transplanted Texan who was president of a major Chicago bank; and William McAdoo, who had been Wilson's son-in-law.

Garner realized that the big problem he faced of turning the trend away from Roosevelt was his own lack of public recognition. Rayburn's campaign line would have been that Garner held "the highest position of any Democrat in public life" and was "doing the job of Speaker and leading the Democrats in the House in a masterly way." But this bland approach did not satisfy Garner.

Over at the Democratic National Committee, Charlie Michelson and Jouett Shouse were conducting a daily press bombardment of President Hoover that depicted him as entirely to blame for the economic depression and painted him as heartless in ignoring the resulting suffering across the nation. While this Michelson-Shouse character-assassination mill would materially help the Democratic presidential nominee, Garner saw that it would have no effect on his own race for the nomination.

So even though he had no basic quarrel with Hoover, he decided to take the lead personally in going after the hapless Chief Executive. He called his own effort at character assassination an attempt to "whittle down Hoover to our size." But later he bragged, "I fought President Hoover with everything I had, under Marquis of Queensbury, London prize ring and catch-as-catch-can rules."

Because of Hoover's overwhelming concern for the welfare of business instead of farmers and workers, Rayburn characterized him in January 1932 as "the toadying master engineer who has proven to be the poorest excuse of a President that we have had in the history of the Republic." [7] But he did not share Garner's strategy of attacking Hoover and fighting him constantly merely for the sake of being considered his principal opponent. To this, Garner shook his head and told him, "Sam, you've got to get your knuckles bloody once in a while."

Hoover knew what Garner's strategy was as soon as he asked Congress to pass his bill to establish the Reconstruction Finance Corporation. "At this time," he said in mellower years, "I was faced with a practical Democratic control of Congress, whose antagonism no man could measure or conciliate. The skirmishing preliminary to the Presidential campaign of 1932 had begun." Garner and his crowd "would not have regretted if demoralization extended through the election."

Rayburn's approach to the RFC bill was to offer amendments to limit a single borrower to $100 million and to ban all fees to middlemen for helping to arrange loans. This was in sharp contrast to Garner's approach, which was to gain headlines as Hoover's leading foe.

All along the RFC's legislative path he tore at the bill so that in its final form it eliminated loans to closed banks to help them reopen their doors, to industry for plant improvements, to farm goods exporters, and to cities for public works projects.

Even then he would not assure House passage of this mutilated bill until it was guaranteed that the names of all borrowers were published monthly. Hoover said this would force him to veto the legislation because creditors and depositors would be alarmed about the stability of the borrowing institutions if they saw the names in print. Finally Garner rewrote the clause so that it required only a confidential report of monthly loans to be sent to the clerks of the House and Senate. And when Hoover agreed to this, Garner put up a new hurdle: House passage would not come until Hoover assured him he could name two of the five RFC governors. Hoover gave his word, and Garner named Jesse Jones, a Houston financial tycoon, and Harvey Couch, an Arkansas utility magnate to the RFC.

Jones and Couch were on the job only a few months when a furor arose. Garner had double-crossed Hoover by making public the lists of loans made by the RFC. According to a Hoover friend and biographer, "at least a thousand banks closed solely because of this publicity," because "an RFC loan was treated by jittery depositors as *prima facie* proof of weakness, precipitating a run." [8]

Garner went after Hoover on other matters as well. There were accusations as in the past of Hoover's "shady association with sugar lobbyists" and charges that the President was totally calloused toward the needs of 3.5 million war veterans. An Adjusted Service Compensation Act, or "Bonus," had been passed in the Harding administration with payment put off for twenty-five years. Its justification was that veterans deserved special compensation for their low service pay during World War I compared with prevailing civilian wages. Hoover, under pressure to pay the Bonus in advance of its due date, proposed instead that money be lent only to poverty-stricken veterans, or an estimated maximum of 15 percent of the total number of veterans. Congress in 1931 had voted to pay 50 percent of the face value of the Bonus immediately, or $1.7 billion, and overrode a presidential veto. Then early in 1932, Garner pushed hard on Hoover to sign a second Bonus Bill, this time paying $2.4 billion in greenbacks without gold backing. But Hoover vetoed it successfully. [9]

At times when Garner sensed that a Hoover position was popular, he would proclaim his support of it temporarily. For instance, after the budget deficit passed a half billion dollars, Hoover asked Congress for higher taxes to balance income and outlay. The Hoover moneymaker was to come through a sales tax and not through an increase in income tax rates. Garner liked this proposal and took it over on his own, for it coincided not only with his own conservative views but this regressive tax was also a favorite of publisher William Randolph Hearst, his chief sponsor for President.

When Garner had become Speaker he assigned Rayburn the task of cultivating small, rolypoly Congressman Fiorello La Guardia, a nominal Republican from New York who led the House's progressive bloc. Rayburn was impressed with the integrity of the aggressive and outspoken La Guardia, and the two became good friends despite La Guardia's conspiratorial view of life in which he saw himself in a perpetual titanic battle against powerful, evil forces. "Fiorello was ready to fight 'Them' to the death, constantly on the alert lest 'They' get him first," said an associate.

It was La Guardia who prevented House passage of the sales tax. When Garner wanted Rayburn to work on La Guardia and weaken opposition to this tax, Sam refused. So at a time when Garner favored a Hoover piece of legislation it failed.

One day speaking in favor of balancing the budget through increased taxes, Garner turned on Hoover the next and introduced three bills destined to skyrocket the deficit. These bills were known as "Garner's Pork Barrel Triplets" and would involve the spending of billions. Among their generous provisions he included the construction of a new post office for every Democrat in Congress; highway, river, harbor and flood control projects from the Atlantic to the Pacific coast; outright grants of $100 million to the states for unemployment relief and the printing of a billion dollars in greenbacks. "The economic effects of this program, gentlemen," he roared before the Ways and Means Committee, "would be wonderful. There can be no doubt about it."

One of the Pork Barrel Triplets got through Congress but was quickly vetoed by Hoover. Garner then pushed another of his bills through the House only to have the Republican Senate vote it down.

Despite his continuing fights with Hoover, Garner knew how to relax late afternoons when he held court in the Board of Education room he inherited from Nick Longworth. There he, his right-hand man Sam Rayburn, John McDuffie, Fred Vinson, Lindsay Warren and a long string of invited guests downed bourbon and branch water in a ritual Garner named, "to strike a blow for liberty." Garner added to Longworth's institution by inviting a succession of freshmen members to

Board sessions. "You get a couple of drinks in a young congressman," he claimed, "and then you know what he knows and what he can do. We pay the tuition by supplying the liquor." [10]

While the sixty-three-year-old, bushy white-eyebrowed Garner was clawing and punching his way into national prominence in the spring of 1932, Sam Rayburn tried to put some order into the Garner-for-President movement. He opened a national Garner headquarters, encouraged the organization of Garner Clubs and his efforts to raise money were aided separately by William Randolph Hearst, who was determined to stop Roosevelt. Hearst not only made a national radio speech backing Garner but he gave him extensive, flowery coverage in his newspaper chain and ordered his Washington correspondent, George Rothwell Brown, to do a quick and heroic biography of Cactus Jack. [11] At first Garner was unable to make up his mind whether Hearst's support was a plus or a minus, because the newspaper publisher had the reputation of catering to the worst side of his readers. But he rapidly reached the conclusion that the publicity was worthwhile.

In the spring of 1932, Rayburn returned to Texas to take a leading role for the first time in a state Democratic convention. Before it adjourned he had been elected chairman of the Texas delegation to the Democratic National Convention destined to meet near the end of June at Chicago.

With the most rabid of Franklin Roosevelt enthusiasts carefully screened out, Rayburn's delegation consisted of an army of 184 delegates and a similar number of alternates committed to Garner. Each delegate could cast a fourth of a vote to make up the state's total of 46 convention votes, and to prevent chaos the unit rule prevailed. This meant that when a majority of those present at a caucus of the delegation voted for one candidate or a position on an issue the entire delegation had to abide by that vote.

Late in June 1932, while Congress was still in session, Rayburn took the overnight train to Chicago to set up the Garner headquarters at the Sherman Hotel, about a half-hour drive from the Chicago Stadium where the convention was to be held. Colonel Gaw, the Windy City's official greeter, was on hand to welcome him and the crowd of convention prominents aboard the train. Garner had remained back in the capital in his Hotel Washington suite and was unreachable by phone to anyone except Sam Rayburn.

The "Stop Roosevelt" movement roared into Chicago in high gear, led by Mayor Frank "I Am The Law" Hague of Jersey City, boss of New Jersey's puppet delegation and principal champion of Al Smith. "Roosevelt, if nominated, has no chance of winning the election in

November," Hague's words of warning to the convention were carried across the nation by the press. "He cannot carry a single state east of the Mississippi and very few in the Far West."

On June 27, a day before the convention was slated to begin, Jim Farley, Governor Roosevelt's campaign manager, grew fearful that his candidate could not corner the necessary two-thirds' vote unless he made a deal with one or more of his rivals. Rebuffed by Garner for a conference, he asked Rayburn to drop by his hotel suite for a talk. "I promised to do everything in my power to secure the Vice-Presidential nomination for Speaker Garner if Texas made the switch," Farley recounted. [12]

But Rayburn was not buying Farley's half offer because he knew that Garner had strong hopes of being the compromise nominee if Roosevelt failed. He did make one concession, however, to Farley. "We don't intend to make it another Madison Square Garden," he said in his laconic fashion. This was in reference to the 1924 convention fiasco that ran to 103 ballots when the front-runners would not compromise.

Mayor Anton "Tony" Cermak of Chicago, the Democratic boss of Cook County, was more than just the host for the convention. Scheming and plotting with Hague and John F. Curry, the Grand Sachem of New York's Tammany Hall, Cermak worked overtime to help win the nomination for Al Smith. Rayburn, who was fully aware that wheeling and dealing and horse trading were integral activities at a convention, had no idea of the mammoth extra activities of these bosses.

Cermak had already printed the tickets of entrance into the galleries, and these were to be handed out only to the Smith crowd. At a nod from a Cermak underling, the galleries were expected to applaud and cheer; at a head shake deafening boos were to fill the stadium. Tennessee Senator Cordell Hull was one pro-Roosevelt speaker who was slated to be drowned out by the spectators. In addition, a Cermak stooge was stationed in the basement with a microphone and loudspeaker to lead the cheering for Smith and the catcalls for Roosevelt.

The bosses also tried to control the convention's machinery by installing a Smith man, Jouett Shouse, fresh from his smear of Hoover, as permanent chairman of the gathering. Again Rayburn stayed out of the power struggle that developed between Roosevelt's choice, Senator Thomas J. Walsh of Montana, the old Teapot Dome exposer, and Shouse. Walsh won by a vote of 626 to 528. Yet even in defeat, the Al Smith forces were not entirely downcast because the Walsh vote showed how far away Roosevelt was from the two-thirds margin or the 770 votes he needed to win the nomination.

When the convention finally got down to its principal business, nine candidates were nominated for president, and Rayburn chose Senator Tom Connally, possessor of an organlike voice, to place Garner's name in the race for ballots. Unable to tie Garner to legislation or to a popular set of political principles, Connally delivered an exaggerated oration "to prove that a really close relationship had existed between President Woodrow Wilson and Jack Garner." [13]

Before the convention, Rayburn had given his delegation strict orders to go to Chicago "in the most dignified manner—no high topped boots, big hats, ballyhoo, etc. I am afraid that if we take our Gray Mare Band that might hurt us." [14] But after his speech, said Connally, "Texas delegates and their friends hopped and jumped around the hall waving their ten-gallon hats, screaming West Texas cowboy yells, while the bands blared 'The Eyes of Texas Are Upon You' and 'The Bonnie Blue Flag That Bore The Single Star.' " [15]

Balloting for the convention's 1,154 votes finally began at 4:28 A.M. on Friday, June 31. On the first ballot Garner got only 90¼ votes compared with 666¼ for Roosevelt and 201¾ for Smith. But Rayburn was not dismayed because Roosevelt was shy of the required two-thirds vote by 103¼. From his knowledge of other conventions, Rayburn also knew that Harding had only 65 votes on the first Republican ballot in 1920 and John W. Davis had just 31 on the first Democratic ballot in 1924.

A second ballot brought Roosevelt only 11½ additional votes, and when the weary delegates recessed at breakfast time after completing the third ballot, Roosevelt had picked up a mere 6 more. The die-hard city-boss Smith backers, publisher Hearst, as well as Farley believed that if Governor Roosevelt failed to get the required 770 on the fourth ballot later that day when the convention reconvened at 9 P.M., he would fade after that.

Just after recess began, Arthur Mullen of Nebraska, Roosevelt's floor manager, asked Tom Connally to have breakfast with him at the shack diner near the Chicago Stadium. Here Mullen asked Connally to work on the Texas delegation to drop Garner and support Roosevelt. Connally said he might consider this if he had assurance that Roosevelt would take Garner as his running mate. Mullen then brought Jim Farley to another meeting with Connally, and Farley shook hands on this bargain, even though Connally told him he lacked authority to speak for Garner. Only Rayburn could.

Farley met afterward with Sam Rayburn, who was well aware that Roosevelt's lieutenants had been dangling the Vice Presidency before several other men, such as Senator Harry F. Byrd of Virginia and

Governor Ritchie of Maryland. "We'll see what can be done," Rayburn told him casually.

Meanwhile Connally had phoned Senators Key Pittman of Nevada and Harry B. Hawes of Missouri, Roosevelt's intermediaries in Washington. Quickly he told them of his talks with Mullen and Farley, and after a short delay Pittman called him back to say he had phoned Roosevelt in Albany. Garner was acceptable on the ticket to the New York governor.

Connally then went immediately to Rayburn to report his activities—Farley's guaranty and Roosevelt's acceptance of Garner—and Rayburn phoned Garner in Washington to tell him what was happening. Connally was on the line, too. But instead of being elated by what he heard, Garner said, "Sam, I want to talk to Pittman and Hawes before I make up my mind. Right now I don't think it's worthwhile to give up the Speakership for the Vice-Presidency."

Rayburn had scheduled a caucus of the Texas delegation for 6 P.M. that same Friday that had already witnessed three ballots on the convention floor, dozens of screaming meetings of other delegations, thousands of political phone calls and frenzied corridor buttonholing in every convention hotel for vote-trading.

So dispersed throughout the city were his Texans that Rayburn was able to reach only about half with word about the caucus. Of these 105, several walked into the caucus snarling that they had heard rumors of a plan to switch Texas from Garner to Roosevelt. "We're gonna stick with Garner!" they bellowed. In the midst of turmoil, seventeen members holding 4¼ votes requested permission to vote for Governor Roosevelt on the next ballot. But a majority shouted them down.

Without instructions from Garner, Rayburn knew he could not propose anything to the delegates. But this situation changed dramatically when a bellboy suddenly appeared and told him he had an important call from Washington. Rayburn left the room, and when he picked up the receiver Garner was on the other end of the line. "Sam, I think it's time to break this thing up," Garner told him. "This man Roosevelt is the choice of the convention."

"Do you authorize me to release the delegation from voting for you for the Presidential nomination?" Sam asked him. Garner said yes. No mention was made of the Vice-Presidency, but since Garner did not say that he intended to stay on as Speaker, his willingness to become Roosevelt's running mate was clearly implied.

"Well, I've just been talking to John Garner in Washington," Rayburn reported back to the caucus. "And John wants you to know that he is out. . . . He released you with no strings attached."

The reaction of some of the delegates was strong. A friend of Rayburn talked nonstop about not running out on Cactus Jack, and several women delegates sobbed. Rayburn tried to calm the ladies by pointing out that no one was running out on Garner since he was no longer a candidate. Finally though, said Rayburn, when the delegation "began to row, I had to squeeze down on them."

This was after an hour of yelling and crying had already passed and Rayburn shouted that he was taking a vote on the question of supporting Roosevelt. A tense rollcall started. "How important each vote was," said Tom Connally, "showed up when the tally was announced. For only by a three-vote margin—54 to 51—did the delegation make its switch to Roosevelt." What might have happened if the absent delegates or their alternates had been present was never determined.

This shift in the Texas vote made Roosevelt's nomination on the next ballot inevitable. Mississippi, which had already decided to lead the convention's slide away from Roosevelt on the fourth ballot, stayed in his column on hearing the news about Texas. Also important was California, which had cast its forty-four votes for Garner on three previous ballots. When William McAdoo, boss of the California delegation, got wind of the Texas change, his personal hopes of getting the vice presidential nomination rose. He jumped into an automobile, raced to the convention before Rayburn, hurried to the platform and announced that California would support Roosevelt on the next ballot.

But the Farley-Mullen-Connally deal held and the vice presidential nomination went to Garner on the first ballot.

If Rayburn thought that all the national attention he had received at Chicago would impress the Fourth Congressional District, he was mistaken. After hobnobbing with the Democratic presidential nominee, who flew out to Chicago to make his acceptance speech, and arranging for Garner to address the convention by amplified telephone, Rayburn came home to the big white house in Bonham to learn that he would have two opponents again in the Democratic primary near the end of July. "It was my thought that I would escape opposition this time," he complained unhappily to friends. "But it seems that that isn't in the cards for me."

He saw from the start that it was not going to be an easy primary. One of his opponents was seventy-three-year-old Choice Randell, who had vacated his House seat to undertake an unsuccessful race for the Senate in 1912. Randell had run against Rayburn two years earlier, in 1930, and had not offered much competition. But he had been working steadily since then, and he could tie up the "old" vote this time. In addition,

Randell, as well as the other rival, were bound to benefit from the national disgruntlement with Congress that could easily be translated into votes to oust everybody holding office.

Then there was the candidacy of Jess Morris from the "old haters' " town of Greenville in the county below Fannin. A young and well-liked reporter and part owner of a printing company, energetic and good-looking Morris posed an even greater threat than Randell to an eleventh term for Rayburn.

Sam realized this painfully when Morris began moving swiftly through the five counties in a campaign based on ridiculing him. He poked fun at Sam's short stature, called him a slacker for not enlisting in World War I, denounced the length of his congressional service, and labeled him a rich snob. [16]

Compared to little Rayburn, Morris jibed, he stood "six feet tall, weighed 215 pounds and [was] able to take care of myself in any crowd, anywhere." Moving from torso politics, he made the point that Rayburn had been feeding from the public trough twenty years already, collecting two hundred thousand dollars that came from the sweat of hardworking people. It was time to cut off his free ride. "He's been there long enough!" he cried. One thing more, Jess Morris yelled, everyone in Washington knew that Rayburn was a snob, and when "he came back from Congress he didn't go to see the common people, but ran around with big shots like Carl Nall in Grayson County and Fred Horton in Hunt County." Yes, Rayburn was a rich man who lived in a "mansion" and had a rich man's contempt for the poor and the needy.

Morris had other campaign stunts to worry Rayburn. He brought his wife and young daughter along on the campaign trail to emphasize his warm family status and call attention to Rayburn's bachelorhood. "And my little girl is 100 percent for her daddy," he told the crowds like a doting father. Then to emphasize that he had bipartisan support in the Democratic primary, he had a Dr. Whitten, a Republican from Greenville, introduce him at some meetings. When Whitten told the audience at Whitewright he was a Republican, said a reporter, it was "a fact he seemed to get much satisfaction out of, to judge from the expression on his face." Still another campaign trick of Jess Morris was his attempt to deflate a Rayburn speech in advance. If Rayburn were coming to a town after him, Morris would shake his head slowly, grimace, and say after exhaling theatrically, "You can expect that Rayburn will be boasting of what he has done. But what has Rayburn done?"

Three weeks before the primary on July 23 Rayburn issued a three-page circular that outlined his record in Congress and warned his district that "a man who will misrepresent his opponent's records is not a man to be trusted by the voters." Then he set off scurrying about the five counties, trying to answer Morris' personal attacks. From town to town and from platform to platform, giving three to five speeches a day, he cautioned voters not to judge politicians with a ruler and a scale. If they had followed the Chicago convention, he said, the good citizens of the Fourth District would know that a short man had done all right. Furthermore, there was a way to prove if he were "a snob and ran around with the big shots." The answer: "Ask the people." As for Jess Morris's cry that it was time for a change, Rayburn countered, why should voters want to change their congressman any more than they would their "doctors, lawyers, tenants, school teachers or bankers?"

What Rayburn noticed most of all during that campaign was the look of worry on the sunburned, lined faces of the farmers who turned out to hear him. They were selling their milk for ten cents a gallon, oats and corn for fifteen cents a bushel, eight-week weaned pigs for fifty cents, cattle for three and three-quarters cents a pound and cotton for four cents a pound. [17] All he could do was commiserate with them. "I live on the farm," he told them. "The savings of my life are invested in farm properties alone." But he knew this statement was not comforting, and when he offered a solution for their troubles it was a negative proposal. "One of the great things that will help the farmers will be to tear from the statute books many laws that discriminate against them."

In 1917, the Texas legislature had passed a law providing that if the winner in a primary failed to get a majority of all votes, he would have to undergo a runoff primary with the candidate who came in second. Rayburn was sickened by the thought that this might be his fate on July 23, 1932.

The important Saturday finally came and voters went to the polls. All that day he waited, fearful that Morris and Randell would collectively get more votes than he and force him into a second primary campaign lasting another month. When the votes were counted at last, Rayburn had 17,895, Jess Morris 10,481, and Randell 6,911. He had squeaked through with 50.7 percent, or with a minute majority of 503 votes out of 35,287 cast.

Rayburn's hairline victory was in the final analysis made possible not by his campaign but by the fact that he had successfully fought a change in his district's boundaries the year before. Because his five counties were sixty thousand persons short of the national average congressional district according to the 1930 census, his opponents in the state legislature in 1931 had tried to tack on a Republican piece of Dallas County to the Fourth

District. Had they succeeded, he would have lost the 1932 contest. But the Texas House and Senate could not come up with the identical boundaries, and the issue was put off until 1933.

The importance of his victory in the first primary was soon revealed. He was to serve as Garner's campaign manager for the Vice Presidency if he got past the primary hurdle. On July 24 came a happy letter from Ettie Garner to Sam, telling him that her husband "left immediately after reading the *San Antonio Express.*" The Garner-Rayburn team was in business. [18]

There was also a telegram from Jim Farley that had come during his campaign, and he could now act on it. On behalf of both Roosevelt and Garner, Farley's wire read, "We greatly need your counsel and help in the direction of the campaign and would appreciate your immediate assistance in the North and East." [19] A letter from Rayburn said he had won by 500 votes plus and was "going to New York." A further request came from Roosevelt, urging Rayburn to join his campaign train through California.

On the national hustings, Rayburn followed the Roosevelt-Garner line that fall. This was what he described as "giving it to Hoover with the bark on." It was a "Hoover Depression"; the unemployed were forced to live in "Hooverville" shacks; Hoover was "responsible" for the depression, "did nothing" to correct it, and wasted billions of dollars doing his "nothing." [20] Conditions were so bad, said Rayburn, "you couldn't find a jackrabbit on the north plains that didn't have two men chasing it. And when they got it into the stewpot, they called it 'Hoover Beef.' "

It was a Democratic year no matter what the speechmakers said. "I accuse the present administration of being the greatest spending administration in peacetime in all our history," was one of Roosevelt's gems. "Their failure to balance the budget is at the very bottom of the economic trouble we are suffering." He also said that from the time of the crash until the end of 1931, Hoover "did absolutely nothing to remedy the situation. Not only did he do nothing himself, but he took the position that Congress could do nothing."

Despite such erroneous comments, the country, in its agony, could not abide another four years of the man who had occupied the White House when the depression struck. On November 8, 1932, Roosevelt won almost 89 percent of the electoral votes and Hoover only 11 percent.

With Garner now out of the House, Sam Rayburn viewed the Speaker's rostrum with greater expectations.

11

The Hundred Days

In the elation of his victory at the national convention, Franklin Roosevelt had called Rayburn to his hotel room in Chicago to thank him for the role he had played. But this was neither the time nor the place to get acquainted properly, and Roosevelt put this off until after he was elected President.

Rayburn finally had his first opportunity to talk more extensively with Roosevelt late in 1932 when the President-elect invited important Democrats to his polio foundation at Warm Springs, Georgia, to confer with him on plans for his coming term as President. By that time Rayburn was disturbed by the unsolicited suggestions being offered by the press and business on how to deal with the nation's economic crisis. Henry Hazlitt, a popular writer, was suggesting that Congress be abolished and replaced with a corporate directorate of twelve men; *Barron's* proposed that "a genial and lighthearted dictator might be a relief"; others called for "an American Mussolini"; while the U.S. Chamber of Commerce argued that "a freedom of action which might have been justified in the relatively simple life of the last century cannot be tolerated today." [1]

In many ways Rayburn and Roosevelt seemed to be opposites. Rayburn was taciturn and frank; Roosevelt, talkative and often evasive. The Hyde Park squire was an only child of an oppressively doting mother. He was born to the comforts of inherited wealth and had the manners of the leisure class; the Bonham farmer, from a large family, poor and grubbing on its few acres, had a frontiersman's wariness and simplicity.

But in other ways they found much in common. They were both born in January 1882 and had the mature yet vigorous outlook of men fifty years old, who had been a long time in politics and had never let the subject grow stale or humdrum. Each, up to that point, was also an economic conservative. In the Hoover-term Seventy-second Congress Rayburn had fought for a reduction in government spending of $210 million, sharp salary cuts for civil servants and consolidation of such government agencies as the War and Navy Departments into one agency. In his presidential campaign, Roosevelt showed kinship with Rayburn when he said: "Let us have the courage to stop borrowing to meet continuing deficits. . . . Bureaus and bureaucrats, commissions and commissioners, have been retained at the expense of the taxpayer." [2]

Although Rayburn and Roosevelt hit it off well at Warm Springs, Rayburn had misgivings about the many hovering professors who formed Roosevelt's "Brain Trust." Newspaper stories and rumors were spreading about the influence they were having on the President-elect.

Rayburn exposed his concern about the advisers on the train trip back to Washington from Atlanta. Walking into the diner, he spied Professor Raymond Moley of Columbia University, who had been at Warm Springs with Roosevelt. Moley, one of the top brain trusters, was a professor of political science and a specialist in criminal law and had worked for Governor Roosevelt as research director of the New York State Commission on the Administration of Justice. His attitude toward professional politicians was that they were inferior beings. Rayburn stopped at Moley's table and said, "My name is Sam Rayburn. We met at Warm Springs."

Moley invited him to join him, and he did, Then, sitting opposite the professor, he suddenly leaned across the table and said gruffly, "I hope we won't have any goddam Rasputin in this Administration." [3] (Rasputin was, of course, the Russian monk who used his religious mysticism to dominate the Czarina of Russia.)

This unexpected remark startled Moley, though Rayburn added that he was not referring to him. But Rayburn went on to say that "the party leaders who helped nominate Franklin Roosevelt were not prepared to tolerate any Rasputin."

The academic, smug Moley later wrote that Rayburn's expression had come from "an authentic interpreter from that vast conglomerate known as Congressional opinion." He added: "Never was advice more gently or shrewdly given."

By Saturday, March 4, 1933, when Roosevelt was inaugurated, unemployment had increased to an estimated 14 million, business stood in chaos, and a financial panic had overtaken the country with a run on banks by worried depositors. A Chicago reporter wrote that "the city seemed to have died." Roosevelt's initial action as President was to order all banks closed. His second was to order Congress into emergency session on March 9, the following Thursday.

When the 313 House Democrats met in their caucus the day before the special session began, the chief order of business was to choose a Speaker. Ever cautious John Nance Garner had run simultaneously for Vice President and his seat in the House in 1932. And even though he won both places, he would not give up his seat in the House until March 3, 1933.

This permitted him to get his final licks at Hoover in the lame-duck session that lasted from December 1932 until the following March. It also should have given him a strong voice in naming his successor. Rayburn was the logical person to win his backing, for he had become one of the most vocal Democrats in the Hoover-period Congresses, had twenty years of service, and was well liked by the members. In addition, he had managed Garner's campaign for the nomination, worked as his floor leader at the Chicago convention and handled his fall campaign for Vice President. For these reasons he believed his chances were excellent to succeed Garner.

First indication of Garner's negative thoughts on the subject came in July 1932 when William Bankhead of Alabama, chairman of the House Rules Committee, wired Rayburn that he planned to run for Speaker if Garner became Vice President. Rayburn replied that his own friends wanted him to go after the Speakership but that he had also been asked to support John McDuffie from Bankhead's state. [4]

McDuffie's length of service was six years shorter than Rayburn's and he was not known for leadership qualities. But (like Rayburn) he was a member in good standing of the Board of Education, and unlike him he was not from Texas. Garner mulled over that last factor and decided that the Lone Star State, possessing a Vice President and five committee chairmen, should not have the House Speaker as well. Bald, bachelor Hatton Sumners, Rayburn's first congressional friend, was now the millionaire chairman of the Judiciary Committee; Marvin Jones, Rayburn's former brother-in-law, headed the Agriculture Committee; Fritz Lanham, Public Buildings; Joseph Mansfield bossed the Rivers and Harbors Committee from his wheelchair; and Rayburn ran the Commerce Committee.

McDuffie was a weaker candidate than Rayburn would have been. But with Garner openly backing McDuffie, Sam dropped out of contention and like a good soldier announced his support for him.

McDuffie's chief opponent was elderly Henry T. Rainey, a white-thatched liberal Democrat from Illinois and Garner's majority leader. While Sam and Cactus Jack buttonholed members to support John

McDuffie, Rainey, wearing a new broad-ribboned flowing black bow tie, trudged from member to member for pledges. When his count was far below what was needed, he made a deal with Joe Byrns of Tennessee, the chairman of the Democratic National Congressional Committee, who was also an active candidate for Speaker. He promised to get his supporters to back Byrns for majority leader if the Byrns followers voted for him for Speaker. This deal proved too much for the McDuffie-Garner-Rayburn forces, and Rainey bested McDuffie in the Democratic caucus by three votes. So the Roosevelt era began with Rainey and Byrns bossing the House. In addition, Texans ran six House committees, for Byrns had also been chairman of the Appropriations Committee, and when he resigned to become Rainey's floor leader, James Buchanan of Brenham, Texas, succeeded him.

Between the time of his inauguration and the convening of the emergency session on March 9, Roosevelt had been working on new banking legislation to end the financial panic and chaos. Frightened, pleading bankers flocked to Washington, crying for any assistance, while at the White House the President and advisers threshed over arguments to nationalize or reform the banking system. Various congressmen, such as Senators Robert M. La Follette, Jr., of Wisconsin, Edward Costigan of Colorado and Bronson Cutting of New Mexico, led the fight to establish a government agency instead of private banks to handle depositing, checking and commercial lending. [5]

At noon on March 9, the incoming Congress was greeted with the new President's banking message and his demand that it proceed swiftly to pass his Emergency Banking Bill. Roosevelt's decision was against nationalization, despite large-scale evidence that banks had milked deposits and engaged in many illegal activities during the twenties. His bill essentially provided that no bank could reopen until it was judged sound by the Treasury Department.

Never in Sam Rayburn's twenty years in Congress did he witness what he saw that day. Roosevelt had sent the only copy of his banking bill to Speaker Rainey. No committee hearing was held on it. Instead Henry B. Steagall, chairman of the House Banking and Currency Committee, read it aloud in the Chamber, stumbling over pencilled-in changes. Debate afterward was limited to forty minutes, but the vote came earlier when Minority Leader Bert Snell stood up and said, "The House is burning down, and the President of the United States says this is the way to put out the fire. . . . I am going to give the President his way." [6] The vote for the bill was unanimous.

SAM RAYBURN

At 7:46 P.M. that same day after the Senate passed it, once it overcame stalling tactics by Senator Huey Long and other banking nationalizationists, it went to Roosevelt for his signature. There was widespread agreement with Professor Moley's assessment of the legislation that "capitalism was saved."

It was Rayburn's understanding that Roosevelt had intended to restrict the emergency session to the passage of his banking bill and then have it adjourn. But his quick success and the continuing economic crisis led Roosevelt to keep Congress in session for what later became known as "The Hundred Days." This was a period that saw a vast array of "recovery" legislation come before Congress.

In his acceptance speech at the national convention, Roosevelt had given his administration the caption, "The New Deal," when he said, "I pledge you, I pledge myself, to a new deal for the American people." Yet his first action after the conservative Banking Bill was to send Congress an even more conservative measure. This was his Coolidgelike Economy Bill, which would cut government salaries by $100 million, veterans' benefits and the military budget by $300 million and various federal spending programs by $200 million.

The bill came to the House on the morning of March 10, the second day of the session, and Speaker Rainey called the Democrats to a caucus to consider it. But opposition to the bill from patronage-hungry Democrats was loud and vigorous, and when Rainey put it to a vote it failed by fourteen.

A defeat for Roosevelt this early in his administration might easily have spoiled his momentum, and Rainey and Floor Leader Joe Byrns asked Sam Rayburn for help because of his popularity with the members and his often-expressed views for retrenchment. Rayburn took the floor and told the House he had served with five Presidents and had always supported their emergency proposals whether they were Democrats or Republicans. The House had to support Roosevelt now and back his program to help "our unhappy country." It was its duty. "My program, your program, is not here. But the program of the man to whom the people of the United States are and must be looking today is before Congress. And what are we going to do with it?"[7] The economy bill passed by a vote of 266 to 139.

The ink was not yet dry on the Economy Act when Roosevelt abandoned the philosophy behind it. For he had reached the conclusion that retrenchment and a balanced budget were not the way to solve the nation's problems. Louis Brownlow, friend and expert on public administration, judged Roosevelt's change as a victory for part of his advisers. In divided camps among his Brain Trust were the "savers" and the "spenders"; the "private enterprisers" and the "government enterprisers."[8] The "spenders" and "private enterprisers" were now more convincing to Roosevelt. Before long, the "government enterprisers" would succeed the "private enterprisers."

Once Roosevelt changed his approach, his New Deal really got under way and the Hundred Days of the session turned into a major spending and function-broadening period. The White House filled up with advisers working from early morning until past midnight planning and developing programs to revitalize the shattered economy. "The men would be working in every room," said Mrs. Roosevelt. "I could not go to bed out of personal curiosity to know what was going on." And what was going on was the writing of fifteen major bills, including those that became the Agricultural Adjustment Act, the Farm Mortgage Act, the Tennessee Valley Authority, Home Owners Loan Act, National Industrial Recovery Act (NRA) with a $3.3-billion Public Works Administration program, a $500 million Federal Emergency Relief Administration program, new banking and securities legislation, an Emergency Railroad Transportation Act and legislation establishing the Civilian Conservation Corps.

Roosevelt's abrupt change in approach did not isolate Sam Rayburn high and dry and marching in another direction because he changed his long-held views just as swiftly. He did so primarily for three reasons. The first was his quick and abiding faith in Roosevelt's leadership. The second was the result of Roosevelt's astuteness in following the Economy Bill with legislation aimed at aiding farmers. The third reason was Rayburn's determination to play a personal role in combatting the depression and reforming the economy.

Rayburn's wavelength kinship with Roosevelt began with the new President's first action in closing the banks. "I know one lady who lived on a farm down in my country who came in to get money out of the bank," Rayburn told a reporter. "They said, 'You can't get any money out. Mr. Roosevelt has closed the banks.' She said, 'I guess Mr. Roosevelt knows best. He is trying to do something for us.' The people knew he was trying to do something about it."[9]

It would have been normal for a President from New York to tackle industrial problems first. But the day after the Economy Bill passed the Senate, Roosevelt began his New Deal in earnest by asking Congress to approve his Agricultural Adjustment Bill. The mountainous food surpluses of the previous year and the number of farm foreclosures had increased while the ruinous, low prices of farm products dropped toward new lows. In later years Rayburn brought astonishment to the faces of rural audiences when he recited existing prices at that time: "Your cotton sold for 4 cents per pound, oats and corn 15 cents a bushel, wheat 28 cents a bushel, a canner cow 1½ cents a pound and a good steer 3½ cents a pound."

Word to Rayburn and other rural congressmen was that a major farm strike led by Milo Reno of the militant Farmers' Holiday Association could be expected in the spring of 1933. Farmers' taking matters into their own hands was not the answer, even though there was some emotional satisfaction in the growing practice of overturning loaded trucks on their way to market, flogging judges in foreclosure cases and setting up spiked barricades to keep sheriffs away.

The AAA (Agricultural Adjustment Act), which was Roosevelt's answer to the plight of farmers, pleased Rayburn. In fact, he called it "the best farm program that was ever passed." What it did was to restrict land put to certain crops, or create planned scarcity in order to raise farm purchasing power. Food processors, such as millers, would be assessed a processing tax, and the proceeds would be used to subsidize cooperating farmers.

Roosevelt also proposed an Emergency Farm Mortgage Bill to ease the calamity of the nation's farmers, who owed $12 billion on their mortgages, through easy refinancing by the Federal Land Banks. After Roosevelt brought up these two proposals plus others for farmers, Rayburn recalled, "When we were down at the White House one morning, President Roosevelt said, 'Now you folks have got what you want. I want a Civilian Conservation Corps.' And out of that grew the CCC, which was very helpful in many ways to the youth of the country. It took them off the streets and gave them a useful life."

The CCC soon sent three hundred thousand unemployed and out-of-school youths to work on conservation projects and in time involved almost 3 million young men. At the insistence of Mrs. Roosevelt a test CCC camp for girls was established in June 1933 on Bear Mountain, New York, but the girls showed little interest in conservation and deserted the camp in such large numbers that the project was abandoned.

Rayburn's role as a New Deal legislator turned out to be major. Yet none of his work dealt with agriculture. Sometimes he relied on almost strong-arm methods to get control of legislation for his committee. Once he walked into the Speaker's office and approached Lewis Deschler, the House parliamentarian, to whom Rainey had assigned jurisdictional disputes. "Could the FCC Bill be referred to my Commerce Committee?"

he asked. While Deschler began mulling this over, Rayburn added, "Even if the rules say it can't, I'm gonna take it."

He did.

Another time Speaker Rainey consulted him directly on where to send a bill affecting business. "I want it," Rayburn said bluntly, and Rainey gave it to his committee.

Unlike some other House committee chairmen who felt inferior to their counterparts in the Senate, Rayburn did not feel any subservience. In Hoover's last year he developed a strong dislike for maverick Senator James Couzens, who was both an inflationist and an obstructionist. It reached a high in February 1933 when Couzens blocked an RFC loan to a Detroit bank that was in trouble. This resulted in a run by depositors that forced the governor to close all Michigan banks. This in turn weakened banks in Ohio and Indiana and brought on the massive runs on banks throughout the nation.

Rayburn's antagonism toward Couzens was so strong that one time on a Couzens railroad bill he told him, "Even if the Senate passes your bill I won't permit the House to vote on it." [10]

In the first Hundred Days of the New Deal, Rayburn was responsible for two vital pieces of legislation. One was the Emergency Railroad Transportation Act, or the Railroad Rehabilitation Act, which he and Professor Moley drafted. "It saved the railroads," said Senator James F. Byrnes, a Roosevelt spokesman in the Senate. [11] Railroads had failed to meet fixed charges of $250 million in 1932 and almost fifty thousand miles of lines were in the hands of receivers. Rayburn's bill barred holding companies from owning railroads, and it established a new rule for setting rates. For the first time the ICC had to consider whether a rate discouraged rail traffic. The bill also safeguarded railroad workers by a provision barring the laying off of any of them.

Another Rayburn effort was his committee investigation that showed the need for federal regulation of interstate buses and trucks. However, Roosevelt refused to give his bill a go-ahead in 1933, and it did not become law until two years later.

Rayburn's other major bill in Roosevelt's first Hundred Days in the 1933 session was the Truth-in-Securities Act. A year earlier at the demand of President Hoover, a Senate committee had begun an investigation of Wall Street and the stock market. Leaders in American financial circles were brought to the committee room to testify, and what came from the lips of J. P. Morgan, Richard Whitney, Clarence Dillon, Thomas W. Lamont and others was a sordid picture of shady practices that bilked the public. There were stories of selling stock below market price to "preferred lists" of friends, the sale of worthless stock to the public, banks that combined their normal commercial deposit and loans business with stockbrokering and the development of holding companies to rig high prices for consumers.

Rayburn also conducted a committee investigation, and what he found was that about $25 billion of the $50 billion of securities sold to the public in the preceding decade were worthless. [12] It was natural that he thought of his Railroad Stock and Bond Bill of 1914, designed to halt the sale of worthless or watered railroad securities to the public by having the ICC issue a "stop order" where warranted.

It was also natural at this time for Supreme Court Justice Louis Brandeis to get in touch with him. In 1914, Brandeis, as an adviser to Woodrow Wilson, had worked with Rayburn on his bill and then helped kill it in the Senate. Now seventy-six, Brandeis was an insider in the Roosevelt camp and he was aware of the success of Rayburn's bill since it was finally enacted in 1920. The Supreme Court Chamber in 1933 was located in a room in the Capitol between the House and Senate Chambers, and the friendship between the two resumed.

Both had the same idea: Why not extend control over the issuance of stocks and bonds to all corporations and not restrict it to the railroads? Roosevelt would be amenable, said Brandeis, because in his campaign speech in Columbus, Ohio, he had said: "The sellers [of securities] shall tell the uses to which the money is to be put. This truth-telling requires that definite and accurate statements be made to the buyers."

This became one of the subjects Rayburn discussed with Roosevelt at Warm Springs, and in January 1933, the President-elect asked Samuel Untermyer, a hard-hitting antitrust lawyer-warrior, to write a bill on this matter. The bill displeased Rayburn, so Roosevelt had Huston Thompson, a former head of the Federal Trade Commission, write it anew.

On March 29, President Roosevelt sent a message to Congress and dispatched the Thompson draft to Rayburn who introduced it in the House. On reading it carefully and listening to complaints from others, however, he decided to make a fresh start.

This time he asked Raymond Moley to work with him on a draft. But Moley, whom Roosevelt had assigned for payroll purposes to the State Department as an Assistant Secretary, was too busy plotting how to take control of the Department from slow-moving, anemic Cordell Hull, the Secretary. So Moley sent Felix Frankfurter, another top Brain Truster, as his substitute. Frankfurter, a little man with an owlish face, was a

112

Harvard Law School professor who had served Roosevelt unofficially as legal adviser when he was governor of New York.

Frankfurter walked into Rayburn's office on April 7 with two young lawyers in tow, who, he said, would help Rayburn. One was James M. Landis, just over thirty and also a professor of law at Harvard. The other was thirty-nine-year-old Benjamin V. Cohen, possessor of a sharp legal mind and a substantial bank account that had been acquired from stock market speculation before the crash.

In three days Landis and Cohen produced a first draft, discussing the intricacies with Rayburn throughout. What the young lawyers used as their model was the British law on the subject. But the British law did not provide for the advance disapproval by a government agency of stock issuance. All it required was full financial disclosure by a firm issuing new securities. Rayburn considered this a serious flaw and he had the two add provisions authorizing the Federal Trade Commission to issue a "stop order" to bar public offering of securities if a company's registered financial statement was incorrect.

In the perfection of the bill, a new lawyer joined the group. He was Thomas G. Corcoran, a brash thirty-three-year-old former law clerk to Supreme Court Justice Oliver Wendell Holmes, the "Great Dissenter." Cohen and Corcoran, who were to form a team in what became known as the second wave of Brain Trusters, were opposites in many ways. While Ben Cohen was a quiet, studious type, "Tommy the Cork" Corcoran was aptly described by Holmes as "quite noisy."

Rayburn grew fond of Cohen and Corcoran, and a close working relationship developed that later extended to other legislation. Said Rayburn, "Taken together these two fellows made the brightest man I ever saw. They never insisted on their views. When I told them what I wanted, they started to work to put it into the legislation, and they wrote it in such a way as to make it stick." [13]

When the draft of the Truth-in-Securities Bill was completed, Rayburn called it the "most technical" he had ever dealt with. When it came before his subcommittee, he had the three young men present to answer questions on the complex subject. After the other congressmen were conversant with its details, he planned to take it directly to the House floor without holding a public hearing. Ray Moley got wind of this, however, and convinced him it would be unfair to the business community not to give it an opportunity to testify.

Reluctantly, Rayburn agreed to give business its say. Leading the array of witnesses was John Foster Dulles of the law firm of Sullivan and

Cromwell, who had a distinguished record as an international lawyer and delegate to various international conferences. Dulles charged into the bill, declared it a wretched piece of legislation. But Rayburn carefully destroyed this star witness by showing that Dulles was neither familiar with his bill's provisions nor its purpose.

Afterward, it sailed through the House while the Senate passed the Thompson Bill. At Rayburn's adamant insistence, the conference committee composed of House-Senate Commerce Committee members accepted his bill instead of attempting to iron out differences between the two. [14] Finally on May 27, 1933, Roosevelt signed it into law.

Like the praising teacher of a promising child, Felix Frankfurter wrote a letter to Roosevelt that was a report card analysis of Rayburn's work on the bill. "He gave himself completely to effectuate the purpose of your message," he said condescendingly. "He worked indefatigably for a law that should be fair to the legitimate interests of finance, while at the same time protecting the credulity and limited knowledge of investors. And the qualities of courage that he showed were no less striking He was keenly aware of the subtle forces trying to defeat your program and was effectively on guard against them." [15]

Roosevelt put the current edition of Rayburn's 1914 bill in simpler perspective. For the first time, he said, the new principle of "Let the seller *also* beware" was a part of American law. [16]

The Rayburn family at the old home at Flag Springs, 1905. *Top row, left to right*: Dr. Frank Rayburn, Sam, Dick, Tom, and Jim. *Front row, left to right*: Will, Abner, William, Martha, Lucinda, Katy R. Thomas, and Meddie R. Bartley.

Sam Rayburn at his desk in the Texas State Legislature, 1907.

Speaker William Bankhead with Majority Leader Sam Rayburn, 1938.

President Franklin Roosevelt with Sam Rayburn and Alben W. Barkley, 1944.

Sam Rayburn confers with John Kennedy and Lyndon Johnson during the 1960 presidential campaign.

Mr. Sam at home in the early fifties.

Three Presidents and a Vice President attend Sam Rayburn's funeral in Bonham on November 18, 1961. It was the first time Truman and Eisenhower spoke to each other since Truman left office in January 1953. (*Courtesy Sam Rayburn Library*)

Speaker Sam Rayburn.

12

New Deal Workhorse

By 1934, Sam Rayburn was describing himself as "a helluva New Dealer."[1] A columnist went further, calling him "a man in the shadows . . . one of the Secret Six who make the wheels go round."[2]

Besides supporting Roosevelt's program and fathering the Emergency Railroad Transportation and Truth-in-Securities Acts, he had enjoyed success on some pet issues during that hectic Hundred Days' session in 1933. For instance, as a freshman in the Texas House in 1907, he had won approval of a bill to insure bank deposits. Twenty-five years later in the Hoover Congress he helped sponsor a similar insurance plan for depositors in national banks. "I believe when a man puts his money in a bank he should know he will get it back, not only for his own benefit but because it will create confidence and stop hoarding," he argued in 1932.[3] He had also promoted legislation to force banks out of the securities business, for this widespread extra-curricular activity endangered the safety of deposits.

Although Roosevelt opposed insuring bank deposits at first, he grudgingly accepted it and it became part of the second banking bill in the Hundred Days. This was the Glass-Steagall Banking Act of June 16, 1933, whose chief purpose was to divorce commercial and investment banking. A Federal Deposit Insurance Corporation was established to guarantee bank deposits up to twenty-five hundred dollars.

Sam Rayburn's role as a New Deal legislator expanded during the five-months' congressional session in 1934.

In the previous year's Hundred Days' session, the first phase of the New Deal had taken place. Emphasis in this phase had been on national planning and on doing something for all segments of the economy to help them recover from the depression blight. The underlying philosophy had been that agriculture, business, industry and labor formed "a true concert of interests" that needed only federal planning and coordination to make the system function properly. Corporate bigness was not a curse, and competition was outmoded.

The best example of this first phase of the New Deal was the National Industrial Recovery Act of 1933. Across the nation, under government sponsorship industries set up NRA codes of fair practices that let them control production, prices, wages and work conditions. Roosevelt blessed this noncompetitive structure: "It is a challenge to industry which has long insisted that, given the right to act in unison, it could do much for the general good which has hitherto been unlawful. From today on, it has that right."[4]

Beginning in 1934 came the second phase of the New Deal.[5] It was not a clear-cut, abrupt change but a gradual and growing shift in emphasis from the "true concert of interests" doctrine with government planning for social management to the Brandeis approach of maintaining private competition through regulatory agencies. This shift came about through the ascendancy of Brandeis protégés among Roosevelt's advisers, and it led a phase-one adviser to declare that Brandeis' goal was "a nation of small proprietors, of corner grocers and smithies under spreading chestnut trees."

Rayburn's big bills in the 1934 session were of a piece with the New Deal's second phase. These were the Securities Exchange Act to regulate stock exchanges and the Federal Communications Act to regulate the communications industry.

In the words of New York Stock Exchange President Richard Whitney the Exchange was "a perfect institution." But a lengthy Senate investigation of its operations during the Roaring Twenties disclosed countless shocking instances of insiders making killings and the public rooked by dishonest brokers and manipulators. Other exchanges, such as the New York Mining Exchange, the Boston Curb Exchange and the California Stock Exchange, were even worse than the Big Board in New York in the frequency of their rigged market fluctuations designed to fleece the investing suckers.[6]

Several of the younger set of Brain Trusters worked on the bill to regulate the stock exchanges, but in the end it became the product of Ben Cohen and Tom Corcoran. After a Roosevelt message to Congress on the subject on February 9, 1934, the fifty-page highly technical bill draft went to Rayburn and Duncan U. Fletcher, the elderly chairman of the Senate Banking Committee.

The explosion from the opposition came immediately after Rayburn announced that his committee would hold early hearings. An aroused business and industrial community, stock exchange officials and brokers flocked to Washington to denounce the bill as "a national disaster." What! Have the federal government regulate and change time-honored trading practices of the exchanges? they scoffed. Or control the amount of margin speculators would have to pay down for stock purchases? Or require the registration with the FTC of old stock being traded as well as new issues?

Rayburn conducted a six-weeks' hearing that exposed him as well as the bill to sharp attack. [7] The elegant Richard Whitney faced the Bonham farmer with contempt, told him that the proposed legislation would "dry up" the securities market and result in "tremendous, if not universal, withdrawal" of American corporations from the exchanges. Rayburn replied: "I am not an enemy of your business. . . . What I want to do is to take the desperadoes out of your field." James Rand of Remington, Rand had a different line. He charged Rayburn with pushing a bill intending to alter the American way of life "from democracy to Communism," while Eugene Meyers, Hoover's head of the RFC, and later publisher of the *Washington Post*, argued that it would bring "state control of industry."

While the emotional hearings went on, the Capitol and congressional office buildings swarmed with lobbyists directed by Whitney. Rayburn called the operation "the most powerful lobby ever organized against any bill which ever came up in Congress." [8] Besides the personal visits to congressmen to sway their votes, there was an ocean of mail and telegrams from home districts against the Rayburn-Fletcher bill. Rayburn's district was not excluded. "Sacks of mail objecting to the bill came from the Fourth Texas District," said Alla Clary, his secretary. Rayburn ordered every letter answered because he wanted to explain his position. But most of his letters were returned to him with the postmaster's notation of "Deceased" or "Moved away." His conclusion: The stock exchange lobby had used old phone books in its phony letter campaign. [9]

As the hearings progressed, he saw a way to weaken the opposition. Moderates among the brokerage and investment houses, such as E. A. Pierce, Robert A. Lovett of Brown Brothers, Harriman, and James V. Forrestal of Dillon, Read, were not adamantly opposed to the regulation of the exchanges. Rayburn gave them ample opportunity to testify, and he told Cohen and Corcoran to work with them in making conciliatory changes in the bill.

On March 20, the two returned a completely rewritten bill to him that proposed the establishment of a new agency, the Securities and Exchange Commission, to take over his Truth-in-Security Act administration from the Federal Trade Commission and regulate the exchange operations. The rewrite also gave the SEC discretionary power to determine the rate of margin that buyers of securities would have to pay in cash. Rayburn, however, would not accept these specific changes and kept them out of the version he pushed through his committee.

There was no letup in the attacks when the House debate took place. Rayburn called them "vicious and senseless." He was especially furious when Whitney's defenders went after Cohen and Corcoran. "They are held up as being somebody from Russia or being tainted with Socialism or Communism," he lashed back in an incredulous tone. [10] But despite the vehemence of his opponents, he won handily on May 5 by a margin of 280 to 84.

The Senate passed the Cohen-Corcoran revision basically, and this required a conference committee of Senate-House members to agree on a compromise measure. Rayburn held out for a while for regulation by the FTC but finally agreed to the Securities and Exchange Commission, claimed one writer, "in order to gain leverage when it came to appointing the commissioners" of the SEC. [11] The conference committee compromise then cleared both houses and was signed by Roosevelt on June 6, 1934.

The new law provided for a five-member SEC commission, and Rayburn sent his suggestions to Roosevelt through Ray Moley, who had been assigned the task of supplying Roosevelt with recommendations. James Landis was the only choice of his that FDR accepted. In turn, Rayburn was far from pleased when Joseph P. Kennedy was chosen as chairman. Joe Kennedy had been a leading stock market manipulator heavily engaged in the very practices the SEC was supposed to prosecute. But Kennedy proved an excellent choice primarily because he had the support of business. There was no trouble getting the twenty-four leading exchanges and their twenty-six hundred members to submit detailed registration material about themselves and the five thousand different securities listed on the exchanges. Nor did the exchanges put up any argument about adopting the trading rules set by the SEC.

Despite his time-consuming work on the Securities Exchange legislation in committee and on the House floor, Rayburn was also heavily involved with several other important bills in 1934. One of these established the Federal Communications Commission to regulate broadcasting and wire communications.

Before then several agencies had handled bits and pieces of the job of regulating wire and wireless communications. Commercial telegraphy had been under the Post Office; railroad telegraphy, the ICC; cables, the State Department; telephones had been essentially unregulated federally; and radio, following the Radio Act of 1927, had been regulated by the Commerce Department. Herbert Hoover, when he had been Secretary of Commerce, had had ninety-eight radio frequencies to allocate to about eight hundred radio stations across the country, and many had ignored his rulings, operating at whatever wavelength they wanted. Los Angeles evangelist Aimee Semple McPherson, a leading violator, once sent him a telegraph that read: "Please order your minions of Satan to leave my station alone. When I offer my prayers to Him I must fit into His wave reception." [12]

Rayburn had as much trouble with members of Congress over the FCC as he did with the industries involved. When Roosevelt disclosed that he wanted to unify regulations of communications, James Mead, chairman of the House Post Office Committee, demanded the bill because the telegraph industry was under the Post Office Department. Otis Bland also wanted it for his merchant marine, radio, and fisheries committee, but Rayburn wrested control for his committee.

Roosevelt's message to Congress on this subject came on February 26, 1934, and Rayburn had new problems when the version he introduced in the House differed markedly from that of the Senate's sponsor, Senator Clarence Dill, the father of the Radio Act of 1927. Each bill contained more than six hundred sections, with Rayburn's measure far less technical or punitive. For instance, where Dill's bill had highly complex rules on certain rate making, Rayburn's version simply said that charges "should be just and reasonable." Yet the bellows of outrage at the Rayburn bill from the broadcasting industry and congressional opponents when he started hearings were intense. This was not "government regulation" but "government management," they cried. Several critics pointed out that at the same time that Rayburn wanted federal controls the broadcasting industry had been asked to set up an NRA code for self-regulation.

With Congress scheduled to adjourn in mid-June, his effort seemed academic when he was only able to clear the bill in his committee by the end of May. [13] But he steered it through the House like an aggressive general. Even then, the strategy talk at the White House was that the bill would have to be dropped in the drive for adjournment.

Yet he plowed on, arranging for a House-Senate conference committee, despite the sharp differences between his and the Dill bill that had passed the Senate. The wrangle was longest on three points: Dill wanted a five-man commission, Rayburn seven; Dill wanted the FCC divided into two agencies—one to control cable and wire systems, the other to regulate radio with each agency head's decisions on technical matters being final—Rayburn's version had three divisions under the control of the commission; and Dill's bill had a censorship section. This said that in case of war or national emergency the President could close wire or radio news stations or censor news passed through them. Rayburn stood firmly opposed to any censorship.

A settlement between Dill and Rayburn looked impossible, especially since Dill felt as though he "owned" federal regulation of broadcasting. But he suddenly gave in on all key points, and the Rayburn conference report quickly won House and Senate approval.

When Roosevelt signed the Communications Act on June 19, 1934, he offered to let Rayburn name a commissioner. At Rayburn's earlier request, Roosevelt had named Dr. Walter Splawn, the former president of the University of Texas and Rayburn's committee assistant, to membership on the ICC. As his statistician, Splawn had hired Rayburn's nephew, Robert T. Bartley, son of his sister Meddie. Rayburn now recommended Bartley for the FCC, but not as a commissioner, and Roosevelt named him director of the Telegraph Division. [14]

Having earned the enmity of the stock exchanges and the communications industry in 1934, Sam Rayburn added the oil industry to the list that same year. Oil companies had been a major political force in Texas since the "Lucas Gusher" came in at Spindletop near Beaumont in 1901. In the rush of Humble Oil's rise to the status of the greatest single enterprise in the state, this subsidiary of Standard Oil bought politicians right and left, including Rayburn's early political hero, Joe Bailey. The constant press by the Texas congressional delegation to please the industry reached a peak in the mid-twenties when the delegation played an important role in establishing the 27½ percent depletion allowance. From his spot as ranking Democrat on the tax-writing Ways and Means Committee and then later as Speaker, Garner had seen to it that only friends of oil were named members of the committee.

The only time the industry lost some of its arrogance came after the discovery in 1930 of the east Texas oil field, the world's richest, with reserves of 5 billion barrels. The gigantic supply coming from twenty-five thousand producing wells, coupled with the force of the economic depression, drove prices down to ten cents a barrel. At forty-two gallons to the barrel, the price was a measly penny for 4.2 gallons.

By the time Roosevelt became President, a Texas law gave the State Railroad Commission authority to determine the amount of oil each well could produce. Production in excess of quotas was called "hot-oil," or illegal oil. While the commission tried to create scarcity and raise prices, many oil producers were shipping hot-oil across state lines and depressing prices further. As a result, oil industry leaders begged Roosevelt for a federal oil czar with power to limit production at the well and shipments in interstate commerce.

Roosevelt liked the idea, had a bill written by the oil industry that would make Interior Secretary Harold Ickes oil czar, and sent it to both houses with a presidential message.

But his expected clear sailing did not occur. Senator Marvel Logan of Kentucky quickly propelled the bill through his Mines and Mining Committee. In the House, however, while he favored federal policing of interstate oil shipments, Rayburn opposed letting the federal government have power to determine production of each well, because he considered this a state function. This placed him in the uncomfortable position of being against his state's chief industry, President Roosevelt and Harold Ickes, who wanted badly to become dictator of the oil industry.

The bill should have gone to the House Mines and Mining Committee, where Congressman Joe Smith of West Virginia stood ready to clear it for House vote in short order. Instead, Rayburn went to Speaker Rainey and talked him into sending it to his committee. By the time Smith discovered it, Rayburn had already begun planned interminable hearings to talk the bill to death. His excuse: He wanted to hear all shades of opinion on the subject.

As the weeks went by, Roosevelt wrote him a letter asking him to report the bill out favorably to the House for a vote. When this did not happen and more time vanished, Roosevelt sent him a second urgent letter. After twelve weeks, the administration and the oil lobby had Congressman Tom Blanton of Abilene confront him in the House. Blanton, a big, heavy man, was the most argumentative member of the Texas delegation and was forever seeking revenge for real and imagined injustices he suffered. "Boys," a west Texas editor once wrote, "when Tom Blanton comes to town, you had better hire a hall, get out the band, furnish the ice water and the crowd. Or he will have your paper stopped."[15]

In his loud voice, Blanton demanded to know when the oil bill would be reported.

Caught off guard, Rayburn fumbled out a reply that he would "very soon."

A few days later, Blanton confronted him again. This time he berated Rayburn and finally yelled, "You know me, Sam. You chloroformed this bill and you know it. Both of us are just alike. We will both bluff sometimes."

"I do not bluff," Rayburn shot back.

Blanton mocked him. "Yes, we do not bluff! But we chloroform oil bills all right. You chloroform them. Now, Sam——"

The crimson had shot up from Rayburn's face to his head as he started to charge across the House Chamber toward Blanton. But Martin Dies, a tall, muscular Texas congressman, leaped up and grabbed Rayburn by the arms. While Rayburn struggled to free himself from Dies' grip, Blanton shouted, "I know you, Sam!" and hurried out of the Chamber. [16]

The Oil Czar Ickes bill died shortly after this confrontation when Roosevelt sent Congress a letter in which he recommended divorcing pipelines from parent oil companies. Oil problems were now so confused that there were no objections as Congress adjourned without taking action on the bill bottled up in Rayburn's committee. The following year Rayburn helped promote the Connally Hot-Oil Bill, which provided a federal penalty for interstate shipment of oil in violation of state law. Within a short time oil prices shot up to one dollar a barrel, and the bitter feeling of the oil industry toward Rayburn diminished.

Ray Tucker, writing in *Collier's* Magazine, drew an accurate picture of the army-tank approach Rayburn had used in the 1934 House session: "Rayburn never budges or gives an inch on the floor and in committee. He prefers to outfight and outargue the other fellow. Since he had to resist powerful pressures from railroad and financial organizations, his success has been surprising. Whereas most important measures got through the last House under gag rules restricting debate and amendments, he pushed his controversial bills through the Chamber without such safeguards." [17]

Fresh from his legislative successes in 1934, Sam Rayburn went home unhappily to the inevitable reelection contest that was already warming up. Now there was more territory to cover in the Fourth District, which had been enlarged from its earlier five counties to seven. Fortunately the two additions—Kaufman and Rockwell Counties—were rural and Democratic. Thanks to the effort of friends in the state legislature, pressure from opponents to dump a large Republican section of Dallas County into his district had been staved off at least until after the 1940 census.

Once again his competitor in the primary was Jess Morris, the young reporter who had campaigned against him in 1932 on the basis of his greater height and bulk and the punching power in his hammy fists, plus a false picture of Rayburn's financial worth. Morris was eagerly back for another try, and this time he had a strong ally.

Rayburn quickly gauged that his chief problem was with vocal segments of the district's farmers, some of whom he considered to be "farming the farmers" while others were genuinely angry with Roosevelt's agricultural program. Of the latter group, many viewed the Agricultural Adjustment Act as a villainous piece of legislation. [18] When Roosevelt sent his AAA bill to Congress in the spring of 1933, his avowed purpose had been to help farmers get higher prices for their crops and cattle by cutting the supply. However, by the time Congress approved the AAA in 1933, that year's crops were already planted. So farmers could not get paid for restricting acreage, and as a result prices continued to be lower than costs. Then in 1934 when prices began rising, Congress amended the AAA to tax farmers who put their excess production on the market. Still another aspect of the AAA that made farmers fume was the decision of Secretary of Agriculture Henry A. Wallace to slaughter 6 million pigs and two hundred thousand pregnant sows, in order to raise meat prices. When no provisions were made to give the meat to the poor, an old farmer in Rayburn's district echoed the view of many of his neighbors in saying angrily, "This is wrong, morally wrong, to destroy food that cannot be satisfactorily consumed, with people here and abroad hungry." Rayburn tried to argue the long-term benefits of the program, but he convinced few.

So his primary campaign against Jess Morris was another chagrining affair. Morris managed to win three of the counties and might have swept Rayburn out of Congress if Sam's friends had not brought out a large vote for him in Grayson County.

While Rayburn was at home recovering from the latest fight for his political existence, Speaker Henry Rainey died in August 1934, a day before his seventy-fourth birthday. Congress was not scheduled to meet until the following January, but ten candidates, including Rayburn, put out feelers to friends in the House for support in succeeding Rainey.

Front-runner was Joe Byrns, the usually mild-mannered majority leader, and although Roosevelt publicly professed his neutrality, he preferred Rayburn. To help Sam's cause, he asked him to deliver a nationwide radio address in early September on the blessings of the New Deal. The speech actually served a double purpose, for besides publicizing Rayburn it was an attack on the Liberty League right-wing business leaders and disgruntled Democrats who had organized to fight a second term for Roosevelt in 1936. Anti-New Dealers were labeled a small group who "make up in vociferousness what they lack in other resources," and the specific turncoats, such as Al Smith and John W. Davis, the 1924 Democratic presidential nominee, "political hacks who have done service for the stand-pat Republicans." [19]

But the prestige gained from the speech was not the most concrete way

123

to win the Speakership. He should have returned to the capital to map his campaign. Instead, when Ray Moley invited him to go on a Mexican vacation toward the end of September, he accepted. Cecil Dickson, an Associated Press correspondent on Capitol Hill and Rayburn's personal friend, wrote him early in October of his concern that he was not in Washington. "I talked to Byrns the other day," he said, "and he told me that he had more pledges than Rainey had before the deal was made in 1932. He is very jittery on one hand and very confident on the other. He and McReynolds [from Tennessee] have buttonholed every member who has been in town and have written numerous letters asking for support." On the brighter side, Dickson noted, "Byrns is scared of the White House angle as far as it affects you." [20] Ettie Garner, the Vice President's wife, also felt some concern that Rayburn was not waging an aggressive fight for her husband's former office. A few days after Dickson's letter, she wrote Sam to "fight to the last ditch." [21]

While a few contenders dropped out and the others stepped up their efforts, *The New York Times* scoffed editorially at the lot: "As matters stand, the Speaker does what the White House tells him to do." [22] But this failed to make any of the remaining candidates collapse in futility. By mid-November, Byrns was estimated to be far in the lead even though Garner was working on his old House colleagues to support Sam, and Marvin Jones, Rayburn's former brother-in-law and a competitor for Speaker, had quit the race on November 11 and announced, "I shall support my colleague, Mr. Rayburn."

By the time Rayburn returned to Washington at the beginning of December, a close contest was shaping up between him and Joe Byrns, due in large measure to the lobbying effort by Garner. In out-of-character fury at Garner's success, Byrns had friends visit the Vice President and tell him that as presiding officer of the Senate he had no business interfering in a House contest. Furthermore, if he persisted, he was warned, Byrns and his supporters would oppose his renomination for Vice President in 1936. Garner decided to drop his effort in Rayburn's behalf.

But this was not the only blow Rayburn suffered. Just as he figured he might possibly edge out Byrns, Joseph F. Guffey of Pittsburgh came to town. Guffey, director of sales for the Alien Property Custodian after the war, had been indicted but never tried for the large money shortages in his accounts. Later he was discovered to have failed to pay several hundred thousand dollars in income taxes. By the time the depression came, he was an oil millionaire who bossed his state's Democratic party and was its Democratic National Committeeman. Then in November 1934, he became the first Democrat elected to the U.S. Senate from Pennsylvania in fifty-nine years. Not yet sworn in, Guffey called a caucus of the Pennsylvania Democratic delegation in the House, and his statement to the press afterward was that all twenty-three would support Byrns.

With the vote of Pennsylvania a crucial factor, Rayburn had no alternative. He told reporters on December 12: "I am no longer a candidate for Speaker. There are no alibis. Under the circumstances I cannot be elected." [23]

Byrns offered him the majority leader post after his announcement. But Rayburn "would not serve under him," said Alla Clary. So Byrns gave it to Bill Bankhead, whom he really wanted, and the Democratic caucus shouted its approval, even though Bankhead lay in a hospital bed, victim of a heart attack.

Yet there was some consolation in Sam's action. If he had chosen to be Byrns' floor leader, he would have been forced to give up his committee chairmanship. In doing so he would have lost the opportunity to run the House's biggest show in 1935. This was the stormy fight over the Public Utility Holding Company Bill.

Nineteen thirty-five was a giant legislative year for the second-phase New Deal. In this eight-months' session the Capitol was a combative scene with battles over an old-age pension and unemployment compensation social security law, a new Banking Act, a "soak the rich" Wealth Tax Act, Rayburn's bill to regulate interstate buses and trucks, a National Labor Relations Act guaranteeing free and secret elections by workers to choose their own collective bargaining agents, and a Public Utility Holding Company Act containing a "Death Sentence."

A six-year Federal Trade Commission study revealed that over the years securities manipulators had gained control of the voting stock of most local gas, light, and power companies at little outlay of their own and had combined them under several layers of dummy corporations, each separately issuing stocks and bonds. These upper-layer corporations milked the assets and profits of the bottom-layer operating utilities and forced rate increases onto consumers. A prime example was the empire of Samuel Insull, a former secretary to Thomas A. Edison, whose holding company covered utilities in thirty-two states and wielded enormous political power through the purchase of state legislatures, governors and senators. One time the arrogant Insull proposed buying the Democratic Party's organization in Chicago for five hundred thousand dollars. [24]

In one holdiing-company system, Rayburn explained to the House, "the pyramiding goes so far as to pile one company on top of another until there are ten corporations in the pyramiding, or the local operating company is nine companies removed from the corporation at the top which controls it along with hundreds of others. In this particular set-up an investment of $1 at the top enables the management at the top to control over $30,000 of book value of the operating companies, or with less than $50,000 to control over a billion dollars of book value." The holding companies, he said, milked the operating companies they controlled by determining "what they shall buy, from whom they shall buy, at what price, and with whom they shall exchange services and contracts for supplies." In addition, by listing the property of the operating companies on their books at highly inflated valuations, they used their fictitious worth to acquire other operating companies.

It was Roosevelt who masterminded the fight against the public-utility holding companies in 1935. He had established a National Power Policy Committee, on which Secretary of Interior Harold L. Ickes served as chairman and Ben Cohen as general counsel, and it was here that Cohen and Tom Corcoran drew up regulatory legislation.

On February 6, 1935, Rayburn and Senator Burton K. Wheeler, his counterpart in the Upper Chamber, introduced the bill and scheduled hearings. But a short time later Cohen and Corcoran asked the two to switch to a new version that contained a provision ordering all holding companies not part of a geographically or economically integrated system to be liquidated by 1938. To arouse the public in their favor, holding companies immediately labeled this addition with the emotionally packed name, "Death Sentence."

At first both Rayburn and Wheeler opposed the drastic Death Sentence, but finally they dropped the first Wheeler-Rayburn Bill, as the legislation was called, and introduced the second Cohen-Corcoran draft. Rayburn's hearings began in March, [25] but long before then the holding companies had launched a mammoth lobbying effort that dwarfed the fight against the Securities Exchange Act the year before. The reason was obvious: The thirteen largest electric-power holding companies controlled 75 percent of all American operating companies, and their ease in draining billions of consumer dollars into their own pockets was threatened.

The most articulate spokesman for the holding companies was Wendell Willkie, president of Commonwealth and Southern, which controlled operating companies in Tennessee, Alabama, Georgia and parts of Florida, Mississippi and South Carolina. A shaggy, tousle-haired, Roosevelt supporter in 1932, Willkie argued that the holding company was needed to supply capital and credit to the operating companies and to give them the benefit of centralized purchasing, insurance, engineering and accounting. In testimony before Rayburn's committee, he charged that Rayburn's bill had already cut the value of securities by $3.5 billion. [26] When Rayburn scoffed at his defense, attacked his purposes and called holding-company executives "high-class, white-gloved desperadoes," Philip H. Gadsden, chairman of the Public Utilities Executives, blasted Rayburn's "spirit of wanton destruction and ruthless vindictiveness in which the legislation was conceived and was now pressed for passage." [27]

During the committee hearings, said Senator Hugo Black, who was investigating lobbyists, the holding companies organized a bombardment of Congress that included more than 5 million letters and 250,000 telegrams in opposition to the bill, plus a steady ringing of members' phones. Harry Truman, new to the Senate and a member of Wheeler's committee, received 30,000 letters against the bill. The Scripps-Howard papers counted 660 lobbyists against the bill in the Capitol.

Even well-known public figures were treated to intimidation when they mentioned the subject. Will Rogers, considered beyond fear, defined a holding company as "something where you hand an accomplice the goods while the police search you." After the holding-company lobby threatened him, he apologized and said he had been too flippant.

Rayburn's office was flooded with the largest number of opposing letters, wires and phone calls. "So much has been said, such a whispering campaign has been carried on, unequaled in my opinion by anything in the last half century," Rayburn told the House. [28] "The fat cats from Texas would cuss me out like I was a horse thief," he said, unruffled by the attack. Editorials in Texas newspapers painted him as a "Socialist." The biggest Texas utility tried a reverse tactic on him. "When John W. Carpenter, President of the Texas Power and Light Company was telling me just how good a friend of mine he was, I knew he had been to a banker in the district and asked him to estimate how much it would cost to beat Sam Rayburn. When this banker told him it couldn't be done, he said they had the money to do anything." [29]

During the hearings, Rayburn met several times with Roosevelt, and the two were frequently on the phone to coordinate strategy. Roosevelt's public pep talks to wavering congressmen was to the effect that the death of holding companies would result in lower rates to consumers and give a larger return to stockholders. Rayburn's was based more on the evils of holding companies: "I find little difference between the state socialists on the one hand who would subject us to the tyrannies of a superstate and . . . the greedy, power-mad managers of other people's property who would subject us to the tyrannies of supermanagement and superindustry."

Rayburn's hearings lasted two months, and the printed testimony came to 2,320 pages. In sharp contrast to Senator Wheeler, whose mean tongue lashed all opponents, an observer described Rayburn's method as "friendly, soft-spoken, discreet . . . he handled deserters, recalcitrant captives and plain and fancy saboteurs in the holding company fight with patience and understanding and skill."[30]

But it was Wheeler's methods that paid off, not his. The bill emerged unscathed from Wheeler's committee and squeaked through the Senate by a vote of 45 to 44 on June 11. The next day's *New York Times* declared: "Stocks decline on news of Senate action on Rayburn bill."[31]

In his own committee, however, Rayburn was a failure. Congressman George Huddleston of Alabama, ranking Democrat, worked with Republican members to strike out the mandatory Death Sentence provision and give the SEC discretionary authority to dissolve holding companies.

By the time the emasculated bill reached the House floor on June 27, the public-utility lobby increased its pressure and its whispering campaign. A story swept through Washington that Roosevelt suffered from brain-damaging syphilis and was "shrieking like a maniac in the middle of the night [with] people rushing to control him."[32]

Again Huddleston led the fight against restoring the mandatory Death Sentence in Section 11, and his principal attack was on Cohen and Corcoran, who, he claimed, had been feeding to Wheeler and Rayburn questions to ask utility executives and pressuring congressmen down one Capitol lobby and up another. In Huddleston's words, the young lawyers were "a corrupt influence in the halls of Congress. . . . Those two brain-trusters, those envoys extraordinary, those ambassadors and plenipotentiaries, this firm of Cohen and Corcoran, late of New York City, now operating in Washington, telling Congress what to do, pointing out to members of Congress what their functions and their duties are, they drew up this bill."[33]

Rayburn's strategy was to get a roll-call vote on the Death Sentence, in hopes that by requiring each member to be on record as to the way he voted most would feel forced to support Roosevelt. Once more Huddleston prevented this, and in an unrecorded vote on June 30 the House defeated the inclusion of the Death Sentence by 216 to 146.

So the House-Senate conference committee was faced with two versions. After a month-long impasse, Rayburn asked the House to instruct its conferees to accept the Death Sentence. But another unrecorded vote made him the loser by 210 to 153.

While the conferees tried to form a single bill from the House and Senate versions, Rayburn made still another move. This was a request to Roosevelt to send him a letter insisting that passage of the Senate version was essential. Once it reached him, he, Speaker Byrns and Majority Leader Bankhead publicized it and used it to exert pressure on stubborn conference-committee members.

Finally a compromise solution that the conferees were willing to accept was drawn up by Felix Frankfurter. Instead of eliminating all public utility holding companies, the Securities and Exchange Commission was authorized to dissolve by 1938 holding companies more than a layer removed from the operating companies that did not perform a useful economic function.

Huddleston led the fight in the House against the conference report, but now Rayburn had the votes and it passed 222 to 112.

When Roosevelt signed the bill on August 26, 1935, the most zealous New Dealers who had called Rayburn "weak and shaky" for not getting the Death Sentence through his committee now praised his leadership. Rayburn, with his prestige enlarged, was given the honor of making a nationwide radio address on the bill. He called it a victory for the "gouged and bullied and lobbied" American people against "a professional, mercenary army, the biggest and boldest, the richest and most ruthless lobby." [34]

13

Struggling Toward the Top

In the course of the first three years of the Roosevelt administration, Sam Rayburn could claim six major pieces of legislation. These were the Truth-in-Securities, Emergency Railroad Transportation, Securities Exchange, Interstate Motor Carriers, Federal Communications and Public Utility Holding Company Acts.

This total was more than most of his colleagues had to their names. Yet he did not feel like a success because he was no closer to his primary goal of becoming Speaker after twenty-two years in the House than he had been at the start of the Democratic takeover of the Lower Chamber in 1931.

When the congressional session of 1936 went into action, a seventh major bill was credited to Rayburn. This was on the subject of rural electrification, a matter of great importance to him.

Roosevelt later claimed that the idea to bring electricity to rural America came to him one day while he was visiting his polio foundation at Warm Springs, Georgia. When Rayburn heard this, he said Roosevelt was in error, that it had been he who had first mentioned the idea to the President, who had not then been aware of the degree to which the farm population suffered because electric companies would not stretch their wires beyond cities and big towns.

Rayburn said that the impetus for the legislation came from his memory of his mother's strained eyes as she tried to read her Bible in the light of the flickering kerosene lamp, and her tired appearance after hours at the corrugated washboard using water brought up from the well in a bucket. He also had statistics to show that his home area and other farm regions across the country were still living in pre-industrial age discomfort. Of the 30,490 farms in his district, only 621 had electricity. In Fannin County, less than 2 percent did. [1]

These statistics came out of an investigation Rayburn's committee had conducted in 1933. [2] But he had introduced no legislation on it at the time. However, when Congress passed the Emergency Relief Appropriation Act of 1935, giving $4.8 billion to the new Works Progress Administration (WPA), Roosevelt issued an executive order establishing a temporary Rural Electrification Administration (REA). Roosevelt's order emphasized giving jobs to the unemployed rather than spreading electrical lines, for 25 percent of the REA's $100 million loan money was earmarked for wages, and 90 percent of the workers had to be taken from relief rolls.

This approach, putting the unemployed to work, failed to satisfy Rayburn. So at the beginning of 1936 he promoted a new REA that focused instead on electrifying farms across the nation. Once again when the legislative machinery began moving, the power lobby poured into the Capitol, fiercely denouncing Rayburn and the bill. Their loud battle cry was that he was fostering socialism, and they insisted that he would be wasting taxpayers' money because farmers did not want electricity. Rayburn called both arguments total nonsense.

As the fight neared a decision in the House, several congressmen from big cities joined the lobby's attack on the bill. But their criticism was leveled against what they called blatant Rayburn favoritism toward farmers. Rayburn's proposal offered 2 percent, self-liquidating thirty-five-year loans, preferably to "farmers' cooperatives and other nonprofit organizations," to construct and operate rural power systems. The big city congressmen demanded that farmer cooperatives make a 15 percent cash down payment of the estimated cost of the power company before any loan was made. Because of the general poverty of farmers, Rayburn knew that his REA would be stillborn, and he would not accept this change. In the end, by stubborn persistence and the help of the administration, he got his bill through the House without any down-payment provision.

But the bill was still not out of the woods. In the Senate, George Norris of Nebraska, the aging, grand old Republican insurgent, now in his fourth six-year term, was cosponsor with Rayburn of the REA. When the two versions went to the House-Senate conference committee, said John McCormack, Norris stubbornly brought on a deadlock over the issue "whether private utilities should have the opportunity to be given REA loans" to supply electricity to rural areas. Norris, a father of TVA, opposed this, for he "wanted all power publicly owned eventually," while Rayburn kept insisting on "a combination of public and private." [3] Norris finally gave in to the even more stubborn Rayburn, and Roosevelt signed the Rural Electrification Act on May 20, 1936.

In 1936, Rayburn considered it his soldierly duty to see to it that Cactus Jack Garner was renominated for Vice President. Even though their political philosophies had grown worlds apart, they were still close friends. Unlike Rayburn, Garner found the New Deal repulsive. He spoke openly about his opposition to the TVA, the unbalanced budgets, relief spending and the prolabor legislation, and he clung to Texas friends who were vociferous Roosevelt-haters. When the public-utility lobby had attacked Sam Rayburn in 1935 over the holding-company legislation, Senator Hugo L. Black had launched an investigation of the lobbyists despite his already burdensome duties on eight committees (Foreign Relations, Military Affairs, Finance, Education and Labor, Rules, Claims, Printing and the Special Committee to Investigate Air and Ocean Mail Contracts). In the spring of 1936, Black released correspondence between Garner and his close friend, Texas oil and lumber millionaire John Henry Kirby. Kirby, a right-wing extremist, was pouring money into his kooky Committee to Uphold the Constitution to promote racist Governor Eugene Talmadge of Georgia for President that year.

"My dear John," Kirby had written Roosevelt's Vice President in one letter Black released: "How long are you going to tolerate the apostasy of the Roosevelt Administration?"

Garner's reply of July 9, 1935, read: "Dear John Henry: Your favor is just called to my attention. You can't do everything you want to and I can't do half what I would like to do. You can't control everybody you would like to and I am in a similar fix. I think that answers your question." [4]

However, the raised eyebrows at the released correspondence did not diminish Garner's potential for a second term. Rayburn knew that Roosevelt was not the least pleased with Garner's sarcastic references to him at cabinet meetings as "Cap'n" and "Boss." Nor were Cabinet members whom he cursed in Roosevelt's presence for hurting his ranching and banking businesses. "Damn you, old Moneybags," he muttered to Treasury Secretary Henry Morgenthau at the meeting table. "Until you came along, Mrs. Garner and I averaged 16 percent on our money, and now we can't get better than 5." But Roosevelt considered him essential on the 1936 ticket because of his continued belief that he needed Garner's vote-drawing power in the South.

Furthermore, Garner's personal publicity emanating from Washington reporters was almost entirely favorable, and it would have jarred the voters if he were dropped. Stories about his frugality made excellent news copy, and Rayburn was the source of several of them. "Sam liked to tell the story about the time one of Garner's constituents asked him to autograph a one-dollar bill," said Senator Tom Connally. "The man said he wanted it as a souvenir, which his son planned to frame and hang on the wall. 'Well, in that case,' Garner is supposed to have replied, 'you give me that dollar bill and I'll write you a check.' "[5]

Garner's parsimony was shared by his wife Ettie, who was also his political partner and whom he had carried on his public payroll for three decades. When admirers from all over the country sent Garner enormous amounts of bear meat, venison, beef and fish, she stored it in the iceboxes at the Hotel Washington where they lived, and she let much of it rot because she would not give anything away. One time a reporter found her on her knees in the Vice President's office, where she was "sorting pecans one by one into three even piles." Inquiry revealed that a pecan grower had sent a crate of nuts to be distributed among Garner, Sam Rayburn and William Bankhead.

In addition to the stories about his humorous tight-fistedness that won him public approval, Garner was highly popular with members of the House and Senate. Although he later remarked that "the Vice Presidency isn't worth a pitcher of warm piss,"[6] Garner was the picture of conviviality at that time. He had two hideaways, one under the Senate Library and the other in the Senate Office Building, and frequently when the House's business finished for the day Rayburn was among those who joined him in "striking a blow for liberty." It was in Garner's "Doghouse," as he referred to his S. O. B. after-hours club, that Rayburn became friendly with first-term Senator Harry Truman of Missouri, who was now a Garner protégé and was generally referred to as "the Senator from Pendergast," because he had been put into the Senate by Missouri Boss Tom Pendergast.

In the spring of 1936, Garner wanted a solid show of support from Texas Democrats who were dividing into several antagonistic factions, and late in May Rayburn took the train from Washington to San Antonio to win this for him. The setting was the Democratic state convention, and as temporary chairman Rayburn used his boss powers and a rousing keynote speech to win a unanimous endorsement of the Roosevelt-Garner ticket.

But fresh from this success for Garner, Rayburn was thrown into another defeat for himself. He was hardly back in Washington when Speaker Joe Byrns died suddenly on June 4. A hurriedly assembled House Democratic caucus took up the question of his successor that same day, even before his body returned to lie in state in the Chamber. By now, Rayburn realized his stupidity for not accepting Byrns' offer to make him majority leader two years before. For this would have put him in line to become Speaker now. Majority Leader Bill Bankhead, his forces well organized, was shouted by acclaim as Speaker before Rayburn's friends could place his name in contention. This now left an opening as majority leader. But Bankhead ignored Rayburn and gave his support to John J. O'Connor of New York, the anti-New Deal chairman of the important Rules Committee, who had come to the House ten years after Rayburn. When O'Connor won as floor leader, another opportunity for Rayburn was gone.

There was little time, however, to brood about his inability to move into the House leadership, for Congress planned to adjourn in only two weeks, and Roosevelt kept in touch with him during that time to discuss strategy at the national convention and the fall campaign. Foreseeing a huge campaign effort by Republicans and Democratic dissidents, Roosevelt asked Rayburn to serve after the convention as head of the Democratic Party's National Speakers' Bureau and to schedule leading Democrats for speeches around the country during the campaign. Chief trouble could be expected from Al Smith and company operating the right-wing Liberty League. Senator Huey Long, the wild man from Louisiana, who had planned to go after the Presidency in 1936, was dead from an assassin's bullet. But his crackpot followers had shifted their allegiance to Charles Coughlin, a rabble-rousing anti-Semitic priest, and the antiblack and anti-Semitic Reverend Gerald L. K. Smith, who had been Huey Long's lieutenant, and the two were putting up a presidential ticket for their Union Party.

After Congress adjourned, Rayburn went to Philadelphia before the opening of the national convention on June 23, and he played an important role in writing the party platform. But instead of going to New York after Roosevelt was renominated to set up his speakers' organization, he returned to Bonham.

And for good reason. Jess Morris was running against him in the Democratic primary for the third time, along with Will Harris, an unknown political quantity. Mrs. Eleanor Roosevelt, not knowing where Rayburn had gone, wrote her husband from New York with some anxiety that the campaign organization was a mess. "Mr. Rayburn should come at once to plan the policy and mechanics of the speakers' bureau," she complained, adding, "I think it would be well to start some Negro speakers, like Mrs. Bethune."[7]

In the meantime, Rayburn was going from picnic to picnic in Texas' steaming July, asking the crowds to "return me to Congress to finish the work of the New Deal which I have had a large part in inaugurating." Jess Morris was up to his old campaign tricks, and in answer to his abusive personal tactics Rayburn retorted: "Any man who will deceive you during a political campaign will deceive you after he is elected."[8]

The primary did not come soon enough for him. When the tally was completed, he breathed with relief, for he received two-thirds of the total with his 30, 907 votes.

Although Mrs. Roosevelt kept inquiring why he was absent from his New York assignment, Rayburn needed some relaxation after the primary, and he went to Dallas with Valton Young, the county agent for Fannin County to take in the dairy show. Watching the judging of Jersey cows, he told Young, "Lavender Lady will win if the herdsman will only let her do her own natural posing. . . . The herdsman's lead rein is too tight." When the man continued to mishandle her, Rayburn, in exasperation, went down to the show ring for a talk with him. The herdsman took his advice, and Lavender Lady won the blue-ribbon grand-champion award. [9]

In the fall, Rayburn kept busy but unruffled as he dispatched Cabinet members, congressmen, and business, labor and religious leaders around the country to talk up the Roosevelt-Garner ticket. His star attraction was Interior Secretary "Honest Harold" Ickes, the self-styled curmudgeon whose blistering tongue made opponents gasp. He was an excellent choice for ridiculing Father Coughlin, who was calling Roosevelt "the great betrayer and liar," and for scoffing at the deafening whispering campaign about Roosevelt's suffering from syphilis of the brain and his "shrieking like a maniac." On the other hand, Roosevelt believed that Senator Burt Wheeler, who had worked with Rayburn on major legislation, was his most important advocate. "Please beg Sen. Wheeler to start speeches key places at once; and this is my request—Will you tell him?" he wrote Rayburn a frantic memo. [10]

Rayburn had strict rules for his speakers. "Lay off the five-cylinder words," was his prime admonition. If Republicans called President Roosevelt a "Communist," his speakers were not to denounce it as "mean, vicious propaganda." The proper reply was to "tell them that it's a hell-born lie."

With about 85 percent of the press backing the Republican presidential nominee, Kansas Governor Alf M. Landon, H. L. Mencken saying, "They can beat FDR with a Chinaman," and the *Literary Digest* polls declaring Roosevelt a loser in November, President Roosevelt and his wife were filled with gloom. [11] But this pessimism was absent in Rayburn, Farley and Garner. Cactus Jack told Rayburn that Mrs. Roosevelt wanted to bet him when they were in Philadelphia that her husband would lose Pennsylvania, and he had assured her: "I got up at six o'clock this morning and walked around the streets. That's about saddling-up time Texas," he explained to her. "But it's early here. The only people up were policemen, cab drivers and night workers. I talked to them and most of them are going to vote the Democratic ticket and none of them have done that before. We will carry Pennsylvania."

"The Democrats haven't carried Pennsylvania since the Civil War," she had argued.

"War Between the States," he had corrected her. "So how about betting me a dollar?" She had shaken hands on the bargain. [12]

Sam Rayburn was thinking about more than the presidential campaign in the fall of 1936. In the back of his mind was a growing plan to win the majority leader's post away from John O'Connor when the House Democratic caucus met right after the New Year.

Following Roosevelt's landslide victory over Landon, Rayburn launched his own campaign. His friends, Congressmen Fred Vinson of Kentucky and Carl Vinson of Georgia, went to work as his campaign managers, buttonholing members in his behalf. Garner, too, from his vice-presidential offices, phoned House members and put in a plug for Rayburn. When friends of O'Connor heard about his activity, they told reporters it was an outrageous interference. But Garner, fresh with his own victory, barked in his pinched voice, "I'm for Sam Rayburn two hundred percent. And I'm going to keep working for him."

Rayburn wanted Roosevelt's public support, but he realized it would lead to animosities that might damage the President's program in the House during the coming year. Furthermore, O'Connor's brother, Basil, had been Roosevelt's law partner from 1924 to 1933 and was currently running his Warm Springs, Georgia, Foundation. Open presidential support would have antagonized Basil. But there was no argument at the White House that Rayburn was the one Roosevelt wanted.

Unable to get open presidential blessing, Rayburn sought it from various Cabinet members who were well considered on Capitol Hill. Interior Secretary Ickes noted in his diary that Rayburn came to see him, and they had "a long and friendly talk" about Rayburn's hopes of becoming majority leader. Ickes, who had contempt for Congress, felt a lingering dislike for Rayburn ever since Sam had thwarted his efforts to become oil czar. "He has pretty much opposed everything I have ever wanted on the Hill," he once wrote in his diary. [13] But this time, he wrote condescendingly that he "got a better impression" of Rayburn than he had on previous occasions. Rayburn, he wrote, "seems to me to be a straight shooter and would be a much better Majority Leader than O'Connor." [14]

Ickes's comment was a pompous understatement, considering he was well aware that Rayburn was a New Deal lieutenant while O'Connor had hardened into a bitter opponent of the recovery program. Nor was O'Connor harmless. As chairman of the House Rules Committee, he wielded a major influence over which bills the House could take up and the form and time of debate. The fate of Ickes' bills in the House depended on the whim of John O'Connor.

After offering bland praise for Rayburn and announcing that he would not interfere in the selection of the House majority leader, Roosevelt left the United States aboard the cruiser *Indianapolis* for Buenos Aires to attend the Inter-American Conference for the Maintenance of Peace. But before his departure, he sent a chit to Tom Corcoran designed to cut down O'Connor's strength. Corcoran was to meet the ship carrying Postmaster General Jim Farley home from a European vacation. Word had reached the White House that on his return Farley planned to release a statement backing his fellow Tammanyite O'Connor. Corcoran was told to give Farley a message ordering him to remain silent on the House contest.

A crucial day came for Rayburn early in December when Senator Joe Guffey, the man who had prevented him from becoming Speaker two years before, called a luncheon-caucus of the Pennsylvania congressional Democrats to decide on either Rayburn or O'Connor for majority leader. Rayburn went to the Mayflower Hotel where the Pennsylvanians met to ask for their support before the session. Then he waited anxiously in the lobby. A reporter who spied him there said he was nattily attired in a Hershey-bar colored suit with a cigar of the same hue.

It would have seemed that he had no cause for concern because Boss Guffey took his marching orders on issues from the White House. As Senator Tom Connally once observed, "Guffey doesn't know what his position is on this bill because Roosevelt's line is busy."

But on the other hand, Guffey was a political ally of John L. Lewis, the shaggy-browed, rumbling Shakespearian-voiced president of the United Mine Workers. Lewis and Rayburn had felt a mutual antagonism since 1922. That year Lewis had taken his six hundred thousand miners out on strike, and his men had beaten twenty-one strikebreakers to death at Herrin, Illinois. Faced with a national coal shortage, President Harding had asked Congress for a Fuel Bill, under which the government would appoint a Federal Fuel Administrator to take over the coal mines, fix prices, and distribute the coal. Rayburn's condemnation of the Fuel Bill and of John L. Lewis for wanting federal control had drawn the UMW chief's lasting ire.

Still another uncertainty about Guffey was that he had proclaimed himself indebted to John O'Connor and his Rules Committee for letting the Guffey Coal Bill go to the floor for a vote.

So Rayburn waited in the Mayflower lobby while inside the dining room the delegation caucused. A few members expressed their resentment at Guffey's presence because he was a senator, but he squelched them. Questioned afterward about the results of the meeting, Congressman John B. Daly with dripping sarcasm told a *Time* Magazine reporter, "Ask Senator Guffey about it. He is the big cheese." [15]

Rayburn had a long wait that afternoon. But it was worthwhile. With three members absent, the Pennsylvanians voted 18 to 6 in his favor, and under the unit rule all 27 votes were his.

To this big push forward came others. Congressman Tom Cullen, a Brooklyn Tammany leader, deserted O'Connor to announce his support for Rayburn. So did bosses Frank Hague of Jersey City and Mayor "Big Ed" Kelly of Chicago.

When the Democratic caucus met privately in the House Chamber on the afternoon of January 4, 1937, O'Connor's supporters engaged in a last-minute lobbying effort, painting a picture of a Southern ownership of Congress—with Garner presiding over the Senate, Bankhead as Speaker and Rayburn as floor leader. But John McCormack of Massachusetts hit back at them with a declaration that the selection of the majority leader should not be based on "what section of the country a candidate comes from but what type of leadership a candidate stands for."

Hatton Sumners, Rayburn's first friend in Washington, nominated Sam, and the voting came soon afterward. Rayburn was the winner, 184 to 127. After twenty-four years in Congress, his boyhood dream of becoming Speaker one day now looked possible.

14

Trials of a Floor Leader

In the course of American history, the House majority leader has not commonly been a publicly visible figure. But this was not true in Sam Rayburn's case. With Speaker Bankhead in failing health, Rayburn frequently had to take on much of the former's duties, such as presiding over the Lower Chamber and determining strategy to push the administration's program through the House. These were in addition to his normal responsibilities of leading debate and keeping the various Democratic factions in line.

Because of his temporary functions as Bankhead's stand-in, Rayburn was often in the papers, coming or going from business visits with Roosevelt in the Oval Office. These were in addition to the weekly congressional leadership meetings Roosevelt inaugurated in 1937, meetings restricted to himself, the Speaker, House majority leader, the Vice President and Senate majority leader.

"I think I know people pretty well when I sit down and look at them," Rayburn said once to a *New York Times* reporter. "I sat across the desk from Roosevelt from 1937 until he died, every Monday morning for an hour. When he heard of the underprivileged, or he heard of some people who were in bad shape, his eyes would just reach up, they would almost sparkle. Roosevelt was really for the underdog. . . . He had a program and he had every bit of courage that a man should have, and then he was about the greatest politician."[1] This was a mutual admiration society, because Roosevelt "often said Sam Rayburn was the most valuable Congressman on the New Deal."[2]

Rayburn's high regard for Roosevelt's purposes and his own desire to be the best majority leader ever were sufficient incentives to help him cope with the nasty situation that confronted him in 1937. The House was top-heavy with Democrats—only 89 of the 435 members were Republicans. With this overwhelming majority, passage of key legislation became more difficult instead of easier, because the Democrats split into sizable factions, all vying for power and all at each other's throat. One large faction of conservative Southern Democrats worked closely with the Republicans and were jeeringly called "Republocrats" by liberal Northern Democrats.

Added to this problem was the general congressional mood of anger with the President directly and administration chiefs who acted as though Congress should be treated like moronic sheep. FDR frequently embarrassed Bankhead by not touching bases with him on his activities. Bankhead would tell reporters he was not expecting a presidential message on a certain subject, said journalist Joe Alsop, and "fifteen minutes later the message came and he was a fool."[3] Once when this occurred, Rayburn warned Jimmy Roosevelt, the President's oldest son and troubleshooter, "Tell your father if I'm ever Speaker this kind of thing won't happen to me more than once."

An instance of the growing congressional desire for some independence was the fierce debate that erupted over Roosevelt's request early in 1937 for a blank-check deficiency appropriation of $1.5 billion for WPA relief operations for the rest of the fiscal year. Furious over being asked to appropriate a large sum of money without a breakdown of its uses, Congress amended the bill to guarantee that a third would be earmarked for specific projects in members' districts. Another amendment slashed two thousand dollars from the ten-thousand-dollar annual salary of WPA chief Harry L. Hopkins, whom many congressmen considered contemptuous of the legislative branch.

Hopkins, an Iowa-born social worker, had managed Roosevelt's relief program in New York State and had followed him to Washington to head in succession the Federal Emergency Relief Administration (FERA), the Civil Works Administration (CWA) and the Works Progress Administration (WPA). He was a sickly, sallow, nervous, ruthless man described by one observer as having "the purity of St. Francis of Assisi combined with the shrewdness of a race track tout." Another said with equal accuracy, "He gives off a suggestion of quick cigarettes, thinning hair, dandruff, brief sarcasm, frayed suits of clothes." Playwright Robert Sherwood, a Roosevelt speechwriter, noted that Hopkins "was generally regarded as a sinister figure, a backstage intriguer, an Iowan combination of Machiavelli, Svengali and Rasputin."[4]

If the Roosevelt relief program had been based on the dole, or a simple, regular handout of money to those who were unemployed, it would not have been very controversial. But early, Roosevelt and Hopkins had decided that the unemployed should work for their money, and this made the WPA political. While the antireliefers tried to make political capital by charging that WPA workers were a mass of lazy leaf-rakers, the truth was that Hopkins emphasized WPA projects such as the building of roads, schools, playgrounds, parks and airports.

Congressmen soon saw that if they could fill their districts with WPA projects and put friends in key homestate WPA administrative positions this would help them at reelection time. The problem was that Harry Hopkins was not too cooperative. Besieged by politicians, he was quoted as saying, "You're getting in my hair!" and "Quit lousing up my office with protests." Such undiplomatic remarks served to arouse critics. The smallest WPA scandal made the headlines, and Hopkins was falsely accused by the press as declaring: "We shall tax and tax, spend and spend, and elect and elect." Yet at the same time that he was denying the politicians the right to turn the WPA into a Democratic political machine for their own use, he was not averse to using the WPA to increase Roosevelt's political strength.

When the House revolted early in 1937 against the WPA deficiency appropriation bill with a cut in Hopkins' salary and specific earmarking of local projects, anxiety swept the White House, and Roosevelt phoned Rayburn for help. Rayburn had taken the call off the House floor and he returned to the Chamber to find it a sea of shouts and arguments.

He walked to the well of the House, his back to the rostrum, raised an arm for silence, and the noise vanished. He had told Roosevelt he would try to get the House to recess over the coming Memorial Day weekend so he could work out a compromise. Yet he realized that if he abruptly made a motion to adjourn with tempers so sharp, the vote would go against him.

So he made a calm, low-keyed plea for reason. He said: "I appeal to the cooler judgment of my colleagues. I appeal to what I know is their fairness. I appeal to their better judgment. I pledge you, for and against the amendments that have been adopted in allotting this money, that between now and the time this bill is taken up for consideration again everything that is humanly possible to be done to bring about an adjustment to every man, to every section, and to every project in this country will be done by me."[5]

In a changed mood, the House agreed by a tally of 167 to 85 to let him search for a peaceful solution, and it voted to adjourn for five days.

From that Thursday until the following Tuesday, Rayburn held a series of conferences with Roosevelt, Hopkins and the leaders of the three

Democratic factions that had jumped on the WPA. Hopkins was told that he could not have a simple blank-check handover from Congress; Congressmen Joe Starnes of Alabama, Wilburn Cartwright of Oklahoma and Alfred F. Beiter of New York were told that revenge on Hopkins through a salary cut was childish.

When the House reconvened, Rayburn told members that Roosevelt had given his word that the WPA would be sensitive to their requests for projects in their districts. At the same time, Hopkins' salary would not be cut and members' demands for using some non-relief workers on the WPA projects would not be honored. The bill then passed without the amendments as a show in the House's belief in Rayburn's integrity.

Rayburn's work to save the administration from itself showed up in many other instances. Harold Ickes was another official whose un-popularity in Congress matched Hopkins'. Once Rayburn learned that Ickes planned to make a speech attacking Congressman Martin Dies of Texas and his House Un-American Activities Committee. Rayburn op-posed Dies's scatter-gun approach of labeling New Dealers as "Reds," but he visited Roosevelt and told him that if Ickes delivered his speech, members of the House would defend Dies and cut the appropriation for the Interior Department. Roosevelt accepted Rayburn's opinion and told Ickes to call off his speech.

But he was not as fortunate when it came to Roosevelt's Court-packing bill. At the peak of his power following his reelection in 1936, Roosevelt soon dissipated part of his strength in an ill-fated war on the Supreme Court's "Nine Old Men," [6] as he referred to them.

The nine justices, six of whom were over seventy and seven of whom were Republicans, had not judged any of the New Deal legislation in 1933 and 1934. But Roosevelt sensed there might be trouble, and he invited Chief Justice Charles Evans Hughes to the Executive Mansion where he tried to talk him into establishing a consulting relationship. Hughes refused. "Mr. President, the Supreme Court is an independent branch of government," he said with finality.

In January 1935, the bad news began when the Supreme Court declared unconstitutional the Connally "hot oil" amendment to the NRA oil code. Then after a shaky 5-to-4 decision barely upholding his devaluation of the dollar, the Court struck down the Railroad Retirement Act to provide pensions for railroad workers, the Frazier-Lemke Act to refinance farm mortgages, the NRA and declared that the president could not fire a member of the Federal Trade Commission.

In 1936 the conservative Court continued its rampage against the New Deal by knocking out the Agricultural Adjustment Act. Then it weakened

Rayburn's Securities Exchange Act by ruling that once a man withdrew his registration statement from the SEC, the agency could not continue its investigation of his business. In other decisions the Court struck down the Guffey Bituminous Coal Commission Act and a New York State law establishing minimum wages for women.

After his election in 1936, Roosevelt said that 1937 "was the year which was to determine whether the kind of government which the people had voted for in 1932, 1934 and 1936 was to be permitted by the Supreme Court to function."

At first, Rayburn did not take this to mean that he planned action against the Court. But on Friday, February 5, 1937, Roosevelt invited him, Speaker Bankhead, Vice President Garner, Senate Majority Leader Joseph T. Robinson and the House and Senate chairmen of the Judiciary Committees—Hatton Sumners and Henry F. Ashhurst—to a White House meeting. Roosevelt spoke about the Court's past decisions and then brought up the various New Deal legislation on the Court's current agenda. These included Rayburn's Public Utility Holding Company Act, the Social Security Act and the National Labor Relations Act.

In view of what could be expected from the "Nine Old Men," Roosevelt said he wanted congressional authority to appoint a new Supreme Court justice up to a total of six for each justice over seventy years of age with ten years of service on the Court who would not retire. If the present six in that category wanted to stay on, this would mean an enlargement of the Court to fifteen members. He also pointed out that the Constitution made no mention of the number of judges to serve at one time on the Supreme Court.

After his explanation, Roosevelt asked for opinions. Rayburn, Garner, Bankhead and Sumners said nothing. The other two, Joe Robinson and Ashhurst, said they were in favor of his proposal. On the return ride to Capitol Hill, bald, wizened Sumners, whose committee would have first crack at the plan, gave an indication of the bill's future when he turned to the others and in a tone of disapproval said, "Boys, this is where I cash in my chips."

Rayburn's reaction at the time was that something had to be done by the Court to sustain the New Deal. In retrospect, however, he believed Roosevelt committed an enormous blunder, that he should have first done a public relations job to create public understanding of the problem; then he should have sought a less combative solution, such as a compulsory retirement bill for justices at age seventy, instead of a measure to pack the Supreme Court with six additional members.

The day after the White House meeting, Roosevelt sent Congress a warring message containing his Court-reform proposal. Rayburn expected Sumners to introduce the bill since it would be sent to his committee, and when Hatty refused, charging Sam with kowtowing to Roosevelt, the firm friendship of a quarter of a century began to dissolve. Rayburn then got Maury Maverick, another member of the Texas delegation, to introduce the bill. But even though Congressman Fred Vinson (later to become a Chief Justice) enthusiastically declared that a majority of the House approved it, Rayburn knew better, and he advised Roosevelt to bypass the House because of Sumner's opposition and have the Senate consider the bill first. Once it passed there, its chances in the House should be better.

Roosevelt agreed to this strategy. As an incentive for his tireless help to pass the bill, Senate Majority Leader Joe Robinson was promised the first vacancy on the Supreme Court. But after the bill reached Ashhurst's Judiciary Committee, Rayburn foresaw major trouble when Garner told him he intended to work for its disapproval. In fact, he learned that after Roosevelt's message had been read to the Senate, Garner stationed himself in the lobby off the floor, shaking his turned-down thumbs for all to see.

While Republican senators remained silent and amused, Democratic resistance to the Roosevelt plan developed. Some Democrats opposed to the bill were in agreement with what the Supreme Court had done to the New Deal. Others thought the bill set a bad precedent for a future reactionary President to enlarge the Court even more until he had a majority. Still others were concerned that the proposal was an invasion of the constitutional independence of the judiciary. Opposition hardened, said Senator Tom Connally, when Roosevelt "dispatched Jim Farley, Harold Ickes, Tom Corcoran and Joseph B. Keenan, an Assistant Attorney General to make discreet threats to various Senators."[7]

While the opposition Democratic senators carried their case to the country and stalled the hearings in Ashhurst's committee, the Supreme Court reacted to Roosevelt's threat by capitulating. In March 1937, it reversed itself on the New York State minimum wage law for women and approved a similar law in Washington State. Then it upheld a revised Farm Mortgage Moratorium Act, the Railroad Labor Act's provisions for collective bargaining and dispute mediation, the National Labor Relations Act, and the unemployment compensation and old age insurance sections of the Social Security law. Almost all these decisions were by a 5-to-4 majority, with Justice Owen Roberts's switch to a pro-New Deal approach making the difference.

After the change in the Supreme Court began forming a pattern,

Rayburn visited Roosevelt on House business and mentioned to him that the mail from his district revealed that his constituents opposed the Court-packing bill. But if he thought that Roosevelt might take the hint to drop the bill, this did not happen, for Roosevelt showed irritation and then boredom. "Looky here, Mr. President! By God, I'm talking to you," Rayburn said sternly. "You'd better listen." But Roosevelt could not be deterred from his fight with the Court.

There were other reasons for Roosevelt to drop his bill. On the same day that the Senate Judiciary Committee reported the bill to the full Senate by a 10-to-8 unfavorable vote, seventy-eight-year-old reactionary Justice Willis Van Devanter announced his retirement. The latter action meant that when Roosevelt replaced Van Devanter he would now have a Court that was 6-to-3 in his favor.

But still Roosevelt persisted with his Court-packing plan like a man on a runaway horse. When White House staffers proposed that he return the action to the House and have Fred Vinson introduce another version, he took this up with Rayburn and Speaker Bankhead. The way to get around Sumner's committee, he suggested, was to use the discharge petition. By getting 218 members' signatures on the petition, the House leaders could bring the bill directly to the floor. Rayburn reacted with fury at this scheme to dump the needless battle in his lap. Harold Ickes, the great diarist, gave his interpretation to Rayburn's opposition in this fashion: "He doesn't want to offend anybody because he hopes some day to be Speaker."[8]

With Rayburn's rejection of his scheme, Roosevelt turned back to the Senate, this time with a revised incentive plan for Majority Leader Joe Robinson. Robinson was not to be given Van Devanter's seat but was promised instead a place on the Court when he succeeded in getting the proposed Fred Vinson draft compromise through the Senate. In this version the retirement age was raised from seventy to seventy-five, and only one new justice a year could be added to the Court for those over seventy-five who did not retire.

It was Roosevelt's hope that Garner would accept this compromise bill and help win Senate approval. But Cactus Jack had no intention of doing this. When he told reporters he had promised to spend a summer holiday with his granddaughter in Texas, Roosevelt, in alarm, sent Rayburn to get him to stay in Washington. Garner, however, was adamant about leaving. He told Sam he was not going to Texas as much over his dislike of the Court bill as he was because Roosevelt had not cut relief spending or taken action against labor unions engaged in "sit-down" strikes inside factory walls. He was especially angry because Roosevelt's legislative lieutenants had defeated a Senate amendment to the new Guffey Coal Act in April that would have banned sit-down strikes. [9]

Garner was already on his way to the mesquite and catclaw plains of Texas when Rayburn reported his conversation to Roosevelt. A short time later a pleading presidential letter went to dusty Uvalde that promised Garner a balanced budget the next fiscal year plus a condemnation of "extremists" in labor and industry if he would return. But the Vice President remained in Texas until Joe Robinson died on July 14, 1937. The latter's health had failed from his exhaustive labor to win Senate approval of the revised Court-packing bill. [10]

After attending Robinson's funeral in Arkansas, Garner came back to Washington and saw Roosevelt. "Cap'n," he spoke bluntly about the Court bill, "you don't have the votes." Robinson's death had signaled the end of the fight, for a week later the Senate voted 70 to 21 to recommit the bill to the Judiciary Committee.

Another massive struggle in Roosevelt's second term that found Rayburn in centerstage was the President's bill to reorganize the executive branch. [11] Overlapping authority and duplication of work had led to public brawling among empire-building agency chiefs. The two outstanding combatants were Interior Secretary Harold Ickes and Agriculture Secretary Henry A. Wallace, each of whom wanted a large part of the other's department moved into his own. Other government activities were widely divided among several agencies and needed coordination and unification. In addition, the President was not authorized by law to have a sufficient personal staff to assist him, nor did the White House have direct control over the federal budget, for the Bureau of the Budget was in the Treasury Department.

Roosevelt started the legislative ball rolling by calling Rayburn; Joe Robinson; Senator Pat Harrison of Mississippi, the chairman of the Finance Committee; Speaker Bankhead and House Ways and Means Committee Chairman Robert "Muley" Doughton of North Carolina to a meeting in January 1937 to unveil his reorganization bill. What he proposed was to establish for the first time in history an Executive Office of the President, giving him a staff of administrative assistants and transferring the Bureau of the Budget here. To this point whatever aides he had were borrowed from other payrolls. As for the rest of the executive branch, all boards and agencies would be consolidated into twelve departments, including the two new Departments of Social Welfare and Public Works.

Everyone present wanted some exceptions made to consolidation. This included Rayburn. "Does this apply to all regulatory agencies? Isn't the

ICC, which is so popular and successful, an exception?" he asked Roosevelt.

"There will be no exception, not one," Roosevelt shot back. [12] If he permitted exceptions, he explained, there would be no point to the bill, which he said was designed to promote economy and efficiency.

A joint committee of both houses was set up to handle the bill, with Joe Robinson and Congressman John Cochran of Missouri, a Rayburn protégé, as cochairmen. But with the fight over Court-packing that year, no action was taken on the Reorganization Bill. The measure seemed further cursed when both Robinson and Cochran died suddenly. However, Senator James F. Byrnes of South Carolina and Congressman Lindsay Warren of North Carolina succeeded them and quick passage was predicted in 1938.

But trouble developed unexpectedly in the new year. The Republican press started a campaign crying "dictatorship" and "Congressional abdication." Several hundred thousand letters and telegrams against reorganization deluged Congress from Father Coughlin's followers and from conservative organizations. Catholic pressure on congressmen charged that the bill would give Roosevelt the power to take over parochial schools. Congressman John O'Connor, still angry with Rayburn for winning the majority leader's post and with Roosevelt for his apparent support of Rayburn, declared that he feared "bloodshed" if the bill passed.

A flabbergasted Rayburn pointed out that Congress had passed strong reorganization bills in 1932 and 1933 with little opposition. But now "a rumble started six weeks ago and the rumble has grown into a storm I do not yet understand," he said. The Senate approved the Reorganization Bill by a slim margin and after a short debate in the House Rayburn wanted a vote before matters got out of hand. But on April 1 when he put forward a motion to close the debate and hold the vote on the bill the next day, he was defeated 191 to 149.

With the attacks on him and his Reorganization Bill reaching new daily highs, FDR found it necessary to write an extraordinary open letter to the American people, defending himself against the charge of planning a dictatorship through the legislation. In a three-point defense he wrote:

A. I have no intention to be a dictator.

B. I have none of the qualifications which would make me a successful dictator.

C. I have too much historical background and too much knowledge of existing dictatorships to make me desire any form of dictatorship for a democracy like the United States of America. [13]

Rayburn was finally able to set the vote on the bill for April 8. Four days before then he went on national radio to explain the bill. The House would pass it, he said doggedly, and the House-Senate conferees would then swiftly "lick it into shape."

But the debate continued to go poorly. When Congresswoman Edith Nourse Rogers, a Republican from Massachusetts, pushed hard on the argument that congressional mail was running heavily against the bill and members should vote accordingly, Rayburn forgot he was supposed to be chivalrous toward women. He told her she was not taking into account the fact that the lobbying was not spontaneous but was organized and orchestrated. Her running-away imagination he said, reminded him of "a man in our State one time who claimed to have been a great soldier. A story went the rounds that during a battle the mule he was riding ran away with him, ran away from the enemy. An orator was making a speech in our state and said that his opponent was a peculiar man, that his imagination ran away with him in peacetime and his mule in time of war. I think the imagination of the gentlewoman from Massachusetts is in flight."

It was this plea not to be hoodwinked by lobbyists that gave him some sorely needed votes, he believed. Then he had a further opportunity when Hatty Sumners came to see him and asked him to be his intermediary with Roosevelt, since the President had stopped speaking to him after the Court-packing fight. The message he wanted Sam to transmit was that Roosevelt would gain an extra twenty-five votes for the Reorganization Bill if he dropped his proposal for a Department of Social Welfare. The reason, said Sumners, was their concern that Roosevelt would appoint the hated Harry Hopkins to run the new Department. After the Reorganization Bill passed, he added, if Roosevelt really wanted a Social Welfare Department, he could request it in a separate bill. [14]

But Roosevelt wanted no part of any suggestion from Sumners, despite Rayburn's opinion that Hatty was right. With this handicap, he prepared for the vote by asking that all congressmen who favored the bill be in town for the tally and those for the bill who were away from Washington were phoned to return at once.

By April 8, Rayburn had done what he could, but it was not enough, for the House killed the reorganization bill by 204 to 196. What galled Rayburn most about his 8-vote defeat was that 108 Democrats had voted against it. It was no consolation when Roosevelt sent him a letter congratulating him for his "fine fight." [15] But to FDR's request that he bring it up again, Rayburn told him that there was no hope for a changed vote that year.

Early the following spring, when other issues occupied the Roosevelt opposition, Rayburn was able to get a modified Reorganization Bill through the House and conference committee, and Roosevelt signed it into law on April 3, 1939. It established the Executive Office of the President, transferring the Bureau of the Budget directly to the White House and gave the chief executive a secretariat for press, correspondence, appointments and Hill liaison, plus six "anonymous" administrative assistants. The claim of Louis Brownlow, who helped write the original bill, was that the establishment of the Executive Office of the President led to the "coordination of the tremendously widespread Federal machinery that enabled the U.S. to win World War II and meet the consequent problems."[16]

The Reorganization Act also eliminated, transferred and consolidated agencies. When Rayburn had said he would have trouble with Roosevelt's proposal for a Department of Social Welfare, the title was changed to the less emotional Federal Security Agency, and it was not given Cabinet status, even though its functions ran a gamut from social security, public health and education to the U.S. Employment Service, the National Youth Administration, and the CCC camps.

Rayburn also effected another major change. The original bill dumped all federal lending programs under the Commerce Department. Haughty Jesse Jones, the big, beefy, white-haired boss of the Reconstruction Finance Corporation, who despised both Roosevelt and Rayburn, could not stomach the thought of finding himself subservient to Harry Hopkins, who was now the Secretary of Commerce. Jones went to Rayburn and begged him to save his independence; and Rayburn did, by providing for an unattached Federal Loan Agency. Later when Jones became Secretary of Commerce, he insisted that the FLA be brought under the Department and this was done.

Still another major domestic struggle involving Rayburn in Roosevelt's second term came over FDR's proposed minimum wage and hour legislation. A storm quickly broke out from several directions over the Fair Labor Standards Bill, as it was called. Businessmen attacked it as an infringement on their right to pay employees whatever they chose, while some labor leaders denounced it because it was ridden with exceptions and set the minimum wage floor at only forty cents an hour, a rate they claimed would become the ceiling in practice.

When the bill went to Congress, opposition came chiefly from Southerners. Garner wanted it defeated, said one journalist, "because he was paying Mexicans in his pecan groves only ten cents an hour." Senator

Pat Harrison in an article in *Collier's* called for its rejection because "local labor in the South, where uncontaminated by outside influences, is, generally speaking, very well satisfied." In the House, only three members of the Texas delegation favored it—Sam Rayburn, Lyndon Johnson and Maury Maverick. Years afterward, in an effort to make his stand on the issue appear heroic, Johnson said inaccurately, "I was one of the three Texas Congressmen who backed the first minimum wage law in 1937. The other two were defeated in the next election."

After a great deal of tugging the Senate passed the bill, and it also cleared the House Labor Committee. Rules Committee Chairman John O'Connor decided, however, not to let it go to the House floor for debate and vote. But he lacked a firm committee majority until Garner had a talk with five Democrats on his committee and they joined O'Connor to bottle up the bill. [17]

At this point the measure appeared dead, but Rayburn would not give in to the smirking O'Connor. One way to force a bill to the floor from the Rules Committee was through the discharge petition that required the signature of 218 members. Only once in the twentieth century had this been accomplished, yet Rayburn set out to do it. For all his coaxing only 22 Southerners signed the petition. [18] However, a sufficient number of Northern members did to bring it to the House floor.

In the debate, Republicans centered their attack on Rayburn for signing the petition. This aroused his ire, and in reply he told them that if their numbers were further reduced in the 1938 election according to the 1932-1934-1936 trend, they would be able to caucus in a phone booth. His comment did not help matters, for when the vote finally came on December 17, 1937, the House decided by 216 to 198 to recommit the bill to its original committee. [19]

This made it necessary for Rayburn to start from the beginning again the following year. But now he was successful, and the bill passed in June by 291 to 89.

Yet even after Roosevelt signed it into law on June 25, 1938, Rayburn was forced to save it from manhandling and extinction in the next several years. For instance, Roosevelt wrote him one time, "I heard a moment ago that the Appropriations Committee has turned down the supplemental estimate of $2 million for the Wages and Hours Administration." He went on to say that if the money was not appropriated he would tell the people that a law was on the books and the Committee "has voted not to enforce that law." [20] Rayburn got the committee to change its action.

Another time, when Congressman Adolph Sabath, who succeeded O'Connor as chairman of the Rules Committee, would not report to the House amendments to the wages and hours law that Roosevelt wanted,

Rayburn resorted almost to tank action. "The Majority Leader literally took Mr. Sabath by the arm, led him to the Committee room, where the rule was resting in a pigeonhole and brought both Committee chairman and the rule back to the floor. Mr. Sabath then interrupted the discussion and filed the rule," reported *The New York Times.* [21]

Rayburn's method of operation attracted a great deal of attention from the press. He had only to walk into the House Chamber at the rear when the legislative day was beginning in order to gauge its mood. He would sprawl comfortably, his elbows resting on the brass rail behind the back row of the benches, and let his eyes and ears tell him what could or could not be done that day. There in the Speaker's chair on the rostrum would be Bankhead or a substitute seemingly inert, and on the floor someone would be holding forth.

From his observation post behind a rail, Rayburn would stand and wait, and soon a steady stream of Democrats would make their way to his side. After each visitor had his whispered say, Rayburn would either give him a few words in reply, flap a hand up or down to show approval or disapproval, or nod or shake his head. To a casual observer from the gallery, he appeared to be a popular member being greeted by a succession of friends. But what he was really doing was giving advice, encouragement or orders on various aspects of that day's business. Members generally found him deadly serious when he was in the Chamber. Yet on rare occasions, standing in the unventilated poorly lighted room, he was not all business. On a warm spring day, he told a member, "God! What I would give for a tow-headed boy to take fishing."

On much of its work on legislation, the House converted itself into the Committee of the Whole, where the quorum requirement for members present was smaller and a five-minute speaking rule applied. The Speaker was barred from presiding over the Committee of the Whole, which had its own chairman. Rayburn saw to it that his friend John McCormack became chairman, and he conceived a plan for McCormack to make the opposition look bad when an inept member was presenting its case. This type of member was allowed to exceed his five minutes by fifteen more. Then McCormack would pound the gavel and exclaim, "The gentleman has only one minute left." Great laughter always followed. [22]

Although Bert Snell, the minority leader, constantly sought to enlarge the Republocrat force and weaken Rayburn's control, he and Rayburn left the floor frequently arm in arm after a head-on debating collision. This was a lesson he had learned from Garner, whose closest friend in the House during the twenties had been "you baldheaded old coot!" as he fondly called Nick Longworth to his face in floor debate.

Rayburn worked closely with Snell after hours to smooth the way for legislation that was not controversial, and this in turn led to their increased friendship. In moments of conviviality, Snell told stories, and one he related was about the 1936 Republican National Convention, at which he had served as chairman. It was here that former President Hoover had delivered a rousing attack on the New Deal that brought an uproar of frenzied approval from delegates. While the applause continued, Hoover left the platform and waited in a nearby room for an expected stampede that would lead to his renomination for President. But Snell knew that Hoover had no chance against Roosevelt, and he stepped to the microphone to announce that Hoover had left the Cleveland Municipal Auditorium to catch a train for New York. [23]

Rayburn did not restrict his Republican friendship to Snell but extended it to others as well if he thought they were in the right. Ben F. Jensen, a Republican new to Congress, was listening to the debate on a housing bill. Jensen had spent twenty-four years in the lumber business in Iowa, and he grew aware of an error in the bill as it pertained to lumber. After the debate had run its course and the bill opened to amendment, he stood up and offered one to correct the mistake. "A point of order was raised against the amendment," he said, "on the ground it was not germane to the bill."

The next thing he knew, while he "was standing [there] redfaced," Sam Rayburn had come to his side. "I did not know what to say or what to do because I had not anticipated that a point of order would be raised against my amendment," said Jensen. "Mr. Sam said then, 'Ask unanimous consent to withdraw your amendment to this section of the bill and offer it to section 9. It will be germane to section 9. You have a good amendment and I want to see it passed.' "

Jensen followed Rayburn's suggestion. "I asked unanimous consent that my amendment be withdrawn to that particular section and at the proper time I again offered my amendment and it was agreed to by the House." [24]

But as willing as Rayburn was to help a Republican in need, he would not permit an attack on Roosevelt to go unanswered. On one occasion after the House passed a farm bill, Jesse P. Wolcott, a Republican from Michigan, read aloud excerpts from Carl Sandburg's two-volume biography of Abraham Lincoln. One excerpt described General Grant as "a bewildered, confused and miserably perplexed man," an apt description of President Roosevelt, Wolcott added.

House members watched as fury crossed Rayburn's face and his bald head turned crimson. Then he stalked across the aisle to the Republican side of the House and shouted, "I'll answer that!"

Total silence descended on the House while he upbraided Wolcott for carrying "partisanship to such a point of personal criticism." He said Presidents were not immune to criticism and that he criticized some in the past, but he had never done so on the Wolcott approach that a President was "a dishonest man or a fool."

Because of Roosevelt's growing dependency on Rayburn as his second term moved along, their work relationship grew closer. Now more frequently, the two men got together in the White House, both chain-smoking Camel cigarettes while they exchanged information and mapped strategy. And during the week there were numerous phone calls and chits from Roosevelt about new problems that had arisen or pep talks for action. In a typical note, Roosevelt wrote one time: "Sam, can you get this bill through on Thursday? FDR."

Sometimes it was a call for help to save a pet agency both had worked hard to create. "I hear Jim Wadsworth will put in legislation to amend the SEC with the help of Clarence Lea [the chairman of the House Commerce Committee]," Roosevelt told him one time. "Don't you think we should step on this and stop it? It would destroy all your good work."[25] Rayburn stepped on the amendment.

There were many failures but there were far more successes. Among the failures was the longtime Roosevelt dream of developing the St. Lawrence Seaway. Rayburn had held a committee hearing on the subject back in 1933, and he was one of a few Southern members to favor it. Others believed it would draw off trade from Southern ports and damage the railroad industry. When Roosevelt learned that Joe Mansfield of Texas, chairman of the Rivers and Harbors Committee, planned to eliminate it from his pork-barrel "general grab-bag bill," he wrote Rayburn plaintively, "I do hope you will do all you can to save the St. Lawrence project in it. . . . The locks could always be put in later on."[26] But Rayburn was unable to rescue it.

As Rayburn found, getting the WPA appropriations through the House without mishap was always an impossibility, and the Court-packing fiasco remained a continual rallying point for the Republocrat coalition of Southern Democrats and Northern Republicans on a host of unrelated issues. Yet by skill and hard work, Rayburn often overcame this strong opposition, as when he helped Marvin Jones win House approval for the Farm Security Act of 1937, which gave federal assistance to sharecroppers, tenant farmers and migrant workers. There was also his work to win a second Agricultural Adjustment Act in 1938 that created the "ever-normal granary" plan to store farm surpluses for sale in poor crop years, a Federal Crop Insurance Corporation to insure crops against natural disasters, and a Food Stamp Plan to provide an outlet for part of the farm surpluses to the urban needy. There were further a public-housing law that he helped pass and a Food, Drug and Cosmetic Bill that he sponsored and won passage for in the House to replace the Pure Food and Drug Act of 1906. Toward the close of Roosevelt's second term when *Life* Magazine asked fifty-three Capitol Hill reporters to name the most influential member of Congress, Rayburn was an easy winner.

The Roosevelt-Rayburn relationship also extended to laying strategy for campaigning. Beyond that, Rayburn made himself readily available to help Democratic congressional candidates by going into their districts to speak for them. Always the Democratic warrior, when he left Washington in October 1938 to invade Republican strongholds, he told White House reporters, "I'm going out to give the doctrine to the heathens." [27]

What he considered a major Roosevelt blunder was the President's attempt that year to "purge" Democrats who had opposed Court-packing and other New Deal programs. Of all those whom Roosevelt tried to defeat, he was successful only in the Democratic primary involving Rules Committee Chairman John O'Connor, who was his chief troublemaker in the House. After his loss, O'Connor ran in the November election in New York as a Republican, and he issued a campaign broadside claiming that Sam Rayburn was supporting him. But Rayburn swiftly issued a denial, and his enemy went down to defeat. [28]

When Roosevelt delivered his annual state of the Union message to Congress in January 1939, he signaled the end of New Deal innovations. "We have now passed the period of internal conflict in the launching of our program of social reform," he said. "Our full energies may now be released to invigorate the process of recovery in order to preserve our reforms."

So it appeared that Roosevelt would finish his term making minor adjustments in the legislation Congress had given him and then retire to Hyde Park. But events were taking place that would preserve the Rayburn-Roosevelt relationship for a long time.

15

Speaker Sam Rayburn

Speaker William Bankhead had been in continuing poor health since he won the top House post in 1936, and though his condition worsened in 1939, he clung tenaciously to the Speakership. With the years going by, impatient Sam Rayburn, now moving into his late fifties, saw little chance of climbing to the top of the rostrum. So he considered working quietly toward another ambition. This was to land a place for himself on the Democratic ticket in 1940.

It was far from being a spur-of-the-moment goal; he had confided it to his sister Meddie in a vague sort of way eighteen years earlier. His desire he said then, was "to achieve my life's fondest ambition—which is about as limitless as the circumstances and location will admit a fellow to cherish with any hope of realization."[1]

Rayburn knew that his chief deficit as a candidate was that he was a Southerner. On the other hand, as his friend Wright Patman of Texas assessed him at the beginning of 1939, he was a fifty-seven-year-old New Dealer with a solid reputation as a legislator and a man of integrity and leadership, and the man best fitted to succeed Roosevelt. *Look* Magazine hailed him as "the most useful member of Congress" that year, and an editorial in the liberal *St. Louis Post-Dispatch* promoted him as the leading dark horse candidate for President at the next Democratic Convention.

Because the two-term presidential tradition was so deeply engrained in the American political system, it appeared certain that the Democrats would choose a new team for their next race. As a result, midway through Franklin Roosevelt's second term congressmen, cabinet officers and governors looked upon him as a lame-duck Chief Executive who would be swept before long into the political discard. Indicative of this were the

troubles he was experiencing winning congressional approval of his legislative program, the growing attacks on his wife and the ebbing praise of
him by other Democrats. As ardent New Deal Senator James E. Murray
of Montana bluntly put it during this period: "There was a time when I
would have bled and died for him, but . . . I just intend to stay away from
him and he can do as he pleases."

But the two-term tradition failed to take into account the spreading
menace of dictators abroad.

Ironically, from the time of his inauguration until he became a lame-
duck President, Roosevelt had had little personal affect on the basic
direction of American foreign policy. From 1935 to 1937, for example, he
had been helpless while Congress established isolationism as the keystone
of the country's international relations. A series of neutrality measures
barred U.S. arms or other military aid to other countries at war, including those under attack or invasion. In October 1937 when Roosevelt
in a Chicago speech merely called for a moral quarantine of aggressors,
the outcry by press and politicians against his words was thunderous.
And when he submitted the Army's budget request to Congress, he knew
it was hopeless to ask for more than a pitiful $250 million.

With nothing to fear from the U.S., Adolf Hitler's Nazi Germany seized
Austria, Benito Mussolini's Fascist Italy dropped bombs at will on
Ethiopia, Francisco Franco's totalitarians brought on a civil war in
Spain, and the warlords of Japan stepped up their regime of cruelty in
China.

But after the Nazis walked into Czechoslovakia in March 1939 and
began a war of nerves against Poland, the lame-duck President took his
first bold stand against the murderous Berlin-Rome-Tokyo Axis.

In a leadership meeting attended by Rayburn, Roosevelt asked
Congress to repeal the arms-embargo provisions of the neutrality laws.
Secretary of State Cordell Hull was to work with Sol Bloom, chairman of
the House Foreign Affairs Committee, to draft the repeal legislation, and
Bloom and Rayburn would get the bill through the House. Then the
repeal bill would go to the Senate to be handled by Chairman Key Pittman of the Foreign Relations Committee.

It was Rayburn's intention to keep an eye on the progress of the bill
drafting. But he became ill that spring with a continuing sore throat and
back pain. Later he wrote his sister Lucinda, "I had my tonsils out in
April and it was some months before my back and knees were normal
again."[2] And when he returned to Bonham for a visit, he hobbled about
with a cane.

His physical troubles cleared up, but what followed in the meantime
on the repeal draft was a disaster. Sol Bloom, a popular, friendly man

who had been a songwriter and music publisher, was relatively unversed in foreign affairs or bill writing. The legislation he and Hull worked up was so ineptly worded that lawyers argued that the language actually retained the arms embargo. To compound matters, John Vorys, a Republican freshman House member, introduced an amendment that reiterated the nation's isolation policy, declaring that whenever the President proclaimed a state of war existed between foreign powers, the U.S. could not export arms to either belligerent.

The vote on the Vorys amendment came on a Friday early in July 1939. Bedeviled by Eastern Democratic congressmen who stayed in Washington only on a Tuesday-through-Thursday basis, Rayburn tried desperately to round up his crowd. But he failed by 2 votes, and the Vorys amendment carried 159 to 157. "Once in, it was impossible to take out," said Cordell Hull, and the bill with the amendment passed 214 to 173. [3]

Because of the botch, Roosevelt's revised plan was to have the Senate repeal the arms embargo in a clean bill and then have Rayburn get the House to accept the Senate version. But later that month Pittman's Senate Foreign Relations Committee tabled any action until the 1940 congressional session, and Roosevelt seemed more of a lame-duck President than ever.

It was after Hitler's invasion of Poland on September 1, 1939, that the two-term tradition began to shake.

Under existing law, Roosevelt's required declaration of neutrality had, in effect, placed the U.S. on the side of the arms-rich Nazis against weak Poland and against England and France, who had come to Poland's aid. This ridiculous situation led Roosevelt to call Congress into special session that same month.

This time Sam Rayburn took vigorous charge of the House fight for repeal of the arms embargo and in view of Key Pittman's alcoholic condition, Senator Tom Connally bossed the Senate battle against isolationist Senators William Borah, Burt Wheeler, Arthur Vandenberg and Gerald Nye. Repeal cleared the House by 243 to 172 and the Senate by 63 to 30. Roosevelt's first significant victory over congressional isolationism had been accomplished by the hard work of the two Texans.

But Rayburn read far more in the action than the needed change in foreign policy. He foresaw the repeal as having a radical effect on the 1940 election. Jim Farley, talking to Rayburn on October 18, 1939, was among the first to hear his opinion. "Rayburn was certain that Roosevelt would be a candidate and would win reelection." he said. [4]

Rayburn's implication was that Roosevelt would want to see the catastrophic crisis through to the end, and the nation would prefer a man trained in the Presidency to hold that office. But after stating this judgment, Rayburn added that if Roosevelt "turned down the nomination . . . it would go to Garner, Hull or me [Farley]."

Although Rayburn believed that Roosevelt would run for a third term, the President's silence on this subject made others bold. In the rush for the big prize, Garner was one of the first to throw his sweaty Stetson into the presidential ring, to the roar of approval from big business and the conservative press. To offset the fact that he would be seventy-two at his inauguration, his backers pumped out the claim that he had "the mental and physical vigor of men 20 years his junior." A jeering detractor commented, "His love of poker, baseball, fishing and his habit of tossing off whiskey neat are hailed as evidence of an earthy Americanism that would withstand the invasions of alien ideologies."

Rayburn's dilemma came when Garner asked him to serve as his campaign director. The two had continued to drift still further apart politically, and Rayburn was well aware that Roosevelt and Garner were no longer on friendly terms. But always the good soldier, Rayburn felt he had no choice and he accepted, even though he realized this would damage his chances to be Roosevelt's running mate. "I am for that outstanding Texan and liberal Democrat, John N. Garner, for the presidential nomination in 1940," he told the press.

When FDR read that Rayburn had endorsed Garner, he was hurt, until he saw that Sam had carefully followed his endorsement with the statement: "History will place President Roosevelt and his accomplishments on the same plane with Washington, Jefferson and Jackson." But the hurt returned when he learned that Rayburn was writing letters to Democratic leaders in various states, asking them to support Garner.

Indication of Rayburn's strained relations with the White House became public when Denison, Texas, in his congressional district, held a "Sam Rayburn Day" celebration. [5] Texas Senator Morris Sheppard wrote to Roosevelt and asked him to send a presidential message for the occasion. Nothing was sent, and afterward White House Press Secretary Stephan Early lamely claimed that Roosevelt was at sea and did not receive Sheppard's request "until after the celebration at Denison had been concluded."

There was still another presidential slur. This involved a Rayburn protégé named Lyndon Baines Johnson. A brash, pushy young man on the make, Johnson had come to Washington at age twenty-three in December 1931 as secretary to newly elected Congressman Richard Kleberg, who was proprietor of the fabulous King Ranch, a piece of property larger than Connecticut. Kleberg was later exposed for collecting kickbacks from his congressional clerks. [6]

Even as a congressional secretary, Johnson had been able to upset Cactus Jack Garner. When Garner was House Speaker, he had made a ruling that he would name all local postmasters in Texas instead of following the tradition which gave this patronage to the state's eighteen U.S. representatives. Johnson passed this story to a reporter, and when the press attacked him, Garner hurriedly rescinded his order. "Who in hell is this boy Lyndon Johnson?" he squeaked.

Lyndon's father, Sam Johnson, had served a term with Rayburn in the Texas House, and the tall, skinny Texan used this as his calling card to meet and become a Rayburn protégé. The father-son relationship that developed became clear when Johnson was rushed to a Washington hospital one time with pneumonia. When he regained consciousness, Rayburn was at his bedside. "Now Lyndon," said Rayburn, "don't you worry. Take it easy. If you need money or anything, you just call on me." This relationship paid off for Johnson in 1935 when, at his pleading, Rayburn went to see Senator Tom Connally and asked him to recommend Johnson to Roosevelt to head the Texas National Youth Administration (NYA), despite the fact that he was only twenty-six and inexperienced. (Senators controlled statewide patronage while members of the House were limited to job recommendations within their districts.)

After two years as director of the Texas NYA, Johnson won election to the House in 1937 at the age of twenty-eight, and he was soon working overtime to win recognition as a protégé of Roosevelt as well as Rayburn. In mid-1939, he had to make a temporary choice between Rayburn and Roosevelt when CIO President John L. Lewis called Garner a "labor-baiting, poker-playing. whiskey-drinking, evil old man." Garner grew concerned that the labor leader had damaged his candidacy, and he demanded that Rayburn get the Texas congressional delegation to pass a unanimous resolution declaring him innocent of Lewis' charges. All members except Johnson were willing to sign such an absolving resolution. For two hours Rayburn spoke privately to him to sign. "Lyndon, I'm looking you right in the eye!" he scolded him. But Johnson had been asked by the White House not to comply, and Welly Hopkins, Johnson's close friend from back home was legal counsel to Lewis' United Mine Workers. So he stunned Rayburn when he shouted in return, "And I'm looking you right back in the eye!" [7] In the end, Garner did not get his resolution and Rayburn, hurt by Johnson's remark, said, "Lyndon is a damned independent boy; independent as a hog on ice."

But he could not remain angry for long at his substitute son, especially when Lyndon and his wife, Lady Bird, invited him to a home-cooked meal or when Lyndon sent him carefully written letters of thanks.

159

Typical was the letter of May 13, 1939, in which Johnson said that two years ago "you walked down the aisle with me and stood with me while I raised my hand and took my oath." [8]

A third Roosevelt slur on Rayburn for supporting Garner's candidacy came in the spring of 1940 and again involved Lyndon Johnson. The year before, principally because of the lobbying of Maury Maverick and Rayburn, Roosevelt had appointed Alvin Wirtz, a Texas New Dealer and private-utility operator, as Undersecretary of the Interior. Wirtz was the third adopted "Daddy" to Johnson, along with Rayburn and Roosevelt. He had handled Johnson's campaign for his House seat in 1937. Early in May 1940, Roosevelt sent Wirtz back to Texas to swing the state Democratic convention, scheduled for the twenty-eighth, away from giving support to Garner. White House aides believed this would not be too difficult a task because of what was happening in Europe: The Nazis had taken Norway and Denmark in April and had moved into Holland, Belgium and Luxembourg early in May. The fall of the European continent to Hitler appeared imminent, and Roosevelt the silent candidate looked more and more like a third-term standard-bearer.

But the composition of the state Democratic convention depended less on such major events than on local politicking. First there were 5,500 precinct conventions that chose delegates to 254 county conventions, and then these county brawls selected delegates to the state convention that picked delegates to the national convention.

Because of the pileup of congressional work, Rayburn stayed in Washington, far from the antlike conventioneering back in Texas. But he tried to effect a compromise in advance by suggesting that one-third of the forty-six delegates to the national convention be for Roosevelt, a second third for Garner, and the rest pledged to vote for Garner only on the first ballot. At the same time, Wirtz was asking the precinct and county conventions to approve a "Harmony Resolution" that pledged delegates to the national convention not to take part in any "stop-Roosevelt movement."

When only a minority of the conventions approved the Harmony Resolution, Roosevelt was disturbed. Aides told the busy President that if Myron Blalock—an oil man, Texas Democratic chairman, and friend of Garner—would personally approve the Harmony Resolution, this would carry weight at the state convention.

Convinced by the fast-talking, conning Lyndon Johnson that young as he was he wielded a great deal of political power in Texas, Roosevelt decided that Rayburn and Johnson should sign a public telegram to Blalock asking him to endorse the administration, propose Garner as a favorite-son candidate and declare his opposition to any "stop-Roosevelt" scheme at the national convention.

160

This idea brought a scowling rejection by Rayburn. The reason was not the contents of the wire but the indignity of having Johnson's name on it alongside his own. Ickes, in high glee and always happy to pound Rayburn, wrote in his diary that Rayburn "did not want it to appear that in a Texas political matter, a kid Congressman like Johnson was on apparently on the same footing as himself, the Majority Leader."

By now panicky about Texas, Roosevelt would not accept Rayburn's rejection and he demanded that he and Johnson come to the Oval Office. Here Rayburn decided that sending the telegram was more important than his injured feelings. In this incident, Roosevelt showed an extremely dark side of his character, for he enjoyed the opportunity to demean the man who had been most responsible for the success of his programs in Congress. Gloating Ickes claimed: "When Johnson and Rayburn appeared in the President's office that afternoon, he told them benignly that they had been good little boys and that they had 'papa's blessing.' He treated them as political equals with the malicious intent of disturbing Sam Rayburn's state of mind." [9]

The upshot was that after a three-hour riot at the Waco convention the telegram's suggestions were adopted. Rayburn was named head of the Texas delegation to the Chicago convention, Lyndon Johnson as vice chairman, Wirtz as a member of the platform committee and Blalock as Texas national committeeman.

As the Democratic National Convention's opening on July 15 approached, Roosevelt continued his official silence about the third term. But from his experience with Roosevelt's interference in the selection of the Texas delegation, Rayburn was convinced he planned to break political tradition. Even if Roosevelt had steered clear of the Texas conventions, Rayburn believed that in view of the French surrender to Hitler on June 20 and the weak condition of lonely Britain against the might of the Nazi air force, Roosevelt's third-term try was inevitable.

He was therefore surprised by the ongoing Alice-in-Wonderland candidacies of Garner, Cordell Hull and Jim Farley. Like busy little bees trying to suck honey from a dead flower, the three men were in telephone touch with each other daily on their candidacies: Hull insisting that Roosevelt had referred to him as the "next President"; [10] Jim Farley repeating that Roosevelt had promised him he would not run for a third term; and Garner having pipe dreams despite his loss to noncandidate Roosevelt by 7 to 1 in the California primary and another defeat in Illinois. "Jim, the two of us can pull together to stop Roosevelt," Farley said Garner had told him.

When the convention got under way in the Chicago Stadium on July 15, Rayburn continued to go through the motions of working for Garner even though he knew his cause was hopeless. At one point when he told

Farley that Garner was not being treated fairly by the convention officials, Farley looked at him dubiously. "I did not take Sam's tears too seriously," he said later, "as he was a red-hot candidate for Vice President." [11]

Roosevelt's farce continued through the keynote speech by Senator Alben Barkley, who read a statement that the President had no desire for a third term and that the delegates were "free to vote for any candidate." But Roosevelt's convention directors, bunglers though they were, had been dashing about, collecting the votes needed for his nomination.

It was all over on the first ballot, at 10:38 P.M. on July 17, with Roosevelt collecting 946¼ votes to 72¼ for Farley, 61 for Garner and 6 for Hull. And when it happened, Rayburn aroused the animosity of the hopeful conspirators by hurrying to the platform and offering a motion to make the nomination unanimous. Farley found it wise to do the same after he saw the response from the convention.

With the presidential nomination settled, the vice-presidential spot now became the big issue. When the convention had opened two days earlier, Roosevelt had given newsmen a list of persons whom he considered acceptable to him for the presidential nomination. Rayburn's name headed the list, followed by Senator Jimmy Byrnes, Governor Lloyd Stark of Missouri—who was then running for the Senate against Harry Truman—and young Supreme Court Justice William O. Douglas. [12]

Rayburn had accepted this to mean that Roosevelt was no longer indignant about his nominal support for Garner and had installed him as his leading choice for his running mate. For this reason he tried to develop support for his own vice-presidential candidacy at the convention at the same time that he was boosting Garner for the presidential nomination. A story in *The New York Times* on July 17 reported: "Rayburn's candidacy gains momentum as Texas delegation fans out to other delegations."

When Roosevelt failed to make known his choice for Vice President following his own nomination late on the seventeenth, Rayburn called a 2:00 A.M. meeting of the Texas delegation in an effort to force the issue. Word of a solid vote of support for him by his delegation was bound to snowball into delegation strength among other states.

But Rayburn's strategy went awry. At the same time that Alvin Wirtz and Lyndon Johnson circulated among the tired Texans to gain a swift vote for Rayburn, Garner's die-hard supporters, who blamed Rayburn for their man's failure, undertook a similar mission in behalf of Jesse Jones, the choice of Jim Farley for Vice President. The collision brought on a shrill war of words that lasted throughout the rest of the night and into the morning. Long after daylight, Johnson ordered a hunt made for missing delegates. One was discovered dead in his hotel bed, several others were ill from overdrinking, and billionaire oilman Sid Richardson sulked because he had been robbed in the elevator.

The belated vote went overwhelmingly for Rayburn (88 to 7), but it came far too late to create the ground swell he had hoped would pressure Roosevelt. Not long after it was taken, Jesse Jones, the cause of the delay, walked into the room to report that Jim Farley had confided to him that Roosevelt had just phoned him and wanted Henry Wallace, the Secretary of Agriculture, as his running mate.

Rayburn did not buy Jones' story, but he told the delegation to keep its decision dangling until word came confirming or denying it. A short time later Roosevelt phoned him. "Sam, I want you to do me a great favor," he shouted in his normal telephone voice.

From his opening remark, Rayburn was certain he was going to tell him he wanted him on the ticket. But Roosevelt continued, "I want you to make a seconding speech for Henry Wallace." After an anguished pause the good soldier Rayburn said he would.

Yet even though he swallowed his hurt and did this, the Texas delegation refused to accept Wallace. Instead, it cast its votes for Speaker Bankhead, who had tottered to the platform to deliver the opening convention speech in a weak, sick voice. Nor was the Texas delegation unique, for the atmosphere in the Chicago Stadium grew ugly, Roosevelt's name was booed, and a revolt sprang up against Wallace—a mystic and nonpolitician who was further suspect because his father had been Harding and Coolidge's Secretary of Agriculture. Only the last-minute plane flight to Chicago by Mrs. Roosevelt and her pleading speech to the convention allowed Wallace to come through narrowly by a measly 627 votes out of 1,100.

Rayburn suffered more humiliation after the convention. In 1938, he had no primary opposition when he ran for his fourteenth term in the House. But in 1940, while his words and face were appearing regularly in the national press he was confronted with an opponent in the Democratic primary. Even though he easily disposed of Dr. Bliven Galbraith by a 7-to-1 margin, the effort was costly in terms of concern and money.

In September he was back in Washington where he was most at home, leading the fight in the House for Roosevelt's expanding defense program. The previous January he had served as the sick Bankhead's substitute at a Jefferson-Jackson Day Dinner in Baltimore, and in April when the Speaker went into the hospital for a time, the House elected Rayburn Speaker pro tem.

But Bankhead recovered to the point that he could travel to Chicago and try for the vice-presidential nomination. His strength was fast fleeing, however, and he suffered a stomach hemorrhage on September 14. His wife and daughter Tallulah, a famous stage actress, rushed to his side, but he died the next day.

When the House met on Monday, September 16, Bankhead's body lay in state in the well of the Chamber before the dais. In this atmosphere, John McCormack introduced a resolution to make Rayburn successor to Bankhead. There was no discussion, no argument. The vote was unanimous.

Rayburn had been in his office, where he had shaved to look his best. But in his nervousness, he had cut his chin, staining his collar with blood. With only a few minutes left before his oath taking, a friend ran frantically down the avenue and returned with a new shirt. [13]

Finally he walked into the Chamber and was sworn in. After 27½ years of service in Congress, he was Speaker of the House of Representatives. In the rush of other events, however, his moment of triumph was crowded off the front page of *The New York Times* by the Nazi airpounding of London, Roosevelt's signing of the military draft, and Republican presidential candidate Wendell Willkie's predicting an American dictatorship if Roosevelt won a third term.

16

Saving the Draft

It was after Roosevelt's overwhelming victory over Wendell Willkie in November 1940 that Sam Rayburn's mettle as the House's forty-fourth Speaker was tested. The question was a simple one: Would he be his own master or a servant of the President?

Later Rayburn was to state that he never served *under* a President, but rather served *with* him. But at the outset the opposite seemed true.

His first crucial test came over the Walter-Logan Bill, which was intended to create uniform procedures among independent federal agencies like the SEC or the FTC. Francis Walter of Pennsylvania, one of Rayburn's leading lieutenants, had written the bill with the help of White House aides, and it was based on the careful reports of the Special Committee on Administrative Law.

Walter's bill passed Congress by its expected large majority, and stunned anger spread among members when Roosevelt vetoed it. One section of the bill had provided for court review of judicial decisions by the agencies, and Roosevelt's belated view was that this would weaken the authority of the independent agencies and make them ineffective.

There was little doubt that the House votes were there to override the veto. But flushed with his winning of a third term and feeling powerful, Roosevelt insisted to Rayburn and Majority Leader John McCormack that his veto had to stand. This created an enormous problem for Rayburn because his standing as Speaker was at stake.

He chose in this instance to be the President's rubber stamp. His whip organization under likeable but tough Pat Boland put a heavy hand on Democratic members to back Roosevelt, and Rayburn and McCormack added their voices in the crunch.

When the veto was sustained, Roosevelt wrote Rayburn a commanding and condescending letter on December 23, 1940, that began "Dear Sam" and ended "always affectionately." In the body of the letter he said, "Courage—just sheer courage—brought that about." He added in a bossy tone that the next Congress would consider important legislation that would require ceaseless labor for Rayburn and McCormack:

> What I want to get across to both of you before the next session begins is that good fellowship for the sake of good fellowship alone, an easy life to avoid criticism, an acceptance of defeat before an issue has been joined, make, all of them, less for Party success and for national safety than a few drag-down and knock-out fights and an unwillingness to accept defeat without a fight.

To cover his tracks from the charge that he was dictatorial and operated with weak congressional leaders, he added:

> I myself must, as you know, be guided by the recommendations of the Democratic leaders of the House, and while in no sense do I want the advice of "yes men," I do want the advice of fighting leadership, with adjective "fighting" underscored.
>
> You and John have an opportunity to salvage much that would otherwise be lost in the coming session, and you and I know that this means day and night work, taking it on the chin, getting knocked down occasionally, but making a comeback before you are counted out. I am saying this for the sake of the Party. I am saying this more greatly for the sake of the Nation. And I know you will understand—and do your best. . . . On the success of that session will depend the future reputation of the President and the Speaker and the Majority Leader. It will not help any of the three to meet with a series of defeats in the next Congress. [1]

So a pattern of total subservience to the President seemed to be set. But Rayburn was too independent and outspoken a man to let it continue.

The crucial test for him came shortly after the 1941 session began when Roosevelt asked Congress to pass his $7 billion Lend-Lease Bill. With the fall of France in June 1940, and Britain left to fight alone for her existence against the Nazi air force, Roosevelt had begun to strengthen the nation's defenses. In one short period, he asked Congress for $6 billion for a military program and spoke of plants turning out fifty thousand planes a year. During 1940, he also appointed a National Defense Advisory Commission of top corporate officials to manage the defense program, named two pro-British interventionist Republicans to his cabinet to head the War and Navy Departments, banned the sale of aviation gasoline and scrap metal to Japan and transferred fifty destroyers to beleaguered Britain in exchange for ninety-nine-year leases on British possessions in the Western Hemisphere. In addition, Congress passed the Selective Service Act, making eight hundred thousand young American males subject by lottery to a year of military training.

The Lend-Lease Bill was based on turning the United States into "the arsenal of democracy," as Roosevelt put it. Under this legislation, he would be able to sell, exchange, transfer, lend, or lease any defense article to a government "whose defense the President [deemed] vital to the defense of the United States." [2]

As expected, the Lend-Lease proposal brought the strong isolationist groups in Congress and the country out in force, for they realized that it would commit the nation to the British cause and increase the likelihood of Nazi retaliation. Roosevelt, in his anger, committed a serious violation of the Constitution when he ordered the FBI to investigate those opposing Lend-Lease with wiretaps and mail-reading. [3]

Rayburn, who was a firm believer in the defense program, assessed the situation carefully. House Republicans had taken a party stand against Lend-Lease, and many Democratic fence-sitters had hard reservations about some of the bill's provisions. Added together, these forces could easily defeat the legislation. Roosevelt's determination to get the bill through Congress intact was foolhardy.

In a visit to the White House Rayburn confronted Roosevelt with his conclusions. The bill was dead, he said bluntly, unless the $7 billion requested came through the appropriations process and not as a blank-check authorization without congressional scrutiny of details. Further, he said, there had to be a two-year time limitation. Secret operations were out; Roosevelt should agree to send trimonthly reports to Congress. There would also have to be a provision requiring the military chiefs to approve all proposed releases of war supplies to other nations as well as a ban on American convoying of lend-lease materials.

Roosevelt argued against Rayburn's demands. But in the end he agreed to make these changes.

Rayburn also had another piece of advice. Lord Halifax, the British ambassador to Washington, was planning to address the Pilgrim Society of New York. With the tall waves of anti-British feeling promoted by isolationists, such as Colonel Charles Lindbergh and Senator Burt

Wheeler, this would stir up additional opposition to the Lend-Lease Bill. The speech to the Pilgrim Society had to be postponed, said Rayburn, "even if Lord Halifax must have lumbago." [4]

This strong suggestion was passed along. A short time later Lord Halifax agreed to postpone his speech and asked Senator Jimmy Byrnes to tell Rayburn that "I think, as he suggested, I may have to invoke lumbago to my aid."

The House had a rough three-day debate on lend-lease. When the vote came, only 24 of the 159 House Republicans would support the proposal. But with Rayburn's changes and Halifax's silence, a sufficient number of Democrats came through to give the bill a tidy margin of 95 votes on February 8, 1941.

Rayburn's action on the Lend-Lease Bill became his normal mode of operation in dealing with Roosevelt. When FDR asked Congress to pass new tax legislation to meet skyrocketing defense costs, he included a section that established compulsory joint income-tax returns for husbands and wives. Rayburn went to see him with advice.

"I think it'll raise hell with all the married women and all the working women," he said, while Roosevelt listened. "And all the Catholic priests and the Episcopalians," Rayburn went on. Roosevelt held a palm toward Rayburn and nodded. He eliminated the compulsory provision in order to cut opposition to his proposal.

Another time when Rayburn learned that Roosevelt had ordered the dropping of defense contracts in Congressman Eugene "Goober" Cox's district in Georgia, Rayburn told him this was wrong. Adolph Sabath of Chicago was chairman of the powerful Rules Committee, but bushy-haired "Goober" Cox bossed it and held a life and death grip over most House legislation. "Cox was the real leader of the Southerners in the House," said Joe Martin, Republican leader after Bert Snell had retired in 1939. "He and I were the principal points of contact between the Northern Republicans and the Southern Democratic conservatives" in collecting votes "against FDR." [5]

In 1938, Roosevelt had included Cox in the list of congressmen he wanted to "purge," and now he had designed reprisals to punish him. Rayburn told Roosevelt that he and Cox were close personal friends. They were so close, in fact, Rayburn explained, that if he wanted to get a bill cleared by the Rules Committee for floor action, he would go see Cox. "Do you really need this one?" Cox would ask. If Rayburn said it was important, Cox would clear it through Rules even though he opposed the bill personally.

"Hell, Mr. President," Rayburn told Roosevelt, "you can't go after

Gene Cox. He's at least five votes on the Rules Committee. He's the difference."

Roosevelt stopped action against Cox.

Rayburn was on his own in 1941 in dealing with one of the most vital events in the Roosevelt era. In May, after Athens fell, FDR had declared a state of national emergency, and a month later when Hitler's armies invaded the Soviet Union he extended lend-lease aid to the Communists. The defense program was starting to boom by mid-1941, raising American spirits as the international situation worsened. But a new crisis was developing that threatened the entire defense effort. The one-year military draft was to expire in October 1941, and the Attorney General pointed out to Roosevelt that his national emergency declaration could not keep the boys in army camps beyond that time. As the law read, draftees could not be retained "unless *Congress* declares that the national security is imperiled."

Trouble developed when the young draftees were asked to volunteer for further service. There were reports that in October the camps would empty, and if legalities were instituted to keep them there they would desert en masse. Draftees were said to have adopted the slogan of "OHIO," or "Over the Hill in October."

Although Roosevelt realized the consequences of losing so large a group of semitrained soldiers, because of the burgeoning national outcry he was willing to let the draft expire on course and revert to the inadequate volunteer system. But when Army Chief of Staff George C. Marshall and Secretary of War Henry L. Stimson persisted in their protests, he agreed to ask Congress to extend the draft.

Rayburn's first thoughts on a draft extension were negative, and Marshall was dispatched to discuss it with him. In his undiplomatic manner, Marshall spoke about details of the proposal, as if the issue were already settled. This infuriated Rayburn, who "blew up over what he regarded as a crude attempt by the Army to force his hand on a draft extension matter that had little chance of passing." [6] But after a few days of further reflection, Rayburn told Marshall he "harbored no hard feelings."

Then came Secretary of War Stimson, whose basic point of view was that the country was divided between a few elitists and a mass of brainless sheep, and he told Rayburn he wanted a draft extension that would hold draftees in the Army for "unlimited" service. Afterward Rayburn informed Roosevelt that Stimson's proposal would only increase the agitation and would never clear Congress. For unlimited service during peacetime would be considered a form of slavery. What he believed might be possible was a bill providing at most for a thirty-month maximum period of service. Roosevelt agreed.

But this was only the beginning of the fight. A behind-the-scenes check of probable votes by Pat Boland, the majority whip, showed that even Rayburn's proposal would lose. The Republicans were making it a party policy to oppose any extension, and many liberal Northern Democrats intended to join them in the vote.

With the lines seemingly drawn, Rayburn ordered Boland and his whip organization to go after converts. But not fully relying on his whip, he also joined the effort, using the approach that was singularly his own. "Mr. Sam is terribly convincing," said a member who was victim to Rayburn's lobbying technique. "There he stands, his left hand on your right shoulder, holding your coat button, looking at you out of honest eyes that reflect the sincerest emotions."

By agreement, Rayburn and Minority Leader Joe Martin agreed to hold the vote extension on Tuesday, August 12. Two weeks before, Roosevelt had been heavily in the news, closing the Panama Canal to Japanese ships, freezing Japanese assets in the U.S., and calling up the Philippine militia after Japan took over southern Indochina. With the growing crisis in the Pacific, Rayburn believed that Roosevelt's personal lobbying with House members would influence some votes. So a week before the draft-extension count, he phoned the White House to request this vital aid. But Roosevelt had left town to meet with British Prime Minister Winston Churchill aboard a ship at Argentia Bay, Newfoundland, for what would become known as the Atlantic Charter Conference.

Without Roosevelt on hand for last-hour lobbying, Rayburn in desperation asked Secretary of State Cordell Hull to send an open letter to the House in favor of the bill. When Hull's letter proved to be a dud, Rayburn realized the entire burden now lay on his own thick shoulders.

With grim determination, he lined up his crew of speakers for the debate and ordered Pat Boland and his whip organization to continue their work to the end. There was no question that log-rolling and pork-barrel inducements were hinted at.

On Sunday, two days before the climactic vote on Selective Service, Rayburn's friends could not find him. He had taken the overnight train back to his birthplace in Roane County, Tennessee. There he visited the log house where he was born and the farm of his grandfather, John Waller. Then he went to the house of relatives near Kingston and asked the old woman who lived there for "an old wash pan and an old sack towel like I used to use." While he washed his hands on the back porch, he was observed staring thoughtfully at the hills in the background.

On Tuesday, shortly before the House vote, Rayburn personally won agreement from four Democrats to support the draft extension. When the bells rang for the roll call, Pat Boland and his assistants were at the doors to do some final vote pleading as members streamed in. Overhead, the galleries were packed with antidraft leaders, soldiers and, as one journalist noted, "pathetic-looking mothers clutching little American flags." [7]

The clerk called the roll in this oppressive atmosphere. After the final name—"Orville Zimmerman"—he started through the second required roll call to pick up those who had not answered the first time around. When this was completed, Rayburn glanced gloomily at the tally total, for he saw that the vote was a tie, or a defeat for the draft extension.

House rules permitted those who wanted to change their vote to come now to the well below the rostrum and get recognition from the Speaker to do so. Rayburn was soon aware that almost all who stood beneath him were Republicans and he knew they intended to switch their votes from Aye to No, as part of Republican strategy to kill the bill. So he beckoned to several Democrats to climb the stairs to his desk and he made a swift plea for them to change their votes from No to Aye.

Lew Deschler was Rayburn's lookout on the vote-switching. When he saw the total become 203 for and 202 against, he quickly handed the tally slip to Rayburn. Without a moment lost, Rayburn shouted, "On this vote 203 members have voted 'Aye'; 202 members have voted 'No'; and the bill is passed!"

A great shout went up from Republican leaders. They insisted that the vote must stay open until all changes and additions be made, as was customarily done. They were hoping to switch still more of the measly band of only twenty-one Republicans who were on record as voting for the extension. But Rayburn coldly said that it was too late for this because the vote results had already been announced.

Then Republican Congressman Dewey Short of Missouri, one of his party's strategists, tried to buy time by demanding a recapitulation of the vote. Rayburn had no objection, and he ordered the clerk to call the names of those who voted "Aye" and those who voted "No." All other names were excluded, and members were not permitted to change their vote.

The moment the recapitulation was completed, Rayburn mumbled, "No correction in the vote, the vote stands, and the bill is passed, and without objection a motion to reconsider is laid on the table."

It took a while for the opposition to realize what Rayburn had done this time. When a motion to reconsider was "laid on the table" it meant that not only had the subject been decided adversely, but it could not be brought up for consideration again except by unanimous consent.

Congressman Short bellowed a complaint that Rayburn was unfair and that the entire vote should be reconsidered. Rayburn told him bluntly he was too late because—as he had already announced—"without objection a motion to reconsider is laid on the table."

Other congressmen demanded to know who had made the motion to table reconsideration, and Republican Carl Andersen of Minnesota protested angrily that Rayburn had never announced "that a motion to reconsider had been tabled."

"The chair has twice stated that he did make that statement," Rayburn said.

"I beg to differ with you——" Andersen cut in, shouting.

Rayburn stared icily at him. Then he silenced Andersen and broke the back of the arguers. "The Chair does not intend to have his word questioned by the gentleman from Minnesota or anybody else." Down came his gavel and the subject was finished.

So the draft was saved. The eight hundred thousand young men in army camps remained in training, and an additional eight hundred thousand were soon on their way into military life.

A few days after the vote, Rayburn decided that the House deserved a one-month recess. He told reporters that he was homesick for "a little place" near his Fannin County home where he wanted to be alone. "I live on a broad highway in a white house, where everyone can find me," he said. "But I have another little place that I call the ranch. It's not quite big enough to call a ranch, but I'm going to be a ranchman anyhow. When I start toward that place—it's about 13 miles from my farm house—the road gets narrower and narrower every mile I go. And when I get to the narrowest part of the road, there is a gate, and there is no telephone out there."

17

The Speaker's Way of Life

By 1941, Sam Rayburn's routine as Speaker was already set, just as his life in general had found relative stability. At night he was in bed by 10 o'clock, and although he belonged to no church, he often knelt to pray as he had as a child. "I stay in bed as long as I can," he said. "Although I don't sleep nine hours a night, I know that when I'm stretched out in bed all my insides are relaxed. Also, I don't worry. . . . I figure that if I can't do my job standing up there's no sense in stretching out and worrying about it all night."

In 1929, a restless Rayburn had moved twice since his honeymoon apartment, first to the Hamilton Hotel and then to the Anchorage Apartments at Nineteenth and Q streets Northwest, just off Connecticut Avenue above Dupont Circle, which became his Washington home for the rest of his life. He started first with a two-room-and-bath walk-up apartment at the Anchorage, but when he became majority leader, the owner of the Anchorage wanted to keep his special tenant, and he ripped out the walls of the adjoining apartment, doubling the size. Once after the New Deal was under way, Raymond Moley visited him and was surprised at his modest place. Rayburn pointed out, "I had this room enlarged a little, and I took another room. My sister [Lou] comes up and stays with me sometimes in the winter."[1] The chief feature the apartment lacked was a kitchen, but the owner operated a restaurant across the street. After Rayburn climbed out of bed at 7 A.M., he phoned there, and a waiter carrying his breakfast soon knocked on his door.

He took pride that the formal suit he had brought to Washington in 1913 still fitted him. As a rule he dressed in black or dark blue tailor-made suits that he bought from a wholesale tailor in Baltimore. His thick shoulders and big chest ruled out ready-made suits, as did his demand for cuffless trousers. His narrow, black size 8½ shoes were always highly polished, and in his somber, immaculate attire, he looked like a capable undertaker. A poker-faced expression was normal for him, and someone once commented on the tragedy of wasting it on a man who did not play cards. Charles Halleck of Indiana, the assistant Republican leader in the House and later the leader, scoffed at those who advanced the theory that his expression was a facade. "His stern demeanor was no veneer to hide a shy and timid nature," said Halleck. [2]

If there was an aspect about himself that he found embarrassing it was his shiny bald head that Marquis Childs, one of his favorite newsmen, described as resembling "a well-polished ostrich egg." [3] When he was provoked, his poker-face stayed unchanged, but his head turned crimson. There was a saying on Capitol Hill: "When Speaker Sam's face gets red, beware; if the red spreads to his bald head, start running." At a convention a basket of pigeons was released in celebration, and one landed on his head, causing viewers to laugh at his plight. He disliked being photographed, for he was convinced editors had ordered cameramen to focus on his top. "That's enough, boys!" he would call to photographers just after they started clicking. A comment he used frequently was: "Did you snap it when I was licking my lips?" Still another tack was to complain about the waste of his time while the equipment was being set up.

No picture of himself ever pleased him. On one occasion he attended the unveiling of a Sam Rayburn portrait. After the windy praise of Rayburn, the string was pulled and the portrait uncovered. Rayburn stepped back and stared glumly at it. Then he muttered in a loud whisper to an aide, "My God, don't you think that's the worst picture you ever saw?" [4] When friends sent him glossy shots of himself to be autographed and returned, he tossed them in a wastebasket and replied, "If I permit a thing like that to be hung up in an office, it will frighten off some old maid who might want to propose!"

He was mollified slightly about his bald head one time when Edward Boyd, a magazine writer, wrote that he had overheard two newsboys in the Capitol discussing it. One asked the other if he knew why Rayburn was so bald and the second newsboy replied, "If you used your head as much as he does, you wouldn't have any hair either."

Only rarely did he view his baldness with humor. One afternoon, for instance, he left his high perch in the House and headed through the Speaker's lobby toward his office. Along the way he passed the hanging painting of Samuel J. Randall, a Democratic House Speaker during Republican President Ulysses S. Grant's second term. Randall had thick dark hair. Studying the portrait momentarily, Rayburn patted his own head in an exaggerated way and told the policeman on guard duty, "There is the second most handsome Speaker in the history of the House."

In the morning, following breakfast and the ritual of winding the gold pocket watch House Commerce Committee members gave him in 1932, he set off for the Capitol. Rayburn collected pocket watches and his sentimental favorite was the present his colleagues gave him when he served as Speaker of the Texas House in 1911. As Speaker of the U.S. House of Representatives he was supplied with a limousine and George Donovan, as chauffeur. However, he customarily walked half the three miles to the Capitol before climbing into the Cadillac that had been trailing him. Then once he arrived at the East Portico entrance on the House side of the Capitol, with his short, swift steps he completed two or three brisk turns around the racetrack walk that lay between the Capitol, Library of Congress and the Supreme Court. The Capitol grounds were rimmed with trees fairly representative of the different sections of the country. In 1949, he planted a white oak on the House area of the Capitol and frequently left his work to measure its changing girth and height like a proud father.

Even though he celebrated his sixtieth birthday on January 6, 1942, Rayburn continued to think of himself as young in body and spirit. "If there's anything I hate more than an old fogie it's a young fogie," he growled one time. In meeting with teenagers from Dallas, he remarked, "Glad to see young people my age." He would know, he said, when he had grown old. That would come "when some day I find myself sitting around with others bewailing the younger generation and talking about how much better we did things in our day. . . . The old complain of the conduct of the young when they themselves can no longer set a bad example." [5]

The principal exception to his early morning routine of going to the Capitol came on Mondays when he went to the White House for the weekly meetings between the congressional leaders and the President. And there were other mornings when Roosevelt asked him to stop by on urgent legislative business or to get his opinion of a forthcoming speech or "Fireside Chat," as FDR's intimate radio broadcasts were known. For instance, a note Roosevelt sent him on September 6, 1942, that read: "Can you come to my study in the White House Wednesday morning? Please keep this very confidential as I want Message and Speech contents to be wholly secret until Monday noon." [6]

Inside the Capitol, Rayburn had two offices, plus an after-hours "Board of Education" hideaway and a private dining room. When he came to work in the morning, he went first to his back office, a three-room suite that faced the Mall and was situated behind the Rotunda in the center of the 751-foot-long building. Rayburn occupied the middle room of the suite and by the time he hung up his Stetson, his secretary, Alla Clary, had been through the mail and was ready to discuss it as well as that day's schedule with him. Mail that could be answered in his name was divided among the stenographers, and the more personal and complex letters were set aside until Saturday to be answered by him directly. "The mail about World War I lasted until World War II," she said.

Miss Clary had started working for him in October 1919 when she was thirty, after having been a schoolteacher and government clerk, and she was with him a total of forty-two years. Lady Bird Johnson, reminiscing to reporters at a dedication of a portrait bust of Mr. Rayburn, cast a pall over the gathering when she said in Miss Clary's presence that "Miss Clary and Rayburn used to have raging battles." Alla Clary contradicted her. "Oh, he threatened to fire me a lot of times, but that didn't mean a thing. He was a wonderful boss, very kind and very considerate." [7]

About 10:30 A.M., Rayburn left his back office and went to the Speaker's formal office across the marble-floor hall from the House Chamber. In the large anteroom sat various aides, including Lewis Deschler, his old friend and House parliamentarian. Miss Clary was there, too, to handle phone calls and the steady stream of visitors, and she occupied the desk just outside the inner room of the two-room suite that was the Speaker's private office.

This was an ornate room with a huge gold mirror hanging over the mantel behind his desk. An immense crystal chandelier from Teddy Roosevelt's White House was suspended from the high ceiling, a red oriental rug lay over the marble-block floor and the furniture consisted of reddish overstuffed, buttoned leather chairs and sofas. On the mantel Rayburn kept pictures of his mother and father, and on the wall were three of Robert E. Lee, the patient, weary-eyed man of the Confederacy. A menacing-appearing black-knobbed shillelagh rested in a corner. This was a gift from Daniel A. Reed of New York, a Republican power on the Ways and Means Committee. Reed, who once lived in the same hotel with Rayburn and sat at his table there for dinner, sent a message with the shillelagh, suggesting that Rayburn use it "to bash Democratic heads."

Once he settled down in his high-backed red leather swivel chair, his day turned into a sea of faces and revealed his art of "pushing, prodding and guiding" the House relentlessly throughout long congressional sessions.

In essence, the Speaker's job boiled down to the business of listening and talking. Asked one time by *Life* reporter Robert Coughlan about the key to successful leadership, he said: "You really can't say how you lead. You feel your way, receptive to those rolling waves of sentiment. And if a man can't see and hear and feel, why then, of course he's lost."

Fortunately, brevity and directness were two of Rayburn's basic characteristics. Even when the President phoned him, he managed to conclude the call in three minutes or fewer. Sometimes in making phone calls, he did not bother to waste a moment to introduce himself. Once when a senator failed to show up for a scheduled meeting, the senator's secretary answered her ringing phone. "Tell him he's late," was all the testy voice said before her phone went dead. The caller was Rayburn. [8]

His big test was to handle and satisfy the swarms of visitors who were already in the anteroom of his formal office when he walked in each morning. But he had an immense ability to get people in and out in a few minutes without giving them the impression they had been shortchanged. He liked to talk to visitors while he rested a foot in a pulled-out desk drawer, and most callers were limited to the length of time it took him to smoke a Camel. On a hard day he smoked forty cigarettes. The bulk of his visitors were scheduled for specific times. But if he were told that a farmer without an appointment and a sweet-smelling banker with one were waiting in the anteroom, he invariably had the farmer sent in first.

It was no ordeal for him to talk to a steady stream of visitors because of his simplicity. He was always unaffected and never burdened by any need to act a role. As a reverse corollary, he was suspicious of those who tried to impress him, flatter him, or use complex reasoning. "If you have common sense, that's all the sense there is," he insisted. "But that's not enough. You have to use it." Another time he said, "It makes no difference how much sense you have if you don't have any judgment." [9]

When a person met Rayburn for the first time, he felt he was being examined by an X-ray machine. In a way he was, because Rayburn manner. Talk was not necessary. "Sam could tell fast if a man had no sense—common, book, or horse," said Wright Patman.

When he carried on a conversation with someone, he always looked directly into the other's eyes, and he was disappointed when that person did not reciprocate. On one occasion in discussing a presidential candidate, he said, "———— is a good fellow, and I like him. But he can't win because the folks won't believe him. I've watched him while we conversed and he has eyes that shift around. He couldn't look a farmer in the eye, and you can't get a farmer's confidence if you don't look at him. A farmer wouldn't believe a word he said, despite the fact that he's a pretty truthful fella."

House members made up the largest group of visitors. They usually came in to discuss their political problems and to seek advice. Sometimes their wives made appointments to see him, and more often than not these private talks were a recital of their husband's overdrinking, gambling, or affairs with other women. Rayburn was a sympathetic listener and, if asked, was ready to call in the errant husband.

Only longtime members called him "Sam" or "Mr. Sam" to his face. Others always addressed him as "Mr. Speaker," despite his informality and his willingness to listen to them. He jocularly offered an explanation for his reluctance to use his status and dominate conversations: "It's better to be silent and pretend dumb than to speak and remove all doubt."

When he spoke it was slowly and distinctly without a drawl, and he emphasized a point by widening the line between compressed lips and slapping his knee a half dozen times. He was always frank, never evasive. "I always tell the truth the first time and don't need a memory to remember that," he said. An offshoot of this truthfulness was his unwillingness to pay a compliment unless it was warranted. Some called this a lack of sophistication. Others, like sophisticated President Roosevelt, found it refreshing.

"Around him a lie never lives to be old," one of his employees said. [10] He even had contempt for those who told white lies. "There are no degrees in truthfulness," Rayburn insisted. "You are 100 percent, or you are not."

If he were irked with a visitor, his gruff voice gave him away. "I've never hated any man," he said, "although I've been temporarily provoked with several." But his rule was never to let House members leave him in an angry mood, "even if you have to jump up and stop them when they're going out the door."

In general he did not tell people off. "The day of pounding the desk and giving people hell is gone," he said. "A man's got to be led by persuasion and kindness and reason."

On occasion, however, he could be extremely blunt. One time he told a congressman who was getting a reputation for meanness: "You remind me of a man I know in North Carolina. He ate some cabbage one day and found that it made him disagreeable. So he ate cabbage every day from then on."

When he gave his word that he would do something for a member, his visitor knew he would carry it out. "Sam stays hitched," Cactus Jack Garner said matter-of-factly. In order to make certain he would not forget his promise, Rayburn would pull an old envelope from his right hip pocket and jot it down. In time the envelope would be completely filled with notations. The scribbling smudged, and the paper grew wrinkled. But the promises were kept.

Rayburn's open-door policy was especially accented for freshmen congressmen. He tried to make them welcome by throwing a special luncheon for them each session, and he attempted to make their path less thorny by giving them an orientation talk at the beginning of their legislative career.

In his lecture he spoke about his own first term in the House, the problems he encountered and the frustration of being at the bottom. He also gave advice on how to comport oneself to be a successful congressman. "When a new member comes in," he said, "he will find his colleagues pulling for him. They want him to make good. If he handles himself well in his first speech or in his committee duties, they are glad and tell him so. But if he falls down in his work or fails to pull his weight in committee or becomes self-important, that fact is noted. If he keeps on the same way, eventually the other members will have no more to do with him than they can help."

The importance of being liked by colleagues was given further emphasis. "You must please the people of your District," he said. "And if you want to be in a position which will enable you to help and please these people, you must also please your colleagues in the House. When you go home make yourself available to the people so that you will know their wishes and they will regard you as their servant and leader. But you must also command our respect."

Most new members found his lecture illuminating and invaluable. A few, however, found it condescending and stifling. Chester Bowles, for instance, coming to the House after serving in a cabinet-level post and as governor of Connecticut, expressed "shock" at Rayburn's orientation talk, which he said was really intended to convince new members to park their brains and blindly "back the leadership." [11]

One widely quoted Rayburn remark that would seem to bear him out was the Speaker's famous comment: "To get along, go along." But this was merely the opening words of his view regarding the reasons new members should cast their votes on legislation.

"I've never asked a man to cast a vote which would violate his conscience or wreck him politically," was his usual follow-up. "And on any piece of legislation if you're convinced in your heart that something is right, do it, go after it, fight for it, even if you find yourself in a minority of one."

At the same time, party regularity, he said, was important when these factors were not involved. "That doesn't imply that anybody has to become a rubber stamp, because when two minds always agree, one of them is doing all the thinking. But when there's an umpire in the game and a rule is made, I learned in baseball that it's a poor player who becomes angry, throws his bat at the umpire and quits the game like a spoiled child."

When Rayburn found a shy Democratic freshman, he went out of his way to make him at home in the House. Far-from-forward Dan Inouye from Hawaii, answered his phone one day and a man grunted: "Inn-oo-way or Inn-way or however you say it, this is Speaker Rayburn. I thought if you weren't too busy you might come around and see me."

The one-armed congressman hurried to Rayburn's office, where Rayburn first said he was welcoming him to Washington and then took him on a tour of the Capitol. As they walked through the House Chamber, galleries and lobby, Rayburn sketched the history of the institution. He also told him that the shoeshine boys in the House barbershop were not required to be tipped but that they should be. Then he took him back to his office. "If you're the right man, you'll do well," he said. "And if you're the wrong man, well, being scared won't keep you from being found out." He added, "We get along here by respecting the needs and integrity of every man in the place." Then for the first time, a gleam of a smile showed. "You know you're the best-known member after me," he told Inouye.

"But why?" Inouye asked, stunned.

"Why? Well how many one-armed Japanese do you think we have in the Congress of the United States?" [12]

When a new member asked for a private meeting, Rayburn was always blunt with his advice. Adam Clayton Powell, the controversial black member from Harlem, went to see Rayburn as a freshman. "Adam," Rayburn began firmly, "everybody thinks you're coming down here with a bomb in each hand. Maybe you are. But don't throw them. Feel your way around. You have a great future." [13] Powell reflected later: "All through the years he maintained his fatherly attitude."

When Powell eventually rose through seniority to top Democrat on the House Education and Labor Committee, several Southern Democrats objected to his becoming chairman because of his color, Miss Clary said. But Rayburn told them firmly, "No, he is going to be chairman. He has the ability, seniority and he is going to be chairman of that committee." [14]

Earlier, Rayburn had fought off racists who opposed seating black Congressman William L. Dawson of Illinois as chairman of the House Government Operations Committee. In that instance, Rayburn checked with the Cook County Democratic machine to make certain Dawson would not be overburdened with home district duties. Then he saw to it that Dawson became chairman.

There was one group of new members he always rode herd on, and these were the freshmen from Texas. "No ten gallon white hats and boots while in the House," he warned them. One member who ignored him and appeared on the House floor in cowboy regalia was motioned outside by Rayburn who delivered a stinging rebuke to him about giving Texas a loudmouth, loud-attire image.

On occasion Rayburn interceded with poorly-educated new members who had become quickly tangled in the congressional ropes. Sometimes he suggested a course of reading, as Champ Clark had once done with him. A few resented the advice. "I don't belong here," Rayburn said one member told him. "I don't know what's goin' on and never will. But you'll never get rid of me," he added defiantly, "because I'm just like my folks at home." Rayburn saw no reason to discuss the matter further with him.

As Speaker, Rayburn no longer served as chairman of the Commerce Committee. In fact, he had given up his committee assignment when he became majority leader in 1937 in order to devote all his time then to managing major bills that reached the floor. While he talked to morning callers in his ornate office, various House committees were investigating legislative proposals and holding hearings. Through committee and subcommittee chairmen, he had a direct pipeline on their activities and problems. In addition, this sort of intelligence system let him know which new members were working and which were loafing. If a member continued for long to be a dead loss, word would drift back to the local Democratic organization and chances were that he would not have party backing next time he ran.

He depended on committee chairmen to handle their committee members, but on occasion he was forced to abandon his aloofness. Late in 1940, for instance, a committee chairman told him that an administration bill had been defeated by two votes in his committee. The significance was that a bill with an unfavorable committee report was as handicapped when it reached the floor as a criminal whose past felonies were related to a jury.

"I'll move for reconsideration," the chairman said swiftly when he saw the smoldering look in Rayburn's eyes.

But Rayburn took charge himself. He talked privately to the members, and when another vote was taken it passed the committee this time by a margin of seven. [15]

Generally he refrained from interfering with a committee's consideration of a bill. But his prestige was so great, said Carl Albert of Oklahoma, that "committee chairmen wouldn't cross him if he went to them and said, 'I want this done.' " [16]

A casual word from him sometimes resulted in important changes in a bill. Congressman Wright Patman of Texas recalled an instance. Patman said he happened to be in Rayburn's office one day when "Bill Robinson of Utah, chairman of the House committee dealing with roads and highways, came in to ask Sam for permission for floor consideration of the Highway Bill." At once, Rayburn asked, "What have they got in there for country roads?"

"We don't have anything that's designated," Robinson told him.

With firm conviction in his voice, Rayburn said, "The bill should be returned to your committee. And have the committee agree to an amendment that will earmark 30 percent of the funds for farm-to-market roads."

"Robinson seemed to agree on the figure," Patman noted, and Rayburn told him, "We will then take it up and pass it."

The bill was changed according to Rayburn's offhand prescription and became law. Said Patman: "There was little rhetoric involved in this kind of leadership and less self-glorification." As for the national effect of Rayburn's simple but steely suggestion, Patman pointed out, "It changed the way of life for farmers. They no longer were stuck at home in the mud, and the conveniences of the cities could now be brought to the country over the all-weather, hard-surface roads." [17]

One thing was certain about his relationship with committee chairmen: They could expect curt, blunt talk from him if they allowed half-hammered, "undigested" bills to pass through their committees and reach the House floor. He insisted that controversial parts of a bill be threshed out in committee and a consensus reached among the differing committee factions so that the House would be spared the nightmarish task of rewriting it through endless amendments when it came to the Chamber.

It was only in extreme cases that he openly took on an entire committee in full public view. One such time occurred when a House select committee—feuding with the Federal Communications Commission, which it was investigating—let it be known that a majority of committee members favored an amendment to a bill that would abolish the FCC. Rayburn decided to intervene personally after the Democratic whip organization found that the House would support this killing of the FCC.

Cancelling his appointments one morning, he walked into the committee's hearing room and asked to be heard as a witness. When this failed to end the attack, he carried the fight to the House floor and spoke at a crucial point for the FCC:

> I think I have a right to speak on the amendment, because I happened to be the chairman of the committee that reported the

bill to set up the Communications Commission and was the author of the bill. Before that time there was chaos in communications throughout the length and breadth of the land.

The telegraph and telephone business had hardly been touched by the agency that was supposed to handle them—the Interstate Commerce Commission. The old Radio Commission was devoting a little time to broadcasting and to broadcasting only.

I do not appeal to your prejudice or to your passions, and I do not respect people of demagogy. But I do want to counsel with your reason. I repeat with all the earnestness I can command. There is only one agency in the United States of America, let me say to you, that has any control over the air of the United States. Do you, by your vote at this time, wish to strike down that only agency?" [18]

The amendment was defeated.

Rayburn's special friendship with two key congressmen assured him a great deal of control over legislation and the committee system. One was Gene Cox, ranking Democrat on the Rules Committee, and the other was Bob "Muley" Doughton, chairman of the Ways and Means Committee.

Cox, a fuming anti-New Dealer, owned the votes of the other four Southern Democratic members on the fourteen-man Rules Committee. With the four Republican members always willing to be helpful to his cause, he, instead of Chairman Adolph Sabath, bossed the committee. This was enough to give Roosevelt nightmares, since Rules determined what bills would reach the House Chamber after other committees had completed action on them and what the debating restrictions would be on the floor. This was the reason Roosevelt had tried to purge Cox in the 1938 Democratic primary in Georgia. But such an effort was unnecessary, for despite his strong personal opposition to releasing a bill for floor action, Cox usually gave in following a Rayburn plea. Yet the threat was always there that the next time he would not. So the ritual of the pleas, while generally successful, was unending.

Muley Doughton's committee handled not only tax and social-security legislation, but its Democratic members determined the House committees to which freshmen Democrats would be assigned. Doughton always deferred to Rayburn's suggestions on where to put the new crop and on committee transfers. It became a truism on Capitol Hill that you had to take an oath to uphold the 27½ percent depletion allowance tax break for the oil industry before you could be assigned to Ways and Means.

Other committee assignments resulted from Rayburn's assessment of a new member or as a reward for good work. Carl Albert—Phi Beta Kappa, Rhodes Scholar and lawyer—said, "Mr. Rayburn bought a lot of alfalfa from my District in Oklahoma that abutted his in Texas, so he put me on the Agriculture Committee." When Clinton Anderson of New Mexico came to the House, he was tucked away on the bottom-level Census Committee to languish after John Dempsey, his predecessor, went to every member of the Ways and Means Committee and denounced him. But the Census Committee soon had life-and-death control over the reapportioning of House seats by states according to the latest decennial census. A major argument developed whether to take one seat from Arkansas and give it to Michigan or let both states retain their old totals. Anderson turned out to be the swing member, and he decided on the status quo. This pleased Rayburn because all seven of Arkansas's House delegation were Democrats while the seventeen-member Michigan crew was overwhelmingly Republican. Afterward, he called in Anderson and asked, "Anderson, how did it happen you didn't get any committee assignments worth a hoot?" [19] A short time later he was reassigned to the powerful Appropriations Committee.

Beyond his indirect authority in the regular standing committees, Rayburn controlled about eight hundred appointments of House members each year. These involved membership on special House committees, joint House-Senate committees, and commissions and international conferences. Selection of Democrats to these lay in Rayburn's hands and gave him a weapon against blatant disloyalty to the party's programs.

The range of the Speaker's activities was even broader. He also had a host of administrative responsibilities. He was the boss of the two House office buildings, where each member had a two-room suite, the Capitol Police Force, the Capitol Bank with millions in assets, the stationery store, the page system, power plant, press gallery, and, of course, the House Chamber. Congressman Joe Martin, who later served four years as Speaker, noted that "no tree can be cut down on Capitol grounds without his consent." [20]

To outsiders Rayburn came across as a man moving casually from one unplanned activity to another, chiefly talking to congressmen, visitors and reporters. But there was nothing offhand about him, because he budgeted each day carefully and, for that matter, the entire session as well. He could generally gauge with remarkable accuracy long before-hand when the session would end. Ingenious reporters who wanted to find out about adjournment day before it was announced would ask the railroad clerk in the Capitol for a look at Rayburn's Pullman reservation for Texas. Rayburn's accuracy on this score was upset occasionally by the endless talkers in the Senate. Once when he was asked about the House's adjournment timing, he launched into a story of the "farmer back home who got tangled up with a bull that had a rope around his horns. A neighbor came by and asked, 'Where are you going?' and the farmer replied, 'Don't ask me. Ask the bull.' " In his own case, said Rayburn, the bull was the Senate. "Ask them."

One reason Rayburn worked so hard without getting tired was that he believed weariness was a state of mind. "If you say you're tired, you will be tired," he advised some congressmen. A more compelling reason was that he loved the House and believed in the essentiality of the work of the legislative branch. Riding with friends one evening alongside the Potomac, he looked up as the lighted dome of the Capitol hove into sight. "How do you like *my* Capitol?" he asked proudly. One January when he took his oath of office, he admitted to the House, "The House of Representatives has been my life and my love." [21]

Such pride was the opposite of the disdain one of his favorite Presidents, Woodrow Wilson, had for the legislature. "Congress is nothing more or less than a big meeting of idle people," Wilson wrote. "In proportion as you give it power, it will inquire into everything, settle everything, meddle in everything. Congress is a despot who has unlimited time, unlimited vanity; who has, or believes he has, unlimited comprehension." [22]

Every morning just before the House met at noon, Rayburn held a five-minute news conference in his formal office. The atmosphere was relaxed because he was a favorite of Capitol Hill reporters. When everyone was inside, he opened the question-and-answer session by leaning back in his red swivel chair and saying, "Shoot!"

Unless he gave permission, his remarks were off-the-record and frank. "You'll have to go elsewhere to get your quotes," he told frustrated newsmen one time when he gave them front-page material. But there were occasions when Roosevelt wanted him to make his remarks on a subject public as a trial balloon for a program he was contemplating.

Rayburn felt kinship with reporters, unlike photographers, whom he believed were in a conspiracy to make him look bad. The depth of his regard for them was revealed when the teen-age daughter of a newsman died. Early the following morning there was a rapping on the reporter's apartment door, and he gaped when he opened it because Rayburn was standing there.

"I just came by to see what I could do to help," he said.

The flustered grieving father replied, "I—I don't think there's anything you can do, Mr. Speaker. We're making all the arrangements."

"Well, have you all had your coffee this morning?" Rayburn asked.

"No, we haven't had time."

"Well," he replied quickly, "I can at least make the coffee this morning."

While he was working in the kitchen, the reporter came in and said, "Mr. Speaker, I thought you were supposed to be having breakfast at the White House this morning."

"Well, I was," said Rayburn. "But I called the President and told him I had a friend who was in trouble, and I couldn't come." [23]

At noon, Sam Rayburn was seated in his high-backed chair on the rostrum, gaveling the House to order. Normally he presented a dignified picture, his back straight and his face immobile. Unlike the Vice President who presided over the Senate like a declawed kitten because of his lack of authority, Rayburn was in charge of the House. When members stood up and asked to be recognized, Rayburn was within his rights to ignore them or choose any of them. In contrast, the Vice President had to give the floor to the first Senator rising.

Rayburn was asked once how he decided whom to recognize when nine or ten congressmen wanted to be recognized at the same time. "There are times when one of the men is on his feet to promote the legislative program," he explained. "The others are on their feet just asking for recognition to speak for a minute or five minutes. It's one of those things you have to be selective on." [24]

There was no question that he frequently used his power of recognition to keep opponents silent. One time, for instance, Rayburn offered an amendment to an unrelated bill that would provide funds to start a new House office building. Clare Hoffman, a Republican member from Michigan, jumped to his feet and yelled for recognition. Rayburn knew that Hoffman intended to make a point of order that his amendment had no connection with the bill and was therefore illegal. But Rayburn would not recognize him and the amendment carried along with the bill on the vote. This was the beginning of what later was called the Rayburn House Office Building. [25]

Another difference between the men on the rostrum in the House and Senate was that Rayburn could join in debate while the Vice President enjoyed no such privilege. Further, the Speaker could vote on every matter before the House; the Vice President, only to break a tie. The Speaker also spoke for the House in dealing with the President, a role the Vice President did not have in the Senate.

From his readings in American history and biography and from his own observations since 1913, Rayburn knew his office thoroughly and understood most of his predecessors, going back to a Lutheran minister named Frederick Muhlenberg, a Pennsylvanian elected Speaker in 1789. Muhlenberg adopted a role of suspicion towards the Presidency and believed that George Washington wanted to establish himself as a royal ruler.

One of Rayburn's favorites was Henry Clay, the longest serving Speaker, who became one the day he took the oath as a House member in 1811. Clay was known as "the Great Compromiser," a title various writers tried to pin on Rayburn. But the Texan considered this description in error. Henry Clay compromised on principles, while he never did, he pointed out. Instead, said Rayburn, his own role was to bring differing factions together to whittle away at their differences until they reached a positive agreement.

Another Rayburn favorite among his forty-three predecessors was Thomas B. Reed of Maine, who pounded the gavel in two Congresses during the 1890s. It was Reed who made a remark that Rayburn thought accurately described the Speaker's status: "The Speaker has but one superior and no peers." Reed made himself dictator of the House by appointing himself to the Rules Committee to control the House's business and by assuming sole power to name or remove members from committees. Reed's trenchant wit was renowned. When a member quoted the famous Henry Clay remark, "I'd rather be right than President," Reed said dryly, "Well, the gentleman will never be neither." In replying to two talkative colleagues, he said, "They never open their mouths without subtracting from the sum of human knowledge." [26]

Although, of course, the "Revolution of 1910" in the House removed Speaker Joseph Cannon from the Rules Committee and ended his stranglehold on committee membership, Rayburn held a high regard for "Uncle Joe," whom he had known personally. Rayburn had none of the institutional powers Reed and Cannon had enjoyed to the hilt, but through his character, strong personality, and friendship with committee leaders he was able to do substantially what they had done.

Carl Albert once observed, "Sam Rayburn ran a very neat House. He was very particular about time and recognition, and he was a very strict parliamentarian." [27] Rayburn kept a sheet of paper with the list of legislative items scheduled for the day on top of his white marble desk, and he seldom left before crossing through every line.

The day started with the chaplain's short prayer, and generally before the Lower Chamber got down to serious business, Sam permitted members to address the House for one minute on any subject and add to their remarks before they appeared in the *Congressional Record*. This was done so that House members could frank the speeches back in their districts. "A politician has to have publicity to live," Rayburn once explained his generosity. But on occasion when his kindness was abused he reacted like an angry school principal. "It costs $85 a page to print the *Congressional Record*," he said coldly one day, cutting off what appeared to be an endless number of tributes to various citizens. "The bill mounts up if we continue to congratulate everybody in the United States."

He was free with his advice on how to be more effective in the House Chamber. A new member, who had been a judge, asked him if he thought he was talking too much.

"Yes," Rayburn grunted.

"What should I do about it?" the man asked.

"Quit it!" Rayburn advised him bluntly.

"I have sat in the Speaker's chair and watched many a Congressman talk himself out of Congress," he told a reporter. [28]

He told Lyndon Johnson who was ineffective in debate, "Slow down when you talk. Why, you talk so fast your voice comes out high-pitched like a choir boy." He advised another member who lost control of himself easily, "Whenever you're mad and ready to say something—wait a minute." Carl Albert was told not to be aimless but to have his own legislative program. "I personally know men," he said, shaking his head slowly, "who have been in Congress a long, long time and there is nothing they can point to that they have accomplished—simply because they never had a program of any kind that was constructive." Still another member was advised, "Try to get all the facts on both sides of a question. Study these facts thoroughly, then make your decision. And stick with it. People lose confidence in a person who is forever making snap judgments and then switching back and forth." [29]

As for his own formula for running the House, Rayburn told Bob Albright of the *Washington Post*, "I ride the horse." One important rule he followed was: "Be reasonable, be fair." He continually cautioned members about bills they planned to introduce. "Legislation should not be designed to punish anyone. It must be fair," he said. "Let's reform without punishing; let's cure without crushing."

He also got after members to raise the standard of floor debate. "Use one-syllable words. Avoid multi-syllable and tongue-twisting words. Remember that the steam that blows the whistle will never turn a wheel." [30] Once after listening to a poor discussion, he declared, "The lowing of my Herefords is the sweetest music I know."

Those who engaged incessantly in lost causes made him scowl. Using

Garner's remark to him several years earlier, Rayburn said that a congressman was not a pro unless "his head had been damn-well bloodied a few times." But Rayburn added that "a man may as well quit if his head is bloodied too often."

He had unusual respect for anyone who mastered most of the House rules and precedents, which he estimated numbered twenty thousand. Eyes of reporters popped when they asked him for his list of outstanding House members and he included slight, frail, sallow Vito Marcantonio of New York, who called himself a Republican but followed a pro-Communist party line. Rayburn's reason was that few members equalled Marcantonio in befuddling opponents through his knowledge of the rules.

The sound of Rayburn's gavel indicated his mood. Oldtimers considered him a "whacker," compared with his predecessors. A heavy thud meant anger; repeated hollow rappings, weary impatience; an echoing blast, finality. His gavels, which came to him chiefly as presents, were almost all well constructed. "I broke the gavel once," Rayburn admitted. "A fella kept talking after his time ran out. Wouldn't sit down. Kinda wish I'd hit him over the head."

In time his collection came to more than one hundred, but occasionally he gave one to an admirer. This was unlike Garner's attitude that each of his gavels was roughly equal in value to the Hope diamond. Once a young congressional employee borrowed a battered old pine gavel from Garner to use while he served as "Speaker" at a mock Congress on Capitol Hill. Some time later the forgetful borrower received a threatening note from Mrs. Garner that read: "Please return or remit." [31]

If he chose, Rayburn could regulate floor activity without relying on his gavel. "Sam Rayburn used to be able to glare people down," said Thomas P. "Tip" O'Neall of Massachusetts.

Or he might "circulate." For instance, when a bill providing for a cooling-off period to stave off labor strikes came to the House floor, Rayburn wanted it debated fully. Experience and instinct told him that with feelings running high an attempt might be made to shut off debate and go directly to a vote. This proved correct when Jennings Randolph of West Virginia, a member of the Labor Committee, won recognition and started to make a motion to do this.

While he was still talking, Rayburn walked down from the dais and headed toward him. With each approaching step Randolph's voice grew weaker. Finally he stopped talking when Rayburn reached him and put a hand on his shoulder. For a short time, with his face set sternly, Rayburn spoke in a low, gruff tone to Randolph, whom he liked. Then still talking, he removed his hand, plunged it into his jacket pocket, and his body rocked back and forth from his heels to his toes. Then he turned suddenly and walked back to the rostrum.

Laughter swept the Chamber as embarrassment crossed Randolph's face. When silence came, Randolph announced he was withdrawing his motion, and he added, "As a legislative son I am always willing to follow the advice of my legislative elders." [32]

When appropriations bills were on deck, especially the pork-barrel rivers and harbors bills that Appropriations Commiteee Chairman Clarence Cannon of Missouri handled, Rayburn made sure he was present to keep the aging bantamweight from throwing punches at those who disagreed with him. He had known Cannon since the Wilson administration when the Missourian had been the parliamentarian of the House under Speaker Champ Clark. The big-nosed little man was the author of *Cannon's Procedure in the House*, a compilation and cross-reference of House rules and precedents. At the outset of the Republican era that followed Wilson, Rayburn successfully lobbied to put an item into the legislative appropriation to retain Cannon on the congressional payroll as an $1,800-a-year messenger. Cannon won election to the House in 1923 and then through the seniority system and his own pugnaciousness he became the fighting chairman of the Appropriations Committee.

Cannon's favorite punching bag was John Phillips, a mild little man from California but the leading Republican opponent of the fat pork-barrel legislation in Cannon's committee. At the slightest provocation, Cannon would rush to Phillips and punch him in the face. [33] "Sam Rayburn always said, 'We've got to get the hell out of here,' just when I got in fights over appropriations," Cannon noted fondly.

There were several members who stopped short of Cannon's physical attacks but enjoyed exchanging insults on the floor. On occasion, when a man was the chagrined loser in the heated exchange he would try for revenge by offering a motion to have the other congressman's words stricken from the *Record*. If this motion carried, the person penalized was also barred from debate during the rest of the day. If a Democrat made this type of motion against another Democrat, Rayburn would come down the stairs from his perch for a conference with him. Almost invariably the motion would be withdrawn and peace temporarily restored.

He disliked various types of congressmen. "Damn the man who is always looking for credit!" he said. "I've always noticed that if a man does his job, and does it well, he will get more credit than he is entitled to." The conceited type was also a pain. To Rayburn this was a dead giveaway that he was not big enough for his job.

Rayburn also had little use for "a man whose change of position changes his position." He was thinking primarily of what happened to congressmen who got on the House Un-American Activities Committee. Back in 1934 he had been helpful to John McCormack in winning House approval for a Special Committee on Un-American Activities. Its original purpose was to investigate the growing Nazi propaganda mill in the United States.

Although McCormack was the committee chairman, he was so busy that he turned operations over to his vice-chairman, Sam Dickstein of New York. Before long, many prominent Jews told White House aides that with Dickstein, a Jew, running the committee, this gave the Nazis ammunition for attacking it. So pressure developed to replace Dickstein with a non-Jew. Martin Dies, Jr., a tall, heavyset man, had come to Congress in 1931 at the age of thirty from the eleven-county Pine Belt District in east Texas. As a protégé of John Garner, he had early won a seat on the Rules Committee, where he had the reputation of a Roosevelt supporter. When the question of revamping the Un-American Activities Committee came up, Garner talked him up to Bankhead and Rayburn, and he became chairman of a new special committee. [34]

To Rayburn's shock, Dies quickly erupted as "a man whose change of position changes his position." Within a short time, Dies was concentrating the committee's activities on putting a Red label on various New Deal officials, union leaders and members of liberal organizations. By 1939, Dies had grown so wild in his charges that Roosevelt asked Rayburn and Bankhead to explain to him that he was damaging the Democratic party. But Dies would not give up the headlines and the public attention he was receiving for his slanders and libels, and Rayburn ended relations with him. [35]

After that, Rayburn tried to abolish the committee. Failing at this, he filled committee vacancies with fair-minded liberals. But in almost all cases, his choices became as rabid Red witch-hunters as Dies, and as embarrassing. One time when the committee was investigating the WPA Federal Theater Project, a witness mentioned Marlowe's *Faustus,* and a committee member asked, "Marlowe? Is he a Communist?"

Every year at appropriation time, said a Rayburn friend, "Dies would strut in to the well of the House, intone the names of government officials, call them Reds and a wrangle of several days duration developed." Rayburn would be angry throughout, and he would consider himself a success if he was able to pare the committee's budget.

At one point, Rayburn thought he had a solution when he put Congressman Francis Walter of Pennsylvania on the committee. For years Walter had called for its abolition, and scuttlebutt had it that Rayburn was grooming him for his successor as Speaker. But liberal Francis Walter was soon out-Diesing Dies. Further, he wanted to enlarge the committee's scope to control legislation dealing with immigration and the issuance of passports. "We're not going to do that," Rayburn told him bluntly, putting him outside the pale with Dies.

One of Rayburn's cardinal principles was that the Speaker had to establish a good working relationship with the minority party leaders in order to get any business done. "It's a wise man who realizes that the church is bigger than its pastor," was the way he put it. Just as John Garner had set the example by establishing personal arm-in-arm relationships with Republicans Nick Longworth and Bert Snell, so Rayburn enjoyed a warm friendship with little Joe Martin, the black-smith's son from Massachusetts, who succeeded Snell as minority leader in 1939.

"Sam and Joe," members referred to them. One time when Massachusetts Democrats asked Rayburn to come to their state to campaign against Martin, he replied savagely, "Well, if I lived there I would work for him."

At the same time he knew that Joe was working closely with bushy-haired Gene Cox and pompous Clif Woodrum of Virginia to effect a coalition of conservative Republicans and Southern Democrats to fight Roosevelt legislation. According to Jerry Voorhis, whom Rayburn put on various committees because of his liberal views, one third of the House Democrats were conservative, and almost all Republicans were.[36] In the Seventy-sixth Congress of 1939-41, for instance, Rayburn's score sheet showed 268 Democrats to Martin's 162 Republicans. But when the coalition held, Martin actually owned a majority. This increased Rayburn's task enormously, yet he was always kind to Joe personally. As Martin acknowledged, Rayburn protected him from attacks by his own party members who wanted to replace him by giving the Republicans "a good deal more patronage, such as jobs around the Capitol, then we, as the minority party, ever would have got otherwise."[37]

Nevertheless, Rayburn's friendship with Joe Martin did not soften his animosity toward the Republican party in general. He remained convinced that Republicans were "bigger haters" than Democrats. "We don't hate their Presidents the way they do ours," he insisted. George Dixon, a talented syndicated columnist on political humor, reported one time that Martin invited Rayburn to view the life-size portrait of himself that hung in the Capitol Hill Club, a private drinking spa for Republican congressmen, party fund contributors and lobbyists.

Rayburn entered the building like a true believer attending an atheist rally. A short while later he pushed legislation through Congress to have the government buy two square blocks on Capitol Hill for new public buildings. The Capitol Hill Club, which was on this land, would have to be demolished, he said with satisfaction.

Rayburn had the ability to change with the times, and in some respects he was ahead of the day. On January 27, 1939, for instance, he gave a speech over television, even though the industry did not come into commercial operation until after World War II. As for the House, when he first took his oath in 1913, the Chamber was unventilated, the lighting abysmal, the acoustics wretched, and engineers agreed that it was only a matter of time before the old roof fell in.

Rayburn was willing to bring in air-conditioning, improve the lighting and acoustical systems, get rid of the brass cuspidors, build a new concrete and steel roof, and replace the narrow, hard benches with roomier ones that had soft cushions. But when it came to the House's rules and method of operating, he was strictly old-fashioned.

He thought the established seniority system was superior to the various alternatives the reformers offered that discounted longevity on committees as the basis for selecting committee and subcommittee chairmen. He also considered voting machines for instant recording of members' stand on a bill a curse that would deprive the leadership of the opportunity to roam about the floor and lobby with members to vote their way or change their vote after the roll call. Reformers constantly talked of "streamlining Congress" by doing these things, and cutting the number of committees, adding hordes of professional assistants and "modernizing the creaking machinery."[38] However, Rayburn remained convinced that broad and detailed reforms would not only weaken the leadership but would take the heart out of the House's tradition of being close to the grass roots. When many of the standard reforms were placed in the original version of the LaFollette-Monroney Bill in 1946, he saw to it that most were removed before he allowed the House to vote on it. Newspapers hailed it as a "legislative miracle," but the fine print revealed that its chief changes brought a pension and raise for members of Congress and an increase in their staffs.

"In the Congressional forum, all is not pure reason," said Rayburn. "There are obdurate, selfish interests, stubborn prejudices and passionate fears. But reason has a way of ultimately triumphing over unreason in the open forum of public opinion."[39]

Early in the afternoon when things appeared under control, Rayburn would have a substitute occupy his chair temporarily, and he would go downstairs to the first floor for lunch. He had his own private dining room and friends and admirers sent him a variety of foodstuffs. Once when he casually mentioned to reporters that he wished he had a Bermuda onion, sacks totalling twenty thousand pounds flooded his offices a few days later. He gave almost all of them away. As a rule, his chauffeur, George Donovan, was under Rayburn's instructions to parcel out excess food to his poor friends. Besides onions, Rayburn's favorite foods were fire-hot chili, fried chicken, turkey, turnip greens, coconut cake and watermelon.

There were parts of afternoons when the House converted itself into the committee of the whole for general debate on a bill and the offering of amendments. Since the Speaker was barred from presiding in the committee of the whole, Rayburn used some of this time to hold strategy meetings in his formal office with the majority leader, Democratic whip and committee chairmen. Joe Martin and a few top Republican leaders also came for private sessions with Rayburn to be kept abreast of the legislative schedule and to search for common ground on bills in order to avoid needless floor clashes.

Whenever the committee of the whole reported back to the House, Rayburn took the chair for the big push of getting administration bills passed. He seldom left the dais to take part in floor debate. Perhaps he did at most a dozen times a year. But when he spoke it was to deliver a "back to the wall" plea because the fate of a "must" bill lay in jeopardy, and he had already done all the behind-the-scenes lobbying he could.

As soon as he reached the well of the House and stood behind the microphone an immediate shout of excitement rang out "Sam's Up!" The members' benches and the gallery seats quickly filled, and a hush fell over the Chamber. While this was happening, he surveyed the hall, looking slowly from one section to the next. When he finally spoke, said Paul Healy of the *New York Daily News*, it was "in a low, conversational tone, in shorthand sentences and in stripped-down vocabulary." His "Sam's Up!" speeches rarely went beyond five minutes, but their impact was generally decisive.

A few months before Pearl Harbor, for example, Roosevelt proposed a bill to arm American merchant ships on the high seas, because Nazi U-boats were firing at and sinking some despite the nation's neutral status as a nonbelligerent in the European war. As Roosevelt revealed to his congressional leaders, an intercepted order from Hitler to his submarine commanders told them to fire on sight against American vessels.

Rayburn's count after the first day of serious debating revealed that with the Democrats divided on the bill and the Republicans set against it, the measure would fail by twenty votes. Because of this he asked Roosevelt to send a special message to the House and told him what his letter should contain.

Fifteen minutes before the debate ended on the last day, Roosevelt's letter came and it was read to the House. "Failure to arm merchant ships," Roosevelt wrote, "would discourage the Allies, cause rejoicing in the Axis countries and bring before the world a picture of disunity in the United States."

When Democratic Whip Pat Boland's final count still showed a losing cause, Rayburn stood in the well before the dais to add his own last-minute "Sam's Up!" warning to the House. "Let me appeal to you," he said simply to the quiet gathering, "whether you love one man or hate another, to stand up today for civilization as it is typified by the United States of America."

The bill passed by 212 to 194, with 190 of the 267 Democrats and 22 of the 162 Republicans supporting it.

In late afternoon when the House adjourned for the day, Rayburn walked down the marble staircase to his first floor hideaway, popularly known as the "Board of Education," the same title Garner had used. Rayburn disliked the name, referring to it as "the room downstairs," but when the name persisted he said, "I guess some fellahs have been educated down there."

The Board of Education was housed in a large room on the south edge of the Capitol that looked out across the avenue at the two House office buildings. It was furnished with overstuffed, leather buttoned chairs, a sofa, frayed rug, fireplace, oil paintings of Rayburn and former Senator Morris Sheppard of Texas—the real father of the Prohibition Amendment —a desk at which Rayburn presided and a refrigerator holding ample liquid refreshments needed to "strike a blow for liberty."

Here the talk centered on politics, though gossip was also exchanged and profane stories told. Rayburn tried to enforce two rules in his Board: (1) Everything was off the record; and (2) the jokes "must not reflect on womanhood." [40] Wayne Aspinall, a Democratic member from Colorado, reported that "Mr. Sam's favorites were the shaggy-dog types of stories."

Views of the Board by participants differed. Said Carl Albert: "Sam Rayburn used it as a sounding board to find out what others were thinking and to learn what was going on." [41] Clinton Anderson saw it this way: "There was a lot of laughter and fooling around. We rarely discussed business." He said that he and Gene Cox played bridge, and sometimes they and others played poker games for good stakes. "Rayburn never played cards," he recalled. "After two or three drinks or more, we'd often go downtown to a Chinese restaurant to eat. Rayburn loved to eat Chinese food. But whatever we did, he was acknowledged to be the boss, to whom we all deferred." [42]

There were regulars of the Board, plus specially invited guests, such as

195

Cabinet members and Supreme Court justices like Bill Douglas and Hugo Black. Dean Acheson, who attended from time to time, mistakenly claimed the hideaway was in the basement of the Capitol.[43] When a relatively new congressman received an invitation from Rayburn, it was considered by his envious friends as a sign of rising prestige.

Among those invited with increasing frequency was Senator Harry S. Truman of Missouri, a grinning, wisecracking man with thick eyeglasses who liked to talk to Rayburn about farming, history and the menace of Wall Street. After two terms as presiding judge of the Jackson County Court (actually county commissioner), his minor political career was seemingly over in 1934 when he was fifty. But his political boss, Tom Pendergast of Kansas City, used machine-gun toting gangsters to win the city election in March, in which four persons were killed. After three well-known politicians refused Pendergast's offer of support as his candidate in the U.S. Senate Democratic primary, he gave it to Truman as a last resort. Investigation revealed that Truman won with as many as seventy five thousand fake votes.

As a result, Truman, as the puppet of a notorious boss, had come to the Senate under a cloud. But Vice-President Garner befriended him and made him a member in good standing of his after-hours club. In this way he met Sam Rayburn, and their association deepened because Truman was on the Senate Commerce Committee that was the counterpart of Rayburn's committee in the House. In 1938, Rayburn helped him push through his first legislation, passage of the Civil Aeronautics Act, even though this removed control over flying from Rayburn's beloved ICC.

Rayburn also began inviting him to his own hideaway and arranged to have him made a member of the fairly exclusive Chowder, Marching and Baseball Club, which got together for lunch and attendance at the Washington Senators' games when Congress was not in session. Truman remained in awe of Rayburn, especially because he saw and spoke frequently to Roosevelt. On his part, Truman could not bring himself to phone Roosevelt directly or make an appointment to see him when it was necessary. Instead, he would phone Steve Early, the White House press secretary, and ask him to handle the matter.[44] On the other side of the coin, Roosevelt had contempt for him as a continuing member of the Pendergast organization and in 1940 supported his opponent in the Democratic primary. Roosevelt went so far as to offer Truman a seat on the ICC if he dropped out of the race.

A few congressmen enjoyed special honors in Rayburn's Board of Education. Said Wright Patman: "Sam let it be known that only two House members had keys and didn't have to gain admittance. I had one key; Lyndon Johnson had the other."[45]

Johnson's relations with Sam Rayburn, his adopted "Daddy," had survived Roosevelt's crude use of him to embarrass his legislative chief. In 1940, for instance, shortly after Rayburn became Speaker, Johnson pestered him to induce Roosevelt to let him manage the committee that raised and parceled out funds to Democratic congressmen running for reelection. Then after the election, Johnson tried to have himself included in the congressional leadership group that met regularly with the President. Failing in this, he talked Rayburn into urging him on Roosevelt as acting secretary of the Democratic National Committee. In 1941, when Johnson ran a losing race for the Senate after the death of Senator Sheppard, Rayburn contributed to his campaign, phoned Texas friends to do their bit for Lyndon and sent a message for publication in home-state papers that he intended to cast his absentee ballot for Johnson. Wearied one time by Johnson's unending pressure and self-pity, Rayburn told him: "I've just received a cheerful letter from a fella whose problems remind me of yours. He said that one of his bald-faced heifers had broken her back and died; some hunters had set fire to his oatfield stubble; a tornado had blown down his windmill; some storms had killed all his chickens; the rain soaked his oats so they couldn't be stored. And he ended his letter with 'Hoping you are the same, I am, truly yours.' "

Sometimes Johnson included Roosevelt and Rayburn in his schemes to gain publicity. "I remember once he had an idea that Roosevelt should give a surprise party for Sam Rayburn," said Tom Corcoran. The idea was to hold a January 6 birthday party for Mr. Sam in the Oval Office. "The President went for it," said Corcoran, "and Lyndon arranged it, brought Rayburn down to the White House on some pretext and all the Texas delegates went with him. He even bought a big Texas hat for the President to give him. I couldn't figure out why he was doing all this. Then the papers came out the next day and there was Lyndon, standing right between the President of the United States and Rayburn. That was the first time I really knew that an operator was loose."

No doubt the reason Rayburn was willing to put himself out for Johnson was his psychological need to have a son and a family. Once when Johnson told Rayburn that his wife was expecting a child, Rayburn burst with grandfatherly pride. "When is Lady Bird expecting?" he asked excitedly.

"Oh, about six months from now," Johnson replied.

Concern broke out on Rayburn's normally unrevealing face. "What about Lady Bird?" he demanded. "Is she all right?" And before Johnson could answer, he went on insistently, "Go call her this minute and see how she's feeling."[46]

Rayburn took little notice of the Washington social whirl. Cocktail parties bored him and dinner parties were dull. "One reason I don't go to these society dinners is that they don't serve chili," he once quipped. Sometimes after his Board of Education finished its session, suggestions were made to go to nearby cocktail lounges. But Rayburn always refused. "It's not that I have any prejudice," he told Pete Brandt of the *St. Louis Post-Dispatch.* "It's just because I don't think a public official should be seen in such places." He said he had seen some generals at a cocktail party and "I wondered then why they weren't using the time to fight the war. Some people might have some such idea if they saw me in a cocktail lounge."

With a warning that he had to be back at his Anchorage apartment by 10 P.M., Rayburn on occasion went for dinner to the homes of friends. He insisted on helping with the meal and ended up preparing the steaks and hot chili. More frequently he had a few politician guests come to his apartment. "Sam would send out to Pierre's on Q Street for dinners," said Congressman George Smathers of Florida, "and he'd also order a special plate of raw onions for himself."[47] When the food came, he sat at the table on a little bench he had used as a child on the farm. If he went out for dinner it was generally to Martin's on Wisconsin Avenue, and he chose a booth near the kitchen door because he said the service was best there.

There were certain formal dinners Rayburn could not avoid, and one was the annual affair for the Speaker the President put on with a smashing array of top-drawer Washington figures. At other White House parties Rayburn showed a tendency to be the first to leave. One spring Roosevelt asked him to bring the entire crew of freshmen members to a party so he could meet and talk to each separately. The evening was still young when Rayburn rounded up the congressmen and announced they were leaving. "Father Sam," Roosevelt protested, "you want to send the boys to bed too early."[48]

His subconscious dislike for parties in his honor proved almost disastrous one time to his reputation for owning an infallible memory. He and Frank McNaughton, who covered the Capitol for *Time* Magazine, enjoyed a leisurely dinner at a Maine Avenue dockside seafood restaurant, and drove afterward to Rayburn's apartment. Instead of taking the usual route up Connecticut Avenue, they went on Sixteenth Street. A crowd in formal clothes was entering the Carleton Hotel, and McNaughton wondered aloud what party might be going on. "Hey!" Rayburn bellowed. "That party's for me"[49]

After a wild ride home, he rushed into his apartment, scrambled into his tuxedo, and raced back in time to take his place as the guest of honor.

On many evenings Rayburn returned to his formal office from Board of Education sessions and worked at his desk until eight or nine o'clock. He also came to the Capitol on Saturdays to put in a full day answering the large load of mail that required his personal attention. Alla Clary had accumulated such letters during the week for this one-day burst.

Rayburn handled this chore in his first-floor hideaway, and his method was to dictate replies rapidly to three stenographers, all of whom took down each reply. Later they divided the letters into three piles, and if one of the stenographers had unclear notes, she could check the steno pads of the others. In this way, Rayburn never had to be interrupted to repeat something while he dictated. [50]

As a rule Rayburn's replies to letters were brief and frank. He gave far more attention to handwritten, pencilled letters than to typed letters on excellent paper from corporation executives. "When someone writes me on tablet paper with a lead pencil I figure what he's writing me about is pretty important to him," he said.

Rude letters were seldom answered in kind. The usual technique was to thank the writer for his "views on matters of public interest." But there were exceptions. Once when a constituent sent him a wire demanding that he take certain action and asserting that he was not doing his job, Rayburn's low boiling point surfaced. "I have received your insulting telegram," he replied. "I think I am perfectly capable of tending to my business and if you would tend to yours, I think it would take most of your free time. The matter has already been taken care of." [51]

So his work week went, a hard, long period that needed his best effort without any letdown. However, it was worthwhile to him not only for the power he enjoyed but because of his belief in a national purpose, which required a well-directed House. It was the Speaker who could take the spark and build a fire and force the proper solution. "Quite without side, without bombast, without pretension," said Marquis Childs, "he works hard in session and out, making the machine go. It is a troublesome, thankless job which somehow Rayburn seems to like."

18

The Speaker's Other World

The private side of Sam Rayburn emerged on Sundays and when he went home between congressional sessions. On Sunday Rayburn awakened an unhappy man away from the noise and excitement of the Capitol. "God help the lonely, for loneliness consumes people," he said lugubriously at the prospect of a day of quiet. For a few years in the 1930s he rushed from his apartment to a golf course just after daybreak on Sundays and sprinted around the holes, whacking balls. But there was no pleasure in remaining a duffer, and he gave his clubs away. So he settled down to a routine of phoning his assistants, begging them more or less to come for a shirred eggs breakfast and to read all the Sunday papers to which he subscribed. By midafternoon when the silence was again stifling he was on the phone once more, this time rounding up members of the Texas congressional delegation to have dinner with him.

Sunday also became a day for fishing. If he could not get anyone else to join him, he donned old clothes, and his chauffeur drove him to his favorite fishing haunts in Maryland and Virginia. But if he could arrange a fishing party, they would leave on Saturday night and sleep in cabins near the lake. Those who went along for the first time were stunned by the change in Rayburn's personality. Solemn, laconic and brief in the Capitol, on the road he was talkative, humorous and a great tease. Then at daybreak on Sunday he would pound and kick the doors of the other cabins, yelling in response to sleepy grunts, "Everybody up! It's late!"

In order to give the fish a sporting chance, he filed the barbs off his lures and hooks. And out on the water, said his assistant H. G. Dulaney, he did not follow the fisherman's basic rule of keeping silent. Instead, he talked softly and loudly to the fish, alternately begging and threatening them if they did not bite. If he caught none, he would exclaim to the air, "They got a message that Sam Rayburn was coming, and they went into hiding."

His least favorite fishing companion was Lyndon Johnson, who talked politics throughout the trip. Harry Truman presented a danger because he could not sit still for long. One time Rayburn, Truman and a few other men went fishing in an extremely cold-water river in eastern Maryland. Truman stood up in the small boat despite the choppy water, and before Rayburn could order him down he fell overboard. After a frightening effort his companions finally hauled him back on the boat, and he wrapped himself in blankets. "You just go on catching the fish, Sam," he called pathetically to Rayburn, "and I'll do the swimming." [1]

Rayburn also liked to hunt, and he and Truman accepted an invitation to do some shooting with Senator Joe Guffey on his Pennsylvania game preserve. Guffey's chauffeur drove the three by limousine to a clearing, and other workers beat on bushes to force frightened deer within gun range of the car. But the hunt was a fiasco because neither Rayburn nor Truman would fire his gun. [2]

There was only one place he headed for after Congress adjourned. "When I get away from Washington," he told Bascom Timmons, an old reporter friend, "I don't want to go anywhere in the world but home." As Speaker he could have traveled anywhere on the globe on the taxpayer's tab. But he had no desire to cross either ocean or run up a fraudulent bill. "I never considered that a few days abroad would enable me to speak with any authority on foreign affairs," he said, in a veiled attack on other members of Congress who did this.

Rayburn continued to ride the leisurely train back to Texas until the late 1940s. "Takes two nights and a day to get home that way, and the best rest I ever get is during that time. I spend most of it reading a Wild West magazine," he said. [3] This was a decided change in his reading from earlier trips when he read biographies and history books.

His fear of airplanes was the result of a harrowing ride in 1935, the only time he had been airborne. "But you've no idea how air travel has improved since then," a friend argued with him. "Why, if you took a trip to Texas by plane now, you'd never go any other way."

"That is exactly what I'm afraid of," Rayburn replied, walking away.

On trips home, Rayburn sometimes made short side excursions to favorite places. The call of his birthplace area in Tennessee was still strong. So was the urge to visit Stratford Hall, Virginia, the gracious plantation where his hero, Robert E. Lee, was born in 1807.

Stratford had originally been patented by Charles II to Nathaniel Pope, a great-great-grandfather of George Washington, in 1656, and lay a few miles below Washington's birthplace at Wakefield on the Potomac. When Rayburn first saw the large Elizabethan-Jacobean house at Stratford in the late 1920s, it was in shocking disrepair. A group of women led by Mrs. Harry Hawes, wife of a Missouri senator, organized the Robert E. Lee Memorial Foundation in 1929 to buy the plantation from its current owner and restore it to its eighteenth-century splendor. Mrs. Hawes, who had heard Rayburn talk about Lee, asked him to be a fund raiser, and he appealed to the Confederate pride of several Texas millionaires for the necessary money. The estate was purchased in 1932, and restoration began, with Rayburn visiting the site from time to time to check on progress.

It turned out to be a costly effort to restore the massive brick house built in an H-plan with four turrets and spacious rooms. Outside the house, the wharf, mill, spring house and formal gardens also needed extensive work. Rayburn personally contributed the breeding stock for the herd of white-faced Herefords at Stratford, as well as a large flock of black-nosed Hampshire sheep. Unfortunately, some wild dogs chased the sheep through the grove of beech trees on the high cliffs along the Potomac, and the sheep fell to their death.

There were still no decent train stops at Bonham thanks to the decision of its citizens decades earlier to keep the railroad traffic out. Only a spur line of the Texas and Pacific reached the town, and connections were terrible. So Rayburn got off the Katy's Blue Bonnet at Denison for the twenty-three-mile ride home by car with members of his family. The Denison end of the trip gave him the opportunity to talk to Colonel Lucius Clay to see how things were going on the Denison Dam project, which he had sponsored in 1937. After years of study, he had thought this was a badly needed program for flood control, irrigation, hydroelectric power and navigation in the Red River region of both Texas and Oklahoma. And he was stunned when the governor of Oklahoma, Leon "Red" Phillips, the Oklahoma congressional delegation and leaders in the state legislature came to Washington to fight it.

Over and over, they emphasized that it would result in the flooding of some of Oklahoma's best farmland. There were also strong hints that this was just another raid on the federal treasury by someone who had been a longtime practitioner of pork barreling. "I've been a member of Congress for 24 years," Rayburn said in cold outrage, "and I have never introduced a bill to spend a dollar of money in the District I represent." To get Roosevelt's support, Rayburn sent him a letter alleging that Oklahoma Governor Phillips had a close relationship with the Oklahoma Gas and Electric Company. [4]

Congress approved the funding of the $54-million project in June 1938, and Rayburn should never have doubted that it would. For his friend, Clarence Cannon, was chairman of the Public Works Subcommittee of the House Appropriations Committee.

In time, the Denison Dam project proved its value. On completion, it produced 270 million kilowatts of power a year. Seven million persons also came annually for recreational purposes to man-made Lake Texoma, which had resulted from the construction of the dam. The lake had a shoreline of five hundred eighty miles. In addition, the project included the establishment of two natural wildlife refuges totalling twenty-eight thousand acres.

When Rayburn finally reached the big white, two-story colonial house on Highway 82, there was little time to sit in any of the seventeen or more rocking chairs or nap on the sleeping porches. Life became physical now, and he was there to help with the work. His brother Tom, the former baseball player, was married in 1941, and he and his bride, Loyce, bought an adjoining 140-acre farm. But Tom still managed the Rayburn family farm next door and showed good production records in corn and cotton, while sister Lucinda (Miss Lou) took charge of the domestic duties.

In 1938, Sam deeded the property over to Miss Lou because of her great devotion to him and the rest of the Rayburn clan. Every January she stayed with him in Washington for several weeks, and he took her to the formal White House Dinner for the Speaker, to other Roosevelt parties and he held receptions in her honor. She was much concerned with his health, because he caught a cold almost every winter and it hung on a long time. One winter she wrote in her diary that Sam's cold "did not make him very agreeable." At the end of another visit to Washington, she confided to her diary, "Always sorry to leave dear Sam. He is so sweet to me."

Miss Lou had no interest in politics, and her scrapbooks were filled with invitations to White House affairs and society-page stories about the clothing worn and the food served at these and other parties. When she was back home, she insisted that Sam fill her in with descriptions of the famous persons he met, and he complied, reserving political letters to his two other sisters, Katie and Meddie. When the Duke and Duchess of Windsor came to Washington as Roosevelt guests, he dutifully sent Miss Lou a rundown on their appearance. The Duke, he wrote, was "very youngish looking, rather a light reddish blond little fellow . . . an engaging personality"; the Duchess "looks exactly like her pictures . . . the slimmest looking person you most ever saw—very narrow, just little—has nice eyes and mouth and a wonderful smile—a brunette with dark blue eyes."[5]

In the mid-1930s, Rayburn used part of his congressional salary to remodel his farm house. He enlarged it to fourteen rooms, removed the front porch, and added a fourth twenty-foot white pillar. The house had six bedrooms upstairs and one down, three bathrooms and a sitting room as well as a living room. Behind the house was a bell on a long pole to call people to meals, peach and hackberry trees, a smoke house, garage, barn residence for farm workers, a large vegetable garden and 160 acres of farmland. There was also a white doghouse, at most times empty because of the folly of owning dogs in a house abutting a fast-traffic highway. When he was in Washington Rayburn worried a great deal about his dogs and was sick when he heard one had been killed.

Shortly after the town loafers called out "Hya, Sam," as he rode past the courthouse square on his way home from Denison, visitors came to the farm in large numbers to see him. It was not necessary to have an appointment. The routine was to walk in through the back porch and wait your turn before seeing him in the adjoining sitting room that had a ceiling fan with long lazy blades. He kept these visits short—like the ones in Washington. Most people came to ask for favors, but through other questions he asked he had a good view of the mood of his district. He never sent out a questionnaire or polled constituents because he believed a congressman should vote his own convictions. Yet he found these personal visits the best way to find out what was concerning people on the everyday level.

Rayburn did some farm work, and if he were in the field shucking corn, visitors who wanted to talk to him would have to walk alongside the wagon and shuck too. One man found him begrimed and sweaty in overalls, working in the corn crib on a torrid day. Rayburn thought it would be too much to ask him to join him.

He always brought some members of his staff to Bonham when he came home, and they worked out of an office above the First National Bank on a corner of the courthouse square in the center of town. They had the large flow of mail to handle, and they helped him with the requests of constituents for aid. "When I used to drive a truck on the Red River project and they owed me $600, he saw to it that I got it," said H. W. Stevenson, also the local gravedigger, who had gone to see Rayburn. Another time a young garage operator from Oklahoma showed up and astounded Rayburn by asking for his recommendation to land a top diplomatic post. "Mr. Rayburn received him courteously and discussed his request gravely," reported Bicknell Eubanks of the *Christian Science Monitor*. [6] Later one of Rayburn's sisters asked him how he had disposed of the mechanic's demand. "I just told him to get in touch with Joe Martin," he said with a chuckle.

Rayburn prided himself as a modern farmer, and he tried to convince Fannin County farmers to follow his lead. For instance, he was always promoting terrace farming instead of straight-row planting, and plowing cornstalks under instead of burning them. But his dubious neighbors were slow to change methods that had been handed down to them by their parents. He also tried to upgrade the Jersey dairy herds in his district by giving away bull calves, and he was a leading force behind the annual Fannin County Fair. His best descriptive powers came into play to whet interest in the Fair's exhibits: "Hogs so big that their legs can hardly hold up their thick bodies, and poultry with carefully groomed plumage." [7]

By 1940, as many people as not who came to the farm to see him were directed to a place thirteen miles north. This was Sam Rayburn's ranch in the Choctaw Indian territory near Lake Crockett, close to the village of Ivanhoe. In the summer of 1937, while the Court-packing fight raged in Washington, he had purchased several worn-out, abandoned, or bankrupt farms for only eight dollars an acre to form a 972-acre parcel.

His purpose was to fulfill his dream of becoming a rancher, and his twin brothers, Will and Jim, five years his senior, helped start the transformation when they enclosed the land with fence posts and barbed wire. Next, Sam and hired workers joined them in creating six pastures with a pond and barn in each. Sam was there between congressional sessions and during recesses to help with the tedious job of felling trees and clearing the heavy underbrush that was killing the grass. On the biggest pasture, which contained six hundred acres, the men took out two hundred acres of timber.

Because of his notoriously inaccurate aim, those who watched him feared for his life when he wielded a double-bitted ax. But he miraculously came through without accident. He was also inept when it came to operating any mechanical gear or cars. "You never knew where he would end when he backed up his pickup truck," said H. G. Dulaney. He had enormous respect for anyone who could parallel-park a car, because he found it impossible. Passengers who rode with him on a highway winced in terror every time he emphasized a point, because he always removed both hands from the wheel to do so.

Much of the early work on the ranch had to be done with caution, for copperhead snakes were common in the area. There were other surprises and dangers. Dilapidated moonshine stills were uncovered, telling the story of the way previous owners had tried to earn a livelihood. The high weeds also brought Sam his only serious accident. Some old bedsprings buried in the weeds tripped him one day and he fractured his left elbow. The news traveled fast, and when he returned to his farm from the doctor's office the President was on the phone, saying he was sending the presidential plane to deliver him to the Naval Hospital at Bethesda, Maryland, for treatment.

Rayburn would not hear of it. "But I wish I could have been thrown by one of those good quarter horses," he apologized. "Then I wouldn't feel so bad about this busted up elbow."

Later there was a communication from Harry Truman: "Anyway, more power to your right elbow."

For his ranch house Rayburn constructed a three-room wood cabin nestled in an oak grove. The living room measured forty by twenty feet and had a large fireplace. At first he used a plank for a table and nail kegs for chairs. But after a while he brought in a twelve-foot table and beds, and he completed the kitchen with running water, a refrigerator and a butane gas range. Specifically barred were a telephone and radio.

When the ranch began taking shape, he purchased 20 registered Polled Hereford heifers plus Old Joe, a bull to sire their offspring. In time he had about 150 white-faced, hornless Hereford cows and a dozen sires. This required a ranch crew, and when he hired Roy Gauntz, his first foreman, he told him how he wanted his business of selling cattle done. "Any fellow who will cheat for you will cheat against you," he told Gauntz.

From the Capitol, he maintained close touch with the ranch by mail, and he told his foreman when to expect him and what he wanted when he reached Ivanhoe. "We can look over and separate some cattle and get some back in the big pasture," he wrote one time. "Another very important thing, I would like to have a good many minnows where we could get our hands on them to do a little fishing two or three afternoons."

"All of the men looked upon him more as a partner than a boss," said Gauntz. One time he baked cornbread and fried a nineteen-pound fish in hog lard for the crew. Buck Henson, his next foreman, said he never had a cross word with Rayburn. "He was always one of the common people. He had no airs. He would come to my place on the ranch for lunch, and he was one of the family." [8] He offered to send Buck's daughter to college, and when she did not want to go, he gave her a job in his Bonham office, and she went part time to a business school in Sherman, Texas.

Despite his years, Rayburn did a man's job on the ranch. Buck Henson recalled that the Speaker and he "cut wood all day long on a very freezing day." Buck said he kept three horses ready for Rayburn at all times. "He helped drive cattle like a ranch hand." One horse was a roping horse: "You had to throw a rope around his neck before you could run up to him and saddle him." Rayburn's favorite was a Palomino quarter horse named Pansy, and when she was twenty-one he said proudly, "When a cow darts quickly to one side, you'd better start grabbing leather because Pansy is going to stay with that cow."

Sometimes Rayburn went too far in living out his rancher's dream. One day a neighboring rancher found him in a corral in the midst of two dozen ugly-acting Herefords doing their best to send him flying. He was trying without success to cut several out and put them in a nearby pasture. "Mr. Sam was cussin' and runnin' against them with a vengeance," said Joe B. Johnson.

"Mr. Sam," he called out, "you're crazy. This country's got too much money invested in you for you to be out there actin' like this. Get up on that fence and let me cut out those cows. If they kill me it won't hurt so much." Rayburn finally gave up and climbed onto the fence. [9]

Rayburn developed a few good friends besides Joe Johnson among neighboring ranchers. One was Erwin E. Smith, who had designed the buffalo nickel for the U.S. Treasury. But Ivanhoe itself had been hostile political country for Rayburn, and it remained so even after he became a rancher there. As he complained to his old friend, Judge S. F. Leslie, in 1944, 95 percent of the vote was always against him. Sherman Eubanks was the "bell-ringer," he said, for the forty Eubanks living in Ivanhoe.

While Rayburn worked conscientiously on the ranch's business, it failed to pay for itself, and he had to subsidize it from his congressional salary of $30,000 a year. All the cattle were carefully bred, registered, tattooed and fed, but the cost of hay, wages, and his generosity to his crew exceeded the $200 to $250 he got for a bull, 25 cents a pound for calves and $100 for steers. Most incredulous, he did not have a savings account at the bank but kept his money in a checking account where it earned no interest.

Yet he loved the ranch. "Man, this is living!" he would stretch his arms, breathe deeply, and exclaim to Buck Henson on returning to the ranch from Washington. He always wanted to show the place off, and his guest list included Cabinet members, judges, congressmen and Bonham neighbors. "Get to my house farmer's early and we'll take a spin to the ranch," was his standard invitation. He took visitors out on horses to inspect the place, and at night while they sat outdoors in rope-bottomed chairs he cut watermelon with a stiletto and ran the conversation.

Despite his love for his ranch, Rayburn could never forget that he liked being Speaker most of all, and to retain that power he had to keep his House seat. So he took the time at home to write letters, phone and talk to his local political organization to maintain its enthusiasm, and he frequently was the dinner or banquet speaker in the towns of his district. He never prepared one of these speeches in advance but spoke extemporaneously, generally holding to serious issues facing the country. This travel about the district was a form of campaigning between campaigns, and he was an unusual politician because he never slapped the back of a constituent, kissed a baby, bragged about himself or told humorous stories. "I tried to tell a joke once in a speech," he confessed, "and before I got through I was the joke." [10]

Rayburn thrived on the many activities that engulfed him when he returned home from Washington. In fact, he could not tolerate having an idle hour between rising and climbing into bed. Once in his spare time he taught an illiterate black farmhand to sign his name. "When he could think of nothing else to do at home in Bonham he would get out all his shoes and polish them," D. B. Hardeman, his administrative assistant, said. One time when he had cleared all his responsibilities and there was no work to do at the moment, he tried to take a nap but was soon up, moving about restlessly.

"If this keeps up," he confessed, "I'll be like old Howard, down south of Bonham. Every day he dressed up and stood around on the courthouse square all morning, just talking. One day a fellow asked an old colored man, 'Say, what does that fellow do?'

"He replied, 'Well, sir, he don't do nothing all morning and he rests all afternoon.' " [11]

But Rayburn had no possibility of becoming another Howard.

19

Second Man in Charge

When World War II came to the United States, it was as if the Japanese and Germans had finally dropped the other shoe, but the Japanese shoe contained a massive bomb. On Sunday night, December 7, 1941, with the shock of Pearl Harbor still numbing the country, Roosevelt called Rayburn and other congressional leaders to his upstairs study in the White House to discuss that day's infamy. What was intended as a briefing session turned into a mean scene. It was the ferociousness of the Japanese attack and the lack of response by the American military in Hawaii despite forewarnings that precipitated the row, with Secretary of the Navy Frank Knox undergoing a roasting from the congressmen. [1]

But the meeting ended with a sense of bipartisan unity that was heightened a few days later when Germany and Italy also declared war on the United States. One important result of the change from a peacetime to a wartime government was that it brought on an even closer relationship between Rayburn and Roosevelt. In a news conference, the President told reporters that "Dr. New Deal" had given way to "Dr. Win the War." In military and foreign affairs, he intended to make his own decisions, seeking coordination with British Prime Minister Winston Churchill. However, on matters pertaining to what legislation was needed to run the domestic war machinery, Rayburn was his partner.

Since the two men had worked so well together in the past, this portended an enormous plus for the duration of the war. This sense of partnership and mutual respect was indicated in January 1942 when Roosevelt and he exchanged birthday greetings on reaching the age of sixty. FDR wrote him on the sixth: "It must be awful to be so old—I don't get there for 23 days"[2]; and on January thirtieth, Rayburn's message read: "I thank God for this day—because I know at 60 years of age you are ripe and strong for the burdens that would crush a less determined and weaker man."

Although neither man considered for a moment the possibility that the United States could conceivably lose the war, the opening period of the fighting was one of continuing disaster. Guam and Wake fell. So did Attu and Kiska in the Aleutians; and Manila was overwhelmed by the Japanese on January 2, 1942. Also German submarines were enjoying a field day against American cargo ships in the Atlantic.

Nor did the Allies have any good news to report. The British lost most of their Asiatic fleet as well as Hong Kong, Singapore and other possessions in Southeast Asia, while the French were completely driven out of Indochina and the Dutch out of the East Indies. In Europe, the Russians, who had been invaded by the Nazis in June 1941, were fighting what appeared to be a losing battle for the Ukraine.

In the midst of defeats of such magnitude, Roosevelt sent Congress a presidential message in January 1942, calling for the production of sixty thousand planes, forty-five thousand tanks and 8 million tons of merchant shipping a year. His prewar policy of "Guns and Butter" was over. Factories would now concentrate on war production.

With a good part of the press scoffing at these production goals as being unrealistic and with Roosevelt heavily involved in military strategy, Rayburn took on the speaking chore defending the administration's program sights. Although Roosevelt considered Rayburn's effort worthwhile at first, he became concerned when he learned that the Speaker had scheduled a talk in far-off Fort Worth. "I feel it my duty to ask you to stay here with me at least until the House has disposed of the much needed legislation," he wrote him, concerned, on February 18. [3]

On the coming of war, an emotional national unity had swept over the nation, with the disruptive America Firster isolationists now among the leading patriots. But as swiftly as ranks closed, erosion soon developed. Pent-up anger toward the New Deal found a wartime enemy in organized labor, which had proclaimed its right to strike even in wartime and to collect overtime pay for more than a forty-hour week. Early in 1942, after a series of mass meetings across the country, a flood of antilabor mail poured into the Capitol, criticizing Congress for not acting against the unions.

As second man in the government next to the President, Rayburn found himself a major target. At first he did nothing, but when congressmen told him they were being intimidated by constituents who said they were going to get them in the next election for letting widespread strikes go on, Rayburn hit back at the attackers. At a news conference in March 1942, he blasted those who were writing the letters. "From every section of the country come letters and telegrams, many of them very insulting," he said angrily. "They charge that Congress is playing politics, that the people are divided. If this is true, Hitler, Mussolini and the Emperor of Japan would have paid a lot of money for what they are getting free. On March 17—Tuesday—there were between 7 million and 7.5 million engaged in war industries. Of these, there were only 100 on strike."[4]

Besides this antilabor hysteria, there were tens of thousands who wrote about huge waste and mismanagement at military posts and war plants and the lack of military equipment for soldiers in training. Some of this war-factory chaos was understandable, for the government's conversion of the economy from peace to war was being attempted swiftly. Some of it, on the other hand, was the work of crooked contractors. In answer to the growing demands that he personally inspect war plants to check on the accuracy of the information sent him, Rayburn's reply was that if he did he would see only machines and ovens and fanbelts and wouldn't understand any explanation of what was going on there. Besides, he pointed out, the Truman Committee to Investigate the War Program was doing this job.

It was Rayburn who had indirectly helped give Harry Truman a jump in status from a Pendergast-machine hack in the U.S. Senate to an important member of the Upper Chamber. Months before Truman had introduced a resolution to form his special committee, Gene Cox had proposed a similar investigating committee for himself in the House. But Cox was so anti-Roosevelt that Rayburn sat on his request and prevented any action on it. Then after Truman began getting headlines with his findings of waste and fraud in war production and government bungling, Lyndon Johnson asked Rayburn to let him have a Johnson Committee so he could share Truman's publicity. But Rayburn shook his head.

As the legislative leader in the war, Rayburn's help to Roosevelt was enormous. It was hectic, exhausting labor, yet Rayburn thrived on it. He agreed with Roosevelt that industry had to be appeased to obtain its full cooperation, and he put through measures to permit business to write off capital expenditures for new equipment and plants in only five years instead of the customary twenty years; eliminate the 8-percent ceiling on war contract profits; bar the General Accounting Office from auditing war contracts or looking into the activities of the Maritime Commission and have the government pay all postwar reconversion costs to peacetime production. Rayburn also helped win funds for twenty new federal wartime agencies that controlled distribution of raw materials, production levels for civilian goods, prices, war propaganda and economic warfare abroad. There were also bills for payroll tax deductions, for prevention of strikes in war industries and for increased income tax rates.

One program he obtained money for was kept secret. This was the project to construct the atomic bomb. [5] Secretary of War Henry Stimson, General George C. Marshall and Dr. Vannevar Bush came to the Capitol one day to see Rayburn, Joé Martin and John McCormack. Marshall and Stimson "sat with their heads down in their chins," said McCormack, while they explained that there was a race between the Nazis and the Americans for a new kind of weapon. "If Hitler's government perfects it before we do, we could lose the war overnight," Stimson muttered. He went on to divulge that the Nazis were working on it in Norway, and a recent British commando raid had set the project back six months. [6]

To get their project under way, the three government officials had illegally taken money from military appropriations. But the amount taken was small, and now they wanted $1.6 billion. When they started to explain the nature of their project, Rayburn cut them short. "I don't want to know," he said, "because if I don't know a secret I can't let it leak out." With no further discussion, he agreed to get their request through the House without any publicity or explanation to members. The only exception was his old friend, crusty, cantankerous Appropriations Committee Chairman Clarence Cannon. Because of the role he played on the floor in promoting money bills, he was told the amount and the need for his secrecy. So the money was quietly appropriated, and work on the bomb went ahead full speed.

In only one major instance did Rayburn oppose an administration wartime measure. This was the Roosevelt proposal to have the Office of Price Administration ration gasoline as well as meat, sugar, fats, coffee and tires. No Texas politician believed he could survive in office taking on the oil industry, which was the largest single business in the Lone Star State. And the oil moguls opposed gas rationing.

When Roosevelt brought up the need to ration scarce commodities, Rayburn supported the view of the industry that "rationing gasoline is like rationing air." Then for six months he held out against including gas rationing within the authority of the OPA. But at that point he saw it was needed to conserve rubber whose imports from the trans-Pacific plantations had ended with the Japanese conquests. When he quit his opposition, it angered many oil executives, and some were to remember this a long time.

Despite Rayburn's continuing defense of Congress, criticism of the legislative branch increased in severity throughout 1942. Friends of his were concerned that the anti-Congress trend might cause trouble for Rayburn in the midyear Democratic primary when George Balch, a Baptist preacher, popped up to oppose him.

The stress of Balch's campaign was noted by one district newspaper in this fashion: "Balch waged a vigorous campaign of slander, and if he were to remain on his knees for the next hundred years it is doubtful that he would get forgiveness for the reflections he cast and the direct untruths he uttered against Rayburn, who stands second to President Roosevelt not only in politics but in the hearts of the people of the country." [7]

But Rayburn was too busy to be worried and he stayed in Washington, where he heard in time that he won over Preacher Balch by more than a three-to-one margin.

In general, the situation for other Democratic House members, however, was not as good in 1942, and the responsibility for this rested primarily with Rayburn. For all the public carping against Congress, most members expected to be reelected until Rayburn forgot he was a politician. Trouble came in October, a month before the congressional elections when Roosevelt sent Congress a message asking that the draft age be reduced to include eighteen-year-olds. Normally with an election approaching, Rayburn would have waited until it was over before taking up so controversial an issue. But he knew that Major General Dwight D. Eisenhower was planning to throw his troops soon into North Africa, General MacArthur's island hopping against the Japanese in the Pacific was ready for action and General Marshall was apprehensive that there would be a shortage of military forces in the global fighting. Under these circumstances, Rayburn brought up the bill quickly, and when it passed, the avalanche of protests from parents bode no good for sitting Democrats who had supported the Speaker.

The effect of Rayburn's statesmanlike act stared him in the face as he looked down from his desk on the rostrum at the beginning of the next session in January 1943. Fifty Democratic members of the last Congress were gone, and his margin over Joe Martin's Republicans was a thin 217 to 206. He realized further that this was not really a working majority, because a third of the Democrats were Southerners and perhaps more than half of them were closely aligned to conservative Republicans.

A crisis developed over the first group of administration bills that came to the floor. When a large number of Southern Democrats failed to show up for the vote, the bills were defeated. Other House Democrats angrily met with Rayburn and demanded that he call a Democratic caucus, give the vote absentees a tongue-lashing and then bind them to decisions on legislation made at the caucus.

Rayburn refused. "There won't be any serious trouble if we just give these fellas time to let off steam," he said. [8] It was his idea that the non-voting Democrats believed that the election had been an anti-Roosevelt display by the public and that they were the true voice of Congress. His solution was to let them talk themselves out on the floor, proceed slowly on bills for a while, and speak patiently to them in private. For reasons incomprehensible to Northern Democrats this worked, and remarkable unity developed among party members.

As this Congress progressed, a strange change was occurring in the country regarding Sam Rayburn. He was becoming an institution. When people thought of Congress the picture in front of their eyes was that of a stern-faced Rayburn, his gavel poised. He had developed into a sort of calm fatherly image whose words of praise were appreciated and whose annoyance with their antics did not go beyond a show of impatience.

It became one of his added duties to keep the domestic complaining from getting out of hand. When he said that the "symphony of sour notes on the noisy, squabble-ridden home front" was an affront to those fighting and dying, the noisy, squabble-ridden home front agreed. "When I hear complaints about the shortages in civilian goods," he chastised the public, "my thoughts turn to the South Pacific where the boys are fighting in sunshine, wind and rain to preserve our liberty. I would despise myself if I complained of any minor inconveniences." [9]

He had more to say. "I am an average American citizen, no better, I know, no worse, I hope, than the average. I have no son to give to this war or the reconstruction of a sad and stricken world when it is over, and I am in the same position as at least 50 percent of the men and women. I am wondering what sacrifices I have made, and I cannot think of a single one. Some people hate President Roosevelt so badly they hope the country will win the war but Mr. Roosevelt will lose it. Which can't be done."

There was a way to spot the home-front "saboteurs of the spirit, or 'Grumlins,' " as he labeled them. A Grumlin, he said, "is a fellow with a big mouth who at breakfast drinks orange juice and coffee, eats cereal, two eggs and toast, then feels sorry for himself as he grumbles at his wife because she has used up her red stamps and was unable to give him bacon." In another definition, he said this was the person who was "afflicted with jaundice of the spine in 1940 and enlargement of the spleen in 1943."

Rayburn also wanted the country to think about the postwar period in a sane fashion. "No matter how much money it costs," said farmer Rayburn, "every returning soldier who wants a farm must be given a start toward owning one." Others should get federal money for education. As for the enemy, he jumped on those who were talking about a need for a soft peace. "Within 60 days after the end of the war," he predicted, "sob sisters and sob brothers will start crying that the common people of Germany, Italy and Japan had nothing to do with this war. This is rot. If it had not been for the common people of Germany, Italy and Japan there would have been no Hitler, Mussolini or Hirohito."

In 1943, Rayburn was getting around the country more than in the past. He dedicated hospitals, a steel mill, a Liberty ship named the *William Marion Rayburn* after his father, collected an honorary Doctor of Laws degree and had his portrait hung in the Texas House.

The Roosevelts were also praising him publicly. Newspapers reported that Mrs. Roosevelt called one of his "lectures" to the U.S. House of Representatives the "most statesmanlike" wartime speech and that her husband had used it to prepare one of his own major speeches. Roosevelt also made public his letter of praise to Rayburn on completing two years as Speaker and singled him out in a news conference for his importance in passing the administration's New Deal and war bills. The FDR letter said in part: "The Speakership has assumed a special importance because of the gravity of the issues with which you have continually had to deal. . . . The country has need of you." [10]

By the beginning of 1944, when interest in that year's presidential election had begun to percolate among Democrats, the party organizations in various states deluged Sam Rayburn with requests to speak at money-raising dinners. Southern congressmen added to the growing interest in Rayburn as a candidate for President by voting him their region's favorite son in January 1944.

In experience, outlook and character, he would have made a fine President. But he was certain Roosevelt planned to run for a fourth term. This became apparent when he delivered the major oration at the Jackson Day Dinner in Washington and described the next Democratic presidential nominee in such terms that listeners knew he was referring to Roosevelt. To head off efforts by the conservative wing to promote its own man against Roosevelt, he warned that the party would not accept "an imitation liberal who points a finger at Wall Street but points a gun at the SEC."

Just as he was convinced that Roosevelt would run again, so did Rayburn believe that he would drop Vice President Henry Wallace from the ticket. The uproar from the party pros was already growing that Wallace was a radical, pro-CIO captive who had not developed any close ties to Democratic organizations in the forty-eight states.

Since 1933, when Wallace began to administer the Agricultural Adjustment Act, Rayburn and he had been friends. They frequently discussed farm problems, and Wallace, who had been an outstanding plant geneticist, sent him supplies of the revolutionary high-yield, high-stamina hybrid corn seed he had developed. Unsolicited letters from Wallace to Rayburn over the years revealed the regard he had for the Speaker. In one letter Wallace wrote, "You are indeed one of the greatest assets the Democratic Party has had over the long years." [11] In another he said, "I have known not a single one who has so completely maintained his integrity." [12]

Although Rayburn never mentioned it, it must have been as obvious to him as it was to many others who had frequent contact with Roosevelt after his return from the Teheran Conference in December 1943 that the President's health was declining. The strain of directing a major war and managing the country, the long hours, daily military briefings, incessant pulls by generals, admirals, department and agency heads, legislators and politicians had worn him down. He looked far older than his sixty-two years—his lined face was ashen, his clothes hung on his wasting body, and he had a hacking cough that would not go away.

Because of his failing health, he should not have run for a fourth term. Yet the party bosses cruelly insisted that he do so because of their conclusion that no other Democrat could win in 1944. While they worked on him at every meeting, he showed ambivalence until after the successful Allied landings in Normandy on the June sixth D-Day when he decided he wanted to be in command to establish the postwar international order. But it was not until early July that he publicly announced he would run again "reluctantly but as a good soldier"; adding: "All that is within me cries to go back to my home on the Hudson." To his wife Eleanor he said jokingly, "I really want to be reelected to a fourth term so I can fire your housekeeper. She's been giving me oatmeal every morning for months now." [13]

Since the Democratic bosses did not expect Roosevelt to live out a fourth term, top priority had to be given to the selection of the vice-presidential nominee. As Ed Pauley, California oil man, commodity speculator and treasurer of the Democratic National Committee, so frankly put it to them: "You are not nominating a Vice President of the United States, but a President."

Although Rayburn was second only to Roosevelt in Democratic stature, the party pros saw clearly that he was his own man and would not be manageable. The man they believed they could handle was Senator Harry Truman of Missouri, who had been getting some publicity running his war investigating committee. So they decided to get him on the ticket with Roosevelt, and the person designated by the "conspirators," as they called themselves, to convince Roosevelt to accept Truman was a young Irishman from Missouri named Robert Hannegan.

Hannegan had been a minor boss in the crooked Democratic machine in St. Louis when he double-crossed the local organization in 1940 by throwing his votes to Truman, of the Kansas City Pendergast machine, in his fight to win reelection to the Senate that year. Hannegan's action provided the margin of Truman's victory in the Democratic primary over

Missouri Governor Lloyd Stark, who had Roosevelt's backing, and it opened a national career for Hannegan. Truman's first reward to Hannegan was to get him a patronage job as collector of internal revenue at St. Louis; then through Truman's friendship with Frank Walker, the chairman of the Democratic National Committee, he had Hannegan named head of the entire Internal Revenue Service; and when Walker resigned his chairmanship, he saw to it that Roosevelt appointed Hannegan as his successor in January 1944.

Constant sniping at Henry Wallace by Hannegan, the city bosses and an FDR staffmember finally yielded a Roosevelt decision to replace him as Vice President. Ed Pauley pointed out that the inside man in this endeavor was General Edwin "Pa" Watson, Roosevelt's military aide. "I had a huddle with him during one of my visits to the White House," said Pauley, "and entered into a conspiracy with him to arrange appointments with Roosevelt for all potential convention delegates who were opposed to Wallace. . . . This went on month after month. Slowly, and little by little, they began having their effect." [14]

But if the ailing President were willing to dump Wallace, this failed to make Truman front-runner as his replacement.

It was Rayburn's view that because Roosevelt had to concentrate on winning the war, he might approve an open convention to chose the vice presidential nominee. So despite his friendship with Wallace, he decided to test his own political following.

In March, he made a campaign tour of the West Coast. Unaware that Ed Pauley was a self-professed "conspirator" for Truman, he asked him to be his guide. He spoke at several Democratic banquets and was greeted everywhere with prolonged cheers. On March 30, Senators Truman, Harley Kilgore of West Virginia, and Mon Wallgren of Washington were in San Francisco on Truman Committee business, and they attended an affair for Rayburn. Said Victor Messall, Truman's assistant, "Truman wanted to be Vice President, but he had to pretend he didn't." [15] "At the cocktail party [before the dinner]," Pauley said, "Truman proposed a toast to Rayburn as the next Vice President of the United States. Later, in an unprepared speech at the dinner, he said the same thing and got a tremendous ovation."

After this successful trip, Rayburn believed that Roosevelt would warm further to his candidacy for Vice President if he had the strong endorsement of the Texas State Democratic Convention. At the same time, he knew that Roosevelt, still unannounced as a candidate for a fourth term, wanted Texas to send a pro-Roosevelt delegation to the national convention in July. If he decided not to run, he nevertheless would want to control the nomination of his successor. So with Texas as the largest

217

Southern State, its backing of Rayburn and FDR would be double insurance for the Speaker.

Alvin Wirtz, the former Undersecretary of the Interior and political godfather to Congressman Lyndon Johnson, undertook both Texas assignments with Johnson as his assistant. Rayburn's ties to both men were strong: to Wirtz as a selfless, tireless worker for Roosevelt programs; and to Johnson as his substitute son. There were many disquieting stories about Lyndon, but as a doting daddy he never asked him about them. One story was that Lyndon urinated in his office sink while dictating to his female secretary. Then there was his use of Rayburn's name to help him get a lucrative radio station license from the FCC, an agency indelibly indebted to Rayburn for its creation. The license for KTBC in Austin had been taken out in the name of Lyndon's wife, and this had required some heavy fabrications to meet the business experience requirement.

There was also Johnson's blatant tie-in with the Brown and Root Company, the oil, natural gas and war plant construction giant. He had openly used a B. and R. company plane as a shuttle between Washington and Texas, and a criminal suit had been instituted against B. and R. for making illegal campaign contributions to him. Early in 1944, newspapers reported that Internal Revenue had assessed a $1.6-million tax charge and fraud penalty against the corporation and was taking it into criminal court for its illegal donations to Johnson's unsuccessful Senate campaign in 1941. Shortly afterward, Johnson went to the White House to plead with Roosevelt for B. and R. [16] The President was amenable because of his hope for Texas political support. He ordered a tax settlement of $372,000 and told IRS to drop the court action.

Strangely, when Johnson left Roosevelt's office and was surrounded by reporters, he took a slap at Rayburn. No, he told them, he had not come to the White House to discuss Brown and Root troubles. He had come solely to make a strong plea to Roosevelt to put Rayburn on the ticket in place of Henry Wallace. In off-the-record elaboration that drifted back to the Capitol, Johnson claimed that Roosevelt was opposed to Rayburn's candidacy, that he said the Speaker knew nothing about foreign affairs, was not acceptable to organized labor, and was essential to the nation as Speaker during the next four years.

To all this, Rayburn did not question Johnson but accepted his silence to mean that the remarks attributed to him were false. On Johnson's part, he stepped up his swarming friendliness toward Rayburn. When his wife, Lady Bird, had her first daughter in mid-March 1944, he phoned Rayburn and told him he was the first person he had called, even before he had phoned his own mother. "It's a red, crying, screaming baby girl!" he bellowed.

Alvin Wirtz went down to Texas alone to start his double assignment, and in May when Johnson joined him for the state Democratic convention at Austin, Wirtz had already botched both jobs. He had sent his people out to work on the Democratic precinct conventions, but disaster had developed when most chose anti-Roosevelt delegations to the next level county conventions. In turn, a majority of these sent delegations to the state convention with instructions to approve a resolution there to order Texas electoral college selectees to vote against FDR, even if he carried the state in the November election. As for Rayburn, Wirtz failed miserably on this score as well. Because he was closely identified with Roosevelt, the county conventions would not endorse him.

When his turn came to plead his case to the state convention, Johnson was treated to continuing booing. After a bloody melee between Texas Regulars (conservatives, anti-Roosevelt Democrats) and Texas Loyalists (pro-Roosevelt Democrats), the minority of loyalists fought their way out of the Texas Senate Chamber, where the convention was being held, and staged a rump convention of their own. As a result, two snarling delegations prepared for another fight at the Chicago convention, and the hopes of Rayburn and Roosevelt for united support from Texas Democrats were shattered. "The state convention was a terrible disappointment to me," Rayburn wrote a friend.

While the Texas imbroglio was going on, the Democratic Party pros were working their conspiracy on the physically fading President. "Don't press him and wear him out," Mrs. Roosevelt pleaded with visitors. [17] Of all the local bosses, only Ed Flynn, leader of the Bronx, wanted Roosevelt to retire because of his health. Yet he dared not suggest this to Roosevelt directly.

After Roosevelt decided to run again, the night of decision on his running mate came on Tuesday, July 11, when he invited the city machine bosses and others to dinner at the White House. [18] Following the meal, the group went to the blue oval study on the second floor where the possible candidates were discussed. Senate Majority Leader Alben Barkley was derided by the bosses because of his age and a suspected lack of loyalty to Roosevelt; former Senator and Supreme Court Justice Jimmy Byrnes was rejected because he had been born a Catholic and was anti-labor and a South Carolina bigot in the eyes of Northern Democrats.

When the talk turned to Sam Rayburn, several brought up the phony issue of the split in the Texas delegation as the reason for denying him any consideration. As Roosevelt made no attempt to counter this point with others in the Speaker's favor, Rayburn's name was unceremoniously discarded.

But there still seemed a remote chance that Rayburn's candidacy would be reopened by Roosevelt when Truman was discussed. While the bosses chorused their enthusiasm for Truman, Roosevelt argued that he was tainted by his association with Tom Pendergast, the Kansas City boss whom the administration had prosecuted and sent to jail for accepting a bribe. Moreover, he thought Truman was too old, and he confessed that he hardly knew him personally, even though he considered his work on his War Investigating Committee worthwhile.

Worn down in the end by his visitors, Roosevelt later gave Bob Hannegan a letter to be read to the Chicago convention, in which he said he would be "very glad" to run with either Bill Douglas (Supreme Court Justice William O. Douglas) or Harry Truman. In a wily move, Hannegan had Roosevelt's secretary, Grace Tully, retype the letter with Truman's name preceding Douglas'.

However, this still did not settle the issue in Truman's favor, because Roosevelt did not plan on being in steady touch with the convention and cracking a whip over its preceedings. Despite secrecy precautions, it was well known on Capitol Hill that while the convention was in progress he would be on his way to a strategy meeting at Pearl Harbor with General Douglas MacArthur and Admiral Chester Nimitz on the war against the Japanese.

This was why it was important for Rayburn to attend the Democratic convention and manage his campaign for Vice Président on the spot. Senator Tom Connally, who was there, came early to the conclusion that had Rayburn been present he and his friends could have offset the bosses. [19] John McCormack, the House majority leader, reached the same opinion that "if he had attended the Convention he would have won the nomination." In fact, said McCormack, "I called him from Chicago to come up, but he said he couldn't leave his District." [20]

In the course of a few weeks in July 1944, Rayburn had to make a decision that would influence his entire political future. If he went to Chicago, there was a good possibility that he might come away with the Vice Presidency. On the other hand, he faced a Democratic primary in his district against two opponents, and he had it "from reliable sources that upwards of $200,000 was being spent to beat me" by the oil crowd, Dallas businessmen, the public utilities and Roosevelt haters. If he went to Chicago and lost the nomination, chances were he would also lose the primary at home. So when John McCormack pleaded with him over the phone to be present at the convention, the second most powerful political leader in the nation had already made up his mind to fight to hold on to his House seat.

The Democratic primary was slated for Saturday, July 22, and by the time Rayburn returned to Bonham after Congress recessed, he found that his well-heeled opponents had been working full time for months to unseat him. One was George Balch, the Baptist preacher from Commerce, who had carried out the slanderous campaign against him two years earlier. The other was G. C. Morris, an intelligent and personable young man. Morris, a drug and stationery employee for McGaughey Brothers in Greenville, had served four terms in the Texas House and was now in the Texas Senate. He was not related to Jess Morris of the same city—who had come uncomfortably close to forcing Rayburn into a runoff race in 1932, using the apalling campaign arguments that he was taller, heavier, younger and better with his fists than Rayburn.

Balch, a man of the cloth, was up to his old tactics of 1942 when he collected 10,000 votes to Rayburn's 35,000. Across the district went his flyers depicting Rayburn as throwing big parties in his apartment where everyone got "pretty well lit up." In further detail, he swore as gospel: "Sam drained his glass, fell over on the bed, rattled the ice in his glass and said, 'Listen fellows, did you know I represent the driest district in Texas and here I am as drunk as a fiddler's wench. I wonder what those old boys back home would think if they could see me now?' "[21]

Despite such entertaining nonsense from Balch, Rayburn's network of friends throughout the district had apprised him that young G. C. Morris was a far more serious threat. Even before Rayburn had returned home to campaign, G. C. had shaken an estimated thirty thousand hands, spoken at dozens of barbecues and passed out tens of thousands of pieces of "literature." Like Preacher Balch, he painted a horrifying picture of Rayburn as a champion of Socialism, accused him of being a willing tool of a radical administration and called the wartime controls part of a Rayburn scheme to expand the tentacles of government.

While Rayburn scrounged about for campaign funds, money was obviously no concern to Morris and Balch. The preacher had crews nailing "No Seventeenth Term" signs on the poles in the district, and Morris blasted Rayburn regularly from high-cost radio programs. Other money was poured into whispering campaigns to go far beyond what Morris and Balch were saying publicly. No man, even if he were House Speaker, was expected to survive a charge of being a "nigger lover," and this kind of charge was now aimed at Rayburn. One whispering campaign had him and Roosevelt being responsible for the Supreme Court decision of April 3, 1944, which declared that Negroes could not be barred from Texas Democratic primaries. Another well-spread mouth-to-ear charge said that since he had had the power to kill it but had not, Rayburn was responsible for the half-million-dollar appropriation to the Fair Employment Practices Committee (FEPC), an agency set up to prevent racial discrimination in war-industry hiring. The *Greenville Herald* in Morris' hometown helped promote this campaign with the disclosure that Rayburn had not voted on the FEPC appropriation, which had passed the House by only four votes. The *Herald* also helped by quoting Rayburn in Amos 'n Andy lingo. When its editorial had Sam saying, "Them am my sentiments," an irate admirer of the Speaker rejoined, "They made Sam Rayburn a nigger." [22]

Rayburn had kicked off his campaign with a speech dedicating the Denison Dam on the Red River, and he intended to run a high-level campaign no matter what Balch and Morris were saying. This worried his friends who were convinced he should strike back. Several suggested that he rake Morris as a draft dodger, because his young opponent had gained exemption from service on the ground that he was a state legislator. One Rayburn supporter wrote Sam that Morris was being introduced at meetings as "a hard fighter," and that Sam should respond with the remark that "this country can use those kind in its armed forces right now."

But Rayburn refused to take the low road. His campaign circular said mildly, "Don't go back to 5 cent cotton—keep Sam Rayburn in Congress."

In the final two weeks, he spent a day each in Rains and Rockwell Counties with a combined tiny population of fifteen thousand and roughly two days each on the other five counties with their 215,000 inhabitants. With a territory larger than Connecticut, it was a taxing ordeal. He wrote to his friend Pat Coon that in Kaufman County he had stopped not only in every town but in every "filling station" as well.

He was on the road on Friday, June 21, the day before his primary when he heard that Harry Truman had defeated Henry Wallace at the national convention for the vice-presidential nomination. On the first ballot, Wallace had led the field with 429½ votes, with Truman second at 319½. The Wallace forces had wanted a recess in order to go after the additional 159½ needed for the nomination. But Hannegan and the other bosses had been exploiting the softness in the Wallace support in the various delegations and forced an immediate second ballot. The contest was even after the first 950 votes; then Truman surged over the top.

Rayburn was in touch with Truman to offer his congratulations; then he braced himself for the vote that would tell if he were still a member of the House.

The contest between him and Morris turned out to be embarrassingly close. It revealed that if the rich anti-Rayburn outsiders had been willing to put more money inside the district, the second most powerful man in Washington would have been sent back to his farm and ranch for good. At the end of that torturous Saturday, he had 22,052 votes; Morris, 16,705; and Preacher Balch, 816.

Letters went out to those who had worked hard to save him. "Bless your old heart and thanks for everything," he wrote to Jim Busby in Sherman. He also did something most unusual for a politician. Instead of pocketing them, he returned several checks from contributors with the notation that all bills had been paid. [23]

After his victory, Rayburn enjoyed some revenge on the Texas regulars, who in fewer than three months had helped eliminate him as a vice-presidential candidate and almost removed him from Congress. Besides the precinct-county-state conventions in the spring, Texas Democrats also held a repeat trio of conventions in September. In the second state convention, winners of the primaries were certified for the November ballot and the governor announced his program and named the sixty-two members of the Democratic state executive committee.

Chiefly through the work of Alvin Wirtz, most of the county conventions sent supporters of the Roosevelt-Truman ticket to the second state convention. Governor Coke Stevenson, a Texas regular who was on a "Hya, Sam"—"Hello, Coke" basis with Rayburn, flew to Washington to beg Rayburn to arrange a meeting with Roosevelt in order to make a compromise.

One Stevenson proposal to the ailing President was a plan to put two sets of presidential electors on the ballot, one for the ticket and the other opposed. For the sake of peace in Texas, Roosevelt was willing to do this, but Rayburn and Wirtz would not agree.

Afterward, Wirtz returned to Texas, where he ran the second state convention like an orchestra. He dumped the anti-Roosevelt presidential electors chosen by the May convention and put in his own. He also expelled Stevenson's state executive committee and replaced the members with people loyal to Roosevelt and Rayburn. As a special offering, he named Rayburn's good friend, Bill Kittrell, to the vital post of committee secretary. Kittrell, a New Dealer on most matters, was a Washington lobbyist who had known Rayburn since the Wilson administration and occasionally helped in his campaigns. "People who wanted to get in good with Sam Rayburn always thought it wise to be nice to Kittrell," said Congressman Wright Patman. Kittrell was also an excellent source of intelligence for the Speaker, according to Patman. "Bill was the only man I ever knew who was knowledgeable about every man who walked through the lobby of the Mayflower Hotel in Washington," he claimed. [24]

So the revenge against the Texas regulars turned out to be an asset for the national ticket. When Roosevelt swept Texas in November with 800,000 votes to 191,000 for Governor Thomas E. Dewey of New York, the state's electoral votes were duly cast for Roosevelt and Truman.

Rayburn's concern over Roosevelt's health increased after the unprecedented inauguration at the White House instead of the Capitol in

January 1945. He found that the new Vice President was also aware of Roosevelt's condition and had been for a long time. "Truman told me about a dream, rather a nightmare he had during the 1944 campaign," Rayburn later recalled. "He said he awoke in a cold sweat for he had dreamed that the President had died and he was called into service."

But Truman had more than a dream. During the campaign he and Edward McKim, sergeant in his old Battery D during World War I and now his assistant, went to a White House showing of a movie, *Woodrow Wilson*. As they were leaving the grounds afterward, McKim remarked, "Hey, bud, turn around and take a look. You're going to be living in that house before long."

Truman nodded. "Eddie, I'm afraid I am. And it scares the hell out of me."

In February the story raced through the Capitol that Roosevelt had died. Rayburn checked it out immediately and learned that Edwin "Pa" Watson, his aide, had died at sea on the way home from Roosevelt's conference at Yalta with Josef Stalin and Winston Churchill. On the other side of the Capitol, when Harry Truman heard the rumor, he left the presiding officer's desk on the dais and rushed to the office of Leslie Biffle, the secretary of the Senate. "I hear the President is dead, Les. What will we do?" he asked in such agitation that Biffle phoned the White House for him. [25]

On Roosevelt's return to Washington, he made arrangements with Rayburn to address a joint session of Congress and the nation on the Yalta Conference. Close up, Rayburn saw he had waxy skin and his jaw hung slack, but his mind was clear. Winston Churchill best described him at that time: "His captivating smile, his gay and charming manner, had not deserted him, but his face had a transparency, an air of purification, and often there was a far-away look in his eyes."

He came to the House on March 1. Rayburn and Truman sat alongside each other on the rostrum while Roosevelt sat at a table in the well of the House. He was not wearing his leg braces that would have permitted him to stand, and he apologized for sitting while he spoke. "It makes it a lot easier for me in not having to carry about ten pounds of steel around on the bottom of my legs." Afterward he apologized further to Rayburn and Truman for his poor performance and said he was going to Warm Springs to recuperate.

It was at a dinner on April 11 that Rayburn confided to friends: "This country is in for a great tragedy, and I feel it's coming very soon. I don't think the President will be with us much longer." Then he added grimly, "I think I'll have a talk with Harry tomorrow. He's got to be prepared to carry a tremendous burden."

According to Lyndon Johnson, Roosevelt had told him he did not want Sam Rayburn as his Vice President because he had no background in foreign affairs. But Truman was actually far less acquainted with this field than Rayburn. Truman had been overseas only once—as a captain of artillery in World War I—and had not served on the Senate Foreign Relations Committee; while Rayburn had listened to foreign affairs debates, studied the issues since the Wilson administration, and had pushed a great deal of international legislation through the House for Roosevelt. Secretary of State Cordell Hull also said he had met with Rayburn several times on the establishment of the United Nations. [26]

As a further drawback, Truman had not been taken into Roosevelt's confidence on the vital foreign issues in the few times he had seen the President since the inauguration, nor had he been briefed by the State Department. Chances were he might not have found time for such briefings because he had developed into Washington's most sought-after dinner and party guest since becoming Vice President. *Time* reported that his heavy party schedule "had Capitol Society writers breathless," and George Dixon, the columnist, wrote that Truman was "the most fed gentleman in Washington." At other times he had gained bad publicity by using an army bomber to fly to Tom Pendergast's funeral in Kansas City and by having his picture taken at the National Press Club, playing the piano with a movie actress sitting on it.

Rayburn felt he was at fault for not getting after Truman earlier, and on April 12 he phoned Truman and asked him to come to his Board of Education when the Senate recessed for the day.

Shortly after 5:00 P.M. Rayburn was presiding in his hideaway, with House parliamentarian Lew Deschler and James Barnes, a presidential assistant and former Congressman. Deschler had just taken a bottle of bourbon and an ice tray from the refrigerator when the phone rang. Rayburn answered it and Stephen Early, FDR's press secretary, asked if Truman were there. Rayburn said he was expecting him, and Early requested him to have Truman call as soon as he arrived.

Truman walked in a few minutes later and mixed himself a drink. After five minutes passed Deschler asked Rayburn, "Wasn't the Vice President supposed to call Steve Early?" It had slipped Rayburn's mind. "He is kind of a pale fellow anyhow, and he got a little paler," Rayburn remembered the change in Truman's face as he and Early spoke. By then Rayburn had an idea what had happened.

When Truman hung up, he set his jaw and said, "Holy General Jackson!" Then he told the gathering, "Boys, this is in this room. Something must have happened. I'll be back soon." [27]

A few minutes later after John McCormack entered the room, word came from the White House that Roosevelt had died of a massive cerebral hemorrhage. Tears of deep grief flowed down Rayburn's cheeks. Then the phone rang again. This time it was Truman, asking Rayburn to come to the White House with John McCormack and other leaders for his swearing in.

When they were gone, Lyndon Johnson wandered in, poured himself a drink, flopped in the overstuffed chair next to the desk, and asked Deschler, "Where's everybody?"

"Roosevelt is dead," Deschler told him. "They're at the White House to witness Harry Truman's swearing in as President."

"I'm going down there!" Johnson bellowed, racing from the room like lightning.

20

Rayburn and Truman

Sam Rayburn was with Truman at the beginning and the end of his Presidency, and during the intervening ninety-three months he served as his chief protector and friend in Congress.

The beginning came shortly after Rayburn told Truman to call Steve Early. Truman, hurrying to the White House at Early's request, phoned back to Rayburn's hideaway, even before he informed his wife of Roosevelt's death, and asked Rayburn to bring other congressional leaders to witness his oath-taking ceremony.

By the time Rayburn reached the Cabinet Room for the swearing-in his own tears were dry, but Truman remembered afterward that "everyone was crying and carrying on." While waiting for Chief Justice Harlan F. Stone, the dazed new chief executive made his first decision: The UN charter-writing conference was to begin on schedule in San Francisco on April 25. Shortly before Roosevelt's death, Rayburn had asked him to name a woman member of Congress to the U.S. delegation, and Roosevelt had replied on April 6, "The Congressional members of the Delegation seem quite opposed to this." [1] Rayburn did not think it prudent to push women's rights with Truman at this moment, and the opportunity vanished. Still in a daze when Stone appeared, Truman had to be ordered by the Chief Justice to raise his right hand with his left hand on the Bible when he repeated the oath in the one-minute ceremony. [2]

There was naturally a question at the outset about the relationship between Rayburn and Truman. On the one hand, here was a new President who had always looked upon Rayburn as his superior. On the other hand, there was Rayburn who had become aware that he had been deprived of serious consideration for the Vice Presidency by Bob Hannegan, Truman's man. He knew that Hannegan had used the split between the Texas conservative and New Deal Democrats as a telling argument with Roosevelt to sidetrack him.

However, both men made the necessary adjustment, even though it did not come immediately. On Friday, April 13, 1945, after his first morning in the Oval Office, Truman already missed the old gang on Capitol Hill, and he phoned Les Biffle, the secretary of the Senate, that he was coming to his office for lunch with him, Sam Rayburn, and top rung holders in Congress. At the session in Biffle's office, after the drinks and the jokes, Truman said he would like to appear in the House the following Monday to address a joint session of Congress. Rayburn considered this too hasty, and suggested that more time should elapse following Roosevelt's burial over the weekend. Others backed a delay, and Truman almost meekly gave in. But he stiffened suddenly remembering he was President and announced he would speak on the sixteenth. [3] On his way out of the Capitol, a reporter called to him, "Good luck, Mr. President."

"I wish you hadn't called me that," Truman replied.

Because of his own long experience in Washington, his close relationship with Roosevelt and his friendship with Truman, Rayburn went to see Truman on Saturday to warn him about some pitfalls in his new job. Roosevelt's body lay not far away in the wood paneled grand reception hall known as the East Room. "I wanted to help the fellah," Rayburn reminisced about that meeting years later to newscaster Martin Agronsky.

So I went down there and said to him, "You don't have anything in the world that I want. I've come down here to talk about you.

"I've been watching this White House for many years. I know some of the hazards here and I want to tell you what your biggest hazard is. . . . You have a lot of people around you here. Some are going to be men of outstanding ability and character, and some are not going to have too much ability. . . . And some aren't going to be able to stand up and battle it out with men of more ability than they've got. And they're going to try to do to you what they've tried to do to every President since I've been here. They're going to try to build a fence around you, and in building that fence around you they'll be keeping the very people away from seeing you that you should see. That's my first bit of advice.

"The next one is about the special interest fellah and the sycophant. If some old boy from Missouri comes out here he transacts his business and he has a ticket on that 6:30 B & O going back to Missouri. He telephones down here and says he wants to pay his respects to the President. They'll say, 'Why you can't see him for two or three days.' So he gets on the train and goes on back.

"But the special interest fellah will come like the king of old. He'd stand in the snow a week because the king has to see the Pope before he can navigate. That fellah will stay around here for a month and he'll come in here sliding on his vest, and, sycophantic, will say you're the greatest man who ever lived, in order to make time with you. And you know and I know that it just ain't so."

"Well, I know I'm not," Truman agreed.

Rayburn had something further to say about their working relationship. "I'll want to see you about two or three little things once in a while," he said. "And I can't afford to walk through those newspapermen out there and say we didn't talk about anything."

"Just any afternoon after five o'clock," Truman said, "come in the East entrance of the White House, over by the Treasury. Walk through there and come up to my study. I'll be in there."

When Truman reached the Capitol the following Monday, the prospect of delivering his first address to Congress and the nation made him shake. Fortunately, Rayburn sized up his predicament as soon as he entered his office where the special ceremonial contingent of congressmen was to meet him and escort him to the House rostrum. After a half hour of calming conversation, Rayburn saw that Truman's normal pallor had returned, and he said it was time to cross the hall to the House Chamber.

Ironically, it was Rayburn who made Truman jumpy again. Following the loud, prolonged applause, Truman drifted into his speech only to have Rayburn stop him. "Just a minute, Harry," Rayburn cut in distinctly over national and international radio. "Let me introduce you." Truman fell silent; then Rayburn declared, "The President of the United States!" and he motioned the nervous orator to begin again.

Truman revealed early what he thought of Rayburn by asking Congress to change the law on presidential succession. The existing statute passed in 1886 provided that if a President were incapacitated or otherwise unable to discharge his duties, the line of succession would go first to the Vice President, then to the Secretary of State, followed by the Secretary of the Treasury and other cabinet members in a designated order.

Truman's request to Congress was to give the House Speaker the top priority to succeed to his office following the Vice President. Then the Senate president pro tempore would come, with members of the Cabinet getting a crack at the Presidency after him. Modest Rayburn considered it doubly unseemly for him to promote the bill. But Hatton Sumners, chairman of the House Judiciary Committee, felt no compunctions and pushed it through the House in just two weeks after Truman sent the measure to the Capitol. However, it took two years of much histrionic senatorial snarling about the slighting of the Upper Chamber by naming their man behind the Speaker before the bill became law. Because Truman had no Vice President, the Speaker stood next in line to succeed him.

Immediately upon taking over the White House, Truman was besieged by top government officials who intended to control the policies of their greenhorn boss through memos, briefings and stealth. Rayburn went to see him one evening in the upstairs oval study and was appalled to find him surrounded by huge piles of papers. "I've got to sign those things," Truman told him glumly. He remarked that the law required him to sign his name an average of six hundred times a day. "But I'm not going to sign them until I've read them. And I've got to read everything before I go to bed."

There was good reason for Truman to be suspicious of everything that came across his desk for signature. One early crucial paper he signed without reading abruptly ended all lend-lease aid to the Soviet Union. When word got out, the Russians screamed that this cut-off of aid was a highly unfriendly act by a professed ally. In private, Truman agreed with Rayburn and Tom Connally shortly afterward that he had made a mistake, but he could not bring himself to rescind the order, because it would have created the impression that he was giving in to Russian pressure. [4]

When Truman took office in April 1945, the war in Europe was rapidly racing toward a satisfactory conclusion. Despite the fact that the defeat of Japan still lay ahead, political discussion concerning the postwar world erupted in Washington and around the country. Part of it involved foreign relations; part, domestic matters.

In a continuation of the Roosevelt policy of working intimately with Congress, Truman had Rayburn, House Majority Leader John McCormack, Senate President Pro Tem Kenneth McKellar and Senate Majority Leader Alben Barkley come to the White House on a weekly basis. These were informal business sessions to discuss proposed legislation, the status and future of bills in the legislative mill, and to hear rehashes of policy briefings Truman had been subjected to previously by administration officials. It was at these meetings that Truman's "containment" policy toward the Soviet Union was early revealed, a policy that Rayburn thought was reached too hastily with a wartime ally who had lost an estimated 25 million lives.

Truman had entered the White House with the notion that the Russian wartime alliance was a prelude to a postwar world of lasting peace and international good will. But only a few days passed before his thinking was severely jarred by W. Averell Harriman, who had been appointed ambassador to Moscow by FDR.

Harriman—whose relationship with the Roosevelts began in childhood when he went to Groton, an elite private school, with Mrs. Roosevelt's younger brother, Hall—was the son of E. H. Harriman, the railroad tycoon. In 1933, FDR brought Averell into his administration as head of the New York State NRA, then advanced him to administrative officer of the entire NRA. Harriman found himself embarrassed on September 15, 1934, when the front page of the *New York Times* reported that he and other officers of the New York Title and Insurance Company had been indicted "for issuing and publishing a deceptive financial statement on the corporation's balance sheet." [5] But nothing happened, and he continued in government service as a member of the Commerce Department's Business Advisory Council. After that he began to take on diplomatic assignments for Roosevelt, eventually becoming ambassador to the Soviet Union, and he was on hand at most of the conferences with Roosevelt, Churchill and Stalin in World War II.

It was shortly after Roosevelt's death that Harriman flew in from his post in Moscow to tell Truman that the Russians had violated the Yalta Agreement, which had called for free elections in Poland. He also charged them with mistreating released American POWs in their fighting sector, installing a Communist dictatorship in Rumania and planning "a barbaric invasion" of Western Europe. Asked what he advocated, Harriman proposed a get-tough policy with the Soviet Union in order to prevent another Munich. [6] An angry Truman tongue-lashed Soviet Foreign Minister Molotov not long after that when he came through Washington on his way to the San Francisco UN Charter Conference. The congressional foursome were told about this, plus news of Harry Hopkins's mission to Moscow. During the war Hopkins had become Roosevelt's foreign affairs troubleshooter. Near death now, he made the trip for Truman to end Soviet intransigence at San Francisco. He also got Stalin's agreement to enter the war against Japan and arranged the Potsdam Peace Conference in July of the Big Three—Truman, Churchill and Stalin.

The failure of the Potsdam Conference to engender much more than massive suspicions among the wartime allies was a major setback to postwar tranquility. Its minor results were to establish a Council of Foreign Ministers, recognize Communist Poland with a part of Germany included in her territory, and work up a reparations and occupation plan for Germany. Its chief result was to solidify Truman's foreign policy toward the Soviet Union for the rest of his Presidency. His words to Rayburn, McCormack, McKellar and Barkley on his return were similar to what he wrote his mother and sister: "You never saw such pig-headed people as are the Russians. I hope I never have to hold another conference with them." He did not.

By the fall of 1945, following the unconditional surrender of Japan, the political climate within the United States toward the USSR became extremely unfriendly. Many organizations, administration officials and military officers called for a "preventive war" against the Russians after they took over the Japanese Kurile Islands and a big chunk of Chinese territory, stole machinery and equipment from Manchurian factories, began installing a border belt of puppets throughout Eastern Europe and threatened other border nations such as Turkey and Iran.

Anxious that the spreading talk of "preventive war" might lead Stalin toward some desperate, idiotic act, Truman asked Rayburn to speak out to assure the Soviet dictator that this was not being contemplated. Most other persons who might do so stood in danger of being called a Communist "tool," but Rayburn's prestige was too great to be damaged.

In a Dallas speech in January 1946 that received national attention he said: "Some people say that we must and will fight Russia. What for? If we should win a war with Russia, what would it profit us? Nothing! What would we lose if we fought Russia and lost? Probably everything! I oppose for us the kind of government Russia has, but the kind of government Russia has is more its business than mine. I think I know one thing, and that is the present government of Russia is better for the common man under the leadership of Stalin than under the Czars. The Czars had only to have an impressed army and a state church—they were the two classes they headed and served. I am utterly opposed to both." [7]

This signal to the Russians that the U.S. government did not intend a Pearl Harbor type of attack on the Soviet Union did not restore friendly relations between the two countries. However, it was another high-level voice that helped lower the danger of a Third World War. For it served notice that the ground rules did not call for the sneak dropping of American nuclear bombs on Russia but for less cataclysmic yet effective means to halt Soviet expansion.

It was Winston Churchill who settled any lingering doubts about American foreign policy early in 1946 with his "iron curtain" speech at Westminster College in Fulton, Missouri, where Truman was among those who heard it. After this, containment became Truman's open policy, and he barred any consideration of it in terms of its effect on domestic politics. Rayburn recalled a White House meeting between Truman and congressional leaders on foreign policy legislation. One congressman brought up the subject of its effect on domestic politics. An infuriated Truman snapped, "Let's get one thing straight! I never want to hear that damn word 'politics' mentioned here again when we're discussing a thing like this."[8]

While Rayburn was generally able to maintain Democratic unity in the House on Truman's proposition that politics ended at the coastline, he had no acceptable homily to use for domestic legislation. As things turned out, Truman enjoyed a honeymoon with Congress just so long as he announced no domestic program. But in September 1945, shortly after V-J Day ended the war in the Pacific, he sent a twenty-one-point New Dealish program to Capitol Hill that sparked legislative turmoil lasting until he left the White House in 1953.

Had Rayburn been asked for his advice before Truman sprang the program on Congress, he would have told him he was requesting far too much at one time—full-employment guarantees for the entire working population, a national health-insurance program, federal aid to education, subsidies for private and public housing, widespread expansion of public power projects, higher minimum wages, extended social-security coverage, increased price supports for farmers, a permanent Fair Employment Practices Committee (FEPC), increased congressional and civil-service pay and continuation of the wartime draft and economic controls.

Although Rayburn agreed with much of this program, he knew from the public denunciation by the Republican leadership and Southern Democrats that only a few items might possibly get through Congress, and then only after wholesale amendments. The one with the slightest chance was the proposal for a permanant FEPC, for any Southern congressman who voted to give blacks the legal means to protest hiring and job discrimination was ending his political life.

On this issue, Rayburn knew from his last election that he had to give tacit support to racial bigotry. But he made his own racial view clear one time when he hired a black man to row him and Frank McNaughton across a freshwater eastern Maryland lake in search of bass. After several luckless hours, Rayburn finally caught a large fish, but, while he was pulling it into the boat, the oarsman accidentally knocked the fish off the hook and it escaped. Rayburn's expression turned sad, but he said nothing. Later he told McNaughton, "I naturally felt disappointed, but then I realized that, but for the grace of God, I'd have been pulling those oars myself today, not he."[9]

When 1946 came, Rayburn believed that the continuing adverse publicity Truman's twenty-one-point domestic program was getting in the press endangered the sixteen-year Democratic control of Congress in that year's elections. In addition, Republicans were promoting the spurious charge that Roosevelt had been personally responsible for Pearl Harbor, New Deal Democrats were yelling that Truman was a scoundrel for ridding his administration of FDR officials, and a national outcry was developing over the slow release of draftees now that peace had come. Furthermore, labor strikes were erupting all over the country, and housewives were furious over the shortage of meat.

To add to all these sour signals, Truman brought on extra trouble for the Democrats in June 1946 by not listening to Rayburn. Congress passed a price-and-rent-control bill far weaker than the measure Truman had requested, but Rayburn advised him to sign it because it was the best he could get.

This was the occasion when Rayburn first learned that "Harry always shot from the hip." Instead of accepting half a loaf, Truman vetoed the bill as inadequate. Food prices now free of controls immediately skyrocketed and rents doubled and tripled. By the time another bill imposed controls two months later, meat dealers, unwilling to accept the price rollback, held meat off the market and added to the anger of housewives against the administration.

None of this affected Rayburn back home, because for the third time since 1912, he had no opposition in the Fourth District's Democratic primary. This rare happening allowed him to concentrate on the problems of worried House Democrats seeking reelection, and in the fall of 1946 he cut records for radio use by sixty Democrats in the tightest races. Then at Truman's request he rode to Missouri with him aboard the bomb-proof Presidential train to campaign with him throughout the state. Missouri had a majority of Democrats in the House, and Truman considered a change as a personal defeat. Along the way west, Rayburn studied the abundant harvest, listened to complaints by voters, and finally grunted his view to reporters, "This is going to be nothing but a goddamned beefsteak election." [10] He was referring to the anger over the meat shortage as the dominant factor.

Rayburn was right. Truman's Missouri sent a majority of Republicans to the House, and the Democrats for the first time since 1931 were the minority party in both the House and Senate.

There was also a harsh, personal blow from the "goddamned beefsteak election." Rayburn was no longer Speaker of the House.

21

The Miracle Election

By 1947, Rayburn had spent forty years in political office, and now with his loss of the Speakership there were rumors he considered retiring from Congress. One piece of gossip was that he had been offered one hundred thousand dollars a year to join a law firm; another, that President Truman would give him a place in his cabinet.

It was a glum time for him, contemplating a future without a gavel in his hand. But one thing he seemed fairly adamant about: "I will not be the Minority Leader," he told reporters, after noting that the Democrats had lost a whopping total of 53 House seats in the November 1946 election and that Joe Martin would boss a House composed of 246 Republicans and only 188 Democrats.

To show he was not making an idle threat, he sent a wire to John McCormack, his majority leader, telling him that he would back him for minority leader in the Eightieth Congress. But when McCormack related this to John Sparkman of Alabama, whom Rayburn had appointed majority whip after the death of Pat Boland, Sparkman found that Southern Democrats opposed McCormack. At the same time, Northern Democrats would not accept any Southerner except Rayburn. So Sparkman undertook a drive to pressure Rayburn to take on the minority leadership. Truman, appalled at the thought that Sam might not be his right hand in Congress, also joined in the pressuring.

The day of reckoning came in January when the House Democrats met in caucus. McCormack gained the floor and quickly moved to nominate Rayburn, and the din for him was earsplitting. "I didn't want the job and I had said I wouldn't take it," Rayburn told reporters afterward. "When I was voted for unanimously I yielded like I figured a good soldier should do." But he wanted no one to call him "minority leader," and his stationery was headed: "Office of the Democratic Leader."

Truman celebrated Sam's decision by attending a mammoth dinner party in his honor at the Texas State Society a few nights later. Dr. Wallace Graham, the presidential physician, had ordered him to stay in bed because he had a sore throat and a fever. But Truman sneaked out of the White House and showed up at the Statler ballroom before the crowd of twenty-five hundred persons. "I just wanted to come here to tell you how much I love you," he told Rayburn.

Soon after Rayburn became minority leader, House Democrats discovered that besides suffering a $7,500 cut in pay, the $2,500 extra expense allowance for Speakers, and the loss of his formal and back offices, he had also lost his limousine and George Donovan, his chauffeur and fishing companion, to Speaker Joe Martin. A few wealthy House Democrats offered to buy him another automobile, but he angrily retorted he would not accept the gift. Finally Congressman Frank Boykin of Alabama asked if he would object to a limousine purchased through widespread contributions of House Democrats. This time Rayburn said with embarrassment he had no objection if contributions were limited to twenty-five dollars.

Within a few days there was more than enough money. In fact fifty Republicans also joined in, but Rayburn insisted that their $1,250 be returned. The car Boykin purchased was a boatlike 1947 Cadillac costing $3,600. Rayburn's only expenses were for the monthly $200 salary for Nick Nicastro, his chauffeur, the car's upkeep and the cost of enlarging the garage on his farm. What pleased him most was the inscription inside the car that read: "To Our Beloved Sam Rayburn—Who would have been President if he had come from any place but the South." [1]

Gloating over Republican supremacy in the House and Senate, *Life* Magazine, which had long praised Rayburn, now went out of its way to belittle him without mentioning him by name. "The opening of the 80th Congress at noon on January 3," said *Life*, "marked a significant shift in the government's center of gravity. In recent years Congress has lost much of its traditional power as part of the American system of checks and balances, had become a combination rubber stamp and whipping boy for the White House and had fallen to dangerously low public esteem. Now it began to reassert its strength and enter into the business of government as a full fledged partner." [2]

The blunt truth was that the Republicans could not believe their good fortune and operated through chaos except for an occasional helpful assist from Rayburn when they were not showing their hatred of Roosevelt,

Truman, labor unions, government employees and intellectuals. For instance, their method for handling Truman's budget request of $37.5 billion in 1947 was to cut departments and agencies by percentage figures instead of analyzing individual programs.

Rayburn was always on hand on the right side of the aisle to debate sour-faced John Taber of New York, the chairman of the Appropriations Committee, whenever Taber had another department up for gutting. Taber, he told the House, behaved like "a man with a meat ax in a dark room."

Only through the logic of his appeals and expert floor bargaining was he able to keep some existing programs functioning adequately. One time he managed to salvage the $20 million Taber had slashed from REA, but he did not fare as well on the school-lunch and soil-conservation programs. Taber also bested him on public housing and aid to education by the simple technique of eliminating all money requests, while other Republican committee chairmen bottled up Truman's health and expanded Social Security programs.

Still another defeat Rayburn suffered came on the tax-relief bill presented by Harold Knutson of Minnesota, chairman of the Ways and Means Committee. Rayburn's figures showed that 40 percent of the benefits went to higher income groups. A family man with an annual income of $2,500 would get a tax cut of only $25, while someone with a $1-million income would enjoy a cut of $103,000. But Congress disregarded Rayburn and passed this tax bill, and when Truman vetoed it, Rayburn was unable to muster the one-third plus one votes needed to sustain the veto.

The Republicans had been eager to get at organized labor for a long time. With the postwar inflation, strikes for higher wages dotted the country like measles. In 1946, Truman had reacted to the strike of three hundred thousand railroad workers by threatening to draft the strikers into the Army. That year Congress passed a bill calling for a thirty-day cooling-off period before a union could strike.

To the Republicans of the Eightieth Congress in 1947 this was only a beginning. Their Taft-Hartley Bill that year would ban the closed shop, jurisdictional and sympathy strikes and mass picketing; make unions liable to lawsuits; force them to disclose financial records; prohibit them from making political contributions; provide for a sixty-day cooling-off period; force union officials to sign affidavits that they were not Communists; and give the President authority to obtain injunctions to prevent strikes in interstate transportation, communications and public utilities.

Rayburn led the House fight against what he called the "punitive labor bill." Almost all of his work was done behind the scenes, and the speech he made on the floor was a pungent two-paragraph affair. The first was a jibe at Republican haste in giving members too little time to study the measure. The second paragraph, filled with single syllable words, added: "I do not know what is in this bill. Few do, or can. But from what I know of it, I know that what you are doing here is not fair. The bill is not fair. I'm not going to vote for it." [3]

However, he could not hold his party, for a sufficient number of Southern Democrats, including his protégé, Lyndon Johnson, joined conservative Republicans to approve it and later to pass it over Truman's veto.

Part of the chaos in the Eightieth Congress was a result of the Republican overeagerness to uncover wrongdoing in the Truman administration for use in the 1948 presidential campaign. As one member described the Republican approach: "Congress opened daily with a prayer and ended with a probe."

Truman provided the initial ammunition. He had been angered in 1946 by Democrat Roger Slaughter, the congressman from his home district who Rayburn told him was an obstructionist on the Rules Committee. As a result, Truman had asked Jim Pendergast, who inherited the machine from his Uncle Tom, to purge Slaughter in the Democratic primary. Jim did such a thorough job that seventy-one Pendergast hacks were later indicted for engaging in ballot fakery. The Republicans in the Eightieth Congress did their best to blame the scandal on Truman personally.

Other running attacks in the Eightieth Congress tried to depict a White House wallowing in scandal. Rayburn left the defense against these charges to Truman. But he joined in excoriating Republicans who were attempting to establish the doctrine that the administration was a haven for Communists.

In several important respects the Eightieth Congress was not obstructionist. The Republicans supported Truman's requests for the establishment of the Central Intelligence Agency and the unification of the military departments into a single Department of Defense. The Republican leaders also showed responsibility in foreign affairs involving Europe. Truman's request for a $400-million Greek-Turkish aid program to keep both countries from succumbing to Communist domination gained some Republican support because Speaker Martin, normally an isolationist, spoke for it. However, this was offset by liberal Democrats and Republicans who opposed the Truman request on the ground that both Greece and Turkey had undemocratic governments. But Rayburn, like Truman, saw the issue as being much too basic to consider the shortcomings of the governments. In this instance, he picked up vital last-minute votes when he made the final speech before the tally and told members, "I trust in our considerations that this thing called isolationism may not again crawl out of the shadows and defeat the hopes of men and break the heart of the world."

The Republican leadership in the House also supported Truman's proposed Marshall Plan to rehabilitate the war-ravaged economies of Western Europe and prevent their falling prey to Communism. But when the Republican rank and file members opposed it, Rayburn led the fight to win passage of the $17-billion four-year appropriation over the loud objections of John Taber. "These are dangerous days. Let us not do too little," he told a hushed House when the whip count showed Taber would win. "I counsel you as an old and devoted friend. I plead with you not to do too little now." The vote showed Rayburn the victor by 148 to 113.

Truman agreed with Rayburn that his friend, Will Clayton from Houston, the Undersecretary of State and the world's largest cotton broker, was the best man to run the program. But Senator Arthur Vandenberg, Republican chairman of the Senate Foreign Relations Committee, had to be coddled in order to gain his support, and Vandenberg flatly insisted he would not approve Clayton. Vandenberg's choice, Paul Hoffman, president of the Studebaker Corporation, was given the Marshall Plan post instead,[4] with Averell Harriman as operating director in Europe.

If 1946 had early appeared to Sam Rayburn as a poor year for the Democratic Party, 1948 looked far worse. The Democrats were never more divided in the twentieth century than they were in this presidential year.

There were the left-wing Democrats who were fearful that Truman was on a nuclear collision course with the Soviet Union. They had flocked to join Henry Wallace's Progressive Party. There were also the labor leaders who blamed the passage of the Taft-Hartley Act on Truman. Then there were the "Never Forget Roosevelt" liberals who decried the dumping of FDR appointees from the top government echelons and the operation of "Truman's witchhunt," as they labeled the government's loyalty program.

Southern Democrats were equally incensed with Truman after he sent Congress a ten-point civil rights message in February 1948. Among the changes he requested were an end to Jim Crow laws in interstate transportation, elimination of the poll tax, protection of the right to vote, a federal antilynching law, and an FEPC. A storm broke out immediately in the Deep South, and fifty-two congressmen from that section declared they would not support him for President.

As on Truman's earlier request for a permanent FEPC, Rayburn knew that his friend's far larger program now made humanitarian sense but absolutely no political sense in an election year. When Truman called him to the White House, handed him his omnibus civil rights bill, and asked him to introduce it, Rayburn took it but said nothing. Later back in his office he dropped it in the rear of a lower desk drawer. In April, with the Southern shrieking increasing, he called a meeting of the Texas congressional delegation and said he was declaring a "moratorium on all civil rights talk" for all of them. He also met with a large group of Southern politicians, swept his arm before him for silence and told them acidly: "All your high-flown political vocabulary boils down to just three words: 'Nigger; nigger, nigger!' "[5]

Rayburn's determination to help Truman get the Democratic nomination that summer seemed a useless exercise in the spring when a large number of prominent Democrats generated a boom for five-star General Dwight D. "Ike" Eisenhower, the American commander of World War II forces in Europe. Eisenhower came across to the American people as an immensely kind and natural sort, without airs, yet undaunted by the Hitler military machine. Rayburn had first heard of Ike in December 1941 from Bill Kittrell, his lobbyist friend, who had taken the Katy's Blue Bonnet from Texas to Washington with Sid Richardson, the oil tycoon, after Pearl Harbor. Kittrell told Rayburn that Richardson had grown weary of just "shooting the bull" on the long ride and asked him to find someone on the train who would join them for some hands of bridge. Kittrell wandered through the train, striking up conversations en route, and returned with a bald, easy-grinning army colonel from Fort Sam Houston, who turned out to be Eisenhower.

Rayburn did not meet Eisenhower until June 1945, when he returned to the U.S. for a round of mammoth parades in his honor. Then the following April when Ike was Army Chief of Staff, they took a trip to Denison, Texas, for a celebration in Eisenhower's honor at his birthplace. As congressman for the district that included Denison, Rayburn was a sort of host.

Along the way they compared notes and found that Rayburn was a barefoot eight-year-old farm boy when Ike was born in 1890 twenty-five miles away in a little wood-frame house next to the railroad tracks. By the time their plane landed, Rayburn also discovered that this third flight had not been as frightening as the first one in 1935 or the second in 1943 when his brother Will died and he had to get home in a hurry.

The visit to Denison was not a happy homecoming for Ike because of the circumstances surrounding his birth. His father, David Eisenhower, had deserted his family in Hope, Kansas, when his general store had failed. Then later repenting, he asked his wife Ida to bring their two sons to Denison where he was working as a shop foreman in the yards of the Cotton Belt Railway. Ike was born in this tough town a year later, and after a short existence in near-poverty the family moved to Abilene, Kansas, where his father worked as a mechanic. Apparently there was something so distasteful about his start in life that when Ike entered West Point in 1911 he listed his place of birth as Tyler, Texas, which was 150 miles from Denison. [6]

On that uncomfortable April 20, 1946, Rayburn took Ike to his birthplace, introduced him to eighty-five-year-old Miss Jennie Jackson, who remembered bouncing him on her knees. Then in front of tireless photographers the two men ate a meal in the tiny dining room. Later they took part in a huge parade and barbecue and listened to speakers praising both of them. Eisenhower's reaction to the day was to whisper to Rayburn, "Mr. Speaker, I've had two meals in two hours and I'm tired."

Truman knew without being reminded by Rayburn that the Eisenhower boom had to be deflated, and best of all by the general himself. As the sitting President, Truman controlled the people who would run the machinery of the forthcoming national convention at Philadelphia. But still, the ground swell for Eisenhower could sweep the professionals aside, just as Wendell Willkie's amateurs had accomplished at the 1940 Republican National Convention.

Truman's problem with Ike as a presidential candidate seemed to be over when the general's name was entered in the New Hampshire Republican primary. For in a letter to the *Manchester* [N.H.] *Union Leader*, Eisenhower declared flatly: "I could not accept the nomination even under the remote circumstances that it would be tendered me . . . life-long professional soldiers [should] abstain from seeking high political office." Yet this clear statement failed to end the Democratic boom for him, because his Democratic admirers interpreted his words to mean that he would only reject a Republican nomination. Among these were the sons of Franklin Roosevelt, a large number of labor leaders, Senator Richard Russell, New York Mayor William O'Dwyer and Cook County (Illinois) boss Colonel Jake Arvey.

Several came to Rayburn to enlist his support for their drive to dump Truman, the sure loser, and nominate Eisenhower on the ground that he was the only one who could save the November election from the Republicans. But Rayburn's reply was that Ike should not be in politics, because he lacked experience, interest and a philosophy. "No, won't do," he said curtly. "Good man but wrong business." [7]

As the pro-Eisenhower boom continued unabated, Truman asked General George Marshall, his Secretary of State, to get a blanket statement of noncandidacy from his protégé. After Marshall backed off from taking part in politics, Secretary of Defense James Forrestal agreed to do this. He phoned Eisenhower, who was then president of Columbia University, and asked him to inform Franklin Roosevelt, Jr., his chief Democratic supporter, to quit promoting him. [8] When Eisenhower did this Rayburn felt small relief, for the boom continued.

As usual as the convention approached, there was trouble among Texas Democrats. Governor Beaufort Jester, a leader in the Southern revolt against "Trumanism," was choleric about Truman's veto of Taft-Hartley, his civil rights proposals and his instructions to Attorney General Tom Clark—a Rayburn patronage protégé—to sue in the Supreme Court for federal ownership of offshore tidelands oil. "Beautiful Jester with the marcelled hair," as he was known, ordered the state convention to send an uninstructed delegation to the Philadelphia convention. Only because this looked too heavy-handed, at the last minute he permitted the inclusion of Senator Tom Connally and Sam Rayburn as Texas delegates.

To help Truman's cause, Rayburn had agreed to boss the national convention as permanent chairman. It was a sullen, defeatest army of Democratic delegates whom he gaveled to order when the Democratic clambake opened at Philadelphia's Convention Hall on the sweltering Monday afternoon of July 12. The last-ditch Eisenhower supporters had been dealt a death blow a week earlier when their man issued his final words on the subject: "I will not at this time identify myself with any political party and could not accept nomination for any political office." Swaying before Rayburn's eyes were signs held by delegates that read: "We're just mild about Harry."

It was Rayburn's intention to make a short speech and move rapidly into the convention's chief business, but the dismal faces he looked down upon from the platform forced him to work as a cheerleader. One after another he asked the convention questions, such as: "Who brought the farmer out of the bankruptcy courts in 1933 and into his prosperity in 1948?" At first he answered his own questions with the loud refrain: "The Democrats." But after a half dozen questions the delegates caught on and began shouting "The Democrats!" back to him as their refrain. By the time he finished, he had evoked an enthusiasm that surprised the delegates themselves.

What was supposed to be a burial ground convention sprang further to life with fury on Wednesday, July 14. Rayburn let Mayor Hubert

Humphrey of Minneapolis have the floor during the vote on the platform, and Humphrey brought on a major confrontation by proposing a strong civil rights plank as a substitute for the platform committee's weak compromise.

Following the shrill debate on one of Philadelphia's hottest days, Humphrey won by a vote of 651 to 582. But his action split the convention. Handy Ellis, a six-foot six-inch delegate from Alabama rushed to the platform and waved his big arm for recognition in front of Rayburn's face. Rayburn knew that to give him the floor meant a continuing anti-civil rights diatribe that could tear the convention apart. So he recognized another delegate with whom he had arranged to call for adjournment until evening.

When the convention reconvened Rayburn still would not let the "Dixiecrats," as the Southern Democrats became known, disrupt the proceedings, and Southern delegates stamped out. After they were gone, Rayburn was heard to say, "Those Dixiecrats are as welcome around here as a bastard at a family reunion." Three days later a Dixiecrat (States' Rights) convention nominated South Carolina Governor Strom Thurmond for President and Mississippi Governor Fielding Wright for Vice President.

While Rayburn took the view that the Southern extremists had acted like spoiled children instead of loyal Democrats, Truman was more charitable. Back in Washington he confided to Secretary of Defense Forrestal that he felt no animosity toward the Southerners for their opposition to the civil rights plank. "I would have done the same thing myself if I were in their place and came from their states," he said. [9]

Had Rayburn wanted the Vice Presidency, there is no doubt he could have had it. The *Greenville* [Tex.] *Banner* on October 19, 1947, carried the story that he had said "No" to Truman's offer to make him his running mate. Shortly before the convention Truman decided on Supreme Court Justice William O. Douglas. However, Douglas rejected the offer and Truman was still casting about for a running mate when the convention began. In order to prevent anti-Truman demonstrations in the galleries during this televised convention, Rayburn had put Les Biffle in charge of doling out gallery tickets. While handling this assignment, Biffle, a Democratic power, also rounded up a majority of delegates who pledged to vote for Senator Alben Barkley for Vice President. [10] Biffle and Barkley then phoned Truman on Tuesday and broke the news to him. At first Truman was angry that he had been outmaneuvered, then he was perturbed because Barkley was seventy years old. Finally he accepted the defeat with as much grace as he could muster under the circumstances. [11]

It was Rayburn's intention to wind up the convention in three days because he could not tolerate long drawn-out activities. On the morning of Wednesday, the third day, he phoned Truman at the White House and told him he expected to have the decks cleared by 9 P.M., at which time Truman could deliver his acceptance speech. This seemed like a wild bit of calculating, considering that the platform was not yet completely resolved, that there had to be nominating speeches for presidential candidates and balloting, and that a repeat performance of this would be necessary for the vice-presidential nomination.

Yet if Humphrey had not precipitated the civil rights fight, he might have met his schedule. As it was, he ran five hours overtime before Truman beat out Senator Richard Russell on the first ballot by 947½ votes to 263, and Barkley had his vice-presidential nomination by acclamation. It was 2 A.M. when Rayburn sent word to Truman and Barkley to come to the platform and speak. The two were in a performers' dressing room facing an alley on the floor below the convention. Rayburn felt sorry for Truman when he stood before the exhausted delegates, his eyes blinking with fatigue. An aide to Truman described his face as "starch white."

But in one sentence Truman changed the entire atmosphere. "Senator Barkley and I will win this election and make these Republicans like it—don't you forget that!" he snapped pugnaciously, and the cheers ricocheted off the walls. Then he borrowed a theme that Rayburn had expressed a year earlier, that the Eightieth Congress was "the worst Congress in my 35 years." As Truman later recalled, "I tore into the Eightieth Congress . . . and I did not pull any punches." When he finished, some of Rayburn's gloom about the November election against New York Governor Tom Dewey, the Republican nominee, lifted, even though the polls had declared Dewey a sure winner.

Once the Philadelphia convention adjourned, Rayburn made a beeline for home for a ten-day drive to save his House seat from two opponents, David H. Brown and G. C. Morris, who was making his second try. Brown was not the chief threat, though there was always the possibility that his votes when added to Morris' would deprive Rayburn of the majority he needed to prevent a run-off election. The unpleasant memory of the 1944 primary was still strong, when young State Senator Morris with opulent backing ran an uncomfortably close race against him.

Once again, according to a local paper, Morris had ample campaign funds that paid for, among other things, an imported "high-powered, high-salaried" P. R. man. Both the Brown and Morris campaigns focused on attaching Rayburn to Truman's civil rights program, with Morris charging that Rayburn was backed by the CIO and Henry Wallace's Progressive Party. Rayburn's friends worriedly begged him to lash out at the two, but he campaigned as usual, ignoring their existence and telling crowds in his low-key fashion that they owed their prosperity to the Roosevelt-Truman administrations. This proved to be the winning approach, for on July 24 he collected 31,559 to Morris' 12,357 and Brown's 5,681.

After this, Rayburn was free to work in Truman's behalf to stem the Dixiecrat revolt and bring the South into the Democratic fold before the November election. But he seemed too preoccupied at the outset to take on this job. The reason was the serious problem swamping his protégé, Lyndon Johnson.

Since the end of World War II, Rayburn had continued to coddle Johnson, in the face of steady pressure for favors from the young man. Johnson had so much energy that, despite a heavy concentration of time and effort to become a millionaire, he pushed on Rayburn continually to help him enlarge his political power. On his behalf, Rayburn, for instance, asked Truman in the fall of 1945 to appoint Senator Tom Connally U.S. ambassador to the UN. The scheme was to empty Connally's Senate seat, making it available to Johnson in an election. But Connally turned down Truman's offer.

With Johnson House-bound for the time being, Rayburn proceeded to add to his regular assignment with the Naval Affairs Committee. First, he appointed him to the Select Committee on Postwar Military Policy. Then after Rayburn helped squelch the generals who were lobbying to place atomic energy matters under military control, he saw to it that Lyndon had a seat on the new Joint House-Senate Committee on Atomic Energy.

Johnson finally ran for the U.S. Senate in 1948. Truman as well as Rayburn gave him his blessing—even though Johnson had voted for Taft-Hartley, calling it an "anti-Communist" bill; had denounced Truman's civil rights program as "an effort to set up a police state"; and had demanded full wartime mobilization for war against the Soviet Union.

On the day Rayburn won his primary, his pleasure was tempered by the fact that Johnson had come in second against former Governor Coke Stevenson. However, since Stevenson failed to get a necessary majority in the three-man field, Rayburn was not totally dejected, for the law required that Johnson should have another chance in the special run-off election scheduled for the end of August.

Johnson's second campaign was geared to a repetition of how much he despised the Truman administration and to a massive slandering of Stevenson. This second primary ended with a vote that brought great consternation to the Johnson camp. Out of a million votes, the Texas Election Bureau gave Stevenson the victory by 114.

But this situation was soon rectified by the dispatching of a Johnson aide named John Connally, plus others, to the sun-scorched south Texas mesquite country. A short time later George Parr, the dictatorial boss of the poverty-stricken Mexican population in three counties near the border, announced he had discovered an error in the vote-count of Box 13 in Alice, the county seat of Jim Wells County. Parr and his father had for decades been notorious for the peculiar vote totals they submitted for their domain. In this instance, George Parr said that Box 13 had understated Johnson's total by 202 votes, putting him ahead of Stevenson in the state by 87. And now Johnson proclaimed himself the winner. "I was beaten by a stuffed ballot box, and I can prove it," Coke Stevenson cried, as he declared his intention not to have his victory stolen from him.

Rayburn did not involve himself in the Johnson-Stevenson imbroglio, except to listen to Lyndon's stories of supposed vote cheating by Coke Stevenson's side. But it was no surprise to him when ex-FBI agents found that the registration signatures of Parr's 202 Johnson additions were signed by the same person, or that some of the names were of dead persons. Nor was he astonished when a state judge in Austin named Roy Archer, whom Johnson knew, issued an injunction forbidding any reconsideration of the final vote-count from Box 13 in Alice.

When the Texas State Democratic Convention convened in mid-September, Rayburn steered clear of the Johnson-Stevenson business, which was the chief issue on everyone's mind. Instead, he concentrated on warning the gathering that there would be either a depression or a war unless Texas Democrats and members in other Southern states supported Truman in November. Johnson's dirty work was left to Alvin Wirtz, his other Texas "Daddy," who labored backstage first to oust the vociferous anti-Truman delegations from Dallas, Houston and three counties. Several fistfights enlivened this effort. Then Wirtz won approval of a resolution placing Johnson's name instead of Coke Stevenson's on the ballot in November against the Republican nominee.

But this did not end the troubles of Rayburn's protégé. Johnson's State Judge Roy Archer had supported him. But now Stevenson went to Federal Judge T. Whitfield Davidson for an injunction to bar Johnson's name from appearing on the ballot. Judge Davidson set a later date for a hearing and sent court agents to examine the election returns from Box 13 in Alice. The agents reported back that the ballots had disappeared. So had the election judges. Davidson's temporary restraining order barred Johnson's name from appearing on the November ballot. Then to add to Johnson's woes, a U.S. circuit court judge said he would not consider an appeal before October 14, long past the legal deadline for putting names on the ballot.

This was the situation when President Truman came through Texas on his nationwide "Give 'Em Hell, Harry" twenty-two-thousand-mile "whistle-stop" train campaign against Governor Tom Dewey. Prominent Texans had told his secretary, "They'd shoot Truman if he went down there, that no-good s.o.b. and his civil rights."[12]But undaunted, Truman entered Texas for nineteen back-platform speeches and some more formal meetings to rail against the "Do-Nothing Eightieth Congress," and introduce "the Boss" (his wife Bess), with a broad wink to the men in the crowd, and "the Boss' Boss" (his daughter Margaret).

Rayburn joined the train at the western end of Texas for the sweep that would be climaxed on September 27 with a presidential stop at Bonham and a reception and meal at his farm. They stopped at Uvalde to visit John Garner, now almost eighty, and Truman gave him a bottle of whisky "for snake bites." Garner was proud of his Senate protege, but the sadness over his wife showed through. "Ettie is bedridden invalid, both mentally and physically," he had written Rayburn earlier that year. [13]

For a short time along the way Lyndon Johnson was aboard to get Truman to make public announcements supporting him. Lyndon had lost twenty-five pounds and was suffering from a severe skin rash brought on by the crisis to his ambitions. His hands shook when he drank a proffered double Scotch, and he chain-smoked cigarettes. Truman, of course, knew of his sorry record on administration bills and his demands for war with the Soviet Union. But he reasoned that he could change in the Senate. In addition, he knew from his own case that a crooked election could put an honest man into the Senate. [14] Then again, anyone who was Sam Rayburn's protégé was all right to him. So at every whistle-stop he threw his weight against Coke Stevenson and asked the crowds to support Johnson.

At San Antonio, George Parr climbed aboard the train for a thirty-minute visit with Truman. Some time before, Parr had been placed on probation after a conviction for income-tax violation. When he was caught altering oil and gas leases, he spent 9½ months in prison as a probation violator. Gossip had it that in this meeting with Truman he asked for a presidential pardon for his help to Johnson. (He later got it.)

Lyndon Johnson had left the Truman train before the San Antonio stop. Then suddenly, a short distance from Bonham, a helicopter flew close to the train, and the frightened engineer applied the brake. After the helicopter landed alongside the tracks, Johnson climbed out and rushed aboard the train to be with Truman and Rayburn in Bonham.

He had much to tell Rayburn. His friend and lawyer, Abe Fortas, had gone to see Supreme Court Justice Hugo Black, and he expected Black to issue an order that said federal courts did not have jurisdiction over U.S. Senate primaries. This would throw out the ruling of Federal Judge Davidson, and the action would revert to the pro-Johnson decision of State Judge Archer. [15]

A crowd estimated as large as forty thousand persons, or almost six times the normal population of Bonham, was on hand to greet Harry Truman in Sam's town. Rayburn had insured this immense turnout by sending a request throughout Fannin County for every community "to organize and come over in large caravans."

Once the Truman train parked in the small, little-used yard of the Texas Pacific Railroad, the festivities began at Rebel Stadium at the high school, where a capacity crowd of fourteen thousand cheered Truman and Rayburn. Then came the reception at Rayburn's farmhouse for the only President to have visited Bonham.

When James Rowley, the Secret Service boss, saw the size of the crowd lining up to shake the hands of the President's family, he insisted that the handshaking be cancelled. It was too dangerous for "Potus," he insisted. "Potus" was the code name for "President of the United States."

"You can't do this," Rayburn insisted. "These are my friends. I know every man, woman and child here. I'll vouch for them personally."

Rowley was finally told by Truman to let the reception go on, with Rayburn doing the introducing of each of his constituents. The Rayburn house had a center hall that ran from the front door toward the back porch, which enabled the crowd to enter, shake hands, and leave without cluttering the house. After Truman had long since passed his campaign record for handshakes, Rayburn yelled to Governor Beaufort Jester, the ardent Dixiecrat, who was present, "Shut the door, Beaufort! They're coming by twice!" [16]

Afterward there was dinner for the Trumans and the Rayburn clan. Surrounded later by the youngest Rayburns on a living room couch, Truman yelled happily, "Sam, I'm up to my knees in nieces!"

The Trumans left the house at 11:00 P.M. to sleep on their train, and in the morning Rayburn went along on the outward swing as far as Whitesboro, where he introduced his friend. Truman, in an attempt to make Rayburn's departure exciting to the crowd, told the audience, "Sam's got an ox in the ditch back in Bonham and's got to get back to the farm." [17]

On November 2, Rayburn was triply happy. Truman had surprised the nation and the pollsters by defeating Dewey, and Justice Black's ruling had made Lyndon Johnson a U.S. Senator.

Later when Truman was out of the White House, he said to Rayburn,

"You know I was for you for Vice President in 1944. If you had got that thing, then I'd still be in the Senate."

"And where would I be?" Rayburn cut in. "They'd have probably beaten me in 1948. You got elected." [18]

The third part of Rayburn's pleasure was his own reward. The Democrats had regained control of Congress, and he was Speaker again.

22

The Victor at Bay

In late 1948, when Sam Rayburn went down to the presidential vacation spot at Key West, Florida, to do some fishing and discuss the forthcoming legislative program with Harry Truman, he noticed a profound change in his friend. Truman's earlier expressions of humility and inadequacy as Chief Executive were gone now that he had won the Presidency by his own effort. [1]

No longer burdened by a need to seek approval from others, he ordered Rayburn and Senate Majority Leader Scott Lucas to purge all Dixiecrats from the Democratic Party in both houses. But Rayburn, who had at one time considered this worthwhile to realign the parties, now saw it as disastrous in the cold light of pragmatic politics. The purge, he told Truman, would eliminate the ninety-two-member margin in the House that the Democrats would hold in the Eighty-first Congress. [2] A much better idea, he counseled, would be to slash the power of the twelve-member Rules Committee, where four Dixiecrats combined with the four Republicans to control the flow of bills to the House floor. Truman reluctantly agreed to this compromise attack on the Dixiecrats.

Joe Martin started the House's year on January 3, 1949, by jocularly complaining to the membership that Sam Rayburn was an "Indian Giver" for reclaiming the Speaker's rostrum from him. [3] In a more serious vein, Martin told reporters that Truman could "get anything he wants from Congress—during the next few months anyway."

Martin's assessment of Truman's chances was based to a large extent on Rayburn's successful action against the Rules Committee the day before. And this in turn was based on Rayburn's recollection of a technique Speaker Champ Clark had used in 1913 and 1914. In those first two Woodrow Wilson years the House and Senate Democrats held "binding" caucuses, in which decisions reached on his New Freedom bills became binding on all Democrats. At the time, an elated Wilson said that this "reduced malcontents and mutineers into submission," and "the silver speech spent in caucus secures the golden silence maintained on the floor of Congress, making each party rich in concord and happy in co-operation."[4] Later, when squabbles over foreign policy predominated, the Democratic caucus became a "conference" without power to bind members.

On January 2, 1949, Rayburn insisted that the Democratic caucus be a binding one on the single proposal to curb the Rules Committee. When this carried, his alteration authorized committee chairmen to bring a bill directly to the floor if the Rules Committee failed to clear it for House action within twenty-one days. "Czar Rayburn," some angered Dixie-crats charged. But when the full House approved this rule change the next day, they stayed bound for fear he would purge them from the Democratic Party and their committee power if they did not.

The man most elated by Rayburn's success was Harry Truman. He showed up that same afternoon at Rayburn's Board of Education for a bourbon and branch water to help him "strike a blow for liberty." Then three days later he was back in the Capitol again to celebrate Sam's sixty-seventh birthday at a luncheon in the Speaker's first-floor dining room. The celebrating had only started when Sam told Harry he had to hurry upstairs to the House Chamber to oversee the electoral college's vote "and see them elect a President." Later that afternoon Lady Bird Johnson hosted a birthday reception for her husband's "Daddy." Truman begged off, because he had to return to the Oval Office to sign his daily average of six hundred documents as the law required.

All this celebrating proved premature, however, for the enormity of Truman's legislative program with its large number of highly con-troversial parts wiped out the benefit of the rules' change. Rayburn saw this when Truman asked him to the White House for an advance look at his state of the Union message and his inaugural address. It was in this particular message that Truman gained a title for his administration: "Every individual has the right to expect from our government a *fair deal*." But his Fair Deal for 1949–50 was an indigestible twenty-four-point program calling for a big civil rights program, repeal of the Taft-Hartley Act, elimination of $4 billion in tax loopholes that included the oil depletion allowance, federal possession of the offshore oil lands, compulsory health insurance, a stiff anti-inflation measure, broadened social security, expanded low-cost public housing and an increase in the minimum hourly wage to seventy-five cents. As for Truman's inaugural address, it called for a step-up in the unpopular foreign-aid program through help to underdeveloped countries under what became known as "Point Four" aid.

Despite his misgivings about Truman's demand for so much in so short a time, Rayburn agreed to help him get grass-roots support for his Fair Deal. This meant frequent trips out of Washington, making one-night stands for his friend. He spoke to 1,600 persons at the Jackson-Jefferson Day dinner in Nashville and to other packed houses in Austin, Texas, and Raleigh, North Carolina, appealing to J. Strom Thurmond's Dixiecrats and Henry Wallace's Progressives to become good Democrats again.

But it was not soft soap that he peddled. He told one Southern audience in straight talk that the South "must give the Negroes a better break if they want to prevent passage of Federal civil rights legislation, such as the FEPC. You can't filibuster forever," he warned his listeners.

Westbrook Pegler, the widely circulated columnist who hated the Roosevelts, added Rayburn to his list at the outset of the Speaker's trips into the South for Truman. "Mr. Rayburn, a Texan," said Pegler, "is a renegade who chose early between the first article of the political and social creed of the South and the paltry satisfactions of success with a degenerate party." [5]

But such mean attacks did not deter Rayburn from these speaking trips or from talking directly to malcontent Democratic leaders. Jimmy Byrnes—former member of the House and Senate, Supreme Court justice and a Secretary of State until the President fired him—was spoiling for revenge by leading a massive Southern revolt against Truman. Rayburn met with him over a full bottle of Jack Daniel's "green label" sour mash in Lexington, Virginia, in June 1949, in an effort to get him to change his mind. At the close of his long pitch, a woozy Byrnes thanked him for his concern but refused to be convinced that the Democratic Party had room for both him and Truman.

All the while Rayburn was making his forays, he never forgot that his chief work to help Truman was in Washington—in the Capitol and in the White House. "We're going to have only one kind of Democrat in this Congress," he told reporters. But he knew that the job of holding the Democrats together called for a Super-Speaker. Gene Cox and Joe Martin were as thick as barber-pole stripes. Beyond this, lantern-jawed Percy Priest, whom he had appointed as Democratic whip, said, "More than 100 of our 263 Democrats got more votes in their Districts than Truman, and they felt they didn't owe him a damn thing." [6]

Rayburn was aware that Cox was always ready to erupt on the floor with a wild anti-Truman tirade that would ruin his shaky Democratic alignment. For this reason he babied Cox and appealed to him directly not to jump off the deep end. There were several close calls, all variations of an earlier experience when he learned that Cox planned an imminent break with Truman. On that occasion he had wagged a finger at Cox and motioned him to climb the rostrum to his desk.

"Gene," he whispered when Cox stood alongside him, "you look all swelled up like a tick. Harry Truman is your friend and you're his friend. Now, don't do it!"

Cox argued, but finally walked down the dais stairs and out of the House without delivering his break-off speech. [7]

Rayburn also had to maintain close watch over Cox to keep him out of physical combat with liberals in the House Chamber. One time Cox pulled the hair of Congressman Will Rogers, Jr.; another time he traded blows with old Adolph Sabath over a Housing Bill.

At the other end of the avenue, Rayburn had to work on Truman to modify his programs in order to have some success with Congress. He did part of this work by phone, letter, and in private, and part in Big Four congressional leadership sessions, the weekly hour-long meetings with Truman that began at ten o'clock on Monday mornings in the Oval Office. When Truman was out of town on a Monday the Rayburn–John McCormack–Vice President Alben Barkley–Senate Majority Leader Scott Lucas meetings with him were by telephone hookup. [8]

The immensely broad range of Truman's program made Rayburn's role as a constructive critic difficult. A Truman memo to Rayburn after one congressional leaders' meeting showed the scope of the topics considered. Wrote Truman:

I'm arranging to send the request for the special appropriations down the latter part of the week.

I've already written a letter to the Chairman of the Ways and Means Committee on tax matters and have sent a copy of it to Senator George.

The request for Emergency Aid to Yugoslavia will be down before the week is out.

I've written letters to Senator Maybank and Congressman Spence of the Banking and Currency Committee on the extension of rent control.

I am this morning sending a letter to the Vice President regarding the Statehood for Alaska.

> The other matters referred to have either passed the House and
> have not passed the Senate or have passed the Senate and have
> not passed the House.

> The most important thing under present conditions is the Aid to
> Medical Education, which is pending in the House Committee
> on Education and Labor. [9]

Since the others present did not view the Truman program with the
same perspective as Rayburn, it made him appear frequently as a nagging
obstructionist. "At Big Four meetings," said Barkley, "Truman sat cross-
legged at his desk, swinging in his chair and chopping the air with his
hands about two feet apart to emphasize a point. He canvassed us on
proposals, and sometimes he had trouble with Rayburn." [10]

The trouble, of course, was his unwillingness to accede blindly to every
request Truman made. "I have been in on White House meetings where
the President, the Majority Leader of the House, the Vice President and
the Majority Leader of the Senate were against me on a proposition,"
Rayburn said in 1951. "I have told them that I thought they were wrong
and ill-advised, but that I would go along and let the rest of the fellows in
the House thrash it out. But when the votes were about even in one of
those meetings I stuck by my guns."

Truman's proposal to reestablish the tough wartime Fair Employment
Practices Committee in the Eighty-first Congress was not an issue Rayburn could ignore. While he and Truman argued about it at Big Four
meetings, Northern liberals and Southern conservatives were spoiling for
war. Finally Rayburn found his own solution and pushed it through the
House. Instead of a compulsory FEPC, Rayburn promoted a voluntary
FEPC in interstate industries. The result was that when the bill passed the
Senate, Truman signed it, and each side claimed it had gained
something.

There was no simple solution when Truman demanded that the Taft-
Hartley Act be repealed, just as the Democratic platform in 1948 had
pledged. Rayburn, who had voted against passage of Taft-Hartley in the
first instance and then to uphold Truman's veto in the last Congress,
found merit in one provision of the existing law and argued strenuously
for its retention. This was the section authorizing the President to seek an
injunction to prevent strikes that affected the national welfare.

Truman could not accept this because of his absolute promise to
organized labor, and he criticized Rayburn's proposal privately in a letter
to Al Whitney, president of the Railroad Trainmen Brotherhood. When
Whitney leaked the letter to reporters, they tried to promote a feud

between Rayburn and Truman. But Rayburn merely shrugged his thick shoulders, and Truman took refuge in a statement that the letter had been misquoted.

The entire matter soon became academic because Republican Senator Robert A. Taft, whom Rayburn considered a small man with an excellent press, was able to keep the Senate from repealing the act.

Only a few parts of Truman's extensive Fair Deal program were washed away by rushing events. This was the fate of his anti-inflation proposals for price, wage, rent and credit controls, over which he and Rayburn had had much discussion at first. But the sharp rise in unemployment early in 1949 and the drop in the cost of living allowed Rayburn to put the bills aside without a Truman protest.

No such ending happened to Truman's proposals regarding the oil industry. In fact, the issue blossomed into a major campaign subject in 1952.

Part of Truman's oil program called for the elimination of the 27½-percent tax depletion allowance. He knew that Rayburn would not lift a finger to help him on this tax reform, but he wanted it discussed as a rallying point for future action. [11]

Of far more immediate interest to Truman was the issue of the ownership of the offshore tidelands and the continental shelf, where great oil stores existed. In a case involving California, the Supreme Court had ruled that the federal government owned the offshore tidelands, or the three-mile belt off the state's coastline. Truman wanted Congress to pass legislation establishing federal ownership over the tidelands off the other states. As a countermeasure, members of Congress, on orders from the oil lobby, were promoting a bill to give the states ownership. The philosophy behind this move was that the states would be easier to control than the federal government.

Rayburn soon found himself pushed by both sides, each angry because he made no move to bring either bill to the floor. Eastern newspapers considered him the slave of the oil industry while Texas papers treated him like a treacherous turncoat. But he ignored the name calling and mulled over middle-ground solutions.

Finally he produced his own bill that he believed would protect the interests of both the states and the federal government. Texas political leaders were claiming inherited ownership from Mexico that put the state's boundary three leagues, or about 10.5 miles, off her coast. Rayburn's bill recognized this, but it gave the federal government 37½ percent of the oil and mineral revenues within this area and half the rights under the continental shelf, which extended almost two hundred miles further in some places into the Gulf of Mexico.

As he should have expected, his proposal infuriated some Eastern Democrats on one hand and oil producers and their political and newspaper allies on the other. The *Dallas Morning News,* for one, referred to him in an open letter as "the enemy" of Texas, [12]while behind the scenes the oil lobby once again undertook to change his congressional district so that it would include a large rock-ribbed Republican area to wipe out his normal margin of victory in elections. But though most members of the state legislature were willing to condemn his proposal, they would not overhaul his political base.

So the tidelands issue remained to fester and swell.

The Fair Deal record was not entirely negative. Rayburn's hard work at maintaining a semblance of Democratic unity paid off with the passage of the minimum wage-increase bill, expanded Social Security and an 810,000-unit low-cost public housing measure. But as the Eighty-first Congress moved along, Truman frequently became impatient with the pace of legislation.

Sometimes he showed this impatience by his efforts to intrude in Rayburn's domain. In a typical instance, when a House subcommittee was dawdling over a bill to provide federal aid to medical schools, Truman bypassed Rayburn and asked the Democrats on the sub-committee to come to the White House for a conference in the Cabinet Room. Dixiecrat Dwight Rogers, a congressman from Florida, was the subcommittee chairman. Right after Truman finished stating the importance of the bill, Rogers started to argue, and the meeting ended in shambles when Truman shouted at him, "That's a fine way to show your appreciation after all I've done for you!"[13]

To Rayburn's chagrin, Truman was often his own worst enemy. He could show great courage in calling for the Berlin Airlift to supply that vital German city after the Russians closed the land approaches; and he could reveal cold-war creativity by the establishment of the North Atlantic Treaty Organization (NATO), the mutual-assistance military pact that was a warning to Stalin that an attack on any of the eleven signatory nations would be considered an attack on all.

Yet he could embarrass his friends by lapses of undignified behavior. There was, for instance, his habit of waking early and writing provocative letters. In one letter he wrote that the Marine Corps had "a propaganda machine that is almost equal to Stalin's." Another time he said John L. Lewis, head of the United Mine Workers, was not worthy of being appointed a "dog catcher." He wrote one member of Congress: "It seems to me that you have been making Macedonian cries or yells ever since I have been in the White House." The most notorious of his letters was one he wrote to a music critic who had ridiculed his daughter Margaret's singing recital. "I never met you," he wrote, "but if I do you'll need a new nose and plenty of beefsteak and perhaps a supporter below."

"My God!" Rayburn gasped when he heard about this last letter. "Why doesn't someone down there in the White House hide all the lead pencils from Harry so he can't find them?"

Despite Truman's embarrassing letters that lessened the stature of his administration and Rayburn's frank comments at Big Four meetings that riled the occasional member of Truman's palace guard who attended them, the strong Harry-Sam friendship was never endangered. Suggestions and requests each made to the other were always taken in good faith because complete trust was present.

Rayburn felt no deterioration of the doctrine of separation of powers when Truman sent him recommendations for House committee posts, nor did Truman when Rayburn suggested individuals for jobs under the President's control. In one letter dealing with vacancies on the Ways and Means Committee, Truman wrote: "It would certainly be a grand thing if we could get a couple of people on that Committee who are favorable to the program in which you and I are interested. I'll talk with you on the subject Monday if you feel inclined." [14] When a vacancy appeared on the Appropriations Committee, Truman suggested "a western man." [15] He also bemoaned the presence on a committee staff of a man whom he called "an almost impossible gentleman to get along with the Executive Branch of the Government. He is one of the men who fed poison to the Republican Committee during the last Congress." [16]

Rayburn was a softie when it came to promising to send Truman letters of recommendation for appointments to government agencies and the bench. On occasion in Truman's almost eight years in office, he even recommended Republicans. One such letter involved Republican Congressman Noble Johnson of Indiana, whom Rayburn recommended for a seat on the board of a federal agency. Truman objected to him in his reply not because of his Republicanism but because of his age. Considering that Johnson was three years younger than Truman, his comment was strange. "A lot of these Boards are suffering from senility," Truman told Rayburn, "and it has been my policy since I have been here to overcome that situation without the slightest reflection on Representative Johnson." [17] But Rayburn persisted, and the following year Truman nominated Johnson to the U.S. Court of Customs and Patent Appeals.

Almost from the start of Truman's elected term as President, he became the subject of abuse and ridicule. The depth of the press attacks was reached by the *Washington Times-Herald*, which called him a "dishonest nincompoop." In reply, Truman said, "I'm saving up for four or five good hard punches on the nose, and when I'm out of this job I'm going to run around and deliver them personally."

In sharp contrast, outside of the attacks by the oil crowd and right-fringe Dixiecrats, Rayburn's national status grew. In May 1949, *Collier's Weekly* awarded him ten thousand dollars for distinguished service, and he turned the check over to a Sam Rayburn Library fund for Bonham and Fannin County. Phi Beta Kappa also elected him to membership that year. Honorary degrees began flowing his way; a chamber of commerce presented him with a prize Palomino quarter horse named "Whistle Stop"; and parties honoring him became too numerous to record. One awesome bash for him was a fifteen-thousand-dollar affair paid for by Congressman Frank Boykin. The "friends of Sam's" guest list totaled 937, and the groaning board sagged under a river of champagne and a buffet of bear, buffalo, elk, antelope, deer, possum, and "Steak Rayburn." [18]

Fortunately, Rayburn remained enough of a skeptic not to take the outpouring of praise too seriously. When Wright Patman and Lyndon Johnson held a luncheon in honor of his sixty-eighth birthday on January 6, 1950, Truman gave him a new hat and remarked to the crowd, "Sam is the only man I know who could stay in Washington over 40 years and still wear the same hat size he wore when he came here." His eyes growing misty with sentiment, he shaped the hat, and set it on Rayburn's head. But Rayburn spoiled the moment by pulling the hat down over his eyes and ears.

The most maudlin show of regard for Rayburn in the Truman era came in January 1951 when he passed the carefully calculated 3,056½ days that Henry Clay had served as Speaker in the early part of the nineteenth century. Member after member rose to praise Rayburn so effusively that he sat bathed in embarrassment. The only humorous note was provided by Bob "Muley" Doughton, the eighty-seven-year-old chairman of the Ways and Means Committee. After praising Rayburn, Doughton suddenly blurted, "I cannot say so much of him as a father. But he's still young, handsome and popular. We still have hope for him in that respect." [19]

Of all the praise that came his way in the Truman era, perhaps his greatest pleasure came from the handwritten note Truman sent him after he made a fighting speech in behalf of an administration program on May 7, 1949.

"Sam," Truman's note said, "you made a wonderful speech this afternoon. You choked me up so I could hardly talk." [20]

23

To the Well with Truman

By early 1950 Sam Rayburn knew what his friend Harry Truman meant when he said that being President was like "riding a tiger. . . . A man has to keep on riding or be swallowed." Almost daily now newspaper editorials and the political opposition were pelting him with charges that the administration was crawling with Communists, fellow travelers and criminals; that he was pulling something crooked by ordering the termite-ridden White House rebuilt almost from scratch; and that he was somehow the villain when Chiang Kai-shek and his dwindling band of followers fled the Chinese mainland for Formosa (Taiwan) in 1949. Even the noncontroversial, bipartisan foreign policy that Truman had struggled to create with congressional Republicans now lay in danger from attacks by Republican isolationists led by Senator Robert Taft and the China Lobby, whose darling, Senator Arthur Vandenberg, declared that his "firm" support of Truman's bipartisan foreign policy was limited to Europe and did not include China. [1]

Rayburn was able for the most part to hold his House flock in line by personal appeals and scoldings, patronage favors and punishment. Said Clinton Anderson, "In his well-organized mind, he [Rayburn] kept accurate accounts on the people he dealt with, rewarding them for political services or punishing them for political slights. Everyone knew he was honest and that when the opportunity arrived for settling a score he would do it fairly and justly." [2]

Unfortunately, Truman had no Sam Rayburn governing the Senate, and here "the knock and smear boys," as Rayburn put it, had a field day with Truman. Senator Harry Byrd of Virginia, a nominal Democrat, was punching holes in the Truman social-welfare budget, killing his proposed $4-billion tax-loophole elimination and waylaying his nominations. Even more disruptive was Senator Joseph McCarthy of Wisconsin, who was hopefully riding the Red-smear circuit to future occupancy of the White House.

Angry over what had happened to his Presidency in only a year and half, Truman wrote Rayburn: "Byrd and his crowd have succeeded in effectively ruining the efficiency of the Government while McCarthy and his crowd have almost ruined the morale of public employees. That may be patriotic and economical but I have my doubts about it."[3]

The most cataclysmic event Rayburn had to cope with in the Truman times was the Korean War, which began in the summer of 1950 and lasted throughout the remainder of his administration. Rayburn had come late and reluctantly to the cold-war concept of containing the Soviet Union. Nevertheless, he supported Greek-Turkish aid in 1947, the Marshall Plan in 1948, and NATO's mutual-defense pact in 1949. He had also come around to the belief that the United States had to be the prime military power on the globe, though he advocated talk and more talk with opponents instead of continual sabre rattling and threats.

While the American cold-war focus was in Europe, trouble came unexpectedly on the peninsula of Korea, which had been temporarily divided at the 38th Parallel following its liberation from Japan after World War II. Despite the agreement at the Cairo Conference in 1943 to create eventually a single, independent Korea, the Soviets had immediately set up a Communist dictatorship in the northern zone while the United States organized a semidictatorship below the 38th parallel under old Syngman Rhee, a longtime Korean exile.

As the years passed, cruelty and a lack of civil rights were common on both sides, as well as fierce border clashes between Rhee's troops and the northern Communists. A UN resolution calling for free elections throughout Korea was ignored in the north and honored on the surface in the south, where Rhee's enemies were barred from the polls. From time to time Truman told the Big Four about his mounting problems with Rhee. These ranged from Rhee's insistence on a personal percentage cut on the value of the free foreign aid shipped to the Republic of South Korea to his ordering the slaughter of fifteen thousand political opponents at Cheju.[4] But despite these shortcomings, Truman's painful conclusion was that "Syngman Rhee may be an s.o.b., but he's our s.o.b."

Beyond the American role as South Korea's creator and the donor of billions in economic and military aid, the relationship between the two countries within the cold-war framework was considered nonexistent by influential administration officials. Secretary of State Dean Acheson and General Eisenhower were on record declaring Korea outside the defense perimeter of the United States. General Douglas MacArthur, with the last fifteen years of his career devoted to Pacific action, went far further, warning that anyone who advocated a land war on the Asian continent should have his head examined.

Rayburn had seen Truman before he flew to Baltimore to dedicate Friendship Airport on Saturday, June 24, 1950, and then on to Missouri to sell a part of his mother's farm at Grandview for a shopping center. [5] It was a peaceful, hot and quiet day in Washington when Rayburn settled down to dictate letters to three stenographers in his Capitol hideaway. He was feeling especially good because he had no opponent in the July Democratic primary. But only three days later, when Truman invited him and other congressional leaders to a Tuesday morning meeting in the White House, his feeling of comfort had vanished, for the nation was rushing into another war only five years after World War II.

At the 10:30 A.M. meeting in the Cabinet Room, Secretary of State Acheson gave a step-by-step rundown of events that had brought this about. [6] Acheson, the recipient of a long battering from Senator Joseph McCarthy, who labeled him pro-Communist, told the congressional gathering he had phoned Truman late Saturday with the news of a large North Korean invasion of South Korea. Truman had wanted to return immediately to Washington, but Acheson suggested that, because there was no word about South Korean counterefforts, he need not cut short his trip home. But there was one thing the United States should do immediately, said Acheson, and this was to ask the UN Security Council to hold a meeting the next day and declare the invasion an act of aggression. Since the Soviet Union had walked out of the Security Council after the UN had refused to seat Red China, its representative would not be present to cast a killing veto.

On Sunday, the UN Security Council did as the United States requested. Then on Monday, after Truman was back in Washington, he had learned that the huge amounts of military equipment and the intensive training he had provided Rhee's military forces were ineffectual in stopping the Communist invaders. So at Acheson's urging, he had taken a step that he believed would aid Rhee yet keep the United States from becoming a full-scale belligerent. This was his order to General MacArthur, in charge of the occupation in Japan, to supply American air- and sea-cover assistance behind Rhee's effort to clear the enemy from the South.

Neither Rayburn nor the other thirteen congressional leaders offered any objections to the actions Truman had taken. However, both Rayburn and Senator Tom Connally stressed the point that all American military action be under the direct orders of the UN. Truman agreed, and later that day the United States won approval of another Security Council resolution that recommended that "members of the UN furnish such assistance to the Republic of South Korea as may be necessary to repel the armed attack and restore international peace and security in the area." [7]

Three days later Truman again asked Rayburn and the same congressional contingent back for another meeting. This time he announced grimly that the United States was engaged in land combat.

American air and sea aid had proved insufficient, and he had ordered a single American regiment into action in Korea. The peninsula may have been outside the U.S.'s defense perimeter, he said, but if the Communists won here they would get the idea that they could overrun other countries without fear of American military action.

Before the meeting began, Truman had asked Senator Tom Connally, chairman of the Senate Foreign Relations Committee, if he should ask Congress for a declaration of war. During the meeting he repeated the question, and Connally gave him the same answer: "You might run into a long debate which would tie your hands completely. You know how they talk," he added, rolling his eyes. [8] Rayburn and all others except Senator Kenneth Wherry of Nebraska concurred that as commander in chief and under the UN banner he could ignore congressional sanctioning of full-scale American involvement in Korea. This was to set a mischievous precedent for future Presidents.

Once the American involvement began, Truman and the congressional Big Four concentrated on wartime legislation. A boost in taxes and the restriction of consumer credit were quickly started. When Truman told Rayburn that his Council of Economic Advisers had proposed a priority and allocation system for materials to war industries plus price controls, Rayburn told him he could get priority and allocation controls approved in a few days if price controls were not tacked on the legislation. The Office of Price Administration had been in a four-year battle with conservative congressmen during World War II, he reminded Truman, and there would be weeks of talk and a major filibuster in the Senate if a new price-control system were advocated.

Truman accepted Rayburn's argument, and the bill did not include price controls. Afterward, Rayburn considered this a mistake, for untended prices soon skyrocketed. Belatedly he tried to correct his error by pushing hard for a price freeze. But the anti-Truman congressional coalition held it up for six months. So in one sense his original judgment proved correct.

Rayburn was pleased to get Congress out of Washington on a two-month recess on September 23. In the turmoil of the first days of the Korean fighting, Truman had given a fast answer at his news conference by agreeing with a reporter who called the war a "police action." When casualties began mounting, this description of the war provided his enemies with ammunition for attacking him. Rayburn's friend, Joe Martin, went so far as to drop a bill in the hopper to cut off Acheson's salary. Other congressmen were using Acheson and Defense Secretary Louis Johnson as punching bags. When Truman retired Johnson for failing to prepare the nation for a hard war and replaced him with General Marshall, Rayburn was infuriated when a Republican senator called Marshall "a living lie."

Despite the strident increase in the political fighting in Washington since the outbreak of war, there was initial optimism among Democrats about the congressional elections on November 7. With his forces pushed down to a flimsy beachhead at the bottom of South Korea, in mid-September MacArthur had daringly moved by sea around the enemy and landed at Inchon, hundreds of miles north on the opposite coast. Then when their supply line was severed shortly afterward, 130,000 North Koreans surrendered, and the area south of the 38th Parallel was free of the enemy by the time Congress recessed.

At the time there was rejoicing among the Democrats over MacArthur's brilliant move because the expected grim prospect of justifying the war to constituents appeared unnecessary. But this sense of relief was short-lived. Truman was in touch with his Big Four and Senator Connally to inform them eagerly that he had instructed MacArthur on September 27 to take North Korea and destroy the North Korean armed forces. "I don't recall that any of us reminded the President that his objective had been only to liberate the Republic of South Korea," said Senator Connally. "And this was also the intent of the UN resolution." [9]

For all the Democratic strategies to sweep the elections on November 7, the deciding factor was totally unexpected. On October 1, an inkling of the role Chinese Communists would play in the congressional elections came from the warning of Chou En-lai, the foreign minister: "The People's Republic of China will not stand idly by and see North Korea invaded."

Truman assured Rayburn and Connally that this was merely talk. But on October 15 when he flew to Wake Island for a conference with General MacArthur, he asked if the general saw a real Chinese threat. MacArthur told him that his own intelligence as well as that of the CIA showed three hundred thousand Red troops in Manchuria across the Yalu River border from North Korea. However, he added, they had no air force and would be slaughtered if they crossed the river to fight his troops.

Events proved him in error. By late October several Red Chinese troops were captured by the Americans as they moved northward, and Russian MIG's were engaging American pilots in air combat. Truman communicated his mounting concern plus his distrust of MacArthur's intelligence sources to his congressional leaders. His equilibrium was further jarred on November 1 when two nationalist Puerto Rican assassins tried to storm Blair House and kill him while he was taking his afternoon nap. The first reports to Texas were garbled, but Truman reassured a worried Rayburn that he had kept his afternoon schedule of appointments without change.

Rayburn was in Bonham on November 6 when radio news carried a MacArthur statement that "men and materiel in large force are pouring across all bridges over the Yalu from Manchuria. This movement not only jeopardizes but threatens the ultimate destruction of the forces under my command." With fear spreading across the U.S., Rayburn's optimism regarding the next day's elections disappeared. When the results became known, the Democrats lost 33 seats in the House, and their margin in the Senate was reduced to only two.

Ironically, while an attack on Truman had proved a productive Republican vote-getter, in one instance a Republican relied on praise by Rayburn. This occurred in Illinois where Everett Dirksen was running against Senate Majority Leader Scott Lucas. Dirksen had quit the House in 1948 because doctors had told him he would soon be blind, and at his departure Rayburn had told the House, "If they are going to send Republicans to Congress, let them send Republicans of the Everett Dirksen kind." Two years later, with his eyesight improved, Dirksen ran for the Senate against Lucas, a Democrat, and used Rayburn's praise on circulars and billboards as a principal campaign weapon. [10]

So far as Rayburn was concerned, the Eighty-second Congress was a wild horse who would not approach the corral even for food. Prospects for patronage and pork barrel could not entice Dixiecrats away from their alliance with conservative Republicans. In fact, with the coalition stronger because of the recent election, the partnership humiliated Rayburn on the first day of the session by restoring the authority of the Rules Committee over bills. No longer could committee chairmen bring bills directly to the floor for consideration if the Rules Committee failed to act within twenty-one days. This dealt a hard blow to Truman because Rayburn had been able to use that power in the last Congress to get floor consideration for the administration's housing, minimum wage, antipollution and National Science Foundation bills.

"MacArthur" was the catchword for the early part of that Congress. The general's alarm on November 6 had proved a few weeks premature, for it was on November 26 that the Red Chinese poured across the Yalu into North Korea and sent the Americans scampering headlong in a disorderly retreat back behind the 38th parallel.

By March 1951, the rollback had been halted and a fairly stabilized line existed near the border between South and North Korea. Truman reported to the congressional Big Four that he was now willing to negotiate a peace at the original boundaries. His chief concern, he said, was MacArthur, who had dropped his earlier view about the folly of fighting a land war in Asia. Since December, the general had been complaining to reporters that Washington was limiting him to a defensive war when he should have been given the opportunity to take on China. "I should have relieved him then and there," said Truman. Rayburn offered no advice, though he disagreed with Truman's assessment of MacArthur as a poor general. [11]

At the next congressional meeting, Truman discussed angrily a public statement issued by MacArthur on March 7 that called for a blockade of the Chinese coast, bombing of her industrial cities and supporting a Chiang Kai-shek invasion of the mainland. This was clearly a case of insubordination, of a general going over the head of a President of the United States. But instead of acting swiftly on the basis of his emotions, Truman surprised the Big Four when he said he would try to set MacArthur straight.

It was Joe Martin who brought the crisis to a head almost a month later when he made public on April 5 a letter MacArthur wrote him in reply to his own suggestive letter. Rayburn knew as soon as he read it that Truman would have to fire MacArthur or reduce the stature of his office as President. MacArthur was calling for a holy war: "If we lose the war to Communism in Asia, the fall of Europe is inevitable. . . . As you point out, we must win. There is no substitute for victory."

Yet Truman waited until April 11 before firing MacArthur, and when he did, the uproar by the general's Republican admirers was enormous: Joe Martin called for Truman's impeachment; young Senator Richard Nixon demanded that Truman be censured and MacArthur get his command back, and Senator Joe McCarthy called Truman a "sonofabitch" who fired MacArthur while he was drunk on "bourbon and benedictine."

There was also an uproar in Rayburn's congressional district after he defended Truman. One letter writer also called Mrs. Truman a traitor, and a Baptist preacher wrote to "Dishonorable Rayburn" that "if the people of the Sherman, Dennison [sic], Bonham area ever elect you to office again, they will be blind, deaf, dumb and ignorant." In his reply, Rayburn said: "Being a believer in God and His Word and the teachings of His Son which was, 'And on earth peace, good-will toward men,' I fear that your conduct will not be conducive to carrying out these things. In other words, I fear that God and His Son traveling with you would be in poor company." [12]

After MacArthur returned to the United States, Rayburn agreed with Senator Tom Connally that their strategy should be to give him every opportunity to defend himself, because to do otherwise would make him a martyr. [13] Kept on the scene to repeat and repeat the same story, the hero would inevitably turn into a bore.

On this basis Rayburn arranged to have him address a joint session of Congress on April 19, a few days after his return from the Orient. There were tears shed by listening congressmen when the dramatic general said, "Old soldiers never die. They just fade away." A short time later Connally helped arrange joint hearings on MacArthur's dismissal before the Senate Foreign Relations and Armed Services Committees. Connally made certain the hearings were closed so that the general, who was a brilliant speaker, would not have a national audience day after day. MacArthur then went on an eleven-state tour to test presidential waters, but by the time he reached Austin, Texas, his audience was not moved emotionally.

However, the Korean struggle did not fade away with MacArthur. In June 1951, Truman reported with pleasure to the Big Four that Stalin was interested in peace negotiations between the U.S. and North Korea. A month later Truman announced publicly that talks were starting at Kaesong near the 38th Parallel. But the fighting did not end, because Truman would not accept the forced repatriation of North Korean POW's. "If I did," he told the Big Four, "the Republicans'd scream for my impeachment."

As a result of this single sticky point, the U.S. forces, which had suffered 50,000 casualties before negotiations began, suffered an additional 80,000 in the rest of Truman's term. Of the 130,000 American casualties, 33,000 Americans lay in graves. An additional 800,000 Korean soldiers were dead, as were 2 million Korean civilians.

Public dissatisfaction with Korea gave impetus to congressional anti-Truman investigations that made Rayburn's control over the House exceedingly difficult at times. Scandals were uncovered in several federal agencies, and congressmen eager for publicity tried to blame Truman personally for them. Truman was surprised when several top officials of the Bureau of Internal Revenue were found to be taking bribes, and even though he fired the individuals concerned and ordered legal action started against them, it became known as a "Truman Scandal." The RFC was also found to be giving loans to cronies of Democratic officials, and the House Judiciary Committee busied itself investigating a host of illegal activities going on at the Justice Department. In exasperation with the proliferation of investigations really aimed at his friend instead of at the wrongdoers, Rayburn commented: "Everyone down my way says Washington is talking too much. They're tired of this investigation and that investigation. There's a time to fish and a time to mend nets."

Other investigations were designed to "prove" that Truman, the relentless leader of containment and the cold war, was "soft on Communism." Rayburn, of course, had no jurisdiction over the hearings run by Senator Pat McCarran's Internal Security Committee or the spoutings of Senator Joe McCarthy. But he had something to say about the House Un-American Activities Committee (HUAC), and he labored to keep it from becoming an American gestapo.

Although he could not control attacks on Truman by HUAC members, he could limit the committee's publicity. Early in 1952, Rayburn read in the paper that HUAC was holding hearings across the country that were being broadcast and televised, letting viewers and listeners know the way some congressmen badgered witnesses. His reaction was to order the committee to get the cameras and electronic gear out of its hearing rooms. Later in a face-to-face meeting with the irate chairman, Francis Walter, his former protégé whom he had put on HUAC to keep it in line, he barked, "There will not be any more committee or subcommittee hearings in Washington or elsewhere televised or broadcast by radio. Period!"

Newspapers criticized him as a man far behind the times for not permitting House affairs to be seen and heard. In reply, Rayburn cited the need to maintain congressional "decorum," that many members would turn into show-business performers if they knew hearings were being televised. Privately, he went further, saying that he did not intend to have individual rights invaded and witnesses tried and convicted outside of court.

Lyndon Johnson, another Rayburn protégé, was among the loudest anti-Truman noisemakers. Fresh to the Senate in 1949, he had charged in his maiden speech that Truman was determined to become a dictator and that only the Southern Senators stood in his path. That same year he also led a vicious attack in a Commerce Committee hearing on Leland Olds, whom Truman had nominated for a third term as chairman of the Federal Power Commission. [14] Johnson acted in behalf of Texas natural-gas interests who wanted Olds out because he had decreed that the FPC should regulate prices. At the hearing Johnson smeared the innocent Olds as a Communist and said that Truman wanted Olds because he hoped to get political support from the "Communist American Labor Party."

Rayburn was displeased with Johnson's McCarthyish attack on Olds and Truman, but with the blind spot of an always-forgiving parent he did not break with him. In fact, he helped reconcile the smoldering President with Lyndon by explaining that Johnson's excuse for his anti-Truman speeches and votes was his need to do so to keep his Senate seat. In 1950 Rayburn even got Truman to offer advice to his protégé when Johnson won Senate approval for a Korean War Preparedness Investigating Subcommittee modeled after Truman's World War II committee.

When Senate Majority Leader Scott Lucas and Majority Whip Francis Myers lost their seats in the 1950 congressional elections, Rayburn helped Johnson succeed Myers as Democratic whip. He did this by phoning the dozen Democratic senators who had once been his "boys" in the House, asking them to support Johnson in the Senate Democratic caucus vote. Unknown to Rayburn, instead of being appreciative Johnson was belittling him in 1951. One instance occurred in a conversation Johnson had with me that year. [15] He wanted a magazine profile of himself and asked me to do it. When I wanted to know if the pitch of the piece would be his availability for the vice-presidential nomination in 1952, he said: "Who wants that? President! That's the angle you want to write about me. You can build it up by saying how I run both houses of Congress right now."

Asked for an explanation of this remark, Johnson said, "Well, right here in the Senate I have to do all of Boob McFarland's work because he can't do any of it. [Senator Ernest McFarland of Arizona was the new majority leader.] And then every afternoon I go over to Sam Rayburn's place. He tells me all about the problems he's facing in the House, and I tell him how to handle them. So that's how come I'm running everything here in the Capitol."

Johnson's Preparedness Investigating Subcommittee was among those Rayburn felt was treating Truman unfairly. But as in other instances he did not scold Johnson after he had described Truman's air-war program as filled with "abuse, misuse and disabuse," or when he hit at Truman for not putting the nation on a full war footing.

By the spring of 1952, the various anti-Truman forces were like the sections of an orchestra, all of them playing fortissimo. From his place on the rostrum, Rayburn had to listen to attacks on Truman for not extending the war to China and for staying in Korea, for wanting to bring Negroes into the mainstream, for being involved in scandals and for being soft on Communism.

There were new sections in the orchestra that spring. One was the screaming group of congressional friends of the oil industry after Truman had vetoed a bill that gave control of the tidelands to the states. Another blast came from the steel industry, which refused to grant the wage increase ordered by the Wage Stabilization Board unless they were permitted to raise the price of steel by twelve dollars a ton. With a strike imminent in ninety-two mills and the Korean War still raging, Truman ordered Secretary of Commerce Charles Sawyer to seize them until a settlement was reached.

Rayburn suffered anguish when he heard that Truman had hastily agreed with a questioning reporter at his news conference afterward that, if he could seize the steel mills in a national emergency, he could also seize newspapers and radio stations for the same reason. This served only to muddy the issue.

On June 2, when the Supreme Court by a 6-to-3 decision ruled that Truman's seizure was unconstitutional, the great body of the business community besides the oil and natural-gas industries joined the anti-Truman orchestra.

With the steel companies in charge of their plants once more and the workers out on strike, Truman was furious at his momentary helplessness. When Secretary Sawyer suggested that he talk with Rayburn, Barkley, McCormack and McFarland to learn "the temper of Congress" on the problem, Truman made his only known unfriendly comment about Rayburn, whose protégé Johnson had recently told the Senate that the President was violating "the plain language of the Constitution." Truman snapped at Sawyer, "They don't know anything about the temper of Congress, and they've proved it." [16] He finally settled the strike after seven weeks by allowing the companies to raise their prices by $5.65 a ton.

Although the general impression across the country was that the federal government was in a state of collapse, it continued to function fairly well. The key reason Truman had what legislative success he enjoyed was the extra effort put in by Rayburn. More often than in past years, he left the rostrum to make his pitch for passage of bills. In addition, while the voting was under way, he circulated on the floor to confront individual members before they cast their votes.

When Truman announced he would not run again for the Presidency in 1952, historians quickly agreed with anti-Truman politicians and newspaper publishers that he would rank among the worst Presidents.

Rayburn disagreed with this verdict and predicted he would one day be ranked among the strongest Presidents. As for his reason, he said with characteristic brevity: "Right on all the big things, wrong on most of the little ones."

24

In the Minority Again

When Harry Truman announced on March 29, 1952, that he would not run again for President, Senator Mike Monroney of Oklahoma told reporters he intended to lead a campaign to win that year's nomination for Sam Rayburn. Monroney, as a House member, had coauthored the 1946 Congressional Reorganization Act with Senator Robert LaFollette, Jr., and although Rayburn had eliminated sections that would have weakened the Speaker's authority, Monroney's enthusiasm for him had not diminished.

By the time Monroney made his announcement, several Democrats were already contesting for the presidential nomination. Front-runner was Senator Estes Kefauver of Tennessee, who had gained national attention with his televised hearings on organized crime. Among the others were Senator Robert Kerr of Oklahoma, an oil and natural-gas operator, who had led the fight to bar the Federal Power Commission from regulating natural-gas prices only to have Truman veto his bill; Senator Richard Russell of Georgia, the leader of the segregationists; and former Secretary of Commerce Averell Harriman, who had first planted the seed for the cold war with Truman.

In looking over the field, Monroney gave this timetable for Rayburn: "Ours is a tenth ballot proposition, not a first ballot one. When a few ballots have gone by and it becomes obvious that none of the candidates is going to get past first base, the delegates will be ready to switch to someone who can get a home run."

At first Rayburn scoffed at Monroney's promotion as well as that of people in his district who organized a "Rayburn-for-President" Club. Three reasons why they were wasting their time came quickly to mind: He was seventy, a Southerner, and he was hated by the oil industry. "I have told my friends that I hoped they wouldn't make a move in that direction," he wrote with much embarrassment, "as I doubted that an effort along that line could be fruitful on account of matters that would take too long to go into."

But as time passed, he realized this would be his last chance to become President, and he decided not to pour too much cold water on his supporters. "Many people have come to me and said they thought I could come nearer to bringing the Party together—North, South, East and West—than anyone else," was his revised approach. "That may or may not be true. Not being a candidate, if such a thing should occur at the Convention in Chicago after a deadlock, they turn to me and ask me to take the nomination, I would, of course, be a good soldier."

Rayburn never discussed his interest in becoming a late-inning pinch-hitter candidate with Truman. Nor did Truman give him any inkling of what moves he was making to control who would get the nomination. Shortly after he decided not to be a candidate in 1952, Truman had told Chief Justice Fred Vinson he would support him at the convention. [1] But Vinson had rejected the offer. Truman then decided on Illinois Governor Adlai B. Stevenson, an intellectual, broad-gauged man and brilliant speaker, who had been an assistant to the Secretary of the Navy during World War II and whose grandfather had been Grover Cleveland's Vice President. Governor Stevenson, however, could not make up his mind whether to accept Truman's offer.

In the meantime, Rayburn's extremely thin chances for the nomination vanished in the quagmire of Texas politics, just as it had in other national convention years. The boss of the miry moor in 1952 was Allan Shivers, the handsome, young lieutenant governor who had become governor in 1949 after Governor "Beautiful Beaufort with the marcelled hair" Jester dropped dead on a train. Shivers had started life poor, but he had been helped to wealth by the father of Lloyd Bentsen, a boy congressman. According to Senator Tom Connally, the elder Bentsen, who considered Shivers a protégé, gave him a "Texas Deal," which was to "sell" him thirteen thousand acres for $25,000 and then buy the property back six months later for $450,000. [2] In addition, Shivers had married the daughter of John Shary—an immensely wealthy rancher, real-estate operator and publisher.

When Shivers purged the Texas Democratic organization with the help of Jake Pickle, his assistant, and then became the spokesman for the oil industry and Dixiecrats, Rayburn saw with horror that Texas could go Republican nationally in 1952 unless the governor were defeated at the polls. The urgency was increased when the Shivers strong-arm plot to force Senator Tom Connally to retire succeeded.

271

Since Lyndon Johnson would not run against Shivers, Rayburn sought another candidate. "Sam Rayburn and R. T. Craig approached me in February 1952," Ralph Yarborough, a liberal Democratic lawyer in Austin, recalled. "Right off, they tried to pressure me to run for Governor against Allan Shivers, but I didn't want to because I intended to run for Attorney General, an office I believed I could win. They persisted, and finally I agreed when they assured me of all the financial help I might need." [3]

At the San Antonio Democratic state convention in May, Shivers owned thirty-five hundred of the four thousand delegates, and in Rayburn's words they were so cowed by Shivers "you could almost hear them 'moo'." Questioned whether he would back Rayburn for the Democratic presidential nomination at the national convention in July, Shivers jeered, "I would like to know what his views are." Congressman Wright Patman, incensed at this slur on his good friend, shot back, "Sam Rayburn's views were well known long before the Governor was born." [4]

Shivers' arrogance at the state convention ran high when he orchestrated a massive booing, which drowned out a resolution that the Texas delegation to the national convention take a loyalty oath to support the Democratic ticket in November. This so aroused fiery Maury Maverick and his small force that they walked out of the convention to the tune of fistfights every foot of the way. Before taking his departure into a heavy rainstorm, Maverick yelled at the Shivercrats, "We will throw you out of Chicago!"

A victorious Shivers shouted after him that he was going to "keep the Democratic Party out of the hands of the ultraliberal, left-wing self-seekers." But soon afterward his arrogance deserted him when he remembered that Sam Rayburn would be the permanent chairman of the national convention. If Rayburn seated Maverick's delegation instead of his own, Shivers realized worriedly he would lose so much face that he would be ruined politically when he returned to Texas.

This led him to fly to Washington to try to convince Rayburn that he was really a good Democrat and that what took place at San Antonio was just the usual political hot talk. Lyndon Johnson was also present to work on Rayburn for Shivers, for Johnson was concerned that Shivers planned to run for his Senate seat in 1954, and a show of friendship might help divert the governor.

But despite Johnson's fervent pitch, Rayburn did not believe Shivers and promised him nothing, for he knew the strange political game Shivers was attempting to play. Not only had Shivers made the Texas Democratic organization a tight bastion for extreme anti-Trumanites, but a large number of Shivercrats had crossed party lines in an effort to control Republican precinct, county, and state conventions. In this way, he intended to send a Shivers delegation to the Republican National Convention as well as to the Democratic Convention.

The purpose of this latter scheme was to promote General Eisenhower for President on the Republican ticket since the general had changed his mind that a military man should not run for public office. In February, Sid Richardson, Rayburn's Democratic friend in the oil industry, had flown to London to sound out the general on tidelands and continental-shelf ownership and to offer the industry's support to his candidacy if he ran as a Republican. [5] Richardson had no need to make a hard sell, for Eisenhower quickly agreed to give up his post as supreme commander of the NATO forces in Europe and become a Republican presidential candidate.

It was Truman's veto of the bill to award ownership of the tidelands to the states that moved the Shivercrats to hysterical behavior at the Republican National Convention early in July. There, the key fight was whether to seat the "Democrats for Eisenhower" delegations from Texas and Georgia or the regular Republican pro-Senator Robert Taft delegations from those states. When the fifty-five Eisenhower delegates were seated, Taft, the front-runner, was doomed, and the stampede for Eisenhower was on.

The Democratic National Convention was slated to start two weeks later in Chicago on July 21, and Rayburn registered early at the Blackstone Hotel. Shortly afterward he told reporters he would recommend to the Credentials Committee that the sixty-two-member Maverick delegation be seated and the equally large Shivers crowd excluded. This brought Lyndon Johnson rushing to his suite to beg him to change his decision. Rayburn's cold comment was that he would if Shivers pledged himself to support the Democratic ticket in November.

Rebuffed by Rayburn, Johnson went hurriedly to Senator Earle Clements of Kentucky, one of his after-hours friends who was now serving as chairman of the convention's Credentials Committee. With speed, Clements' committee voted unanimously to seat the Shivers delegation.

Then Johnson went to Frank McKinney, the Democratic National Committee chairman to cement the Clements committee decision. Easygoing McKinney ruled that, because the convention on opening day had passed a resolution binding all delegations to a loyalty pledge, the fact that Shivers had not walked out showed he considered himself bound.

Outmaneuvered by Johnson while he busied himself with preparation for the convention's chief work, Rayburn had deep misgivings about Clements's handiwork and McKinney's strange logic. His concern was justified after the convention when Shivers announced that he could not bind the coming Texas Democratic convention in September to resolutions passed at the Chicago national convention. "I went to Chicago unpledged and unbowed, and I still am," he said triumphantly, his Democratic face saved by Johnson and his organization poised to plunge into the task of winning Texas for Eisenhower.

Beyond the Johnson-Shivers trickery, once the national convention got down to matters involving the party platform and the Democratic ticket, Permanent Chairman Sam Rayburn was solemnly in charge of the 1,231 delegates. His no-nonsense control made him a national hit with the immense television audience. TV cameras caught Claud Gilmer of the Texas delegation trying to attract Rayburn's attention by fanning the air above his head with his banner. But Rayburn knew that Gilmer wanted to cause a ruckus over the civil rights plank in the platform, and he called on someone else. When one playful delegate started a small campfire in an aisle of the Chicago Amphitheatre to cook a meal, Rayburn called out in a voice designed to prevent a panic yet end the foolishness, "Will Mrs. O'Leary please leave and take her cow with her." Other playful and troublesome delegates found themselves propelled outdoors after a slight nod from Rayburn to a sergeant at arms. One time he restored peace after flashing tempers by ordering the singing of the Lord's Prayer.

Rayburn gave the delegates security with his firmness and his lack of hesitation in laying down the law. On one occasion, Congressman James Roosevelt of California, the eldest son of FDR, called loudly for recognition and declared Rayburn in error for tabling a motion to adjourn. In a smug tone he quoted a paragraph from the rules book that unmistakenly said that a motion to adjourn had to be considered and could not be tabled.

Cameras focused on Rayburn, who seemed at last to have sawed off a tree limb on which he had been sitting. But no visible concern or contrition showed on his face. "He didn't read far enough," he told the convention at last. "The chairman is not attempting to table a motion to adjourn—but a motion to adjourn to a *specific time*." Loud applause and laughter followed.

The arrival of the television age gave Rayburn the opportunity to add to the prestige of other Democrats. Senator William Benton of Connecticut, one of the first to oppose Senator Joe McCarthy's tactics, faced a hard reelection fight because McCarthy planned to invade his state. For this reason, Rayburn allowed Benton to make a televised speech at the convention to help himself back home. [6]

After the nominating speeches were over and Rayburn's gavel smashed down hard, the high point of the convention's life began. Vice President Alben Barkley, then seventy-four, coveted the nomination, but his hopes vanished when labor leaders said they opposed the "Veep," as he was called. Senator Estes Kefauver had impressive primary victories to buttress his candidacy, but Illinois Governor Adlai Stevenson had Truman's backing as well as Rayburn's. In fact, Rayburn was one of Stevenson's most enthusiastic supporters. "He's a combination of Woodrow Wilson and Franklin Roosevelt rolled up into one!" he told Alla Clary.

Truman had remained in Washington to catch the voting on TV when it began on Friday, July 25. He smugly assumed that his instructions to various aides in Chicago as well as Stevenson's floor managers would put Stevenson over the top without much effort. After the first ballot, however, neither he nor Rayburn, standing on the convention-hall platform, was happy when Kefauver had the lead with 340 votes. Stevenson was second with 273; Senator Richard Russell, next with 268; Averell Harriman, fourth with 123½; and ten others divided 214½ votes.

A worried Truman sent Rayburn word that he was on his way to Chicago, and on the presidential plane *Independence* his concern mounted as he watched the second ballot. Kefauver maintained his lead with 362½ votes, Stevenson remained in second place with 324½, Russell was third with 294 and Harriman had 121.

At the close of the second ballot, the Kefauver crowd smelled victory and wanted the third to begin. But Rayburn, fighting for time so that Truman could get to the amphitheatre to consult with the bosses, called a recess for dinner.

During this open time, a grim Truman arrived and held a meeting immediately with Rayburn and other influential convention figures in Rayburn's private room behind the stands. He ordered the Harriman backers to shift all their votes to Stevenson on the third ballot, and he demanded that key delegation chairmen be phoned to switch their delegates from Kefauver to the Illinois governor. "If I had not flown to Chicago," Truman said later, "Stevenson could not have been nominated."

The job was done before the third ballot got under way. With precision, the entire block of Harriman votes shifted into the Stevenson column, and the Kefauver support dwindled. Senator Paul Douglas of Illinois, who championed Kefauver and detested Truman, realized soon after the voting began what was taking place. In a hurried conference with Kefauver, he told his man to bow out before the rundown of the states was completed and throw his votes to Stevenson. In this way,

Kefauver's show of generosity could be rewarded by a grant of the vice-presidential nomination.

Quickly the two raced up the stairs to the platform, and Kefauver asked Rayburn to interrupt the roll call so he could make a statement. But Rayburn realized immediately what Kefauver had in mind, and he ordered the two men to take seats on the platform and be quiet until the third ballot was finished. So the two sat before the convention and TV viewers in full humiliation while Stevenson won the nomination on that ballot.

Only a few hours later, at 1:00 A.M. on Saturday, Rayburn presided at another meeting that included Truman, Stevenson and more Democratic bigwigs. He went down the list of vice-presidential possibilities and belatedly had a kind word to say for Kefauver as a hard campaigner. "He could run like a scared wolf," Sam said. But Truman thought that Senator John Sparkman of Alabama, a mild Southerner, would balance the ticket, and after Rayburn praised Sparkman, his former whip, Stevenson agreed to take him as his running mate. Later Stevenson claimed that Rayburn had "urged" him to take Lyndon Johnson. [7]

On that same day, the Texas primaries were held, and Reagan Brown, campaigning against Rayburn, finished his repetitious charges that his opponent was part of an administration that stood for graft, socialism, federal ownership of the tidelands, high taxes, and inadequate supplies of ammunition to win the war in Korea. "Pink thinking," he labeled Rayburn's political approach. "Rayburn is 70 years old," he had reminded voters over and over again. "He makes $30,000 a year, has been in Washington 40 years. Let's give a young man a chance and have a change."

But the Fourth District gave the absent Rayburn 23,942 to 12,471 for young Brown, and returned him for his twenty-first term in the House.

Shivers' warfare against Rayburn, in abeyance during the Chicago convention, was reinstalled immediately afterward. Ralph Yarborough, running against Shivers in the gubernatorial primary, had infuriated Shivers by calling himself "a Rayburn Democrat." Then when Yarborough ran a close race despite limited resources and organization, Shivers blamed Rayburn.

While the Shivers attacks on Rayburn mounted, Adlai Stevenson—just as Wilson, Roosevelt and Truman had before him—tried without success to fathom what to expect from important Texas in the presidential election. In an urgent letter to Rayburn on August 11, 1952, he wrote:

> Some time I hope we can talk by telephone about the situation in Texas, which mortifies me. I am beset by pressures

on the Tidelands oil issue and alternately assured that Texas is safe, etc., etc. Moreover, I have little information as to what will happen at the State Convention in September. [8]

Rayburn's suggestion was that he talk directly to Governor Shivers, the key figure in Texas politics, and not react to rumors and gossip. Word about Rayburn's suggestion reached Shivers, and in a show of arrogance he sent Stevenson a message insisting that he tell him his policy on the tidelands disposition. Stevenson's reaction was to invite the Texas governor to visit him at the Governor's Mansion in Springfield, Illinois, on August 23. Shivers went in search of an excuse to come out openly for Eisenhower, and Stevenson, who could not be devious or use political double-talk, gave him what he was after by declaring himself in favor of federal ownership of the tidelands.

When Rayburn heard about the meeting, he knew instinctively what Shivers planned to do at the state Democratic convention in Amarillo on September 9. In an effort to hold Texas for Stevenson despite the expected anti-Stevenson hoopla at the convention, he made a statewide radio speech five days before. He was certain, he told listeners, that Stevenson would in the end work out a fair compromise on the tidelands that would satisfy Texas. "Granting that Stevenson is wrong on this question," he posed an extreme possibility, "does that make Eisenhower and the reactionary-isolationist Republicans right on every great issue?"

He closed on this note: "Please think these things over, and I trust that you will heed the counsel of an old friend who for 40 years has worked with no other purpose than to serve to make your path a little smoother and your burden a little lighter."

But it was one old man without money trying to offset a young governor with a political war chest of $5 million. Shivers was the darling of his robot Democratic state convention on the ninth, and he showed his contempt for Rayburn by ordering a resolution approved calling on "all Democrats who have pledged support to Stevenson and Sparkman to reconsider their action and actively support Eisenhower and Nixon."

Even when newspapers across the state applauded the Shivers declaration, Rayburn would not admit defeat for Stevenson. He helped make a big show of the opening of state headquarters for Stevenson in Dallas on September 22, where he derided "Democrats for Eisenhower" who "could *shiver* but not dance to the music of the Democratic hoedowns." [9]

He also managed the Stevenson campaign in Texas and urged him to speak in the state, promising to introduce him at Dallas and have Lyndon Johnson introduce him at Fort Worth, retiring Senator Tom Connally at Houston, Maury Maverick at San Antonio, and eighty-three-year-old

Cactus Jack Garner at Uvalde. Lyndon Johnson was the only one who hesitated. First he phoned Shivers to ask if he objected, and only after Shivers said no, he reluctantly agreed to host the Fort Worth rally.

Rayburn traveled down the state by train with Stevenson, and at each stop the crowds were large and enthusiastic. "My hopes for Stevenson were reinforced," said Tom Connally, who was also on the train. [10]

So were Rayburn's hopes until Eisenhower spoke at Detroit on October 24 and said he would "go to Korea in person if elected and put an end to the fighting." Stevenson had considered making a similar announcement but had dropped the idea. Now with Eisenhower's ownership of this statement, his election seemed certain.

November 4, 1952, was a dreary day for Sam Rayburn. Eisenhower took 53 percent of the 2,075,946 votes in Texas and carried the nation by more than 6 million. The first Republican since Herbert Hoover was President, and Rayburn's beloved House as well as the Senate also belonged to the GOP. For the second time since 1940 he had fallen to the lowly position of minority leader.

Later a bitter Truman, unwilling to recognize that the popular general was unbeatable, assessed Stevenson's personality and campaign tactics as the reason for the Eisenhower victory. "What a political ignoramus I was for in 1952!" he wrote Rayburn. "Nobody but me to blame." [11]

25

The Politician and the General

At the beginning of the Eisenhower administration in 1953, Sam Rayburn had a measure of the length of time he had served in Congress. Adolph Sabath, who had come to the House in 1907, was dead, and Robert "Muley" Doughton, a congressman since 1911, had recently retired at the age of eighty-nine. So of all the 434 members who had served with Rayburn at the time Woodrow Wilson became President in 1913 he was the sole survivor still on the job in 1953, and as such he was the dean of the House.

But being dean was little consolation for the loss of the Speakership. Nor was he happy about the new administration that was taking over. And for good reason. Harry Truman, in his final days in office, had been treated to great indignity by General Eisenhower and his assistants. An order had been sent him to wear a Homburg at the inauguration and to pick up the President-elect at the Statler Hotel for the ride to the Capitol. Truman told Rayburn he had agreed to wear a Homburg even though he disliked this type of hat. But he would not break the long tradition that had the President-elect pick up the outgoing President at the White House. As a result, Eisenhower was forced to drive to the Executive Mansion, but he rudely stayed in the limousine instead of going to the door to greet Truman.

When he was asked to comment later about Ike, Rayburn said dryly, "I like President Eisenhower. He was born over here in Denison, in the Congressional District. And I have been told that he was a good baby."

Rayburn had a far less charitable opinion of Richard Nixon, Eisenhower's forty-year old Vice President, whom he described as "that ugly man with the chinkapin eyes. He has the cruelest face of any man I ever met." He agreed with Truman that "Nixon probably never read the Constitution, and if by chance he had he did not understand it." [1]

Part of Rayburn's opinion of Nixon was colored by the vicious way he campaigned for public office. His name-calling campaign in 1946 for Jerry Voorhis' House seat and his job on Congresswoman Helen Gahagan Douglas in the 1950 Senate race far exceeded even the slanderous campaigns so commonplace in Texas. Then there was his recent campaign for the Vice Presidency that led Rayburn to tell Senator Harley Kilgore, "He never campaigned against Adlai Stevenson and John Sparkman—only against Stalin and Alger Hiss, and once in a while Harry Truman." [2]

Another reason for Rayburn's dislike of Nixon stemmed from the way he mistreated witnesses who appeared before the House Un-American Activities Committee and his quickness in calling people Communists. Rayburn was particularly disgusted one time when he heard that Nixon had come down from the HUAC dais to shout at a frightened little tailor from Baltimore who was testifying.

Rayburn's mood could easily have led him to hamstring the Eisenhower administration from the outset. This would not have been a difficult undertaking because of Joe Martin's thin majority and Rayburn's knowledge of rope-tying parliamentary procedures. "I know how to cause trouble if I want to, for I know something about the rules of the House and the rights of the Minority," he warned Republican members after they had angered him by condemning the Democratic Party in floor speeches. [3]

However, he had no intention of functioning as a roaring obstructionist as he had in the Hoover administration. "Any jackass can kick a barn down, but it takes a carpenter to build it," he told House Democrats. "We will go along with the Republicans as long as their legislation is good for the country." [4]

So for the most part he stomached the pomposity and continuation of the campaign rhetoric by the Republicans in order to give the new administration a chance. At the same time he knew that to pick on Eisenhower no matter what the justification was politically unwise because the President with the friendly grin and upheld fingers in the "V for Victory" signal was immensely popular with the public.

As a result he made no reply speech when Eisenhower came to the Capitol on February 2, 1953, to deliver his first State of the Union message and spoke piously about establishing integrity as if to imply that this was absent in the Truman administration. Nor did he offer a rebuttal when Eisenhower said in the same speech that he was rescinding a

Truman order of June 1950 and was "unleashing" Chiang Kai-shek to attack the Chinese mainland. The Truman order to the U.S. Seventh Fleet had been issued to protect Formosa (Taiwan) from Chinese Communist attacks and to hold Chiang's army to Formosa in order to keep the Korean War from enlarging. Eisenhower knew and so did Rayburn that Truman had later told the fleet to ignore his order to "leash" Chiang.

The chief planks of the Eisenhower legislative program as expressed in his state of the Union address were to balance the budget and cut taxes. Applause for these declarations was generous, but in the weeks that followed, Rayburn sat behind his microphone at the minority leader's seat on the floor, amused at the growing consternation among the Republicans when they saw that the recession that came in with Eisenhower barred either course. Yet this failed to stop old Dan Reed of New York, chairman of the House Ways and Means Committee, from taking Eisenhower at his word and promoting a $3 billion tax-cut bill. "The Republican Syngman Rhee," White House aides denounced Reed.

As the Eisenhower-Reed impasse developed, Rayburn called a Democratic caucus to lay out party strategy in dealing with intra-Republican squabbles. With the shadow of a smile floating over his face, he said that since the administration had charged Truman with maintaining a swollen budget and high taxes, it should stew in its own righteousness. So while Rayburn and his Democrats sat back, administration Republicans were forced to expend much energy, time and angry emotions before sidetracking the Reed bill. Afterward, a relaxed Rayburn told reporters with mock concern, "The Republicans haven't done much—I feel sorry for them actually."

As Rayburn assessed the new administration, its chief troubles stemmed from three causes. First of all, Republican congressional leaders were frozen from long practice in the stance of political "outs." This meant that while they were skilled at railing at the executive branch, they were amateurs when it came to marching with the President. "Maybe that's the result of these last 20 years that we spent in the wilderness," Joe Martin conceded.

The second problem was the presence of a President who had no political experience beyond occasional appearances as a Defense Department witness before congressional committees and participation in ceremonial functions with NATO-country chiefs of state. Besides, his mind was geared to the military way of life, and civilian life was really unknown to him. "Ike was in the Army 44 years," Rayburn said. "I've been in Congress 40 years, and I still don't know all the answers on domestic and foreign problems. But even if I did, that wouldn't qualify me to lead an army."

The third Republican problem was Eisenhower's inept Cabinet, dubbed by the press as "eight millionaires and a plumber." [5] Their rudeness and contempt for congressional committees and lack of understanding of the legislative process were big minuses. So was their unwillingness to take orders from Eisenhower. "I ask them to have something by the next Cabinet meeting, but they come empty-handed and claim I never asked them to do it," Eisenhower once told me. [6]

"If ever there was a man who needed help it's my friend, General Eisenhower," said Rayburn. "He has the least helpful Cabinet of any President I have ever known. There are no men in the Cabinet who have had political experience except a little fellow named McKay [Secretary of the Interior] who was governor of Oregon."

Secretary of Labor Martin Durkin—the plumber and a Democrat—lasted only nine months because of his Fair Deal views. The other cabinet members ranged from conservatives to right wingers. Secretary of Agriculture Ezra Taft Benson considered Rayburn a dangerous radical and the chief enemy of his program to slash farm aid. [7]

For the most part, Rayburn kept to his party dictum on administration-initiated bills. Joe Martin, however, claimed that Rayburn actually encouraged intraparty squabbles among Republicans. Mr. Sam, he said, would pass word to a Republican committee chairman bucking an administration bill that he would line up Democratic votes behind him. Rayburn would give him Democratic support "when he didn't need it, but he could not get it when he did need it."

But there were times when he jumped into Republican debates because of his sheer anger at insults flung at his party. Once for instance, when a health bill he supported was under consideration, a Republican congressman stood up and claimed that full credit for it belonged to the Republicans, that the Democrats were never interested in the health of Americans. Rayburn almost choked with fury, and at the height of his rage he foolishly declared the bill dead. And it was for that session of Congress.

At other times he rushed in when he saw that basic Roosevelt-Truman era legislation was in jeopardy. Roosevelt's Reciprocal Trade Agreements Act of 1934 came up again in 1953 for an extension, and a majority of House Republicans opposed a continuation of the authority of the President to negotiate tariff-reduction executive agreements with other nations.

Instead of lining up support for extension quietly, Rayburn attacked the isolationists directly in one of his "Sam's up!" short talks. "This eternal

Republican solicitation of the American manufacturer makes me tired," he tried to shame the opposition. "They are unwilling at all times to heed the great chorus of sad cries ever coming from the large, yet poor class, the American consumers."

His success in winning the renewal was matched by his joint work with Joe Martin to stave off a proposed cut of $2 billion from the mutual security, or foreign-aid, bill by isolationists. Yet despite his important assistance on such key Eisenhower bills, his help was not reciprocated when it came to his own pet legislation. On the administration's bill to strip the Southwestern Power Administration of authority to transmit electricity from government dams in Texas, Arkansas and Oklahoma to REA cooperatives, he fell forty votes short of saving this New Deal institution. The utility lobbyists had made this a personal battle against Rayburn, and they had the support of the House leadership. As Rayburn admitted afterward: "I'm sure the utilities in that neighborhood are laughing because when I took a licking on this one they said, 'We didn't do much but we did a job on that so-and-so Rayburn.' "

There is little question that Eisenhower would have fared better in Congress his first year had he sought a good working relationship with Rayburn. But unlike Mr. Truman who courted Republican leaders of Congress, Eisenhower operated in his first five months in office as if Democrats did not exist. His initial realization of their existence came belatedly in June after George Rothwell Brown of the Hearst newspaper chain wrote a column in which he said Rayburn had expressed curiosity about the furnishings in the "officers' club" at 1600 Pennsylvania Avenue. [8] Eisenhower, who prided himself on never reading a newspaper, was told about Brown's column by Jim Hagerty, his press secretary. To make amends, in the course of the next few days he invited Rayburn to lunch twice. But in both instances he steered clear of political subjects. Nor did he set up a regular line of communications with Rayburn.

Two basic Eisenhower actions in his first year left Rayburn with mixed feelings. One involved the Korean War, which had dragged on painfully since mid-1951 when Truman had not acceded to the Communists' POW-return demand. Eisenhower later claimed that his threat to use nuclear weapons shortly after he became President in January 1953 brought Communist approval of a truce by mid-year. [9] But Rayburn knew that the death of Stalin early in March had triggered a determination by the new Soviet leaders to end the fighting. Nor did he publicly contradict Eisenhower's claim that he had secured excellent truce terms, even though he knew they were no better than those Truman could have had in 1951. [10]

The other action involved the long controversy over the ownership of offshore resources. Congress gave Eisenhower the Submerged Lands Bill, awarding control of the beds of territorial waters to the states. In the case of Texas, this meant 10½ miles of seabed. At the same time, Congress approved the Outer Continental Shelf Land Bill, giving the federal government jurisdiction over the underwater lands extending from the territorial limits to roughly one hundred to two hundred miles beyond. The oil industry and Texas Governor Shivers hailed the action as a great triumph, unlike the earlier Rayburn compromise that they had condemned. But as events proved, the Rayburn proposal—for revenue sharing by the federal and state governments of both areas—would have actually given the industry more profit and the states more revenue.

During Eisenhower's first year, one of Rayburn's few sources of pride was the fact that Texans controlled the Democratic contingents in both houses of Congress. Following Barry Goldwater's defeat of Ernest McFarland, the Senate majority leader, in 1952, Lyndon Johnson won the contest to replace him as Senate Democratic leader in the Eighty-third Congress.

But Johnson was more than the Senate's Democratic leader. He was also a multimillionaire businessman. From his vantage point on the Senate Commerce Committee in 1952, he was able to browbeat his way to a TV channel license in Austin from the FCC. Not only that, the FCC granted him a monopoly in the Texas capital by barring all others from acquiring a competitive license. With his earnings from his earlier radio station and now the TV station, Johnson branched into other radio and TV stations in various cities, and into banking, businesses, real estate and ranching. Rayburn, who was never privy to Johnson's far-flung financial activities, was pleased when he learned that he had purchased a ranch. "Thank God!" he said. "Now Lyndon will talk about something else besides politics."

When Rayburn returned to Washington for Eisenhower's second year, it was not with any optimism for what lay ahead. He knew from the Republican mood in the House he would have to put in an increased amount of time defending Roosevelt and Truman from the charges of Republican extremists. He would also have to continue to fight rearguard actions to hold off destruction of New Deal and Fair Deal programs and help Ike against Republican isolationists.

Having gone through a similar situation in the late 1920s, eighty-five-year-old Jack Garner sent Rayburn a letter of sympathy and backbone straightening a few days before the session got under way:

Dear Sam,

I just want to write you this word of encouragement for the year
54. I pray that you may have health and success in your service
to your country for you have the hardist [sic] task and the
greatest opportunity of any minority leader in this country. May
the Lord give you wisdom and courage.

Your Friend
Jno. N. Garner

P.S. Ben [sic] in bed for past 4 days with bad feet—will be O.K.
in few days. [11]

Just as Rayburn expected, the Republicans started the congressional
year by leveling cannon balls at Roosevelt's Yalta Agreement and at
Truman for supposedly coddling Communists during his administration.
Rayburn tried to blunt the attack of the Republican "blabbermouths"
engaging in "rot sewer politics" with a harsh warning that he was "tired
of it being open season on Democrats." But he could not silence the
meanness, because national hysteria existed over the communism issue,
thanks to Senator McCarthy, and the Republicans saw too much political
mileage to be made to stop what they were doing.

To a large extent Rayburn blamed Eisenhower for the continuing
smears. During the 1952 campaign, Ike had spoken from the same
platform with Senator William Jenner of Indiana who had called General
George Marshall, his military sponsor, "a front man for traitors." Then
shortly before his inauguration, Eisenhower, in his farewell address to the
faculty at Columbia University, went out of his way to declare a holy war
on communism. Once in office, his Secretary of State, John Foster Dulles,
buttressed this outlook by declaring that the U.S. intended to liberate
"captive peoples." Further, copies of a letter Eisenhower wrote to
Secretary of Commerce Sinclair Weeks circulated on Capitol Hill and
showed his adherence to McCarthyism regarding government employees.
In the letter, he said that the occupants of the better jobs had been chosen
by his predecessor because of "their devotion to the socialistic doctrine
and bureaucratic controls practiced over the past two decades." [12]

Rayburn also believed that Eisenhower's shabby treatment of Truman
was taken as a signal by some Republicans to make it open season on the
ex-President. When Eisenhower was in Kansas City in October 1953,

Truman phoned his suite and said he would like to come by and pay his respects. Eisenhower did not acknowledge the call.[13] Truman told Rayburn, "They put investigators on me and everyone around me to find something wrong." What Attorney General Herbert Brownell thought would be damning proof that Truman was a friend of communism was that his top Treasury economist, Harry Dexter White, was an alleged Communist spy. The *New York Times* ran the story on page one on November 7, 1953. Eisenhower did not protest when Congressman Harold Velde, Republican chairman of HUAC, subpoenaed Truman to appear before his committee on this issue. But Truman refused to go and denounced the administration for accusing him "of knowingly betraying the security of the United States."

With these Republican attacks intent on destroying him completely, Truman rather pathetically wrote Rayburn a justification of his career one time: "Most people don't know that I save [*sic*] the taxpayers from 10 to 15 billion dollars when the Senate had me under control, that the national debt of the nation was reduced 26 billion up to Korea and that I have tried always to be a good public servant."[14]

1954 was a hard year on the House floor for Rayburn. It was one crisis after another—defending the preceding Democratic administrations, fighting off the Bricker amendment that would have tied the President's hands on treaty making, joining congressional leaders to convince Eisenhower not to send American troops to Indochina to take over the French war against the strong insurgents in its colony, saving the 1955 appropriation for the Southwestern Power Administration and the REA, preventing passage of an Eisenhower bill that would have freed stock issuances of middle-size companies from SEC jurisdiction, and losing the floor struggle against passage of the administration's bill providing tax relief for the rich.

Rayburn also prevented the passage of the administration's bill providing statehood for Hawaii on the grounds that Alaskan statehood should have been included. White House advisers had wanted only Hawaii to become a state, because they were convinced it was a Republican bastion while Alaska was a Democratic stronghold. On the positive side, Rayburn helped secure passage of the St. Lawrence Seaway, a project FDR had yearned for in vain.

There was one day, however, when kinship ran high among all members. This was on March 1, 1954, when Puerto Rican nationalists in the House gallery fired into the Chamber and wounded five congressmen. The only comic relief was the sight of two badly overweight members, Frank Boykin and Martin Dies, scrambling to get out the same small door during the shooting and becoming wedged in place. "Say, Martin," Boykin asked Dies afterward, "who was that guy who got caught between us in the doorway?"

In 1954, while the McCarthy-inspired hysteria was rampant, Rayburn took on a major load of returning the Democrats to power in that year's congressional elections. Long before the primary races shaped up, he had traveled extensively to speak at fund-raising dinners for the party, and as summer approached his sister Miss Lou made him promise to go to a clinic in Hot Springs, Arkansas, for a total physical examination before extending himself further. The clinical tests were extensive and especially pleasing to his ego. When he returned to Washington, he reported that the doctor had asked him his age after reading the results. "You say you're 72," the doctor said in surprise. "No, you're not. At least your body isn't. Physically you're a man of 55." [15]

Rayburn had an opponent in the Fourth District's Democratic primary, a man by the name of A. G. McCrae, who had worked for the Texas Power and Light Company. But McCrae was such a lightweight that Rayburn considered him a minor nuisance. His concern was with Lyndon Johnson, who had developed a rash and elevated blood pressure because of his fear that Governor Shivers would run against him in the Democratic senatorial primary in July. However, Rayburn's anxiety for Lyndon disappeared when Shivers decided to run for another term as governor.

An interesting feature of that year's primary was the use candidates made of Rayburn's name. Ralph Yarborough, running once more against Shivers, again proclaimed himself a "Rayburn Democrat." Others bragged of the high regard Rayburn had for them, while Johnson quoted him extensively. "The difference between Republicans and Democrats is that we don't hate their Presidents. That's what Mr. Sam says," Johnson told audiences. "Do right; make yourself available; and tell about your product. That's the way to be elected. That's what Mr. Sam says, and that's what I do."

Rayburn and Johnson won handily while Shivers was forced into a runoff election with Yarborough. In this second contest Shivers's margin was not only small but suspicious. "I was counted out by the border county dictators," said the Rayburn Democrat Yarborough after the late vote named Shivers the winner. [16]

By the time the fall campaigning for Congress went into forward gear around the country, the Senate's special committee to investigate Senator McCarthy had ended its hearings and recommended that the full Senate censure him on two counts. Although Senate Republican leaders decided not to act on these recommendations until after the election, Rayburn hoped that the campaigns would take the committee's verdict into consideration and be clean.

This was not the case, however. Eisenhower gave Vice President Nixon full rein to evolve and direct the Republican theme, and he chose McCarthyism. Rayburn should have expected this, for Nixon had been using that line throughout his Vice Presidency. In a TV speech, for instance, he had used the following rhetorical question to blacken Truman's Secretaries of State by innuendo: "Isn't it wonderful finally to have a Secretary of State who isn't taken in by the Communists?"[17]

Setting the example for the Republicans, Nixon spoke up and down the West Coast and through the Mountain States, calling the Democrats "soft on Communism." He grew hoarse labeling Democratic candidates as being "all from the left-wing of their Party . . . enthusiastically dedicated to the Socialist left-wing policies of the ADA [Americans for Democratic Action] and the Truman Administration." On platform after platform he charged that the Communist Party "had determined to conduct its program within the Democratic Party," and he claimed that the Republicans were "kicking the Communists and fellow travelers and security risks out of government . . . by the thousands."[18]

Both Rayburn and Truman reacted angrily to such foul tactics. "My back is getting tired," Rayburn told reporters. "I can stand charges of crime and corruption. But charges suggesting treason are unforgivable."[19] Truman's language was stronger: "I don't like Nixon and I never will. I don't even want to discuss him. He called me a traitor, and if I'm a traitor the United States is in a helluva shape."

In his travels to speak for Democratic candidates, Rayburn sensed the continuing enormous popularity of Eisenhower, and he traded on it. The election of a Democratic Congress was a necessity, he claimed, because "it's up to us to save Eisenhower from the Republicans."

This theme worried local Republicans to such an extent that they begged Eisenhower to quit playing the nonpartisan President and join Nixon. Eisenhower finally agreed, and in a single day the presidential plane carried him 1,521 miles for speeches in Cleveland, Detroit, Louisville and Wilmington.[20] He appeared ill at ease spouting a mild form of McCarthyism, and his tone lacked conviction when he declared that a Democratic Congress would bring on a "cold war of partisan politics" between him and them.

Although several Democratic leaders wanted Rayburn to retaliate with a slashing attack on Eisenhower, he refused because he knew this would dim prospects for a Democratic victory. Instead he and Johnson sent Eisenhower a telegram that they made public. Their conciliatory message read: "It takes two to make a cold war. There will be no cold war against you by the Democrats."

The Rayburn theme that the Democrats were Eisenhower's true supporters went on until election day. "Out of 164 votes in which his views prevailed during the last Congress," Rayburn hammered away on this line, "the President needed and received his margin of victory from Democrats on 121 votes." At the same time he was careful not to overdo this show of fondness for Eisenhower for fear it could turn off many Democratic voters. "A fella can spend too much time on the golf course when he's needed to mind the store," he dropped a frequent anti-Ike remark to balance his praise. And when an audience responded enthusiastically, he added a comment on Eisenhower's vacillation: "One week defense spending was to decline, the next it was to rise; the Air Force was to have fewer fighting wings, then suddenly more fighting wings; universal military training was out one day and back in the next."

There was little surprise when the country voted a Democratic Congress in November 1954, though the reasons were difficult to appraise. Certainly Rayburn's approach was important. So was the speaking campaign of Adlai Stevenson into thirty-three states. Also important was the negative effect of "McCarthyism in a white collar," as Stevenson labeled the Nixon name-calling method. [21] But there was also some validity in Eisenhower's conclusion that "there were just too many turkeys running on the Republican ticket," and it was difficult "to work up much enthusiasm for many of the Republican candidates." [22]

Sam Rayburn's margin of votes over Joe Martin was small but it was sufficient to reclaim the ornate formal office of the Speaker for the Eighty-fourth Congress. It also meant that he could move from the minority leader's smaller "back office" to the larger Speaker's back rooms behind the Rotunda. But he met Joe Martin in the hall before the Congress started, and his friend looked sad.

"Joe," he told Martin, "Ah'm tired of all this shiften' around. What do you say we each keep the same room we got now?"

"You're the Speaker, Sam. Whatever you say," Martin replied.

So in a gesture of friendship Rayburn let him keep the Speaker's back office. [23]

It was soon after he had regained control of the House that an odd incident occurred. He was seated at his desk on the rostrum with the House in session one afternoon when a woman walked into the chamber, climbed the rostrum, leaned over him, and said, "I'd like to address the House." After gulping, he replied, "I don't think that would be a proper thing to do," and he beckoned to the sergeant at arms to escort her out. "Darndest thing I ever heard of," he said. Later the woman told John

Holton, his administrative assistant, the reason for her strange action: "I've just finished reading Senator Tom Connally's book, *My Name is Tom Connally*, and he did a lot of unusual things." [24]

Rayburn's return to the Speakership and Lyndon Johnson's new status as Senate majority leader heralded a significant change in their relationship with the White House. Even though they were of the opposing party, Eisenhower was now forced to deal with them regularly on his program and policies. As he was to discover, this was less of an ordeal than dealing with Republican leaders, whom he also saw on a scheduled basis.

Besides their mutual love of Bermuda onions and their admission of embarrassment over their bald heads, Eisenhower was closer to Rayburn in age, and for that reason he felt more kinship with him than with Johnson. He had also known Rayburn a longer time, and as he enjoyed admitting, Rayburn had always addressed him as "Captain Ike" before he had become President. [25] Another thing he liked about Rayburn was that, unlike Johnson, the Speaker was not an endless chamber-of-commerce expounder of the wonders of Texas. In 1953, when Johnson was calling him Texas' first President, Eisenhower had bravely denied this in a talk to the Texas State Society in Washington, "Just because a cat gives birth in a stove, that doesn't make the kittens biscuits," he argued.

But Eisenhower found more profound differences between Rayburn and Johnson. The Speaker was blunt, honest, and to the point with his opinions. He was also concerned when foreign problems were discussed whether the United States was acting as a statesman or as a war-desiring bully. As Eisenhower put it: "Sam Rayburn was always anxious to make certain that the United States would do everything possible to negotiate. Senator Lyndon Johnson, on the other hand, appeared to be anxious to be able to take some action, visible to the world, to indicate we had—or the Senate had—strengthened our Armed Forces." [26]

In general, Captain Ike found his sessions with Rayburn and Johnson far easier to take than those with his Senate Republican leaders. In the six months that Senator Robert Taft was majority leader before his death in mid-1953, his typical response at White House meetings was a display of outrage at the erosion of the party's 1952 platform by Eisenhower. At one meeting Taft lost his temper, banged a fist on the table, and accused Eisenhower of "taking us right down the road Truman traveled." [27] Eisenhower later said that others present "had diplomatically given me time to cool off before answering . . . Senator Taft's attack." [28]

His situation did not improve when bulky Senator William Knowland of California succeeded Taft. "It would have been difficult to find anyone more disposed to do battle with much of the President's program in Congress," Eisenhower's chief of staff Sherman Adams recorded about Knowland. [29] One time Eisenhower readily admitted, "I will spend hours here in the office staring out these windows, sometimes a little hopelessly, with Senators Dirksen or Millikin or Knowland here, to tell me what industries I have to protect with higher tariffs—or how the folks back home don't like these big bills for Mutual Security."

In contrast to what he had to put up with in his dealings with Republican leaders, Eisenhower's "aims and hopes actually received more sympathy from the Democratic leaders in Congress," said Sherman Adams. According to Adams, he often invited Rayburn and Johnson to his second floor oval room in the residential part of the White House where over "a drink and a canape Eisenhower smoothed the road for many of his goals and legislative purposes." These invitations scarred Vice President Nixon, who complained bitterly to friends that he was never invited upstairs at the White House during the entire eight years that Eisenhower was President. [30]

Eisenhower also found it worthwhile to honor Rayburn's recommendations for government jobs. He held to this policy for years until Rayburn asked him to retain his old friend, Edgar Witt, a former Texas judge, on the Federal Indian Claims Commission. Ike's letter of rejection pointed out that Witt was eighty. "It is indeed difficult for me to decline to go along with a personal suggestion of yours affecting an individual in government," he wrote Rayburn. "Indeed, I cannot recall any case of doing so during the past seven years. [31]

As a token of their new relationship, Rayburn sent Ike a heifer named Amanda Busta Blackbird VI as a present for his Gettysburg farm. Delighted with the young cow, Ike asked if he could change the name. "I think that as Texans we are agreed that 'Bluebonnet' is precisely the correct name." [32]

But the Rayburn-Eisenhower relationship was far from a smooth love feast because of the underlying view each had of the other. In private, Rayburn's observation was that Captain Ike's militarylike chain-of-command approach in running a civilian government and his unabashed admiration for wealthy men were improper. Furthermore, he saw his boredom when the vital details of legislation were discussed; and like Truman, Rayburn found Eisenhower's extraordinary gush of words and unrelated rivers of thought incompatible with the orderliness his job required. [33]

As for Eisenhower, he could not quite understand how Rayburn could accept most of his foreign program yet label his domestic program "as forward looking as yesterday." Nor could Eisenhower bring himself to trust a Democrat, even Rayburn, with advance notice of his legislative proposals. This was actually laid bare at one of Eisenhower's news conferences when a reporter quoted Rayburn as saying that "every time there is a message from the President coming to the Congress the press gets it in advance, but I don't hear it until it is on the floor."

Eisenhower's low boiling point brought anger to his face and he snapped: "I doubt that the Speaker has to bring to me any complaints about my office through a roundabout course of communications. He and I have been personal friends for years." [34]

Early in 1955, Eisenhower showed his trait for taking for granted the Speaker's yeoman work to save his foreign legislation and attacking Rayburn's efforts to promote opposing domestic bills. Once again when Eisenhower's proposal for a three-year extension of the Reciprocal Trade Agreements Act came to the House, Rayburn knew that dozens of members from various states planned to offer crippling amendments. About half the Texas delegation, for instance, clamored for one that would severely limit oil imports into the country.

To prevent the stampede that would ruin the act, he brought a roll call vote on the question to bar all amendments. Even though his gag rule lost by a vote of 207 to 178, he would not admit defeat. Instead, he walked to the well of the House for a "Sam's up!" short sermon, then followed it up in the morning by making a personal appeal to twenty freshmen members whom he had invited to breakfast. Even so, he needed two more roll-call votes before he won the gag-rule issue by the single-vote margin of 193 to 192.

Not long after this bill cleared, Rayburn took on the job of saving Eisenhower's Formosa Resolution. With the country far from recovered from World War II, Truman had taken the nation into the Korean War in 1950, using as his justification the "domino theory" of the cold war. But the prevention of that first domino from toppling did not stop the Communists from taking action in other countries. The crisis had moved on to Indochina, and then in the fall of 1954 the Chinese Communists began shelling the Nationalist Chinese islands of Quemoy and Matsu a few miles off the coast and threatened to invade Formosa, the Chiang Kai-shek stronghold.

Hysteria overtook the United States, especially after Secretary of State Dulles proposed an attack on Chinese mainland airfields and Senator Knowland a blockade of her long coastline. The prospect of another costly war in which the United States had not been involved in the foreaction looked imminent. Early in March 1955, Eisenhower acknowledged the extent of the crisis to Rayburn when he told him that he and Dulles were "living 24 hours a day with the question of what to do if something happens in Quemoy and Matsu. This is the most difficult problem I've had to face since I took office." [35]

In the end, Eisenhower decided against the Dulles-Knowland proposals because either would bring the United States "to the threshold of World War III." But he wanted no display of American weakness or indifference. So he proposed to Congress that it pass a Formosa Resolution which would give the President authority to use U.S. troops to defend Formosa, the Pescadores and "related positions." [36]

Rayburn's decision to support the Formosa Resolution brought a large delegation of House Democratic liberals storming to his office in opposition.

"Eisenhower doesn't need the resolution. He already has the power to do it without our approval," Rayburn countered their demand. "But I want to show the world we have a united country."

"This is just a method to suck the Democrats in on whatever trouble he decided to get us in around Formosa," one congressman threw at Rayburn.

"Maybe so," Rayburn said tartly, "but the country comes first, and we're not going to play politics. I remember how the Republicans patted Truman on the back when he first went into Korea and then kicked him in the pants afterward. We're not going to do that."

"Okay," another congressman piped up, "we'll pass his resolution but only after we debate it a few days so the country will know the facts."

Rayburn shook his head. "No, we're not going to debate it," he said flatly. "I don't want one word said against this resolution when it gets to the floor of the House."

His standing among Democrats was revealed when the resolution was called on the calendar a short time later. There was no debate, and only a single Democrat voted in opposition.

Rayburn received no congratulations from Eisenhower for his work to save these foreign-relations bills. But when he introduced and put through the House legislation to cut twenty dollars from each taxpayer's bill, Eisenhower denounced him to the country for "some kind of height in fiscal irresponsibility." [37] Referring to Rayburn and the supporters of this measure, he wrote a friend that "the demagogues are gunning for me." [38]

So incensed was he over Rayburn's tax proposal that he acted childishly at the White House Correspondents Dinner where Rayburn was seated a few chairs away from him at the main table. Eisenhower kept up a continual chatter, but so pointedly did he ignore Rayburn that after a while Mr. Sam stood up and walked out of the Statler ballroom.

When Sid Richardson heard about Eisenhower's rudeness, he phoned Rayburn in an attempt to straighten out the matter. "What does Ike mean by saying I'm 'irresponsible?' " Rayburn barked. "When I put through the Reciprocal Trade Bill they thought differently down at the White House. When I passed that Formosa Resolution for him it saved Ike's neck. But when I push a $20 tax deduction to give the little fella a break, I'm 'irresponsible.' "

"The trouble with Eisenhower," Richardson tried to explain his bridge partner's action, "is he probably didn't even know you passed the Reciprocal Trade Bill for him. The boys around him forgot to tell him. Don't forget, Ike never reads the newspapers." [39]

The ill feeling between Rayburn and Eisenhower faded eventually, though Rayburn was openly critical to Eisenhower's face regarding his political ineptness on other occasions. For example, in 1956 when the always-unpopular foreign-aid bill reached the floor, Eisenhower depended on Joe Martin to shepherd it through the House. The Foreign Affairs Committee had recommended a sharp cut of funds for the Mutual Security Bill, and Rayburn was appalled when Martin's stewardship to regain the original appropriations request consisted chiefly of reading a letter from Eisenhower just before the vote. He was not surprised that the House by a 2-to-1 margin voted to cut $1.1 billion from foreign aid.

The next time he was at the White House he scolded Eisenhower. He told him his letter was "ineffective," and that he should have met with the committee and House leaders before the committee took up the bill. "Why your advisers didn't tell you about this legislative rule of thumb is something I can't answer. But it's much easier to influence committee action before damage is done than it is to undo such damage after a committee has acted."

"No doubt about that," Eisenhower said, arguing that he had called a meeting on the bill at which "Congressman Richards, the committee chairman, was there." Obviously Eisenhower believed that James Richards was the head of a chain of command and would pass along a course of action for the other committee members. Eisenhower also said members of the Republican leadership in the House had attended that meeting.

"That may be so, but it's not what I'm talking about," Rayburn said disgustedly. "I was talking about the Democratic leaders of the House, such as Mr. McCormack and myself. We weren't asked to this meeting you speak of."

Another instance of Rayburn anger with Eisenhower came when Eisenhower sent a message to Congress, implying that the Democrats were not loyal Americans. Rayburn made a blistering House speech in reply that led to Eisenhower's call that he come to the White House. "We've been friends too long to have a falling-out. What made you so mad, Sam?" Ike asked, puzzled.

Rayburn handed him his message to Congress with the mean passages underlined heavily.

"Did I say that?" Eisenhower gasped. [40]

Another open Rayburn display of irritation with Eisenhower occurred a few years later at the presidential signing of the proclamation declaring Hawaii a state. John A. Burns, the Democratic delegate to Congress from Hawaii who had worked long in Washington for statehood, was not invited to the ceremony, and this aroused Rayburn's wrath. "In that case I won't go myself," he said angrily. "No one has done more to achieve statehood for Hawaii than Jack Burns. And no one has a better right to be present at the proclamation signing. Well, if they're counting Jack Burns out, they can count me out also."

When Burns heard about Rayburn's intention, he hurried to his office. "I appreciate your friendly support," he said. "But forget about me. I can stand the snub. In the interest of Hawaii and its people—and for my sake—I'm asking you to go to the White House on this occasion."

Rayburn finally agreed without enthusiasm to attend.

He was standing behind Eisenhower when the presidential signature went on the proclamation, and afterward Eisenhower turned with a grin on his face and offered his pen to Rayburn as a gift. "I don't believe I want that," Rayburn said stonily, making no move to accept the pen.

It was a difficult moment until Congressman-Elect Dan Inouye from Hawaii whispered desperately to Rayburn, "Mr. Speaker, maybe Jack Burns would like that pen."

"Well, maybe he would at that," Rayburn agreed reluctantly. "He's certainly entitled to it." Then he said to Eisenhower, "I'll take that pen after all. I'd like to give it to Jack Burns."

Afterward, he confronted Secretary of the Interior Fred Seaton, an onlooker at the signing scene. "This was inexcusable and pretty small," he chewed him out. "The White House deliberately ignored the man who had the most right to be here today." [40]

26

Rayburn and Johnson

Behind the closed door of Sam Rayburn's Board of Education, amid the political banter and the bourbon strikes for liberty, Lyndon Johnson began talking about the Presidency following Adlai Stevenson's defeat in 1952. After Johnson's reelection to the Senate in 1954, his appetite for the White House became insatiable.

By his lopsided victory that year, he wiped out much of the taint that had stalked him since his first election to the Senate in 1948. The obvious vote steal in the runoff primary that broiling summer had led an army of detractors to jeer at him as "87-Vote Johnson" and "Landslide Lyndon." But now that seemed to be over. In addition, the party's victory in the off-year elections moved him up a high notch in the congressional hierarchy. Instead of being the ruthless, tricky and able minority leader taskmaster and boss of the Senate Democrats, he was now the ruthless, tricky and able majority leader dictator of the entire Upper Chamber.

It was natural at this point for Johnson to turn to Rayburn for help in fulfilling his ambition, and his "daddy" did not scoff at him despite the long list of political dirty laundry of which he was aware. It was not pleasant to read in the papers that Johnson claimed he had supported some of Franklin Roosevelt's New Deal programs because he had been "a young man with more guts than brains" and that he was still bad-mouthing Harry Truman and criticizing Eisenhower for not relying entirely on swift, powerful military action instead of using diplomacy to put out Communist brush fires anywhere in the world.

But Rayburn ignored all these sour truths. Lyndon Johnson was like a wild son, beyond parental control, but still a son no matter what he did. There was also the pride in watching the boy rise from lowly clerk to a congressman to unchallenged leadership of the U.S. Senate. Not least of all, Lyndon provided a lonely aging man with his only source of family life in Washington—except for the few weeks each winter when Miss Lou came up from Bonham for the capital's social season. Sometimes after a long, hard day he would spend the evening at Lyndon's house and relax with his family. The only stipulation he made was that no one "turn on that blamed television set." [1]

Rayburn's initial move in Johnson's presidential quest came almost on the heels of the 1954 congressional elections when he took the train to New Orleans. This was in early December of 1954 when the Democratic National Committee met to name a new chairman. After the 1952 convention, Adlai Stevenson had ousted Frank McKinney, Truman's national committee chairman, and arranged for the appointment of his longtime friend, Stephen Mitchell, a low-key Chicago lawyer, as McKinney's successor. Following Stevenson's defeat, Johnson with foresight had gone to work on Mitchell, a rank political amateur and carefully created an amicable relationship with him for future use.

Unfortunately, the Johnson effort was wasted when Mitchell resigned after the 1954 congressional elections and called the New Orleans meeting of the national committee to choose his successor. This made Rayburn's trip to Louisiana of great importance to Johnson, for if Mr. Sam could get the committee to select a friendly chairman, Johnson could use him to secure the presidential nomination in 1956.

By the time Rayburn walked into the meeting room, however, the 105 committee members had already nominated four persons. It was quickly apparent to him that the winner would be Paul Butler, an outspoken, rabidly anti-Eisenhower Indiana attorney, who was in Stevenson's corner. Rayburn tried to make use of his personal prestige by asking the committee to delay the vote for two months. But committee members, no matter how highly they regarded him, saw no point in any delay and voted Butler into the chairman's seat. [2] At that moment, Rayburn recognized Stevenson as having a major headstart for 1956. He also saw future problems for Johnson because Butler despised him.

This unusual partisan display in Johnson's behalf by the Speaker raised some eyebrows at the time. But his standing among Democrats remained so high that a few months later party leaders decided to forego the annual Jefferson-Jackson Day dinner in Washington and hold a one hundred-dollar-a-plate Sam Rayburn Day dinner instead. Over 3,700 persons—including Harry Truman, Adlai Stevenson, Mrs. Eleanor Roosevelt and Mrs. Woodrow Wilson—paid homage to him, and the net take that Paul Butler carried away came to three hundred thousand dollars.

Besides the Butler problem, Rayburn saw other weaknesses in Johnson's candidacy. The first was his Southern antecedents. The Supreme Court decision on May 17, 1954, declaring school segregation unconstitutional, dealt a heavy blow to the national aspirations of all Southern Democrats by focusing attention on the poor treatment of blacks below the Mason-Dixon Line.

Another weakness in Johnson's candidacy was his state of health. Rayburn was concerned about his excitability, the way he drove himself, his inability to relax and his overeating and overdrinking. He was always scratching a rash of some kind and trying to breathe through aching sinuses. Internally, he suffered from a variety of pains. Hardly had he been elected majority leader in January 1955 than he had to go to the hospital to have a kidney stone removed. He was out of the Senate two months in recuperation, and when he returned, he was more high strung than ever. He related to Rayburn his fury at Adlai Stevenson who came by his office and was like a vulture asking for his support in 1956. "I can't commit myself. I might have an awkward situation in Texas," he said he had scolded Stevenson.

Far worse physical trouble was yet to come. On June 18, 1955, while on a ride with Senator George Smathers, Johnson suffered severe chest pains. [3] Some weeks later doctors agreed he had been the victim of a heart attack. But at the time, old, genial Dr. George Calver, the Capitol physician, diagnosed his trouble as a case of indigestion. Filled with concern, Rayburn suggested to Lyndon that he quit eating double meals at each sitting and slow his hectic pace because he looked "all worn out."

But Johnson ignored the advice, and on July 2, he underwent a massive heart attack at the Virginia estate of George Brown, boss of the huge Texas concern of Brown and Root. This was the company that had provided him over the years with much of his campaign funds. In exchange, Johnson had helped arrange a $100-million cost-plus federal contract for B & R to build the Naval Air Training Station at Corpus Christi and other lucrative contracts to construct factories and hundreds of destroyer escorts. Still another deal was one in which the federal government turned over to it the government-built Big Inch and Little Inch Pipelines that supplied the East with natural gas.

By the time Rayburn learned of Lyndon's heart attack, his protégé was lying unconscious in shock at the Bethesda Naval Hospital. In late August, more than forty pounds lighter, Johnson returned to the LBJ Ranch, and so far as Rayburn could judge his presidential quest was over.

But he failed to reckon with Johnson's will for power. President Eisenhower, who had gone to Geneva, Switzerland, in September 1955, for the first summit conference with the Russians in a decade, suffered a severe heart attack on his return from Europe. With the likelihood that he would not run again in 1956 if he survived, Vice President Nixon loomed as the leading Republican candidate for the nomination. This was now a different ball game to Johnson, and his hopes revived.

A few days after Eisenhower's heart attack, Adlai Stevenson came to Austin to speak at the University of Texas. Rayburn met with him for a talk at his hotel, and he was much impressed with his statesmanlike views. This was reinforced further at the school where Stevenson gave a brilliant speech and drew prolonged applause.

Afterward, Rayburn accompanied him to Johnson's ranch where they were to be overnight guests. To Rayburn's embarrassment, Johnson spent part of the evening telling Stevenson he was not the voice of the Democrats nationally.

In the morning Johnson called a news conference for the trio and completely dominated the outdoor session with reporters. Each time Stevenson started a reply to a question, Johnson took over and completed it for him. They had not discussed politics, Johnson insisted, going on to tell the newsmen, "I like Ike."

Asked if he believed Texas would go Democratic in 1956, Stevenson got as far as, "It's my opinion—" when Johnson bellowed, "I think Sam and I are in a better position to answer that question." Another reporter questioned Stevenson about a possible change in Democratic policy in dealing with the administration because of Ike's recent heart attack. Stevenson barely opened his mouth when Johnson bawled, "I will continue to act on the basis of what is best for the country."

At the end, Stevenson told the reporters, "I'd like to come back to Texas and either talk or listen—whatever they'll permit me to do." One journalist noted: "The reporters laughed. Rayburn smiled slightly. Johnson squinted into the sun."[4]

Not long after this unpleasant visit, Stevenson wrote tongue-in-cheek to Rayburn, "I think I came back with a better perspective and at least some little understanding of the intricacies of the political life in Texas."[5] But he did not let Johnson's overbearing manner toward him and possessiveness toward Rayburn keep him from developing a closer relationship with the Speaker. On January 10, 1956, he tried to establish further kinship by asserting that each had suffered from the brutality of the *Dallas News*. "I was reminded [of] what Benjamin Franklin wrote to his sister in 1767 when she was concerned with the abuse he was receiving: 'When I am on the road and see boys in a field at a distance pelting a tree, though I am too far off to know what tree it is, I conclude it has fruit on it,' " he wrote Rayburn.[6]

He followed up this letter with another two weeks later, trying to get "Dear Sam" to accept his candidacy as an accomplished fact. "Just a note," he wrote, "to say how very grateful I will be to you for any advice and counsel you find it possible to give me during these coming months of campaigning. . . . So if you will drop me a line now and then, I will do my best to make full use of whatever suggestions you make." [7]

Although Rayburn's political senses told him that Stevenson was bound to win a second nomination, he believed, nevertheless, that Johnson should go to the Chicago convention in August 1956 as Texas' favorite-son candidate. The big bonus involved here was that this could convince Stevenson to take Lyndon as his running mate. And even if he did not, Johnson's prestige as favorite son might put Texas back into the Democratic column in November.

As he sized up the home-state situation, nothing could be accomplished until the control of the Texas Democratic party was taken away from Governor Shivers. A weak start had been made when Wright Morrow, Shivers' man on the Democratic National Committee, turned out to be an Eisenhower supporter. Rayburn insisted that he be replaced, but Shivers would not agree. Finally after the national committee said that Morrow could no longer attend its meetings, Paul Butler arranged a summit conference with Shivers and Rayburn in March 1955 at the Speaker's Washington apartment to discuss a successor to Morrow.

Shivers came out the winner because Butler backtracked in the interest of party peace. An agreement was reached there to replace Morrow with Lieutenant Governor Ben Ramsey, a Shivers man who claimed he had not voted for Eisenhower in 1952. In addition, Butler promised not to seek a loyalty pledge from the Texas delegation at the next Democratic National Convention.

Later, when Johnson praised the agreement, Rayburn scowled. For if the governor continued his control of the state's Democratic trappings while voicing his support for the Eisenhower administration, all was lost in Texas. "What goes around the Devil's back will some day come around under his belly," he warned Lyndon on the folly of appeasing Shivers any longer.

The time had come to slug it out toe to toe with Shivers, and Rayburn began by guiding Texas liberals into forming their own organization to work within the party to oust the Shivercrats from power. In November 1955, the liberals were so far along that they held their first statewide convention at Waco with Rayburn in attendance. They called themselves the Democratic Advisory Council of Texas (DAC), and Byron Skelton, the newly elected chairman, bravely denounced Shivers and the "corruption in Austin."

While Rayburn considered the primary function of the DAC to end Shivers' control of the party by electing a majority of the delegates to the state convention the following May, he also saw the DAC as a help to Johnson. He revealed this to reporters in March 1956 when he said flatly that "Lyndon will be Texas' Favorite Son for President at this year's National Convention and he will serve as chairman of the Texas delegation." He also borrowed Franklin Roosevelt's description of Al Smith in calling Johnson "a happy warrior," adding that "he [was] the best man to prevent a repetition of chaos."

This statement made Shivers realize that Johnson, at Rayburn's prodding, might stop cringing before him. In addition, if Rayburn helped Johnson gain these two ends, Shivers saw an end to his own power in the state.

He struck back on the nationally televised "Meet The Press" show on March 25. After some mean remarks about Rayburn, he made a sarcastic promise to support Johnson if only he knew his views on such issues as federal aid to education, states' rights and desegregation. But even if Johnson answered these to his satisfaction, he threw out a new hurdle, "If he is supported by the DAC I could not support him."

Three days later back in Houston, Shivers revealed he considered Rayburn his real enemy by making a vicious attack on him in a speech there. Rayburn was "an angry, confused and frustrated man," he denounced him, "a Democrat first and an American second . . . cynical and calculating . . . a brass collar Democrat" who followed the party without using independent judgment. In a divisive move, Shivers also called out, "Lyndon, I'm for you, if you're for us."

Allan Duckworth of the *Dallas News* reported that when Rayburn heard about Shivers' speech he turned "hotter than a 98-cent toaster."[8] Later he calmly told newsmen: "Perhaps he [Shivers] became frightened at the prospects he envisioned—defeat. He appears to realize he is on a leaking boat which may go down at any time. It appears that he didn't want to endorse anything that Byron Skelton or that terrible Sam Rayburn stand for. . . . But if I was as alarmed and cruel as Shivers, I might say Shivers likes Shivers better than anything else, but I wouldn't say that about any man." In a further jab at Shivers, he added, "I do not have to go into Democratic primaries, but when I do I feel morally bound to support the nominees of the primaries."

At this point Rayburn felt that he had done as much as he could for Johnson on his own, and he told him so. Johnson would now have to join in and take on Shivers. "He might turn out to be a paper tiger," he encouraged him. "He might fall over if you blow on him."

With Rayburn's urging, Johnson finally opened the competition

301

between himself and Shivers for control of the Texas delegation by making a statewide TV speech on April 10. Afterward, Shivers hooted, "I might still back him if he will stop playing footsie with Sam Rayburn and the leftwingers of the DAC and PAC (the CIO's Political Action Committee) who are trying to take him into camp."

The Democratic Advisory Council was already organizing at the precinct level for the party's precinct conventions that would send delegates to the county conventions, which in turn would choose delegates to the state convention on May 22. There was some puzzlement among DAC members when Johnson mailed out a half-million "Dear Friends" letters and sent his own 176-man team throughout the state to gain support in the precinct conventions. This personal organization was directed by John Connally, his former congressional secretary and radio-station employee and now the young lawyer for Sid Richardson. But the DAC leaders felt in the end that the Johnson group created double insurance against a Shivers victory.

Shortly before the crucial precinct conventions on May 5, Rayburn broadcast an appeal that they reject Shivers as head of the Texas delegation in Chicago because if they did not, this would be "the kiss of death to any hope of making Senator Johnson the Democratic nominee." Johnson, leaning heavily on Rayburn's reputation in his campaign, had been describing Texas history as the period "from Sam Houston to Sam Rayburn." No slouch at name calling, Shivers rejoined with the comment that his opponent's true appraisal of Texas history should have read: "From Santa Anna to Sam Rayburn."

The precinct and county conventions were smashing victories for Johnson, but when the state convention began on May 22, Rayburn, who had intended to direct it, was there only for the opening rally. "I felt it was my duty to be with my sister rather than to be in a big crowd like that where I would have been unhappy," he wrote a letter of explanation to Paul Butler, who was watching the Texas picture carefully. [9]

There was good reason for him to be with Miss Lou because she was fast dying of cancer. "I have already had my flowers. Please, no flowers," she sent word to her friends. [10]

This tragedy for Rayburn was multiplied when his nephew, Charles Rayburn, son of his late brother Jim, died after an emergency operation, and then Charles's mother—wife of Sam's brother—suffered a fatal heart attack when she heard about her son. Coupled with the death of Miss Lou on May 26, Rayburn's attendance at three family funerals left him in a state of shock.

In the meantime the Democratic state convention went about its business. In the absence of Rayburn's temperate force, Johnson first went savagely after the Shivercrats to gain his twin goals of bossing the Texas delegation in Chicago and going there as the "favorite son" candidate for President. But after he won both objectives, he struck equally hard at the DAC liberals, or "Red-Hots" as he derisively called them, by defeating their motion to replace the Shivers-appointed State Democratic Executive Committee.

The furious DAC struck back once they recovered from Johnson's fast play. Ben Ramsey was to quit his post as Texas' Democratic national committeeman, and originally Johnson had agreed with Shivers to replace him with Congressman Joe Kilgore, a Shivercrat. However, Rayburn had angrily rejected Kilgore. So Johnson next made a deal with the DAC "Red-Hots" in which their president, Byron Skelton, would get Ramsey's seat on the national committee, while young Beryl Ann Bentsen, the wife of former Congressman Lloyd Bentsen, who was a Shivercrat, would become national committeewoman. In a free-for-all at the convention, the DAC candidate, Mrs. Frankie Randolph, a rich Houston liberal, defeated Mrs. Bentsen and an observer correctly noted that nothing had changed in Texas politics: "The Democratic Party of Texas today is a series of armed camps."[11]

All in all, Rayburn was pleased with the accomplishments of the state convention despite the erratic behavior of his protégé. First, Allan Shivers was now eliminated from the national convention; and second, he no longer had a voice on the national committee.

But beyond those two pluses, Lyndon's hopes for the presidential nomination were not really closer to realization. There were good reasons for this. One was his failure to get national campaign money from the oil industry, and for this Rayburn knew he was partly to blame. Another reason was Lyndon's unwillingness to develop further than being a Southern Democrat.

In 1955, Johnson had suggested to Rayburn that they get a bill through Congress to free natural-gas production from federal price control. Truman had vetoed an earlier bill to do this, but now the Eisenhower administration had assured the oil and gas industry that it favored it.

Rayburn's personal experience with the industry had been, of course, rather unpleasant at times, especially when it came to financing his primary opponents, lobbying in Austin to redistrict him out of the House and subverting Texas Democrats to back Eisenhower. Yet he was still a Texan and Johnson's chief supporter, and he expressed initial faith in Congressman Oren Harris, chairman of the House Commerce Committee and sponsor of the Harris-Fulbright Bill, who claimed that the well-head cost of gas was a mere 10 percent of the final cost to consumers.

But this faith diminished when big city mayors testified that the bill's passage would raise prices to consumers $12 billion a year. And his enthusiasm dipped still further when Houston oil men peppered him with phone calls demanding that he hurry things up. "Why don't you call Eisenhower since some of you have done so much for him," Rayburn told each without showing the anger within him for their arrogant lobbying.

In July 1955, after a pulling and hauling of members, Rayburn helped the bill squeak through by the vote of 209 to 203. But Johnson had suffered his heart attack, and it was not until the next session of Congress in January 1956 that he made the Harris-Fulbright Bill the first order of business in the Senate. However, his dream of unlimited oil campaign money vanished in February when Senator Francis Case of South Dakota told the Senate that a lobbyist had tried to buy his affirmative vote for twenty-five hundred dollars.

Despite the Case disclosure, the bill passed the Senate. But Eisenhower confounded everyone when he vetoed the bill on the narrow ground of the proffered twenty-five-hundred-dollar bribe, even though his veto message said the legislation was "needed." [12]

Afterward, reporters asked Rayburn if he planned to promote a new natural-gas bill. With a poker face he replied, "We passed a good gas bill once and he vetoed it. What kind of a bill he would sign, I don't know. There's no use going up the hill if you have to roll down again."

Eisenhower did make a request for a new gas-price-control-removal bill. But Rayburn sent him word that "the time and conditions are not favorable." The issue was now dead, even though Johnson worked doggedly on Rayburn to revive it. In a bitter speech in the Senate he said, "When a gas and oil bill comes in here, everybody says it's crooked, for the same reason they think a girl on the street after midnight is probably up to something. But for me, I don't accuse a girl until I see her doing more than walking."

An even larger matter had convinced Sam Rayburn that Lyndon's candidacy was sunk for 1956. In March, Senators Richard Russell, John Stennis, and Sam Ervin had composed a "Southern Manifesto," a document declaring war on the Supreme Court's desegregation decision of two years earlier. The authors went about collecting congressional signatures of support for their handiwork, but none approached Rayburn because his view that Supreme Court decisions were to be obeyed was well known. Rayburn also advised Johnson not to sign it, even though nineteen senators had, for it would have ruined him as a national politician.

Johnson had not signed it, but another test of his stand was soon working its way through the congressional machinery. This was the

Eisenhower administration's Civil Rights Bill of 1956. This four-point bill proposed to establish a bipartisan Civil Rights Commission to look into charges that blacks were not permitted to vote and were threatened with job losses if they tried, a Civil Rights Division in the Justice Department to bring action when civil rights were violated, new legislation to help enforce voting rights and amendments to existing law to allow the federal government to bring civil as well as criminal action against those repressing the civil rights of others. [13]

Rayburn had surprisingly little trouble getting the bill out of the Rules Committee to the floor for a vote on July 23, and it passed overwhelmingly by 279 to 126.

Senate liberals knew that if the bill were referred to the Senate Judiciary Committee—chaired by James Eastland of Mississippi, a signer of the Southern Manifesto—it was dead. For this reason Senator Paul Douglas, a civil rights champion, headed immediately for the House Chamber when he heard that the bill had passed there. It was his intention to "walk the bill" back to the Senate Chamber alongside the delivery clerk and move swiftly on his return that it not be sent to Eastland's committee.

But Johnson had learned of his plan and posted his own messenger at the exit door of the House with instructions to bring the bill to the Senate floor on the run. By the time Douglas returned empty-handed to the Senate Chamber, the Civil Rights Bill had been already referred to the Judiciary Committee, and Johnson stood revealed as a sectional politician.

By the time Sam Rayburn reached Chicago for the national convention that August, it was apparent to him from private talks with party leaders that Stevenson was an almost certain winner on an early ballot. One who was galled by this probability was Harry Truman, who had come to Chicago determined to be a spoilsport. Truman was championing Averell Harriman for the nomination and was telling everyone who would listen that Adlai Stevenson was a "defeatist," who would not carry nine states against Eisenhower.

Rayburn's unwillingness to join Truman in a last-minute stand against Stevenson had no effect on their friendship. In the years since he had left the White House, Truman had remained in close touch with Rayburn, offering advice and praise at every opportunity. Once when Sam made a major national address, Truman wrote him of his fury with NBC: "This 'good for nothing' Station left out some of the principal parts of it." [14]

But even though Truman seemed as cocky and energetic as ever and grinningly told about his trip to England a short time before to get an honorary degree at Oxford, Rayburn knew he felt outside the main political swirl now. This became most pronounced on Sunday, August 12, the day before the convention was officially slated to begin, when President Eisenhower sent his plane to Chicago to haul the Democratic leaders back to the White House for an urgent conference on foreign affairs. As a man no longer in office, Truman was, of course, left behind.

Egypt had nationalized the Suez Canal on July 26, and a Middle East crisis had begun. In the next two weeks, while the dictatorial Egyptian President Gamal Abdel Nasser threatened further actions against British and French interests, both these countries wanted the United States to join them in ousting Nasser from office. Eisenhower had asked the Democratic leaders to return to Washington to discuss the deteriorating situation.

During the entire ride to Washington, said Carl Albert, "Lyndon Johnson spoke all the way to get support from Sam Rayburn for his candidacy. Sam was very quiet. 'I've given you all the help I could and I want your support for the Presidency,' Lyndon kept saying." [15] It was an embarrassing ride for everyone on the plane, listening to Johnson's bellowing like a spoiled child. But there was silent applause for Rayburn, who ignored him completely.

When the Democratic National Convention opened the following day, Rayburn was on hand in the International Amphitheatre with his two-tone yew gavel to help him serve as permanent chairman again.

Large banners appeared, held high by marchers, and they read: "Mr. Sam is Mr. Democrat" and "Uncle Sam Rayburn." His head turned scarlet, and he pounded his gavel hard while he said sternly into the microphones, "There will be no parades because I am not a candidate for anything."

Standing in the glare of the blanching TV lights and looking down from the platform into the tumultuous scene on the convention floor, he worked from long experience and instinct to keep things moving along. There were nine candidates to be placed in nomination and extolled, each by two praise singers. Typical of what Rayburn was forced to endure was the John Connally speech for Lyndon, calling him a man "who knows people and they love him, and from that love burns an unquenchable flame of trust."

The dimensions of the Stevenson steamroller were just as large as Rayburn had guessed they would be. On the first roll call on August 16, the former governor of Illinois collected 905½ of the 1,372 votes and won his second presidential nomination with ease. Johnson's total was 80.

After the ballot was completed, Rayburn treated the vast American watching public to a page from "Rayburn's Rules of Order for National Conventions." To a motion that Stevenson's nomination be made unanimous, he hit his gavel, and in a continuous rush of words called out: "Those in favor say Aye, there are no Noes, it is unanimous."

As the convention gathered momentum before the presidential nomination, Stevenson and his aides had been assuring several hopefuls in private that he wanted each as his running mate. In some instances, backers of would-be vice-presidential nominees were in contact with him. In Johnson's case, he wanted Rayburn to tell Stevenson to put him on the ticket. But Rayburn thought that Stevenson should decide on his own man without pressure, and he refused to do so. A story Stevenson passed around later, according to an aide, was that Rayburn approached him after hearing that Adlai planned to take a Catholic as his running mate. "Well, if we have to have a Catholic," Rayburn was supposed to have said, "I hope we don't have to take that little ———— Kennedy. How about John McCormack?"[16] But if Rayburn would have promoted anyone, it would have been Johnson.

Rayburn was standing on the platform when a Stevenson aide told him that Adlai wanted him to come to an urgent half-hour meeting at his headquarters at the Stockyard Inn. Rayburn assumed that Stevenson wanted to tell him whom the nominee would be. When he walked in, he found Stevenson, Jim Finnegan, his campaign manager, Lyndon Johnson, Paul Butler, Chicago Mayor Richard Daley and a half dozen other politicians.

Without wasting time, Stevenson said he had no name to offer but wanted to throw the nomination open to the convention. He said that Rayburn reacted "vigorously and profanely."[17]

"It's the most damnfool thing I ever heard of," he sputtered. "People will say you lack decisiveness, that you can't even pick your own candidate; that if you were President and there was a crisis in the Formosan Straits, you wouldn't be able to make up your mind some night on whether to send in the Seventh Fleet."

Paul Butler also thought it a poor idea because the convention might decide on a weak candidate. But Stevenson was adamant, and Rayburn finally told him, "All right, if your mind's made up, give me your arm and I'll take you out there and introduce you to the convention."

Johnson did not want to get into the free-for-all, and the chief battlers for the vice-presidential nomination became four members under his direction in the Senate: Estes Kefauver (whom Truman was heckling as "Cow Fever"), John F. Kennedy, Hubert Humphrey and Albert Gore. Each of the four had campaigned all night long in the scramble, with

Kennedy's father from his vacation spa on the French Riviera telephoning without stop all city bosses at the Chicago convention.

Rayburn wanted to get the show over with quickly to avoid open warfare, and he put into play other devised on-the-spot sections from his "Rules of Order for National Conventions." There were to be no demonstrations or more than two seconding speeches, with each limited to two minutes. Senator George Smathers, making a seconding speech for Kennedy, said, "I was only halfway through when Sam Rayburn started poking me in the back with his sharp gavel. I had the clock right in front of me and I knew I had plenty of time left. But he kept poking and poking, and the gavel can get quite uncomfortable. . . . So I finished up fast." [18]

On the first ballot Kefauver led, Kennedy was second and Gore third. Johnson had cast Texas's vote for Gore, whom he detested. On the second ballot he planned to switch to Kennedy, whom he had contempt for, and on the third to his friend, Hubert Humphrey.

On the second ballot, a Kennedy steamroller developed and his count reached 648, just 40 short of the majority he needed. Kentucky asked to be recognized in order to transfer its 30 votes from Gore to Kennedy. But instead Rayburn called on Tennessee, and Gore announced his state was changing its vote from himself to Kefauver. Then John McCormack rushed down an aisle to the platform and shouted, "Sam! Sam! Missouri!"

Bedlam broke out. Rayburn pounded his gavel and recognized the chairman of the Missouri delegation. This yielded another switch from Gore to Kefauver and broke the back of the Kennedy drive. Other states swiftly changed their votes to Kefauver, and from a loser he was suddenly the winner.

Had Rayburn taken it upon himself to defeat young Kennedy? The answer would never be known.

After the Chicago conclave, Rayburn wrote about the convention to Frankie Randolph, his state's national committeewoman: "There were no brawls, no fist fights, there was no pulling and hauling at state standards, and everyone looked to be at their best. It seemed that everyone wanted to get a winning ticket and go home and work to elect it." [19]

There was a second Democratic state convention scheduled for September in Fort Worth to confirm the results of the state primaries and plan for the national election. Rayburn went there as head of the Fannin County delegation with the hope of uniting the battling factions behind the national ticket. But Johnson was also there as head of his county delegation, and as boss of the convention's machinery, he came to do war on the "Red-Hots" in the DAC, whom he believed had damaged his bid in

Chicago. "I was not in the know-how of those who were running the convention because they did not consult me about any procedure," Rayburn wrote afterward to a long-time supporter who accused him of complicity in the "stealing of the Fort Worth Convention." The man who had run the national convention was without power at the state convention.

While Rayburn sat by in embarrassment, Johnson in steaming anger worked overtime shredding the power of the DAC. Byron Skelton, the national committeeman, followed his orders and told the delegates that the DAC, which he had headed, was no longer needed. Mrs. Frankie Randolph and her duly elected county delegation were ousted from the convention. Mrs. Kathleen Voigt, a liberal from San Antonio, who had passed out copies of a pamphlet charging Shivers and governor-to-be Price Daniel with a "deal" to steal the convention, lost her job as director of the Democratic Campaign Committee. Liberal Judge Woodrow Wilson Bean, head of the El Paso County delegation, who promised Johnson he would oppose seating Mrs. Randolph and then changed his mind, was the victim of this blunt talk from Johnson: "Woodrow Bean, I'm going to give you a three-minute lecture in integrity. And then I'm gonna ruin you." Johnson also had Bean's delegation unseated.

In the primary contest for governor, Rayburn had supported Ralph Yarborough (the "Rayburn Democrat") against Price Daniel, the ally of Shivers and Johnson. For the second time Yarborough was swindled out of the election by last-minute border-county votes that gave Daniel a 3,500-ballot margin. At the Fort Worth convention, Rayburn talked to Daniel about supporting the Stevenson-Kefauver ticket and won Daniel's promise. But hardly had the civil war at Fort Worth ended when the Democratic Daniel came out for the Eisenhower-Nixon ticket.

There was no doubt in Rayburn's mind that with the splintering of the Democratic ranks in Texas and the championing of Eisenhower by the next Democratic governor, Stevenson would have trouble carrying the state in November. But as the campaign moved into its final two weeks, he grew suddenly optimistic that Stevenson would carry not only Texas but the nation as well. In an enthusiastic letter to Harry Truman, he prophesied:

> If we can carry all the South, which I think we will, and the border states, which I think we will, we do not have to pick up but about two large states and some of the smaller ones, like Rhode Island and Massachusetts, and we will be in there.
>
> With all things considered, Stevenson has Eisenhower on a

tough spot about firing off these hydrogen bombs. I made a speech in Memphis last Saturday night in which I said that I thought everything should be done to stop the destructive results of these bombs. I also challenged Mr. Eisenhower to state whether or not if England or Russia, who also have the H bomb, were to ask him to a meeting to try to make an agreement, if he would accept. I also issued a statement from Washington today on the same subject, which will be in the papers before you receive this letter. [20]

But Rayburn's optimism faded because of events in the Middle East. After border clashes among Jordan, Egypt and Israel, Israeli forces invaded the Sinai Peninsula on October 29, followed by British paratroop landings at the Suez Canal and French action inside Egypt. The great concern that swept across the United States of an America being drawn into the war damaged Stevenson's candidacy. For a country with a military man as President seemed fortunate at the moment. Eisenhower's pressure on England and France to agree to remove their troops on November 6 obviously had its effect on the national election, which also occurred that day.

When the political dust settled in 1956, it brought a respite from the campaign's name calling by Vice President Richard Nixon, who Rayburn said was "cruel" to truth and reputations, and who Stevenson declared was "a poisoner of campaigns." It also revealed that luckless Stevenson was not a man for the times because he had carried only nine minor states.

But Congress remained in Democratic hands, and despite his age Rayburn looked ahead hopefully to 1960.

27

The Mission That Failed

Sam Rayburn was three days short of his seventy-fifth birthday when the Eighty-fifth Congress convened on January 3, 1957, and from his age one might have expected him to loosen his tight reins over the House and take things easier. But 1960 loomed beyond the horizon as a crucial year for his protégé Lyndon Johnson, and he had to help him make a legislative record and build delegate strength before the next convention. There was an equally compelling reason why he could not hand over part of his responsibilities to others. His aggressive leadership was as much a part of him as eating or sleeping.

At the very start of this Congress, he lived through a worrisome time with Johnson, whose entire career seemed to teeter on the brink of a single Senate vote. When the results of the 1956 elections showed a neck-to-neck division between the Democrats and Republicans in the Senate, Rayburn agreed with Johnson's plan to have Senator Price Daniel resign his seat on the day he was sworn in as governor of Texas. This would give him the right to choose his successor. But out-going Governor Shivers would not agree to this and insisted that Daniel resign his Senate seat before that day. When Daniel finally consented, Johnson was furious because Shivers had been quoted as saying he would appoint a Republican.

After turning Johnson into a nervous wreck, Shivers finally confided to him that on January 15 he planned to appoint a Democrat named William Blakley, an archreactionary half-billionaire who controlled Braniff Airways. This would give Johnson a 49-to-47 margin in the Senate. But before he could bellow out a happy "Yahoo!" he wailed despondently to Rayburn on opening day that he was going to lose his job as majority leader. Frank Lausche, the Democratic governor of Ohio who had just been elected to the Senate, was telling reporters he would probably vote for Republican Senator William Knowland for majority leader and not for Johnson. If he should do this, it would result in a tie vote and allow Vice President Nixon to cast a ballot, or the clincher for Knowland.

It was a dramatic scene on the Senate floor when the voting came for majority leader. Lausche hesitated when his name was called, then voted against Knowland. Johnson was saved.

If Rayburn lacked enough problems at the beginning of Eisenhower's second term, Democratic National Committee Chairman Paul Butler was eager to add to them. Before the new Congress convened, he had announced the establishment of a national seventeen-member Democratic Advisory Council, which would take on the job of determining party goals and legislative policy. [1] As he put it with his customary lack of graciousness, the congressional Democrats (meaning Rayburn and Johnson) had failed to take on "the true role of an opposition party from 1952 up to the [1956] Presidential campaign."

Butler's undiplomatic statement went on to declare that the DAC intended to remedy this dismal situation under his direction as its chairman. But there would be congressional input into its work, he conceded, for he was appointing eleven members of Congress, including Rayburn and Johnson, to serve on the DAC along with Adlai Stevenson, Mrs. Roosevelt and others.

Rayburn's response to "Butler's brainstorm" was not long in coming. Neither he nor Johnson would join the DAC, because it was an attempt to dilute their lawful duties and authority as elected public officials. He went further with reporters, telling them he was sorry he had saved Butler after the 1956 Democratic convention when Stevenson had wanted to replace him with Jim Finnegan, his campaign manager. He had gone to Stevenson's room when he heard the news and had told him bluntly: "It's pretty late in the day for such action. We have enough differences in the Party now without making new wounds."

Stevenson had grudgingly agreed to retain Butler, who then proceeded into a three-month war with Finnegan while Stevenson campaigned against Eisenhower. Now Butler, in charge of the DAC, began a four-year rain of criticism against Rayburn and Johnson.

Ironically, while Butler was attacking Rayburn for being too moderate in philosophy and too kind to Eisenhower, Rayburn was being attacked at the same time by the conservative, racist Democrats in the House for being too liberal. Leader of this pack was Howard W. Smith of Virginia, chairman of the Rules Committee, who was determined not to permit any "leftwing-radical-Communist" civil rights, health, education, labor or housing bills to reach the House floor.

Before "Judge" Smith had become the top Democrat in seniority on the Rules Committee, Rayburn had depended on his old friend Gene Cox, Smith's predecessor, to get enough other reactionaries on the committee to release bills for floor consideration. But "Goober" Cox died on December 24, 1952, and after two years of Republican domination, Smith became chairman of the twelve-member committee in 1955.

From the beginning of Smith's reign, the committee split 6-to-6 on bills Rayburn considered important, with two of the eight Democrats—Smith and William Colmer of Mississippi—voting with the four Republican members. Because a tie vote kept a bill from leaving the Rules Committee, Rayburn now depended on Joe Martin to persuade either of the two more moderate Republicans on the committee to change his vote. Martin did this on occasion because of his friendship for Rayburn but not as frequently as Rayburn wished and sometimes only after the Speaker sweetened the deal with more patronage for Republicans.

In 1956, Rayburn had worked closely with Martin to squeeze Eisenhower's four-point civil rights proposal out of Judge Smith's committee only to have Lyndon Johnson kill the bill in the Senate by sending it to Eastland's Judiciary Committee. Following Eisenhower's plea for the same bill in his State of the Union Message at the beginning of 1957, Rayburn had a similar arrangement with Martin.

But old Smith, shrewd and clever, believed he had a way to prevent floor action on civil rights. His technique was simple: He refused to call a meeting of his committee.

Rayburn's persistent efforts to meet with Smith were met with excuses by his staff that he was not available. Finally Smith left Washington to escape Rayburn's pressure. On his return some time later he told reporters that he had gone to his 170-year-old dairy farm in Fauquier County to inspect a barn that had burned down. "I knew Howard Smith would do most anything to block a civil rights bill," said Rayburn on hearing this excuse, "but I never knew he would resort to arson." [2]

Smith could not hold out forever, and in late spring his committee reported the bill to the House. This was not an easy time for Rayburn because more than one hundred Southern Democrats, including the entire Texas delegation, were churning with anger at this second go-around on civil rights legislation. But he continued to work with Joe Martin, and the Eisenhower bill carried by 286 to 126 on June 18, despite the opposition of 107 Democrats. "It's going to be a long pull to reeducate our people [in the South] to be sure they will do the just and fair thing,"

Rayburn said afterward. But he predicted that in time the South would accept civil rights for blacks, and he scoffed at the KKK who threatened to burn another cross in front of his Bonham farmhouse, just as they had in 1956, three days after the House passed the bill the first time. [3]

Rayburn knew that the 1957 Civil Rights Bill faced the same problem in the Senate as in 1956, and his protégé Lyndon was again the key figure.

Just as he had done in 1956, Johnson, with the help of Senator Richard Russell, tried to ship the bill to Eastland's Judiciary Committee and certain death. But this year, even though Johnson had the support of Southern Democrats and reputed Northern liberals, such as Senators John Kennedy and Mike Mansfield, his point of order failed by a vote of 45 to 39. [4] So the bill stayed in the Senate Chamber for direct action.

A filibuster followed—sixty-six speeches in eight days—and when the force of the wind abated, the advocates of the Eisenhower bill had not been traumatized. Johnson was now left with no alternative except to put through the weakest bill possible, and he did so with the aid of lawyers Dean Acheson and Ben Cohen from the Roosevelt-Truman administrations. The heart of the Eisenhower measure was Title Three, which permitted the Attorney General to bring suit for *any* violation of civil rights. This included segregation in schools and elsewhere and job discrimination. Johnson won a vote to eliminate Title Three entirely.

What remained was Title Four, which was restricted solely to voting rights. Under the original Title Four, a federal judge could issue a criminal contempt citation if a person found to be repressing the voting rights of another person disobeyed a court injunction to cease and desist. Johnson's alteration would remove this authority from federal judges and guarantee a jury trial for anyone cited for contempt after disobeying an injunction. Since no Southern jury would convict a white man for violating the voting rights of a black, Deputy Attorney General William Rogers said Johnson's new Title Four "handed a policeman a gun without bullets." [5]

When Johnson's bill passed the Senate on August 2, the House voted not to accept his amendments. This sent the bill back to Judge Smith, who, Eisenhower was told, "was content to keep it." [6] At this point, he said, Sam Rayburn phoned the Oval Office and told him, "The Democrats are willing to talk it over."

The result was another Johnson amendment of Title Four, and this watery version passed both Houses. The new change let a federal judge decide if the injunction violator should have a jury trial in a criminal contempt case involving voting rights. If he decided against a jury trial the maximum punishment was six months in jail and a fine of one thousand dollars. Eisenhower signed the bill, even though it did not contain Title Three.

Directly as a consequence of this weak voting rights bill and the continuing high-handed manner in which Howard Smith and his Rules Committee directed legislative traffic, Rayburn picked up another troublesome problem. About one hundred liberal House Democrats formed the Democratic Study Group (DSG) to gain political clout for their views, and Rayburn was the man who caught their complaints when they were frustrated. He counseled them, gave them sympathy, talked to Joe Martin, passed out more patronage to hungry Republicans, and a few of the bills favored by the Study Group were sprung loose from the Rules Committee. But the frustrations grew, and so did the carping at Rayburn.

In the congressional elections in November 1958, the Democrats won a landslide victory in the House, taking 282 seats to only 153 for the Republicans. This was the largest majority since 1936, but it did not make Rayburn happy. "I'd just as soon not have that many Democrats," he told his Board of Education. "They'll be hard to handle. It won't be easy."

The hardest group to satisfy was the Democratic Study Group, now numbering almost 125 Democrats, who agreed with *The New York Times* that the last election was "a sweeping victory for liberalism." Chet Holifield, a Los Angeles haberdasher and spokesman for the DSG, called on Rayburn before the Eighty-sixth Congress began to discuss his group's program. But nothing could be done, Holifield said, unless Howard Smith could be bypassed.

What the Study Group demanded was Rayburn's help to restore the twenty-one-day rule and cut the number of signatures required for a discharge petition. The twenty-one-day rule, which Rayburn had enjoyed for two years in the Truman administration, allowed the chairman of a standing committee to bring a bill his committee had reported out directly to the floor if the Rules Committee failed to do so in twenty-one days. As for the discharge petition, it required 218 signatures to yank a bill away from the Rules Committee. Only twice in forty years had it been successfully used.

Rayburn saw that either proposition Holifield demanded would polarize the Democrats only a year before the 1960 election. So he offered as an alternative the promise that he would persuade the Rules Committee to send all major bills reported out by the standing committees to the House floor during the 1959–60 congressional term.

"What shall I tell the others who want these rules changed?" Holifield asked, as if Rayburn had not already given him his promise.

"Tell 'em everything I've told you," Rayburn said, irked, and repeated his assurance. [7]

"If we have a meeting, the reporters will be ready to blow that Little Rock thing wide open," said Holifield, bringing up another subject.

He was referring to the political aftermath of the Little Rock,

Arkansas, confrontation in the fall of 1957. When the federal courts ordered the local high schools to integrate, Governor Orval Faubus had called on the National Guard to keep black children out, and Eisenhower had dispatched a thousand paratroopers to enforce the courts' order. Congressman Brooks Hays—a Baptist preacher, humorist and friend of Rayburn—had served as intermediary between the White House and Faubus, and when he came up for reelection in 1958, he was punished by segregationists who elected one of their own, Dr. Dale Alford.

It was the Democratic Study Group's intention to fight the acceptance of Hays' successor at the Democratic caucus and then afterward as a member of the House. There was also pressure on Rayburn from Adlai Stevenson to do so. [8] But again Rayburn viewed this as a polarizing move, and he used his own solution on the problem. This consisted of phoning Alford and ordering him not to attend the caucus. He also told him not to come forward with all other members to be sworn in on opening day of the new Congress. "I'm going to let you be seated only provisionally after all the others take the oath," he added, "and if you get to keep that seat it will depend on the outcome of an investigation of your election."

Rayburn soon found that he could not keep his promise to the DSG to get all major bills released by the Rules Committee and brought to the House floor. And the reason was Charles Halleck. The two Republican moderates on the Rules Committee were no longer in Congress, but Rayburn had been counting on Joe Martin to see that two like them would be assigned to the committee when he had given Holifield his assurance. Suddenly, however, Joe was no longer minority leader.

Halleck, in Congress since 1935, was a scrappy, highly partisan Republican, who had served as majority leader in the Eightieth and Eighty-third Congress under Joe Martin as Speaker. When Martin reverted to minority leader in 1955, Halleck asked Eisenhower for his support in fighting him for that post at the Republican caucus. Eisenhower refused that year as well as in 1957, because he thought that an internal fight would make the House Republicans a helpless lot. But following the Republican debacle in the 1958 congressional elections, which he blamed to a large extent on Joe Martin instead of the economic recession, he agreed to support Halleck.

Martin had a feeling something was in the wind when he received a gushing letter of praise from Eisenhower late in the preceding Congress after the passage of the foreign-aid bill. Talk around the Capitol was that too effusive Eisenhower praise generally was followed by a hammer blow. "Dear Joe," Ike's letter began: "What you and Sam [Rayburn] and the rest of the leadership did as a team in this difficult situation was very impressive to me. It was a tough situation you faced in the House, and I think you have every reason for personal satisfaction with the way you marshalled the boys on our side of the aisle."[9]

Shortly after New Year's Day in 1959, one of Martin's friends told him to appoint Gerald Ford of Michigan as his assistant leader in order to hold the support of young Republicans. But Martin saw no need for this because he expected no trouble.

The blow came on January 6 when Halleck challenged him for leadership at the House Republican caucus and won 74 to 70. A stunned Martin charged that "Nixon's people actively opposed me." Then he included several White House aides among the plotters, and added that his friendship with Rayburn had been held against him by Eisenhower.

Rayburn was attending a birthday party in his honor at the Women's National Democratic Club that day when a short, square-faced man, suffering from a blood clot in a leg, came limping into the room. "Joe!" he called out to his sad-looking friend. He hurried across the room and threw an arm around Martin.

"Do you have a cubby-hole for me anywhere, Sam?" Joe Martin wailed.

"Joe, you can have anything you want," he told his old friend, and his remark brought tears flowing down Martin's round cheeks.

Halleck's ascendancy in the Republican ranks immediately complicated Rayburn's existence. Unlike Joe Martin, Halleck was more concerned with creating an opposing Republican solidarity than he was with working out compromise arrangements with Democrats. By nature tricky, "he was always trying to put something over if he could," Alla Clary quoted Rayburn. [10]

When the two new Republican members he appointed to the Rules Committee were not moderates like the two who had departed, Rayburn knew he was in for trouble, not only from the Democratic Study Group but from Howard Smith and Halleck as well. His first major test came over the multi-billion-dollar Housing Bill that went from the Banking and Currency Committee to Judge Smith's twelve-man crew. After a severe recession had hit the country early in Eisenhower's second term, the Democrats, led by Rayburn, had proposed housing legislation that would provide jobs for a half million persons. This was in 1958, and when Howard Smith prevented action, House liberals tried to get the necessary two-thirds vote to suspend the rules and bring the bill up for action on the floor. But they failed by six votes, and the bill lay stalled until the next Congress.

In February 1959, Judge Smith served notice that the bill was still in a coma when he publicized the rigid 6-to-6 vote on it in the Rules Committee. Reporters asked him about Sam Rayburn's pledge to the

Democratic Study Group. "I'm not bound by it," Smith pulled the long, black stogie from his heavy lips and muttered. "I didn't make an agreement with these men or give assurance to anyone."

But Rayburn had, and his prestige was on the line. He waited until after the Easter recess to act, sending Smith an open letter in which he said that his committee was damaging the nation's economy. As a follow-up, Rayburn told reporters he had the votes for both the suspension of the rules and a discharge petition. This was a bluff, yet it served to get two of the Republicans on Smith's committee to cross Halleck and change their votes.

So the bill was reported out, but Rayburn realized he could not repeat his performance too many times in this Congress. Then to spoil even that victory, after the bill had passed the House and Senate, Eisenhower vetoed it. A second try with a reduced program was also vetoed. Only on the third go-around, with the bill hardly more than a shadow of the original, did Eisenhower sign it into law.

Frustrated by the dearth of legislative successes in 1959 despite the "mandate" of the last election, liberal publications charged Rayburn with being an "Eisenhowercrat" in disguise. One claimed that he and Johnson had "snuggled into the strait jacket offered them by the Administration, instead of accepting the challenge to meet the country's needs." [11]

The truth was that Eisenhower had become still another serious problem for Rayburn during his final years in office. This was far more the case in domestic than in foreign affairs, though whenever Rayburn offered objections in foreign matters, Eisenhower showed displeasure as if he were violating the rules. Eisenhower told his son John the entirely specious explanation that Rayburn's objections to strong American actions abroad resulted from his need "to appease Denison isolationists." [12]

Early in his second term, Eisenhower had asked Rayburn to promote a congressional resolution calling for economic sanctions against Israel for not giving up the Gaza Strip taken from Egypt during the second Arab-Israeli War. "Speaker Rayburn flatly refused," Eisenhower noted angrily, and the issue died in the House. [13] To his evaluation of Rayburn as appeasing Denison isolationists, Eisenhower now added an equally foolish explanation: "I found it somewhat dismaying that partisan considerations could enter so much into life-or-death, peace-or-war decisions."

At that time Eisenhower also wanted congressional approval of the "Eisenhower Doctrine." This would permit him to give economic and military aid to Middle East nations under Communist pressures and send American troops into any of them upon request to save them from "armed aggression from any nation controlled by international Communism."

Rayburn offered a simpler "Eisenhower Doctrine" of only thirty-four words that did not contain the sabre-rattling cold-war rhetoric or the economic-aid program. [14] But when Eisenhower objected to it, he pushed the original draft through the House, despite the demand by Paul Butler that he let it die. Afterward, Eisenhower forgot about the help he had received from Rayburn and complained about the "grumbling of some opposing Congressmen" and "the countersuggestions of some leading Democratic foreign policy thinkers." [15]

It was in 1958 that Eisenhower decided to invoke his Doctrine, and he called congressional leaders to the White House. There he confided that a Communist-inspired uprising was taking place in Lebanon, and its President had asked for American intervention. While militant congressmen backed his decision to send American marines into Lebanon, Rayburn spoke up and said he was concerned that Eisenhower "might be getting into something that was strictly a civil war." [16]

Eisenhower bristled at this, and the next day he sent in the marines. Three months later when he pulled the troops out, he claimed that the action had ended the rebellion. However, a year later when Rashid Karami, the premier of Lebanon, came for a White House visit, he confided that he had been the rebel leader! [17]

On a personal matter, Rayburn had a difficult exchange with Eisenhower over a presidential health bill. In three successive years Eisenhower had suffered a major heart attack, an ileitis operation, and a stroke. For this reason he wanted Rayburn to sponsor a "temporary President" bill so that the Vice President could take over his job during the time he was incapacitated.

"I won't do it," Rayburn told him. "We've got along since 1789 without it. Besides, if you send up a special letter to Congress on this subject, people are going to start talking about your health and your quitting office." What he did not say was that he was concerned that Ike might use the legislation if it passed, and this would make Nixon President.

Eisenhower spoke long and fast in his characteristic way of talking at machine-gun speed. But Rayburn was unmoved. Later Eisenhower wrote a secret memo to Nixon that laid out a special procedure by which Nixon would unofficially assume the Presidency on a temporary basis if he became seriously ill again. [18] A decade later this memo was the framework for Section 3 of the Twenty-fifth Amendment.

The Rayburn-Eisenhower relationship took a sharp turn for the worse in the 1959–60 congressional term. Secretary of State John Foster Dulles, who had enjoyed a rather free hand in running foreign affairs, developed cancer and died early in 1959. Dulles' illness left Eisenhower as his own Secretary of State, and he grew less happy with Rayburn's advice. For instance, when a new Berlin crisis with the Soviet Union was approaching in the spring of 1959, he did not appreciate Rayburn's words of caution: "Let's do all the talking we can. I would rather talk than fight."[19] Again Eisenhower blamed the mythical "Denison isolationists" for controlling Rayburn on foreign affairs.

Nor did Eisenhower appreciate Rayburn's attempt to interfere in the Summit Conference with Khrushchev, the Soviet leader, in mid-May of 1960. A CIA U-2 spy plane had been shot down over the Soviet Union and the pilot captured on May 1. Despite grave doubts that Khrushchev would attend the Summit, Eisenhower went to Paris for the conference. While he waited to see what the Communist leader planned to do, he received a telegram from Rayburn, Lyndon Johnson, Adlai Stevenson and Senator William Fulbright for delivery to Khrushchev. The telegram asked the Soviet boss not to "torpedo the Conference." This drew Eisenhower's hot temper and his charge that Rayburn and the others were trying "to interfere in the day-to-day conduct of foreign relations."[20] He waited until Chairman Khrushchev had scuttled the meeting before an aide delivered the wire to the Soviet embassy in Paris.

On domestic legislation, the Rayburn-Eisenhower relationship was torpedoed by Ike during his last two years in office. Rayburn was indirectly responsible, because early in 1957 he told Chairman Oren Harris of the House Commerce Committee to set up a special subcommittee to study the way the regulatory agencies were operating.

Dr. Bernard Schwartz, special counsel to this Legislative Oversight Subcommittee, hit pay dirt in 1958 when he found that Sherman Adams, the former New Hampshire governor who was Ike's White House chief of staff, had intervened with the Civil Aeronautics Board for Murray Chotiner, Vice President Nixon's campaign adviser.[21] Further investigation proved more damaging. Governor Adams, who Eisenhower claimed was "cleaner than a hound's tooth," was discovered to have accepted large sums of cash and expensive gifts from a New England textile manufacturer in exchange for favors from the Federal Trade Commission and the Securities and Exchange Commission.

After long public roasting, Adams finally turned in his resignation in September 1958 and left Washington. With Adams gone, Eisenhower no longer had a trusted aide upon whom he could unload domestic matters. Since Dulles was ill by that time and Eisenhower had to take over much of his work, he did not relish the thought of doing the same in the domestic sphere. So he took the lazy man's approach to the Presidency in this area.

"Every sort of foolish proposal will be advanced in the name of national security and the 'poor' fellow," he confided his expedient approach to Charlie Halleck and Senate Minority Leader Everett Dirksen at their first leadership meeting of the Eighty-sixth Congress on January 13, 1959.[22] He added that he was sending Congress an economy budget worked up by Budget Bureau Director Maurice Stans in which government spending was balanced with revenues at $77 billion. If Congress went beyond the budget on any item, "I'll respond with a veto," he explained his lazy man's scheme to the two men. "And if the veto is overridden," he gloated, "I'll propose a tax increase to cover the increase in spending." There was a way to put the Democratic spenders on the defensive when it came to social legislation, he advised Halleck and Dirksen. "In health, education and welfare," he said, "I'll insist that spending more money does not necessarily hasten progress."

Rayburn did not disagree with the Democratic Study Group that the cities were badly in need of large-scale slum-clearance projects, that crime and disease needed to be attacked, pollution levels lowered, education improved, air flight made safer and dozens of other overdue solutions devised for the many problems facing the nation.

But between Howard Smith's intransigence and Eisenhower's lazy man's veto approach, he could not deliver on his promise to the DSG. Committees held long, painstaking hearings on bills and reported them out; then they went to Judge Smith's Rules Committee and the clamor came from the DSG for Rayburn to spring them loose. After using threats and patronage to get even a fraction out of Rules, he had to see the bills through to House passage and send them to the Senate for committee and floor action there. And after all this effort and time, an approved bill would reach the Oval Office desk only to have Eisenhower scratch a quick veto on it.

It turned into a nightmare of a congressional session. Besides the housing and urban-renewal bills, Eisenhower vetoed legislation covering a wide range of subjects from price supports for farm products to public works and water-pollution controls. Not until September 1959, almost ten months after the session began, were Rayburn and Johnson able to get enough votes to override a veto.[23] A Herblock editorial cartoon in the *Washington Post* depicted a happy Eisenhower speaking to defeated-looking Rayburn and Johnson: "Tell the men they may keep their horses; they will need them for spring plowing," the victorious general is generously saying to his congressional Robert E. Lees.

Eisenhower called his lazy man's weapon "my veto pistol," and from a minor firing of this pistol during his first six years in office, he now quickly amassed a total of 181 vetoes. "What this country needs most is leadership," Rayburn attempted to expose the negative nature of the administration. But Ike had merely to grin in public and flash his patented two-finger "V for Victory" sign, and the applause was deafening. In the face of national grumbling with the lack of government response to vexing problems, his popularity rose steadily in the polls to a high of 71 percent by the end of 1959.

When Eisenhower's vetoes showed no sign of slowing up, Lyndon Johnson personally began slashing the money amounts in committee bills in order to avoid them. For example, he cut the airport-aid bill by a vital $100 million. In another instance, despite the economic recession, he eliminated a bill to provide additional weeks of unemployment compensation beyond the existing limit, thus forcing untold thousands of persons to go on welfare. Other important Democratic bills suffered similar fates.

It did not take long for Paul Butler and the Democratic Advisory Council to condemn Johnson's method and include Rayburn in their scathing comments. In June 1959, the DAC turned its wrath on the "time-consuming efforts to water down proposed legislation to the limits the President might accept." Then on July 5, Butler called Rayburn and Johnson "soft on Eisenhower," and added pointedly, "I hope we will be laying a bill upon the President's desk even though knowing in advance that he may veto it, and letting it be known we will take the issue to the American people." [24]

A sympathetic Harry Truman wrote Sam Rayburn three days later, "I notice that Paul Butler is 'firing from the hip' without consultation with any Democrat that counts." [25] But Rayburn did not want sympathy. He was furious with Butler, not only because he was made to appear as a bill appeaser to avoid a veto but because he considered it a deliberate attempt to damage Johnson's candidacy for the presidential nomination the following year.

A phone call brought Butler to the Capitol for a meeting with him and Johnson. Reporters in the Speaker's outer office heard Johnson bellowing angrily for an hour. Then the three came out. "We had a very friendly meeting," Rayburn told the newsmen. "There was no loud talk . . . no violent disagreements . . . no fighting and scratching."

"It was a pleasant and constructive meeting; it ought to do a lot of good," Johnson added.

When the photographers came forward to take their pictures, pale, downcast Butler said to Johnson and Rayburn: "Let's try to look happy together." [26]

As rancid frosting on top of his cake of troubles with Butler, Eisenhower, the DAC, the House's Democratic Study Group and Judge Smith's Rules Committee was Rayburn's running quarrel with architects and historians over the extension of the east front of the Capitol. This was the spot where Presidents for more than a century had been inaugurated; and when Rayburn proposed extending this section and the long stairway before the center Rotunda thirty-two feet out from the building, a loud cry went out that he wanted to "deface the historic Capitol."

He was called a "vandal" and a "destroyer of our heritage." His reply to this was that the sandstone exterior of the building in the Rotunda area was crumbling. Besides, he added, he agreed with the original designers, who had thought that a Rotunda at the edge of a building made it look lopsided.

While a large-scale lobbying effort was under way against Rayburn's proposal, Eric Sevareid interviewed him, and at the end he said, "My brief reading of history teaches me that Sam Rayburn of Texas usually gets what he wants on this Capitol Hill. I suspect, Mr. Speaker, the east front will be changed." [27]

Sevareid was right. Congress approved the extension of the east front, and Rayburn asked Eisenhower to lay the cornerstone on July 4, 1959, using the same silver trowel George Washington had used to lay the Capitol's cornerstone in 1793. After he finished his chore of lifting a spadeful of earth, Ike wanted to know where the pink cornerstone came from. He was surprised when Rayburn said, "Texas," adding dryly, "The courthouse in Denison, the place of your birth, is a good example."

In 1959, the race was on for the top prize at the next Democratic National Convention. Senator Hubert Humphrey was championing the poor and the disadvantaged. Senator Stuart Symington was hitting at Eisenhower for the "missile gap," claiming that the Soviet first, in sending its Sputnik into outer space in October 1957, showed the lag in American missile science. Johnson was spreading the pitch to magazine and newspaper profilers of his awesome domination of the Senate and the pillar he represented against "Imperialistic Communism," a term he borrowed from Eisenhower. When Eisenhower invited Soviet leader Nikita Khrushchev to visit Washington on September 15, 1959, Johnson told reporters he had induced Rayburn to help adjourn Congress on September 12 in order to avoid having to invite Khrushchev to address a joint session of Congress.

Rayburn watched with concern as Senator Kennedy emerged as the front-runner. "I am grateful to Mr. Sam Rayburn," Kennedy was saying sarcastically. "At the last Democratic Convention, if he had not recognized the Tennessee and Oklahoma delegations when he did, I might have won that race with Senator Kefauver—and my political career would now be over." [28]

It was Kennedy's firm belief that Rayburn opposed his candidacy because he was a Catholic and because of his youth. "Sam Rayburn may think I'm young," he complained, "but then most of the population looks young to a man who's 78."[29]

Rayburn did not believe that the country was ready to elect a Catholic President, and he thought it preposterous that "the boy," as he called him, was at the head of the pack for the presidential nomination. For one thing, he thought of him as a sickly little fellow; for another, he had considered him a cipher in his six years in the House and not much more than that in the Senate, where he was a continuing truant from committee hearings and floor debate.

"When Kennedy came to the House by the election of 1946," he recalled, "he had a swarthy, dark-yellowish complexion. It looked as if he had had that Pacific fever. And he looked so spare. I had no idea how tall he is. I looked upon him as a little fellow. He went to the Senate in 1952, and someone asked me a while back if at that time I felt that Kennedy would ever be President. I said, 'No,' thinking about him as I had seen him in the House."[30]

The real reason, of course, why Rayburn opposed Kennedy's candidacy was that he wanted Lyndon Johnson to get the nomination. As stories came to him of the intensive campaigning by Kennedy across the country, he asked Johnson to do the same, but Johnson decided to stay in Washington and rely on his record as boss of the Senate. "In the past 40 months," Kennedy told reporters when he announced officially for the Presidency in January 1960, "I have toured every state in the Union."[31] Stories also came to Rayburn about the money Kennedy's father, old Joe Kennedy, was spending to establish a nationwide organization for his son and curry support from local politicians. This was the same Joe Kennedy whom FDR had appointed chairman of the SEC. In those days, Rayburn had come to his house in Rockville, Maryland, and showy Joe had taken him upstairs to see the gold bathtub.

The political influence of the elder Kennedy's millions worried Rayburn as much as Johnson's determination not to enter any presidential primaries. Even when Senator Vance Hartke said he could carry Indiana and Senator Jennings Randolph thought he would defeat Kennedy in West Virginia, Johnson would not budge. His retort was that every Democratic leader in the House and Senate was for him and would influence the selection of delegates back home. But as Kennedy observed, "Johnson had to prove that a Southerner could win in the North, just as I had to prove that a Catholic could win in heavily Protestant states. . . . When Lyndon said he could win in the North, but could offer no concrete evidence, his claims couldn't be taken seriously."[32]

Within the narrow confines Johnson worked for the nomination, Rayburn still saw victory if there were no public displays of antagonism toward him by party leaders. That was why he fumed when Paul Butler, supposedly neutral, attacked Johnson indirectly in a speech at New York University, in which he predicted Kennedy would win the April 5, 1960, Wisconsin primary and go on to take the nomination at the Los Angeles convention on the first ballot.

Rayburn was also unhappy when he heard that Walter Reuther, head of the United Auto Workers, was opposed to Johnson. One day when Reuther came by his office to discuss labor legislation, Rayburn pointed to a chair and said, "Sit down. I want to talk to you. I'm sick of the labor leaders ganging up on Johnson."

Reuther was surprised by the scathing attack and countered weakly, "Look, Mr. Speaker, don't include me in that sentiment. I'm not against Lyndon Johnson. I want a winner. I don't want eight more years of Republican rule. I'll take anybody the Party names."[33] Then he escaped and resumed working for Kennedy.

Besides the necessity for a Democratic candidate to have labor support, Rayburn knew the importance of home-state party unity from his own sad experiences in 1940 and 1944, and he wanted Johnson to have shoulder-to-shoulder backing in Texas now. But this was not to be. Fortunately, little news of this intrastate fighting was reported in the outside press.

The crux of the Texas trouble was Johnson's hatred for Ralph Yarborough and Mrs. Frankie Randolph, the national committeewoman who led the liberal Democrats of Texas (DOT), which had succeeded the Democratic Advisory Council of Texas. In 1957, with Rayburn's support, Yarborough, who still called himself "a Sam Rayburn Democrat," won the other Texas seat in the U.S. Senate. "I'm glad I could finally win with him," said Rayburn at the time, "because I lost with him when I voted for him four times before this."

Once Yarborough took his Senate seat, Johnson slandered him constantly to reporters and other senators, gave him poor committee assignments and ignored his legitimate requests for patronage. Little wonder that at the start of the 1960 session Yarborough joined the liberal rebellion in the Senate against the majority leader's one-man rule; or that later when Rayburn asked him to announce his support of Johnson for President, he refused. Unaware of what Johnson had been doing to him in the Senate, Rayburn said he was sorry he had not protested when Yarborough campaigned as a Sam Rayburn Democrat. "All this was worth 100,000 votes," he snapped. As a result, he made no protest when

Johnson kept Yarborough off the Texas delegation to the Los Angeles convention and ousted Mrs. Randolph from the National Committee.

As the precious weeks of 1960 began disappearing, Rayburn urgently demanded that Johnson announce his candidacy, in order to develop an organization. But even after Kennedy took the Wisconsin primary on April 5 and started on his sweep of seven primaries, Johnson would not announce. Almost in desperation, Rayburn asked John Connally to establish a "Johnson for President" headquarters in Washington to direct the corralling of support for him before the convention.

Rayburn officially opened the headquarters at the Ambassador Hotel on June 2. And during the rest of the month, Connally, Bobby Baker, who was Johnson's protégé and Senate aide, Oscar Chapman, who had been Truman's Secretary of the Interior, and India Edwards distributed a mountain of "All the Way with LBJ" buttons, made phone calls, issued propaganda and had polls conducted for their man. Kennedy was the enemy, and an open letter to him described him as an "absentee Senator," too young and inexperienced for the Presidency. John Connally added his own touch separately, charging that Kennedy suffered from a fatal disease.

Harry Truman was as much disturbed by the successful preconvention campaigning of the young senator from Massachusetts as Rayburn. Until recently his communications with Rayburn had been over his desire to get Congress to pass a relief bill for Presidents out of office. As one of his letters to "Dear Sam" read: "I'm not asking for help, relief or a pension—only justice. I don't need any pension but if my library is accepted the rent part of my overhead will cease. But I'll still need three clerks, telephones, telegraphs and postage." [34]

By June 1960, Truman's communications with Rayburn were strictly on the race for the presidential nomination, and his tone was one of alarm and defeat. "I am disturbed about how this thing has worked out and as you know, all I am trying to do is to help the Democratic Party," he told Rayburn. "You and I had a conversation once when we decided on two men that were capable of being President of the United States under present conditions; one was Lyndon Johnson and the other, was Stuart Symington. It looks as if this Convention has been packed against both of them and it is almost impossible for me to stand a situation like this. I want to talk to you again before the Convention meets to see what the proper answer might be." [35] He was so upset that he signed his name "Harry Truman," crossed it out and wrote "Harry" beneath it, and said in a p.s., "You see what habit does!"

Johnson finally made a few speeches, traveling to the Appalachian area for three days and flying in and out of Idaho and California like a tornado. Not until July 5, only six days before the convention was to start, did he announce his candidacy.

He expected to win, he told a disbelieving Rayburn. One of the private polls gave him 500 delegates, and while this was not the 761 he needed for the nomination, he felt it was high enough to help stop Kennedy on the first ballot while he picked up delegates from Symington and Stevenson—and even from Kennedy—and go over the top a few ballots later. "I can see it all now," one of Johnson's assistants piped up. "Johnson will be standing in the hotel room after he wins the nomination, and he'll say, 'We want Sonny Boy [Kennedy] for Vice President. Go fetch him for me.' "

Early in the year, Rayburn had decided to give up his role as impresario of Democratic National Conventions and come only as a delegate with a seat on the floor in the Texas section. As his successor as permanent chairman, he had suggested Congressman Hale Boggs of Louisiana. But when Paul Butler fought this on the ground that this constituted a partisan move for Johnson's candidacy, Rayburn proposed Florida Governor LeRoy Collins, a racial moderate. Collins, a prematurely gray, young man with a pleasant manner and a ready smile, visited Rayburn after his acceptance for pointers from the master's "Rules of Order for National Conventions"; and he learned techniques for hastening votes, curtailing demonstrations, rapping the gavel with authority, getting rid of troublemakers and acting the grim boss. "Above all," Rayburn warned him, "a convention can get away from you in a hurry if you don't watch out."

While he told reporters he was giving up the management of the national convention in order to concentrate on helping Lyndon Johnson's candidacy, there were other reasons. In 1959, his eyesight had begun to fade, and stronger prescription glasses could not correct the situation. Buck Henson, his ranch foreman, became acutely aware of his eye trouble when Rayburn drove him from the farm to the ranch on a visit home. "He couldn't drive straight, but weaved back and forth on the road," said Buck. [36] Alla Clary said that his eyesight became so poor "he didn't know anyone until they were right up to him. If someone stopped him and asked him to read something, he'd say, 'Oh, I forgot my glasses. You read it to me.' " [37] Another aide said that members of Congress were not aware of his eye problem because "he had an excellent memory for voice recognition." He also depended on oral briefings to tell him the details of legislation, and his remarkable ability to retain what he heard helped cover up his handicap.

By mid-1960, his bull-like state of health was also fading. He attributed this to his age, his disappointment over Johnson's weak try for the nomination, his troubles with the Democratic liberals, and his failure to meet the country's needs because of the snowballing Eisenhower vetoes. In only a single instance did Eisenhower praise him for winning the full amount of money requested, and this came over the foreign-aid bill of 1960. Wrote Eisenhower: "I feel impelled to let you know how gratified I am, and encouraged, that the mutual security authorizing legislation came through the Congressional process without serious injury to the level of funds projected for the coming fiscal year. Your support was, of course, a major factor in achieving this result and I thank you for it, not as much personally but, more importantly, officially because this program is so vital to our security and to the buttressing of freedom throughout the world." [38]

Rayburn left Washington early to have some time to rest at home before the convention opened on July 11. He had told Johnson to go to Los Angeles in advance of the Democratic gathering in order to work on the delegations as they arrived. But Lyndon ignored him. "I was up to Mr. Rayburn's house during this time," said Buck Henson. "They called him from Washington and wanted him back for a short business. But he said, 'I'm not coming. My shirts just hang on me and I've lost weight, and I'm just not coming at this time.' " [39]

He was feeling better when it came time to leave Bonham for Los Angeles, but he was not happy, for his political sense told him that Jack Kennedy had more than an even chance to win on the first ballot. He was outdoors ready to climb into his six-year-old Plymouth for the ride to the airport when a young friend asked him whom the Democrats would nominate. He did not say, "Johnson." Instead, he attempted a smile and called out, "A winner!" [40]

By the time he reached the Biltmore Hotel on Grand Street, he was apprised that the efficient crew of Kennedy operators were greeting the arriving delegations and joining them in their deliberations. Asked by reporters if he had seen Joe Kennedy, who had come to Los Angeles to continue to work for his son, Rayburn said resignedly, "I haven't seen him, but he's in the bushes around here."

When Rayburn strolled into the Sports Arena Convention Hall for the opening on Monday, July 11, the delegates gave him a standing ovation. Acting Chairman Paul Butler rapped angrily for order, and Rayburn ignored him, walking about and shaking hands with his host of friends before taking his seat, which was second from the aisle in the Texas delegation's large section of the floor. "It's not as lonesome as sitting up there," he said, pointing to the platform.

Wednesday, July 13, was the day of reckoning. The nominating speeches began at 4:00 P.M., and Rayburn spoke for Johnson. It was a florid assortment of words of the type he had always detested when he had had to listen to the bombast as a prisoner on the platform. In his words, Johnson emerged as "a tall, sun-crowned man who stands ready now to lead America."

After the nominating speech for Adlai Stevenson by Senator Eugene McCarthy of Minnesota, Governor Collins revealed himself as an apt student of the Rayburn convention rules when the demonstration for Stevenson would not end. Collins ordered the lights turned out. Those who watched Rayburn when noise engulfed the Sports Arena at other times called him a backseat chairman, for he kept pounding an imaginary gavel for order. Once when Collins rapped his gavel ten minutes in a fruitless attempt to restore order, Rayburn's clenched fist went up and down simultaneously.

The first ballot began at 10:07 that evening. Through the first twelve states, Johnson surprised Rayburn by running as well as Kennedy. Then the shift came with Illinois, where Chicago boss, Mayor Richard Daley, gave 61½ of his state's 69 votes to the young senator from Massachusetts.

At 11 P.M. it was all over. Rayburn's understanding of Kennedy's true strength had proved correct. On the first ballot, he had gone over the top with 816 votes to 409 for Johnson, 86 for Symington, and 79½ for Stevenson. Yet despite Rayburn's expectancy, he suffered terribly as the vote for Kennedy grew, and when it ended he was a picture of misery. But afterward, when reporters asked if he would support Kennedy, he said fiercely, "Of course! I'm a Democrat."

Later that night Rayburn phoned Johnson and told him of his premonition that Kennedy was going to ask him to take the vice-presidential nomination. "It would be a terrible thing to do. Turn it down."

Rayburn's instinct was right. Kennedy phoned Johnson early the next morning and made an appointment to see him a few hours later. It was obvious from his tone that he planned to ask him to go on the ticket. Johnson then phoned Rayburn and told him of the call, and Rayburn repeated, "Turn it down."

When word spread in the Texas delegation about the morning's events, Wright Patman rushed to Rayburn's suite. "Sam was in the bathroom in his shorts, and he was shaving," Patman said. "He was blistering mad about Lyndon's even considering the Vice Presidency, and he shouted at me, 'It will ruin him for the future.' "[41]

In the meantime, the senator with the worst record for absenteeism called on the Senate's boss. And when he returned to his suite, he had an incredulous expression. "You just won't believe it," he told his aides. "He wants it!"

Kennedy then went to see Rayburn, and the Speaker stared into his eyes for signs of sincerity when the young man explained why he wanted Lyndon on the ticket and promised he would make him a working Vice President. "Well," said Rayburn, "up until 30 minutes ago I was against it. . . . You know, Jack, I am a very old man . . . in the twilight of my life, walking down into the valley. I'm afraid I was trying to keep him in the legislative end where he could help me. I can see that you need him more. I yield on one condition . . . that you go on the radio or television and tell the people you came to us and asked for this thing." Kennedy said he would.

Rayburn phoned Johnson afterward, telling him to accept. "I'm a wiser man this morning than I was last night. Besides that other fellah [Nixon] called me a traitor, and I don't want a man who calls me a traitor to be President."

Labor and liberal delegates threatened a revolt when they learned of Johnson's selection for second place. John McCormack was determined to head off this opposition, and from the floor he yelled for a voice vote on Johnson's nomination. An ugly argument started because the procedure called for a roll call of the states unless a two-thirds vote could be mustered to suspend this rule. Governor Collins saved the situation by using another of Rayburn's convention techniques. He ordered a voice vote on suspending the rules, ignored the roar of noes, and announced that with more than two-thirds in favor "the motion is adopted and Senator Lyndon B. Johnson of Texas has been nominated for the Vice Presidency of the United States by acclamation."

The 1960 campaign actually began in the Capitol in August, and Rayburn was embarrassed because he had helped bring this sorry situation into being. Before the convention, when Johnson thought he would win the presidential nomination, he induced Rayburn to recess Congress instead of adjourning and call a special session in August so he could return triumphantly from the convention and dominate the scene.

But now the Senate majority leader was the second man on the ticket, and the man who had never held any power in the Senate was the majority leader's leader. Kennedy had to offer a program in this post-convention Senate and promote it, even though he had neither the standing among the other Senators nor the time to do anything. Equally embarrassing, the presiding officer during this two-week session was Vice President Nixon, the Republican presidential nominee.

Nor was Rayburn's lot in the House much better. In this abbreviated session, twelve members of the Democratic Study Group used much of the time to denounce the Rules Committee and demand its reform because Smith would not release the school-construction bill. Rayburn went to work in earnest on Judge Smith to release this bill so it could go to a conference committee and become a solid achievement of this August Congress. But Smith would not listen, and Rayburn felt greatly relieved when the session ended on September 1 and everyone fled Washington.

That fall, despite doubts about his stamina, Rayburn booked a heavy load of speechmaking within Texas because if Kennedy failed to carry the state, it would reflect on his wisdom in pushing Lyndon on the ticket. He hit hard at the oil crowd for duplicity and at Bible Belters who opposed Kennedy on grounds of their religious prejudice. At some places he concentrated on attacking Nixon. After his speech at Fort Worth, the *Star Telegram* reported: "Mr. Democrat basted the Republicans in general, and Richard Nixon in particular, with hot sauce at a barbecue for Party failthfuls." [42]

The polls showed early and late that the twenty-four Texas electoral votes would play a crucial role in the November election. Since the chief uproar in the state was over Kennedy's Catholicism, he traveled there in September to eliminate religion as an issue in the campaign. Several stops were planned with the major speech to be given to the Greater Houston Ministerial Association on September 12 over national television.

Rayburn was on Johnson's plane to meet Kennedy at El Paso the day before, and it turned into a nightmare of an experience for him. Johnson's plane landed first, but before he and Rayburn climbed out, a curt radio order from Kennedy flying in from California told them to remain aboard until his plane landed.

Kennedy's *Caroline* did not touch down until an hour later, but long before then, said a Johnson aide, Lyndon's anger was so great that "in pool-room language he fumed because Kennedy was late." Finally after Kennedy took his cheers, they got out of their plane, and while Kennedy spoke, "Johnson sat glumly on the platform." Afterward, unable to take out his fury on the head of the ticket, "Johnson was in Sam Rayburn's face, crying out some terrible woe and emphatically poking the Speaker's chest with that stabbing forefinger. The Speaker looked tired and faintly agonized." [43]

But Rayburn quickly forgave Lyndon for his outburst and Jack Kennedy for his arrogance because the uppermost issue was the election of the ticket. So he went on to Lubbock, San Antonio and Houston with the two, encouraging unity and friendliness. At Houston, where Kennedy gave a superb speech and fielded questions well from the ministers, Rayburn was enthusiastic about the results. "As we say in my part of Texas," he gave his view of the encounter, "he ate 'em blood raw!" [44]

After this came barnstorming by the three and Senator Yarborough in other Texas places, and Rayburn was now the principal speaker for the Democrats. He slammed at religious bigotry and he spoke about the country's future under the party. Later, heading East, Kennedy sent him a telegram tribute: "In past 2 days you made the most effective speeches delivered in the entire campaign. I am deeply indebted."[45]

Following Kennedy's narrow win over Nixon on November 8, the most complimentary comment Rayburn could muster about the unproved victor was, "That boy grows on you." What made him happiest of all was that after eight years in the shallows, the party was in command again.

28

Not a Fur Piece from Flag Springs

The pull and haul of the 1960 campaign left Sam Rayburn extremely tired, and he developed such a heavy cold that Dr. Joe Risser, his local Bonham physician, ordered him into the hospital. Rayburn grumbled and complained not so much against the doctor but against himself, for this was only the second time in his life he had ever been in a hospital bed. The other occasion had been twenty-one years earlier, back in the spring of 1939, when he had his tonsils removed.

When he left the hospital, Dr. Risser tried to humor him. "You'll live to be 106," he assured him.

"I'll settle for 104," Rayburn chuckled. [1]

But age was creeping up on him, and he knew it. His skin was wrinkled, his weight was continuing to drop, his speedy gait of the past had become slow, and his eyesight was dimmer than a year ago. Even before the Los Angeles convention, he could not ride his favorite quarter horse in the local rodeo as he always had but took a seat in a pony cart pulled by a pair of gentle Shetlands. Then again in October, campaigning for Johnson and Kennedy in Pasadena, Texas, near the spot where Sam Houston captured Santa Anna, he settled for an automobile to lead the parade and not a horse.

Another sign of creeping age in Rayburn's case was his increasing interest in formal religion. Although for nineteen years in his younger days he had been a Sunday-school superintendent in a Baptist church, he had never become a member, but did his praying privately.

However, at the age of seventy-four, shortly after his sister Miss Lou died in 1956, he had joined the Primitive Baptist Church and was baptized at the church in the town of Tioga. This particular sect of Baptists were known as "Hard-Shell" and stemmed from the Pilgrim

Church of Predestinarian Regular Baptists, which had first appeared in Texas in 1834. [2] Eyebrows raised when newspapers publicized his joining what was considered in some quarters as an odd religious sect. To persistent questioners Rayburn replied that it had been his father's church, and to the curious he said patiently, "Yes, the Hard Shells are feet-washing Baptists, but just as Jesus washed the feet of his disciples so the members of this sect wash each other's feet."

During the 1960 campaign, when the issue of Kennedy's Catholicism raged in the South, Rayburn had made good use of his own church membership to combat it. "I'm a Hard-Shell Baptist," he declared. "And they say we're about the most prejudiced people in the whole country on this issue. But look at me. I'm not prejudiced."

In imitation of President-Elect Franklin Roosevelt, who had requested Democratic leaders to travel to Warm Springs, Georgia, to discuss ways to get the country moving again, President-Elect John Kennedy summoned party leaders to his father's large home in Palm Beach, Florida, for the same purpose near the end of 1960. Unlike Roosevelt, Kennedy was openly cocky about his ability to run the country. "I don't know anybody who can do it any better than I can," he told reporters. [3]

Rayburn had gone by train in 1932, but now Kennedy sent his private plane, the *Caroline*, on December 19 to whisk him across the South for two days of talk on the "New Frontier" legislative program.

Across a time span of twenty-eight years, Rayburn recognized other similarities. Roosevelt had his brain trusters, Kennedy his task forces. Roosevelt had his "First Hundred Days," an umbrella-type name to signify the awesome list of anti-Depression legislation he had won from Congress in his first spring as President. Kennedy also hoped for his own "First Hundred Days." Said an aide: "In almost every critical area of public policy, comprehensive Presidential messages and some 277 separate requests would be sent to the Congress in Kennedy's first hundred days." [4]

Lyndon Johnson and Mike Mansfield, the Senate's new majority leader now that Johnson was Vice President, had also come to Palm Beach to participate alongside Rayburn in the talks with Kennedy and his staff. The subjects ranged from antirecession bills, housing, education, and highways to regulatory agencies, foreign aid, and defense. Rayburn had been in Congress before Kennedy was born, but as President-elect, Kennedy took charge of the discussions, huckstering many of the reports written by his nineteen task forces, and expressing his ideas on legislative techniques. This had its amusing aspect to Rayburn and Johnson because Kennedy had floor-managed only a single bill during his fourteen years in

Congress and had botched it. This was his anti-labor-racketeering bill of 1959 for which a harsh antilabor bill was not only substituted for his but became law.

Rayburn never bothered to contradict Kennedy's talkative and know-it-all assistants when they talked about legislative matters. But afterward, when Johnson praised their brain power, he said bitingly, "Well, Lyndon, they may be just as intelligent as you say. But I'd feel a helluva lot better if just one of them had ever run for sheriff."

Before the meetings ended, Kennedy told Rayburn he was greatly concerned about the House Rules Committee. If its 6-to-6 tie votes continued, he said anxiously, "nothing controversial would come to the floor. Our whole program would be emasculated." [5]

The old House warhorse agreed. He asked Kennedy to "stay out of the fight," and assured him he would settle it effectively.

Even though Congress was not scheduled to meet until January 3, 1961, Rayburn went early to Washington, burdened by the grim truth that young Kennedy's hopes rested primarily on his shoulders. Congressman John Blatnik of Minnesota, a leader of the Democratic Study Group, was on hand to greet him and reemphasize Kennedy's concern. Blatnik wanted to remind him that he had failed to keep his promise in the last Congress to get all major bills out of Judge Smith's Rules Committee and to the floor for a vote. The DSG was not going to tolerate this situation any longer and had its own solution: Purge Bill Colmer, the ranking Democrat on the Rules Committee, who invariably joined Howard Smith and the four Republicans in voting against releasing DSG-supported legislation, and replace him with a tie-breaking liberal Democrat.

There were others, including Lyndon Johnson, who thought that purging Colmer was a good idea that could be justified on political grounds. Colmer, the Democrat, had supported Nixon and not Kennedy in 1960. But Rayburn did not like this approach. First of all, he had not taken any action against the Dixiecrats who had deserted Truman in 1948. Nor had he purged Adam Clayton Powell, chairman of the Education and Labor Committee, who had deserted the Democrats to support Eisenhower in 1956. Second, a Colmer purge would doom the Kennedy program, for it would push Southern Democrats into a tighter alliance with Republicans.

But the problem could not remain static, and on New Year's Day he called Howard Smith to his office and told him bluntly that the 6-to-6 bill-killer votes had to end. He offered the wily Virginian a choice—either Colmer would be purged or three new members would be added to the

Rules Committee, two Democrats and one Republican. Smith drawled out a sharp no to both.

So the fight began in earnest. The following day Rayburn tried to put pressure on Smith to choose the latter solution by telling reporters he favored purging Colmer. This led Smith to send agents to Rayburn with a counteroffer. If Rayburn took no action, Smith would agree to give up the Rules Committee's control over sending bills approved by the House to conferences with the Senate. In addition, he might magnanimously (he said) agree to let a total of five Kennedy bills go to the House floor for action in the 1961–62 congressional sessions. Smith dropped by later in person to repeat his offer. Rayburn told him this was no answer because the New Frontier program would be a large legislative package.

If Rayburn had wanted to purge Colmer, he knew he had the votes to do this in the Democratic caucus where the liberals outnumbered the conservatives. On the other hand, to add members to the Rules Committee required a vote by the whole House. Should he lose this vote, he realized that Smith would emerge as the undisputed dictator of the House.

"On tough decisions, Mr. Rayburn almost became a loner," said Carl Albert, the majority whip. "He didn't say anything for four days on the Rules Committee dilemma. Then he said that purging Colmer was going too far." [6] His solution was to be the far more dangerous course of seeking House approval to pack the committee.

When Rayburn scheduled a vote on the House floor for January 26, the fight became a war. Carl Vinson of Georgia, Rayburn's oldest friend in the House and chairman of the Armed Services Committee, made a quick count and told Sam that about half the 99 Southern Democrats would support him. If these were added to the 164 liberal Democrats, the total would still fall short of the necessary House majority. Some Republicans would have to support enlargement, or it would lose.

Charlie Halleck struck a heavy blow when he announced that the Republican Policy Committee had voted against enlargement of the Rules Committee. Halleck also said he had told freshmen Republican congressmen that he would not decide on their committee assignments until after the Rules Committee packing issue was voted on.

Rayburn asked Halleck to come to his office, and with his head turning crimson, he warned Charlie, "That's a game two can play. You better think twice. For one thing, I'll use my authority as Speaker to select the Republican members of all special and joint committees. I have that power, but I haven't used it."

Halleck feigned a tone of abject helplessness and threw up his hands. "You know I have to follow whatever our caucus decides."

"Yes, I know all about that," Rayburn said sarcastically. "But when you told Howard Smith you would back him . . . that was no caucus decision." [7]

There was more trouble as January 26 approached. A check of Carl Vinson's vote count showed him far too optimistic. In addition, congressmen were being flooded with mail from the National Association of Manufacturers, the American Medical Association, the Chamber of Commerce and the Farm Bureau in opposition to enlargement, and their lobbyists were everywhere to intimidate members. The *Washington Post* reported that one congressman changed his decision four times. In order to buoy his forces, Rayburn told the Democratic caucus on January 17: "I've received thousands of letters opposing this change. About 80 percent, I might add, came from people who voted for Richard Nixon."

On January 25, Rayburn saw he would probably lose, so he postponed the showdown vote until the thirty-first. Halleck screamed against this, but Judge Smith found it amusing. Once more he promised to allow five Kennedy bills to go to the House, and told newsmen the reason for the delay: "They must be afraid they haven't the votes."

With the need for more votes from any source, Rayburn did not object during this five-day period when Kennedy and his aides joined the struggle. Their noisy, publicized lobbying was heavy-handed and amateurish in the overlay of patronage jobs and federal projects they offered, compared to the quiet work of Joe Martin. He visited Rayburn at a time when Charlie Halleck was cracking the Republican whip to hold his crew together behind Howard Smith. "I'll line up as many people as I can for you," old Joe promised Sam. "And I think you'll be surprised by the number who will."

Monday, January 31, found the galleries packed and a charged atmosphere below on the House floor. Debate was limited to an hour. Howard Smith renewed his offer to permit a vote on five Kennedy bills if he won, and he promised not to go to his farm to "milk cows" during the session. Rayburn came down slowly from the rostrum to the well of the House to make his plea for enlarging Smith's committee.

Then came the roll-call vote. At the 300 mark, Smith was even with Rayburn. The House was morbidly quiet. But at the end, Rayburn squeaked through by the narrow margin of 217 to 212. Only 35 of the 99 Southern Democrats had supported him, while 22 Republicans from Joe Martin country had. Cheers emanated from the winners. "Well, we done our damnedest," Smith muttered, acknowledging defeat. [8]

Kennedy's inauguration had come in the midst of the Rules Committee fight. From the beginning of the year until the oath taking, Rayburn found time each day to go outdoors and urge workmen to finish the east-front alteration before the twentieth. The polishing of the marble and the erection of the temporary wooden stands moved swifter under his watchful eye. On the big day, after an eight-inch snowfall was cleared away, the contrast between the old Speaker and the young President on the platform stood out clearly: one fumbling through the words as he administered the oath to Vice President Johnson; the other issuing a call to youth. "Let the word go forth from this time and place, to friend and foe alike, that the torch has been passed to a new generation of Americans," said Kennedy.

But Rayburn had no intention of fading away at the demand of the young. Early in the New Frontier he had his confrontation on this issue when he recommended Sarah Hughes, a one-time local judge in Texas, to be a federal district judge. The thirty-five-year-old Attorney General Robert Kennedy, brother of the President, crossed through her name because she was sixty-four. One day he went to Rayburn's office to find out why a bill in which he was interested was frozen in the House Judiciary Committee. "That bill will pass as soon as Sarah Hughes becomes a Federal judge," Rayburn said tartly.

Kennedy's reply was that she was an old, old woman. "Sonny, everybody seems old to you," Rayburn explained, staring harshly into his eyes.

A short time later her name was submitted to the Senate, and she was confirmed. Kennedy's bill was also reported out by the committee. [9]

Following Rayburn's enormous battle and ultimate victory over Judge Smith, the Democratic Study Group and the press expected a mammoth New Frontier program to be steamrolled through the House. But nothing of the kind occurred, for the Rules Committee fight revealed that the struggle was just beginning. "With Rayburn's own reputation at stake, with all the pressures and appeals a new President could make, we won by five votes," Kennedy moaned, after the success against Smith. "That shows what we're up against." [19]

What he was up against was that while the Rules Committee could now be expected to release most New Frontier bills for House floor action, each major bill would require as much work for passage as was involved in the Rules Committee packing fight. Each piece of legislation would come to the House Chamber needing sixty or more votes from Southern Democrats and Republicans.

Because of this situation, Kennedy agreed with Rayburn at a Tuesday morning leadership meeting that he should proceed carefully, more so in the House than in the Senate, where the problem was not as acute.

"There is no sense in putting the Presidency on the line on an issue, and then being defeated," said Kennedy. [11] The Peace Corps was a case in point. This was the program that did more to endear him to the young than any other. Kennedy knew it would have lost in an early vote. So he created it by executive order months before he dared ask Congress to establish it by statute.

A measure of the work involved to get Kennedy bills through the House was revealed when Rayburn tried to win approval for an increase in the minimum hourly wage from $1.00 to $1.25 and an extension of coverage to an additional 4.3 million workers. Southern Democratic leaders were not going to stand for this step-up for blacks and poor whites, and they joined conservative Republicans in writing a substitute bill. This would cut back the wage increase to $1.15 and extend coverage to only 1.3 million.

When the Rules Committee sent the Kennedy bill to the floor, the anticoalition was so strong that its substitute bill passed instead, with a thirteen-vote margin. But like the Rayburn of the old days, this setback did not stop him.

With Carl Albert of Oklahoma, his Democratic whip, and his friend Carl Vinson, Rayburn helped write the compromise Albert bill that retained Kennedy's $1.25 but cut new coverage back to 3.6 million. When Carl Vinson showed him convincing proof that enough Southern Democrats would support the Albert bill to win passage, Rayburn confidently ran it out for a vote to replace the victorious coalition bill. But it lost by one vote, 186 to 185.

Enraged, Rayburn investigated the reason for the loss. Three liberal Democrats were found to have been drinking beer in the House restaurant at the time of the roll call. Seven others had been too lazy to walk from their offices to the House Chamber. All caught unshirted hell from him.

But even with this second defeat Rayburn refused to quit. When the anti-coalition's bill went to the House-Senate conference committee to iron out the differences with the Senate version, Rayburn decided on the House members. The compromise that returned to the House for a final decision on May 3 was actually the Albert bill. This time Rayburn took no chances and it carried 230 to 196. [12]

There was a similar haul and pull on other controversial Kennedy bills. An emergency price-support program for the 1961 corn crop at $1.20 a bushel passed the House by a vote of 209 to 202 only after Rayburn appealed personally at the last minute to 7 members who opposed it. The Housing and Area-Redevelopment Bills also required much oral work by

Rayburn before they passed. The Area-Redevelopment legislation, which proposed federal aid to distressed areas suffering from substantial unemployment, had been discussed by committees for four years. In 1961, when it finally became law, Kennedy's aides had rewritten the bill into such a mess of vagueness that Pasadena, California, one of the richest cities in the country, was able to qualify as a "distressed area."

Other controversial Kennedy bills could not be budged from committees without more time than Rayburn could expend on this task in the first half of 1961. For instance he could not persuade Wilbur Mills, chairman of the Ways and Means Committee and one of his protégés, to let the Medicare Bill out of his committee. Mills was the author of the Kerr-Mills Act, passed in the Eisenhower administration, which provided for medical care for the aged who agreed to a means test. In contrast, Medicare provided for short-period hospitalization for the aged under the Social Security system. With additional time to talk to Mills, Rayburn believed he could clear Medicare from Ways and Means before the session ended. He also felt this way about James Delaney of New York, a liberal on the Rules Committee. The Senate passed the administration's Federal Aid to Education Bill and the House Education and Labor Committee had reported it out favorably. But Delaney saw the bill as anti-Catholic legislation, and his was the swing vote that produced the negative 8-to-7 count in the Rules Committee and kept it from the House floor.

Although Judge Smith worked within his new restrictions to keep Kennedy bills from going to the House floor, there were times that he tried to get even with Rayburn by asking the Rules Committee to send bills the Speaker opposed to the Chamber. One of these would permit the televising of House proceedings. But on Rayburn's orders the eight Democratic pro-Speaker votes kept it bottled up in the Rules Committee. Afterward when Smith saw Rayburn, he wreathed his face in mock injury and shook his head. It was too bad, he said, now that he had accepted the Rayburn brand of democracy for his committee Rayburn had abandoned it.

For Rayburn's ceaseless toil, Kennedy paid him the ultimate compliment in relating the story of a phone call to him at the White House when he was in Canada, Lyndon Johnson in Southeast Asia and Secretary of State Dean Rusk in Geneva.

"Who's keeping the store?" the caller demanded, after saying that he had tried to reach Johnson and Rusk.

"The same man who's alway kept it—SAM RAYBURN!" the operator retorted. [13]

Despite his vigorous activity in the January war with Judge Smith and the springtime work on the controversial parts of Kennedy's modest domestic legislative program, Rayburn knew that his health was continuing to slip. The exhaustion he had felt after the November election returned in closer waves, and the pain in his back was deeper. He went home to Bonham over a weekend, and he told Buck Henson, "I've got lumbago." Buck's impression was that "he felt really worse than he wanted you to know."[14]

The tired feeling made him give up his morning walk partway to the Capitol from the Anchorage, as well as the two or three brisk turns around the oval path beyond the new east front. No longer did he measure the girth and appraise the height of the white oak he had planted in front of the House side of the Capitol on October 11, 1949. George Dixon, the syndicated columnist, spied him one day on a Capitol balcony, rising to his toes and rocking back on his heels. "Getting the kinks out of my back, George," he explained his reduced form of exercise.

The condition of his health brought other changes in his daily routine. In the morning when he reached the Capitol, he proceeded to his back office as usual, but he lay on the sofa while his staff read the mail to him. "Near noon," said Alla Clary, "he would get off the couch and straighten his back and walk around to the other office."[15] Now he could not avoid public display, and like the old political trouper that he was he held his bantering new conference and then went to the House Chamber to preside.

Those who saw him daily were not aware of the physical change for a long time, because he did not let down on the job or curtail his social activities. There was the formal White House dinner in his honor, the Texas crowd's party for him at the Mayflower, attendance at a Red Mass with Kennedy, a talk at a boys' school. He also continued his travels for the party, speaking at Jefferson-Jackson Day dinners in Raleigh, North Carolina, and Birmingham, Alabama, where he extolled the young President.

Back again in Washington, he made the time to mount a drive in behalf of Sergeant Alvin York, a famous World War I hero, now bedridden and poverty-stricken in Rayburn's native Tennessee. The Internal Revenue Service claimed that York owed $172,000 in back taxes and penalties from the sale of his book and the movie made from it. After meetings with IRS officials, Rayburn succeeded in whittling York's debt down to $25,000. Then he put $1,000 into the donation pot and asked the public to help out. Within a week there was money to settle the IRS bill plus an extra sum for York.

Not a man to discriminate, Rayburn also helped retired President Eisenhower, who was relaxing at his Gettysburg farm and the Augusta, Georgia, National Golf Club. Eisenhower wanted his five-star military rank returned to him and asked Rayburn for his aid in winning congressional approval. "I learn of your intention to revert to the 'Captain Ike' appellation when next we come together," Eisenhower wrote, like a man wanting a favor from someone with power. "I would like to have the opportunity to mix you a 'Bourbon and Branch Water.' " [16]

Rayburn was able to whip this through in short order because Eisenhower agreed to forego the military pay and allowances that came with the five-star rank and accept the benefits of the act Rayburn had pushed through Congress for Harry Truman in 1958. This was the law for former Presidents that provided twenty-five thousand dollars a year for life plus fifty thousand dollars a year to run an office. On March 21, a day before Kennedy signed the bill restoring him to a General of the Army, Eisenhower wrote his thank-you note to Rayburn. [17]

On another military matter, Rayburn was not the least bit kind. The Civil War Centennial celebration, financed by the federal government, occurred that year. When Rayburn heard that various Civil War battles were to be recreated, he was furious at the possibility of reopening old North-South wounds by this stupidity. As a member of the Civil War Centennial Commission, he demanded that the official who had thought up the battle idea be fired, and this was done.

That spring, Rayburn also gave his support to William Blakley campaigning against John Tower, a Republican, to fill the Senate seat vacated by Lyndon Johnson, who had cautiously run simultaneously for the Senate and the Vice Presidency in 1960 in order to retain a political post if Kennedy won or lost. Rayburn dismissed Tower as a "pipsqueak," but he was puzzled by Blakley. "Blakley was one of the hardest men to help I ever saw," he admitted after Tower won. "He never did say what he was for. He was against everything." [18]

By May, when his pains and weariness held him to his back office couch until the last possible moment and curtailed his hideaway Board of Education appearances, he had his own skirmish with healthy young congressional wives. A majority of the wives of House members sent him a petition requesting a long summer recess so their families could be together back home. Rayburn was outraged that they would put a vacation ahead of their husbands' congressional work. "This is the greatest nonsense I ever heard of!" he exploded, killing the request.

A Kennedy assistant noticed that he was growing "increasingly grumpy and uncommunicative." [19] There was little question of this in his relations with the White House. He was angry and hurt at reports that the mention of Harry Truman's name brought gales of arrogant laughter. He was also offended at the treatment meted out to Lyndon Johnson by Kennedy aides. Youngsters, who would have been afraid to talk to him as Senate majority leader, now called the Vice President "Lyndon" to his face.

At the Chicago convention, Kennedy had assured Rayburn that he would "use Johnson's finesse in handling people on an international level." Yet once he was in office, Kennedy had waited until April to give Johnson a foreign assignment, and it was only the piddling job, Lyndon complained to Rayburn, of representing the United States at the independence celebration in Senegal. Then the next month Kennedy told him to visit South Viet Nam, which was not only little but dangerous.

Johnson had fought for two weeks against this trip. "Mr. President," he told Rayburn he had argued with Kennedy, "I don't want to embarrass you by getting my head blown off in Saigon."

"That's all right, Lyndon," said Kennedy, "if anything happens to you out there, Sam Rayburn and I will give you the biggest funeral in the history of Austin, Texas." [20]

Rayburn was also out-of-sorts with the White House after the disastrous Bay of Pigs venture against Castro's Cuba, and he did not like it when Kennedy was depressed and without self-confidence at leadership meetings for weeks afterward. Then again he was grumpy in June when Khrushchev bested the inexperienced young President at their Vienna meeting and Kennedy complained of backaches and headaches at the next few Tuesday morning leadership breakfasts. Nor was he happy when Kennedy reacted to Khrushchev by producing national hysteria with talk about nuclear war and a request that Congress and citizens start a crash program to build fallout shelters.

In June, Rayburn found he had no appetite, not even for onions or chili. He experienced a frightening moment one afternoon when he lapsed into temporary unconsciousness while presiding over the House. But he quickly recovered, only to have it happen again in July.

Time Magazine carried a story that he intended to retire. He denied he had any plan to quit and insisted that he felt "fine." He had a long question-and-answer session to be used as an article in *U.S. News and World Report,* and he spoke about his job in next year's congressional session. He was asked about his view of his fellow citizens. "I have absolute faith in the American people," he said. "I believe that more than 95 percent of the American people have more good in them than bad. And when properly appealed to, they will respond—now as they have in the past. I think we will come through in a fashion that will make us all proud." [21]

Periods of dizziness claimed him in July, the pounds fell off faster, yet he did not take a day off. On July 16, it was mind over matter as he came off with a forceful appearance with Bill Lawrence, American Broadcasting Company reporter, on "Issues and Answers." Lawrence described him as "one of the great men of our time."

Now the pains grew worse, and in early August he went to see Dr. Calver, the Capitol physician. But he refused to undergo a detailed examination, and he convinced Calver that he had "a bad case of lumbago."

The cowed doctor prescribed aspirin and mustard plasters, but the pain grew so bad that Rayburn knew he had something more serious than lumbago. Yet his friends apparently did not see the change in him, nor did he mention it.

Lyndon Johnson was visiting him in his apartment on the night of August 17 when the phone rang. Kennedy wanted to talk to Johnson. "Lyndon," he asked, "are you available to go to Berlin?" [22]

The Communists had begun to erect the "Berlin Wall" to keep East Germans from escaping to West Berlin, and Kennedy wanted Johnson to fly there to assure the West Germans they could count on American support. Johnson replied that he had a weekend fishing date with Rayburn. But Rayburn spoke up and said that they could fish another weekend.

It was incredible that Johnson, who prided himself on his powers of observation, could not have noticed what was happening to Rayburn. But for that matter neither did Joe Martin until he got a phone call from his old friend one afternoon to visit his office. When he walked in, Joe was surprised to find a photographer in Sam's office, for he knew how much Sam disliked having his picture taken. Sam said he wanted pictures of the "two living Speakers," and this also struck Joe as being strange because Sam still kept in touch with ninety-two-year-old John Garner, another "living Speaker." But he said nothing and posed next to Rayburn sitting wanly in a chair.

It turned out to be Rayburn's way of having a personal farewell with Martin. For the next day he told a shocked House he was going home at the end of the month for medical tests. To quiet the handwringing display of concern, he said, "I'll be back. I want to die with my boots on and my gavel in my hand."

Some wondered why he did not stay in Washington and undergo tests at the excellent N. I. H. facilities or the Bethesda Naval Hospital. But he supplied the answer when he told Congressman Jim Wright of Texas, "Bonham is a place where people know it when you're sick and where they care when you die."

He drew his monthly pay of $2,912.66, of which the take-home sum was $1,583.14 after the $1,100 federal withholding tax plus his retirement pension payment were extracted. As he always did, he deposited his salary in a checking account where it drew no interest. Then he paid his next month's rent of $267.50 at the Anchorage and sent a round-trip airline ticket to Dr. Joe Risser, whom he wanted to accompany him home to Bonham. [23] Only three of his ten brothers and sisters were alive, but they were too old to come to Washington for him.

On his last day in Washington, he held his daily news conference as usual at five minutes to noon. George Dixon reported that he faced the reporters and asked, "You know how things were yesterday?"

"Yes, Mr. Speaker," they chorused.

"Well," said Rayburn dryly, "they're the same today."

Once he was home in Bonham, Dr. Risser examined him and gave him drugs to build up his strength and relieve the harsh pains. No matter how sick he was, he insisted on visiting his ranch. He also went a few times to the Sam Rayburn Library, dedicated in 1957. His foreman and fishing companion Buck Henson was in anguish at his physical deterioration but not surprised at his determination. "He was a man who hated to give up," he said.

Rayburn also kept up with the work of the House. He had seen to it that John McCormack was advanced to Speaker pro tem in his absence. But from the time Rayburn left Washington until Congress adjourned on September 27, 1961, not a single bill of importance had advanced in the House. Senate Majority Leader Mike Mansfield issued a summary of the legislative record of that Congress. He listed 203 Kennedy proposals sent to the Hill and applauded the young President's record, which showed that 124 had won approval. But of these, almost 75 percent were noncontroversial bills, such as the extension of the Wool Act and the establishment of an International Travel Service in the Commerce Department. [24]

Back in Washington, Congressman Richard Bolling of Missouri, whom Rayburn considered one of the brightest lights among the Democrats, blamed Speaker Sam's absence as the cause of the collapse of the House's work. Bolling also foresaw immense trouble for Kennedy's program in the Congresses that lay ahead. Rayburn had "left the House in a shambles institutionally," said Bolling. He ran a "one-man operation," dominating the House—its members and its legislation—though he lacked institutional power to do so. Over his long career, he had accumulated all sorts of IOU's from members by his kindness, courtesy and favors, and he used these to make the House appear to be working. No other Speaker could hope to duplicate this." [25]

Near the close of September, when Dr. Risser's drugs were not helping him, Rayburn told his ranch foreman, "Buck, I'm going over to Dallas to Baylor Hospital there. But I won't be gone for more than a few days."

So many members of his family had died of cancer that by then he came to a conclusion about his own trouble. He went over his will, and what he possessed was minor. "There are no skeletons in my closet or ghosts under my bed," he once said, for he had never taken advantage of a single opportunity to enrich himself through his powerful political connections. Nor had he ever taken an honorarium or any traveling expenses for addressing any organization. He owned no stocks or bonds, and his total savings at the moment consisted of fifteen thousand dollars in his checking account. There was also the ranch, reduced now to 879 acres, that had cost him eight dollars an acre, the 125-acre family farm and two other farms totaling 315 acres south of nearby Ector. Last, but not least, there was the 1947 Cadillac, still in his garage, that House Democrats had given him.

On his bedroom wall, he had hung his own epitaph. These were the final lines from a favorite novel, *Eben Holden* by Irving Bacheller, and they read:

I ain't afraid
'Shamed o' nuthin' I ever done.
Alwuss kep' my tugs tight,
Never swore 'less 'twas nec'sary,
Never ketched a fish bigger'n it was
Er lied 'n a hoss trade
Er shed a tear I didn't hev to.

On October 2, thin and weak, he walked slowly into Baylor Medical Hospital in Dallas and began tests. The diagnosis was that he had a malignancy that had spread rapidly throughout his body. There was no hope for recovery.

Johnson, Kennedy and Truman paid calls on him after the bad news was made public. When Truman left his friend's bedside, he told reporters outside in a breaking voice, "Sam's in good hands in a Baptist institution." Afterward he wrote a pathetically over-cheerful letter to Sam's widowed sisters, Katie and Meddie: "I don't know when I have enjoyed a visit more than I did with Sam a day or two ago." [26] Rayburn's grandnephew also visited him, and Rayburn confided, "Robert, this is the damnedest thing that has ever happened to me."

At the end of October, he was taken back to Dr. Risser's hospital in

Bonham, a wasted little figure almost unaware of his surroundings. Townspeople took his illness as a personal tragedy, work faltered and a heavy sadness settled over Bonham. Finally he died on November 16.

More than thirty thousand persons crowded into the town for his funeral. Congress sent a delegation of 105 members, and three Presidents of the United States and a future President—Truman, Eisenhower, Kennedy and Johnson—came.

Truman had reached Bonham early because, he said, he wanted "to walk around the square to shake hands with Sam's friends." And to many he said, "Sam Rayburn was a man who made his friends proud and his critics ashamed."

Judge Marvin Jones, Rayburn's one-time brother-in-law and House colleague, was also there. Reporters wrote up his assessment of Rayburn. "Sam wasn't a meteor," he said. "He was a star."

Rayburnisms

Any fellow who will cheat for you will cheat against you.

If a man has good common sense, he has about all the sense there is.

There is an old proverb that the old complain of the conduct of the young when they themselves can no longer set a bad example.

It's easy to be an obstructionist; it's hard to be a constructionist.

A man whose change of position changes his position is lost.

The greatest ambition a man should have is to be just.

The size of a man has nothing to do with his height.

We must meet things worthwhile more than halfway—they will not come to us.

The steam that blows a whistle will never turn a wheel.

It's better to be silent and pretend dumb than to speak and remove all doubt.

When two men agree on everything, one of them is doing all the thinking.

I always tell the truth the first time and do not need a good memory to remember it.

RAYBURNISMS

Any man who will deceive the voters during a political campaign will deceive them after he is elected.

Without vision, nations perish.

A man who becomes conceited and arrogant wasn't big enough for the job.

There are no degrees in truthfulness. There are no degrees in honesty. You are 100 percent or you are not.

Damn the man who is always looking for credit. If a man does his job, and does it well, he will get more credit than he is really entitled to.

Any jackass can kick a barn down, but it takes a carpenter to build it.

There is a time to fish and a time to mend nets.

I have found that people respect you if you tell them where you stand.

It is a wise man who realizes that the church is bigger than its pastor.

We're Democrats, you know, and nobody can boss us. And we fight like hell.

A fellow who eats high on the hog can expect to have a few chitlings.

Why should a fellow try to throw a big calf when he's still stomping and running? Wait until he is easy to throw.

I came within a gnat's heel of remaining a tenant farmer.

If you say you're tired, you will be tired.

I have greater trust in people who send their congressmen postal cards and handwritten letters on tablet paper than those who send telegrams.

Some men ripen earlier than others and burn out early. Powder will flash but it won't burn.

A brilliant uninformed orator is no match for a poor speaker who is informed.

The real test of a man is the way he carries success.

I think that the entire political leadership of the country is guilty of underestimating the American people.

Never use sarcasm. It detracts from the other man's dignity, and anyone you ridicule will remember it thirty years later.

Whenever you're mad and ready to say something, wait a minute.

You think you hate a man only because you don't know him.

If you can't lead by persuasion, you can't lead at all.

The American people, when properly appealed to, respond.

Once you have lost the people's respect, it is very hard to regain their esteem.

——was the hardest fellow to help I had ever seen. He never did say what he was for, only what he was against.

To get along, go along. But I've never asked a man to cast a vote that would violate his conscience or wreck him politically.

If there is anything I hate more than an old fogie, it's a young fogie.

People don't do things for you because you've done things for them; it's what they've done willingly for you that cements friendship.

Legislation should never be designed to punish anyone.

Notes

Chapter 1
THE LAND OF HARDSHIP

1. Sam Rayburn Letters, 1944, Sam Rayburn Library (hereafter abbreviated SRL).
2. John A. Wyeth, *That Devil Forrest*, p. 18.
3. Address delivered by Sam Rayburn at Oakwood Cemetery, Martinsville, Virginia, May 6, 1951.
4. Sam Rayburn to Zach Gray, May 9, 1961, SRL.
5. Andrew Sparks, "Why Tennessee Claims Sam Rayburn," *Atlanta Constitution*, May 28, 1961.
6. Bela Kornitzer, *American Fathers and Sons*, p. 213.
7. Valton Young, *The Speaker's Agent*, p. 56.
8. David L. Cohn, "Mr. Speaker," *Atlantic Monthly*, October 1942, p. 77.
9. See John D. Hicks, *The Populist Revolt*, and C. Vann Woodward, *Origins of the New South, 1887-1913*.
10. Kornitzer, op. cit., p. 214.
11. U.S. Congress, House, *Congressional Record*, 87 Congress, 2 Session, January 18, 1962, pp. 505-506.
12. Kornitzer, op. cit., p. 226.
13. See Sam Acheson, *Joe Bailey: The Last Democrat*.
14. Joseph Alsop and Robert Kintner, "Never Leave Them Angry," *Saturday Evening Post*, January 18, 1941.
15. Alfred Steinberg, *Sam Johnson's Boy*, p. 10.
16. *Congressional Record*, 76 Congress, 3 Session, September 19, 1940, p. 18747.
17. Ralph McGill, *Atlanta Constitution*, November 17, 1961.
18. On the Mayo Normal College see James M. Bledsoe, *A History of Mayo and His College*, Dallas, (Harben Spots Co., 1946).
19. Sam Rayburn, *NEA Journal*, March 1960.
20. D. B. Hardeman, "Unseen Side of the Man They Called Mr. Speaker," *Life*, December 1, 1961.
21. Sam Rayburn to Walter C. Nash, September 17, 1949, SRL.
22. Valton Young, op. cit., p. 32.
23. Rayburn to Nash, September 17, 1949.

NOTES

Chapter 2
SPEAKER OF THE STATE HOUSE

1. Rayburn Reunion with Lannius Class, SRL.
2. Sam Rayburn to H. B. Savage, April 26, 1916, SRL.
3. Louis W. Koenig, *Bryan: A Political Biography of William Jennings Bryan*, p. 165.
4. Claude Bowers, *My Life*, p. 69.
5. Ibid., p. 69.
6. Tom Connally and Alfred Steinberg, *My Name is Tom Connally*, p. 48.
7. Dwight Dorough, *Mr. Sam*, p. 75.
8. R. Bouna Ridgway to Lyndon Johnson, SRL.
9. Ray Stanley Loney, *Sam Rayburn*, (M.A. Thesis, East Texas State College, 1962).
10. Texas Legislature, Bailey Investigating Committee, *Proceedings and Report*, 30 Legislature, 1907.
11. Joseph W. Bailey to Sam Rayburn, 1909, SRL.
12. Joseph W. Bailey to William and Martha Rayburn, August 4, 1916, SRL.
13. R. Bouna Ridgway to Sam Rayburn, SRL
14. University of Texas, *Yearbook*, 1908, SRL.
15. *Dallas Morning News*, October 6, 1961.
16. Bryan Blalock to Sam Rayburn, 1957, SRL.
17. Texas, House of Representatives, *Journal*, 31 Legis., 1909.
18. Martha Rayburn to Sam Rayburn, March 15, 1909, SRL.
19. *Austin Daily Express*, January 10, 1911.
20. Texas, House of Representatives, *Journal*, 32 Legis., 1911.
21. Scrapbook of Lucinda Rayburn, SRL.
22. *Bonham Daily Favorite*, July 16, 1912.
23. *Houston Post*, November 17, 1961.

Chapter 3
TO CONGRESS

1. *Dallas Morning News*, March 12, 1911.
2. *San Antonio Express*, January 28, 1911.
3. See *Austin Daily Tribune*, February—March 1911.
4. Texas, House of Representatives, *Journal*, 32 Legis., 1911.
5. Scrapbook, 1912, SRL.
6. *Bonham* (Tex.) *Daily Favorite*, July 16, 1912.
7. Ibid.
8. U.S. Congress, *Congressional Directory*, 1913.

Chapter 4
A YOUNG CONGRESSMAN

1. U.S. Congress, *Congressional Directory*, 1913.
2. Joseph Alsop and Robert Kintner, "Never Leave Them Angry," *Saturday Evening Post*, January 18, 1941.
3. Sidney R. Bland, "Alice Paul and the Great Suffrage Parade of 1913 in Washington D. C.," *Records of the Columbia Historical Society of Washington, D. C.*, 1971-72, 1973, pp. 657-78.
4. U.S. Congress, House, *Congressional Record*, 61 Cong. 2 Sess., March 19, 1910, pp. 3292, 3426-39. See also George W. Norris, *Fighting Liberal, An Autobiography*.

5. Allan Michie and Frank Rhylick, *Dixie Demagogues*, p. 30.

6. Ibid., p. 23.

7. Ibid., p. 33.

8. George Rothwell Brown, *Washington Herald*, January 8, 1933.

9. Alben Barkley to author, January 19, 1949.

10. *Congressional Record*, 70 Cong., 2 Sess., January 5, 1929, p. 1194.

11. Alla Clary, to author, February 21, 1975.

12. Ibid.

13. *Congressional Record*, 63 Cong., 1 Sess., April 8, 1913, p. 1321.

14. *The New York Times*, June 4, 1961, VI, p. 32.

15. W. S. Ragsdale, *U.S. News and World Report*, October 23, 1961, p. 70.

16. *Fort Worth Record*, June 1913.

17. House, *Congressional Record*, 87 Cong. 2 Sess., January 18, 1962, p. 508.

18. Cordell Hull, *Memoirs*, p. 60.

19. Ibid., p. 83.

20. Sam Rayburn to H. B. Savage, April 26, 1916, SRL.

Chapter 5
RAYBURN AND WILSON

1. Cordell Hull, *Memoirs*, p. 51.

2. U.S. Congress, House, *Congressional Record*, 63 Cong., 1 Sess., May 6, 1913, p. 1247.

3. Adolph Sabath to author, October 6, 1949.

4. *Sherman* (Tex.) *Sentinel*, and *Texas Republic*, May 17, 1913. Scrapbooks, SRL.

5. Sam Rayburn to his family, May 25, 1913, SRL.

6. C. S. Potts, "Texas Stock and Bond Law," *Annals of the American Academy of Political and Social Science*, May 1914.

7. Alfred Lief, *Brandeis*, p. 292.

8. Ray Stannard Baker, *American Chronicle*, p. 253.

9. House, *Congressional Record*, 63 Cong., 2 sess., June 2, 1914, p. 9688.

10. *The New York Times*, May 17, 1914, II, pp. 10-11.

11. Ibid., June 6, 1914.

12. Woodrow Wilson to Sam Rayburn, June 9, 1914, SRL.

13. Martha Rayburn to Sam Rayburn, June 16, 1914, SRL.

14. Sam Rayburn to Kate Thomas, August 26, 1914, SRL.

15. Sam Rayburn to William and Martha Rayburn, "Sunday," 1914, SRL.

16. *Denison* (Tex.) *Herald*, Scrapbooks, SRL.

17. Sam Rayburn campaign card, 1914, SRL.

18. Sam Rayburn Scrapbooks, 1912-1955, SRL.

19. Arthur Link, *The New Freedom*, p. 416.

20. Bascom N. Timmons, In a seven part series, *Fort Worth Star Telegram*, October–November 1961.

Chapter 6
WARTIME CONGRESSMAN

1. Allan Michie and Frank Rhylick, *Dixie Demagogues*, p. 171.

2. U.S. Treasury Department, R. Duane Saunders, address before the Industrial Payroll Savings Committee, Washington, D. C., January 12, 1965.

3. John T. Flynn, *Know Your Congress*, p. 134.

4. Tom Connally and Alfred Steinberg, *My Name is Tom Connally*, pp. 54, 88-89.

NOTES

5. Bascom Timmons in a 7-part series, *Fort Worth Star Telegram*, (Part 2) October-November 1961.

6. Martha Rayburn to Sam Rayburn, January 14, 1915, SRL.

7. E. B. Smith (contractor of Rayburn farmhouse, 1914–15) to Sam Rayburn, SRL.

8. Sam Rayburn to Lucinda Rayburn, February 7, 1915, SRL.

9. Sam Rayburn to W. A. Thomas, February 1922, SRL.

10. Martha Rayburn to Sam Rayburn, January 14, 1915, SRL.

11. Arthur Link, *Campaign for Progressivism and Peace, 1916-1917*, pp. 140-41.

12. Speech, Sam Rayburn Scrapbooks, SRL.

13. Woodrow Wilson to Andrew L. Randell, July 11, 1916, SRL.

14. Joseph Bailey to William and Martha Rayburn, August 4, 1916, SRL.

15. H. G. Dulaney to author, September 6, 1974.

16. U.S. Congress, *Congressional Directory*, 65th Cong., 1st Sess., 1917.

17. Connally and Steinberg, op. cit., pp. 89-90.

18. *Denison* (Tex.) *Herald*, 1913, SRL.

19. Louis W. Koenig, *Bryan: A Political Biography of William Jennings Bryan*, p. 527.

20. Dwight Dorough, *Mr. Sam*, p. 151.

21. Ruth Cranston, *The Story of Woodrow Wilson*, pp. 170-71.

22. Ray Stannard Baker, *An American Chronicle*, p. 285.

23. Charles A. Beard, *Rise of American Civilization*, vol. 2, p. 64.

24. Paul H. Douglas, "War Risk Insurance Act," *Journal of Political Economy*, May 1918.

25. House, *Congressional Record*, 65th Cong., 2 sess., February 22, 1918, p. 2540.

26. Raymond Brandt interview with Sam Rayburn, *St. Louis Post-Dispatch*, February 11, 1951, SRL.

27. Beard, op. cit., p. 670.

Chapter 7
REPUBLICAN DOLDRUMS

1. Herbert Hoover, *The Ordeal of Woodrow Wilson*, p. 16.

2. Francis Russell, *The Shadow of Blooming Grove*, p. 306.

3. Ibid., p. 335.

4. *Boston Transcript*, November 1, 1924.

5. John Hays Hammond, Jr., to author, February 16, 1955.

6. Sam Rayburn to W. A. Thomas, January 10, 1919, SRL.

7. Woodrow Wilson, Proclamation Relinquishing Government Control of Railroads, December 24, 1919, Messages and Papers of Woodrow Wilson, *Review of Reviews*, vol. 2, 1924, p. 1159.

8. Russell, op. cit., pp. 456-57.

9. J. J. Huthmacher, *Massachusetts People and Politics, 1919–33*, p. 58.

10. Russell, op. cit., p. 437.

11. Sam Rayburn to Medibell Bartley, April 17, 1921, SRL.

12. U.S. Congress, House, *Congressional Record*, 67 Cong., 1 Sess., July 20, 1921, p. 4150.

13. House, *Congressional Record*, 67 Cong. 1 Sess., June 10, 1921, p. 2405.

14. Russell, op. cit., p. 487.

15. Sam Rayburn to Kate Thomas, February 2, 1922, SRL.

16. Sam Rayburn to W. A. Thomas, February 19, 1922, SRL.

17. See David Chalmers. *Hooded Americans:* and W. P. Randell, *KKK.*

18. U.S. Congress, Senate, Committee on Privileges and Elections, *Senate Election Cases, 1913-1940*, 76 Cong., 3 Sess., Doc. 147, pp. 200-206.

19. Sam Rayburn Speech, Scrapbooks, SRL.

20. Tom Connally and Alfred Steinberg, *My Name is Tom Connally*, p. 139.

21. *Congressional Record*, 68 Cong., 1 Sess., December 3, 4 and 5, 1923, p. 8ff.

22. Coolidge Acceptance Speech, 1924.

23. Speech, Coolidge to American Society of Newspaper Editors, January 1924.

24. Joseph Martin, *My First Fifty Years in Politics*, p. 49.

25. *The New York Times*, June 4, 1961, VI, p. 32.

26. Booth Mooney, *Roosevelt and Rayburn*, p. 16.

27. Sam Rayburn to Kate Thomas, January 30, 1927, SRL.

Chapter 8
A CLUTCH AT HAPPINESS

1. Martha Rayburn to Sam Rayburn, January 14, 1915.

2. Valton J. Young, *The Speaker's Agent*, pp. 15-16.

3. Alla Clary, Tape, SRL.

4. *Atlanta Constitution*, May 28, 1961, pp. 10-11.

5. Sam Rayburn to Lucinda Rayburn, Sunday, October 19, 1927, SRL.

6. Alla Clary, Tape, SRL.

7. Tom Connally to author, May 1953.

8. Alla Clary, Tape, SRL.

9. S. F. Leslie, Tape, SRL.

Chapter 9
COMMITTEE CHAIRMAN

1. Tom Connally and Alfred Steinberg, *My Name is Tom Connally*, p. 118.

2. Arthur Mullen, *A Western Democrat*, p. 242.

3. *Breckinridge* (Tex.) *American*, October 8, 1928.

4. Sam Rayburn Scrapbooks, SRL.

5. Walter Splawn, "Rayburn of Texas," *Bunker's Magazine*, January 1929.

6. Allan Michie and Frank Rhylick, *Dixie Demagogues*, p. 28.

7. Alla Clary, Tape, SRL.

8. *Washington Post*, Potomac Section, June 24, 1973, p. 32.

9. Eugene Lyons, *Herbert Hoover*, p. 196.

10. Calvin Coolidge's Veto Message of the McNary-Haugen Bill, 1928.

11. *The New York Times*, June 4, 1961, VI, p. 32.

12. Cordell Hull, *Memoirs*, p. 132.

13. Herbert Hoover, *Memoirs*, p. 307.

Chapter 10
IN THE KINGMAKING BUSINESS

1. Eugene Lyons, *Herbert Hoover*, p. 245.

2. Rayburn campaign sheet, 1932, SRL.

3. Tom Connally and Alfred Steinberg, *My Name is Tom Connally*, p. 135.

4. Cordell Hull, *Memoirs*, p. 132.

5. Sam Rayburn to T. W. Davidson, January 26, 1932, SRL.

6. Sam Rayburn to L. T. Carpenter, January 12, 1932, SRL.

7. Sam Rayburn to T. W. Davidson, January 26, 1932, SRL.

8. Lyons, op. cit., pp. 314–15.

9. Herbert Hoover, *Memoirs,* pp. 287–90.

10. Neil McNeil, *Forge of Democracy,* p. 82.

11. Allan Michie and Frank Rhylick, *Southern Demagogues,* p. 37.

12. James Farley, *Behind the Ballots,* p. 134.

13. Connally and Steinberg, op. cit., p. 141.

14. Sam Rayburn to Wellington Brink, June 12, 1932, SRL.

15. Connally and Steinberg, op. cit., p. 141.

16. *Bonham Daily Favorite,* July 9, 1932.

17. Valton Young, *The Speaker's Agent,* p. 17.

18. Ettie Garner to Sam Rayburn, July 24, 1932, SRL.

19. James Farley to Sam Rayburn, July 12, 1932, SRL.

20. Lyons, op. cit., p. 297.

Chapter 11
THE HUNDRED DAYS

1. William E. Leuchtenburg, *Franklin D. Roosevelt and the New Deal,* p. 30.

2. Eugene Lyons, *Herbert Hoover,* p. 295

3. Raymond Moley, *After Seven Years,* p. 83.

4. Sam Rayburn to William Bankhead, July 25, 1932, SRL.

5. Robert M. LaFollette, Jr., and Edward Costigan to Franklin D. Roosevelt, March 9, 1933. Franklin D. Roosevelt Library.

6. *Congressional Record,* 73 Cong., 1 Sess., March 9, 1933, p. 76

7. *Congressional Record,* 73 Cong., 1 Sess., March 10, 1933, pp. 213–214.

8. Louis Brownlow, *A Passion for Anonymity,* p. 391.

9. *The New York Times,* June 4, 1961, VI, p. 32.

10. Paul Mallon, column, North American Newspaper Alliance, February 3, 1934.

11. James Byrnes, *All in a Lifetime,* p. 81.

12. U.S. Congress, House, Interstate and Foreign Commerce Committee Federal Securities Act, *Hearings,* 73 Cong., 1 Sess., March-April, 1933.

13. Raymond Brandt, "Speaker Rayburn," *St. Louis Post-Dispatch,* February 11, 1951.

14. Arthur Schlesinger, *The Coming of the New Deal,* p. 442.

15. Felix Frankfurter to Franklin D. Roosevelt, May 24, 1933, SRL.

16. Franklin D. Roosevelt, *On Our Way,* p. 45.

Chapter 12
NEW DEAL WORKHORSE

1. *Business Week,* "Sam Rayburn: Using 42 Years of Savvy to Help the Democrats," December 4, 1954.

2. Paul Mallon, column, North American Newspaper Alliance, February 3, 1934.

3. Sam Rayburn campaign circular, July 10, 1932, SRL.

4. Franklin D. Roosevelt Public Papers, 1933.

5. On the first phase of the New Deal, see Arthur Schlesinger, *Coming of the New Deal;* second phase, Rexford Guy Tugwell, *Democratic Roosevelt.*

6. U.S. Congress, Senate, Banking and Currency Committee, *Stock Exchange Practices, Hearings,* 73 Cong., 2 Sess., 1934, pp. 6437-66.

7. U.S. Congress, House, Interstate and Foreign Commerce Committee, *Stock Exchange Regulation, Hearings,* 73 Cong., 2 Sess., 1934.

8. *Washington Post*, March 16, 1934.

9. Alla Clary, Tape, SRL.

10. *Congressional Record*, 73 Cong., 2 Sess., May 4, 1934, p. 8013.

11. Schlesinger, op. cit., pp. 466–67.

12. Herbert Hoover, *Memoirs*, pp. 142–43.

13. U.S. Congress, House, Interstate and Foreign Commerce Committee, *Federal Communications Commission, Hearings*, 73 Cong., 2 Sess., 1934.

14. *The New York Times*, September 8, 1934, p. 13.

15. Tom Connally and Alfred Steinberg, *My Name Is Tom Connally*, p. 124.

16. U.S. Congress, House, *Congressional Record*, 73 Cong., 2 Sess., June 15, 1934, pp. 11,792-94.

17. Ray Tucker, *Colliers*, January 5, 1935, p. 49.

18. A good source on the AAA: Schlesinger, op. cit., chap. 2–5.

19. *The New York Times*, September 13, 1934, p. 24.

20. Cecil Dickson to Sam Rayburn, October 6, 1934, SRL.

21. Ettie Garner to Sam Rayburn, October 12, 1934, SRL.

22. *The New York Times*, October 4, 1934, p. 22.

23. Ibid., December 13, 1934, p. 17.

24. Charles W. Van Devander, *The Big Bosses*, p. 261.

25. U.S. Congress, House, Interstate and Foreign Commerce Committee, *Public Utility Holding Companies, Hearings*, 74 Cong., 1 Sess., 1935.

26. *The New York Times*, March 15, 1935, p. 2.

27. Mary E. Dillon, *Wendell Willkie*, p. 61.

28. U.S. Congress, House, *Congressional Record*, 74 Cong., 1 Sess., August 1, 1935, p. 12,266.

29. *Paris* (Tex.) *News*, December 8, 1935.

30. Marion Ramsey, *Pyramids of Power*, p. 273.

31. *The New York Times*, June 12, 1935, p. 6.

32. Eleanor Roosevelt to author, July 9, 1957.

33. Mary Dillon, op. cit., p. 66.

34. Sam Rayburn, Radio Address, NBC, August 30, 1935.

Chapter 13
STRUGGLING TOWARD THE TOP

1. *Congressional Record*, 74 Congress, 2 Sess., April 9, 1936, p. 5284.

2. U.S. Congress, House, Interstate and Foreign Commerce Committee, *Rural Electrification, Hearings*, 1933.

3. John McCormack, Tape, SRL.

4. Allan Michie and Frank Rhylick, *Dixie Demagogues*, p. 39.

5. Tom Connally and Alfred Steinberg, *My Name is Tom Connally*, p. 91.

6. *Time*, September 9, 1974, p. 46.

7. Eleanor Roosevelt to Franklin D. Roosevelt, July 16, 1936, Franklin D. Roosevelt Library.

8. Sam Rayburn, Speech at Leonard, Texas, July 18, 1936, Sam Rayburn Scrapbooks, SRL.

9. Valton Young, *The Speaker's Agent*, p. 24.

10. Franklin D. Roosevelt to Sam Rayburn, September 17, 1936, in Elliott Roosevelt, ed., *FDR, His Personal Letters, 1928–1945*.

11. Eleanor Roosevelt to author, July 16, 1957.

12. Alfred Steinberg, *Mrs. R.*, p. 235.
13. Harold Ickes, *Secret Diary*, vol. 1, p. 491.
14. Ibid., vol. 2, pp. 9–10.
15. Tom Connally to author, March 18, 1953.

Chapter 14
TRIALS OF A FLOOR LEADER

1. *The New York Times,* June 4, 1961, VI, p. 32.
2. *Washington Evening Star,* January 5, 1941.
3. Joseph Alsop and Robert Kintner, "Never Leave Them Angry," *Saturday Evening Post,* January 18, 1941.
4. Robert Sherwood, *Roosevelt and Hopkins,* p. 1.
5. *Congressional Record,* 75 Cong., 1 Sess., May 27, 1937, p. 5082.
6. Tom Connally and Alfred Steinberg, *My Name is Tom Connally,* pp. 184–95.
7. Ibid., p. 188.
8. Harold Ickes, *Secret Diary*, vol. 2, p. 174.
9. Allan Michie and Frank Rhylick, *Dixie Demagogues,* pp. 39–40.
10. Connally and Steinberg, op. cit., p. 192.
11. See Louis Brownlow, *A Passion for Anonymity.*
12. Ibid., p. 391.
13. *The New York Times,* April 3, 1938, IV, p. 1.
14. Ickes, op. cit., p. 357.
15. Ibid., p. 358.
16. Brownlow, op. cit., p. 416.
17. Michie and Rhylick, op. cit., p. 63.
18. Richard Henderson, *Maury Maverick,* p. 173.
19. *Congressional Record,* 75 Cong., 2 Sess., December 17, 1937, p. 1835.
20. Franklin D. Roosevelt to Sam Rayburn, August 2, 1939, SRL.
21. *The New York Times,* August 3, 1939, p. 4.
22. Scrapbooks, 1912-1955, SRL.
23. Eugene Lyons, *Herbert Hoover,* p. 350.
24. U. S. Congress, House Document No. 247, 87 Cong., 1 Sess., 1961, p. 31.
25. Elliott Roosevelt, ed., *FDR: His Personal Letters, 1928-1945,* p. 1139.
26. Ibid., p. 1238.
27. *The New York Times,* October 15, 1938, p. 6.
28. Ibid., November 5, 1938, p. 6.

Chapter 15
SPEAKER SAM RAYBURN

1. Sam Rayburn to Medibell Rayburn Bartley, April 17, 1921, SRL.
2. Sam Rayburn to Lucinda Rayburn, 1939, SRL.
3. Cordell Hull, *Memoirs,* p. 648.
4. James Farley, *Jim Farley's Story,* p. 205; and Hull, op. cit., p. 861.
5. Sam Rayburn Day Celebration at Denison, Texas, August 22, 1939.
6. *Washington Evening Star,* June 6, 1944.
7. Harold Ickes, *Secret Diary*, vol. 2, p. 699.
8. Lyndon B. Johnson to Sam Rayburn, May 13, 1939, SRL.

9. Ickes, op. cit., vol. 3, p. 168.

10. Farley, op. cit., p. 230.

11. Ibid., p. 265.

12. *The New York Times,* July 16, 1940, p. 1.

13. Alla Clary, Tape, SRL.

Chapter 16
SAVING THE DRAFT

1. Franklin D. Roosevelt to Sam Rayburn, December 23, 1940, SRL.

2. Tom Connally and Alfred Steinberg, *My Name is Tom Connally,* pp. 241-44.

3. William C. Sullivan, "Personal Observations and Recommendations on Privacy," *Final Report,* Roscoe Pound-American Trial Lawyers Foundation, June 8, 1974, p. 95.

4. James Byrnes, *All in One Lifetime,* p. 116.

5. Joseph Martin, *My First Fifty Years in Politics*, p. 84.

6. Forest C. Pogue, *George C. Marshall, Ordeal and Hope,* p. 148.

7. David L. Cohn, "Mr. Speaker," *Atlantic Monthly,* October 1942, p. 77.

Chapter 17
THE SPEAKER'S WAY OF LIFE

1. Raymond Moley, *After Seven Years,* p. 242.

2. U.S., Congress, House, *Congressional Record,* 87 Cong., 2 Sess., January 23, 1962, p. 486.

3. Marquis Childs, *I Write from Washington,* p. 109.

4. H. G. Dulaney to author, September 7, 1974.

5. Sam Rayburn, Commencement Address, University of Virginia, May 30, 1955.

6. Franklin D. Roosevelt to Sam Rayburn, September 6, 1942, SRL.

7. *Washington Post,* April 19, 1973.

8. Lyndon Johnson to author, September 22, 1951.

9. Robert Albright, *Washington Post,* June 11, 1961.

10. Valton Young, *The Speaker's Agent,* p. 65.

11. Chester Bowles, *Promises to Keep,* p. 272.

12. Dan Inouye, *Journey to Washington,* p. 278.

13. House, *Congressional Record,* 87 Cong., 2 Sess., January 18, 1962, p. 514.

14. Alla Clary, Tape, SRL.

15. *Houston Chronicle,* January 1, 1941.

16. Carl Albert, Tape, SRL.

17. Wright Patman to author, March 1, 1975.

18. *New Republic,* July 10, 1944.

19. Clinton Anderson, *Outsider in the Senate,* p. 37.

20. Joseph Martin, *My First Fifty Years in Politics,* p. 182.

21. House, *Congressional Record,* 77 Cong., 1 Sess., January 3, 1941, p. 7.

22. Woodrow Wilson, *Congressional Government,* pp. 44–45.

23. Robert Coughlan, "Proprietors of the House," *Life,* February 14, 1955, p. 93.

24. Sam Rayburn, interview on "Capitol Cloakroom," CBS, January 30, 1951.

25. *Louisville Courier-Journal,* July 27, 1962.

26. See Samuel McCall, *Life of Thomas Reed.*

27. Carl Albert, Tape, SRL.

NOTES

28. Paul F. Healy, "They're Just Crazy About Sam," *Saturday Evening Post*, November 24, 1951, p. 70.

29. Unpublished Sam Rayburn manuscript, SRL.

30. *The New York Times*, September 22, 1940.

31. Allan Michie and Frank Rhylick, *Southern Demagogues*, p. 28.

32. Jennings Randolph to author, September 22, 1966.

33. John Phillips to author, August 21, 1950.

34. Martin Dies, *Martin Dies Story*, p. 59.

35. See Walter Goodman, *The Committee*.

36. Jerry Voorhis, *Confessions of a Congressman*, p. 63.

37. Martin, *My First Fifty Years in Politics*, p. 9.

38. Raymond Lohr and J. W. Theis, *Congress*, pp. 8–9.

39. See Lawrence Chamberlain, *The President, Congress and Legislature*. And George B. Galloway, "Next Steps in Congressional Reform," *University of Illinois Bulletin*, December 1952.

40. *Congressional Record*, 87 Cong., 2 Sess., January 18, 1962, p. 502.

41. Carl Albert, Tape, SRL.

42. Clinton Anderson, *Outsider in the Senate*, p. 40.

43. Dean Acheson, *Present at the Creation*, p: 97.

44. Victor Messall to author, April 20, 1960.

45. Wright Patman to author, April 17, 1967.

46. House, *Congressional Record*, 87 Cong., 2 Sess., January 18, 1962, p. 508.

47. George Smathers to author, October 10, 1967.

48. Robert De Vore, *Washington Post*, March 1, 1943.

49. Edward Boyd, "Mr. Speaker," *American*, April 1955, p. 90.

50. H. G. Dulaney to author, September 6, 1974.

51. Sam Rayburn Letters, SRL.

Chapter 18
THE SPEAKER'S OTHER WORLD

1. Harry Truman to author, February 10, 1960.

2. Victor Messall to author, April 5, 1960.

3. Bascom N. Timmons in a series on Sam Rayburn, *Houston Chronicle*, October 17, 1961.

4. Sam Rayburn to Franklin D. Roosevelt, January 1939, SRL.

5. Sam Rayburn to Lucinda Rayburn, September 29, 1941, SRL.

6. Bicknell Eubanks, *Christian Science Monitor*, November 1, 1961.

7. Valton Young, *The Speaker's Agent*, p. 63.

8. Buck Henson, Tape, SRL.

9. Dwight Dorough, *Mr. Sam*, p. 421.

10. Edward Boyd, "Mr. Speaker," *American*, September 1955.

11. D. B. Hardeman, "Unseen Side of the Man They Called Mr. Speaker," *Life*, December 1, 1961.

Chapter 19
SECOND MAN IN CHARGE

1. Tom Connally and Alfred Steinberg, *My Name Is Tom Connally*, pp. 248–50.

2. Franklin D. Roosevelt to Sam Rayburn, January 6, 1942, SRL.

3. Franklin D. Roosevelt to Sam Rayburn, February 18, 1942, SRL.

4. Sam Rayburn, News Conference, March 1942, SRL. And Joseph Martin, *My First Fifty Years in Politics*, pp. 100–101.

5. Henry Stimson and McGeorge Bundy, *On Active Service*, p. 614.

6. John McCormack, Tape, SRL.

7. Sam Rayburn Scrapbook, SRL.

8. *Washington Post*, March 1, 1943.

9. Sam Rayburn, speech at Terrell, Texas, August 1943, SRL.

10. Franklin D. Roosevelt to Sam Rayburn, September 16, 1942, SRL.

11. Henry A. Wallace to Sam Rayburn, August 18, 1956, SRL.

12. Henry A. Wallace to Sam Rayburn, November 8, 1961, SRL.

13. Eleanor Roosevelt to author, July 16, 1957.

14. Jonathan Daniels, *Man of Independence*, pp. 237–38.

15. Victor Messall to author, May 3, 1960.

16. Robert Sherrill, *The Accidental President*, p. 172.

17. Eleanor Roosevelt to author, July 16, 1957.

18. Daniels, op. cit., pp. 240–43. Alfred Steinberg, *Man from Missouri*, p. 204.

19. Tom Connally to author, April 7, 1953.

20. John McCormack, Tape, SRL.

21. Sam Rayburn 1944 Campaign, SRL.

22. Sam Rayburn 1944 Campaign letters, SRL.

23. Sam Rayburn Letters after 1944 Congressional Campaign, SRL.

24. Wright Patman to author, April 17, 1967.

25. Leslie Biffle to author, August 23, 1951.

26. Cordell Hull, *Memoirs*, vol. 2, pp. 1670–96.

27. Harry Truman to author, February 10, 1960.

28. William S. White, *The Responsibles*, p. 31.

Chapter 20
RAYBURN AND TRUMAN

1. Elliott Roosevelt, ed., *FDR, His Personal Letters, 1928–1945*, p. 1580.

2. Walter Millis, *The Forrestal Diaries*, p. 43.

3. Leslie Biffle to author, October 4, 1950.

4. Tom Connally to author, April 7, 1953.

5. *The New York Times*, September 15, 1934, p. 1.

6. Harry Truman to author, February 10, 1960.

7. *Dallas Morning News*, January 5, 1946.

8. Jack Bell, *Splendid Misery*, p. 352.

9. Edward Boyd, "Mr. Speaker, the Dynamo of Capitol Hill," *American*, April 1955, p. 100.

10. William S. White, *The Responsibles*, p. 51.

Chapter 21
THE MIRACLE ELECTION

1. Paul Healy, "They're Just Crazy About Sam," *Saturday Evening Post*, November 24, 1951.

2. *Life*, January, 1947.

NOTES

3. U.S. Congress, House, *Congressional Record*, 80 Cong., 1 Sess., April 17, 1947.

4. Papers of Arthur Vandenberg, p. 393.

5. Lewis Chester, *An American Melodrama*, p. 279.

6. See West Point records.

7. Harry S. Truman, *Memoirs*, vol. 2, p. 187.

8. Walter Millis, *The Forrestal Diaries*, p. 404.

9. Ibid., p. 458.

10. Leslie Biffle to author, November 9, 1950.

11. Alben Barkley to author, March 21, 1951.

12. Victor Messall to author, April 5, 1960.

13. John Garner to Sam Rayburn, May 27, 1948, SRL.

14. Victor Messall to author, April 6, 1960.

15. Letter from Justice Hugo Black to author, December 9, 1968. Black denied he had shown favoritism to Johnson. He insisted he had held an impartial hearing with Johnson's and Stevenson's lawyers and had based his decision solidly on the constitutional merits.

16. Margaret Truman, *Harry Truman*, p. 33.

17. *Sherman* (Tex.) *Democrat*, September 28, 1948.

18. Dwight Dorough, *Mr. Sam*, p. 447.

Chapter 22
THE VICTOR AT BAY

1. Harley Kilgore to author, August 3, 1950.

2. Leslie Biffle to author, January 17, 1951.

3. *Congressional Record*, 81 Cong., 1 Sess., Jan. 3, 1949, p. 9.

4. George Galloway, "Next Steps in Congressional Reform," *University of Illinois Bulletin*, December 1952, pp. 12–13.

5. Westbrook Pegler, *New York Journal*, January 3, 1949.

6. Percy Priest to author, June 14, 1949.

7. Neil MacNeil, *Forge of Democracy*, p. 433.

8. Charles Ross to author, July 17, 1950.

9. Harry Truman memorandum to Sam Rayburn, November 17, 1950, SRL.

10. Alben Barkley to author, August 28, 1950.

11. Walter George to author, July 25, 1956.

12. *Dallas Morning News*, March 25, 1951.

13. John Maguire to author, August 8, 1950.

14. Harry Truman to Sam Rayburn, April 27, 1951, SRL.

15. Harry Truman to Sam Rayburn, December 1, 1948, SRL.

16. Ibid.

17. Harry Truman to Sam Rayburn, December 2, 1947, SRL.

18. Paul Healy, "They're Just Crazy about Sam," *Saturday Evening Post*, November 24, 1951.

19. *Congressional Record*, 82 Cong., 1 Sess., January 31, 1951, p. 781.

20. Harry Truman to Sam Rayburn, May 7, 1951, SRL.

Chapter 23
TO THE WELL WITH TRUMAN

1. Arthur Vandenberg, Jr., ed., *The Private Papers of Arthur Vandenberg*, pp. 519–29.

2. Clinton Anderson, *Outsider in the Senate*, p. 40.

3. Harry Truman to Sam Rayburn, August 15, 1950, SRL.

4. Alben Barkley to author, April 26, 1951.

5. Charles G. Ross to author, July 17, 1950.

6. Tom Connally to author, May 5, 1953.

7. *The New York Times*, June 28, 1950, p. 1.

8. Tom Connally to author, May 5, 1953.

9. Ibid.

10. Drew Pearson and Jack Anderson, *The Case Against Congress*, pp. 101–2.

11. Alben Barkley to author, April 26, 1951.

12. Sam Rayburn Letters, 1951, SRL.

13. Tom Connally to author, June 9, 1953.

14. Robert Sherrill, *The Accidental President*, pp. 155–65.

15. Lyndon Johnson to author, September 22, 1951.

16. Charles Sawyer, *Concerns of a Conservative Democrat*, p. 270.

Chapter 24
IN THE MINORITY AGAIN

1. Harry Vaughan to author, September 8, 1950.

2. Tom Connally to author, April 7, 1953.

3. Ralph Yarborough to author, May 2, 1966.

4. Wright Patman to author, April 17, 1967.

5. Dwight D. Eisenhower, *Mandate for Change*, p. 21.

6. Sidney Hyman, *William Benton*, p. 478.

7. Arthur Schlesinger, *A Thousand Days*, p. 52.

8. Adlai Stevenson to Sam Rayburn, August 11, 1952, SRL.

9. *Dallas Morning News*, September 23, 1952.

10. Tom Connally and Alfred Steinberg, *My Name Is Tom Connally*, p. 360.

11. Harry Truman to Sam Rayburn, January 11, 1957, Harry S. Truman Library.

Chapter 25
THE POLITICIAN AND THE GENERAL

1. Harry Truman to author, February 10, 1960.

2. Harley Kilgore to author, June 5, 1952.

3. House, *Congressional Record*, 83 Cong., I Sess., April 21, 1953.

4. Alla Clary, Tape, SRL.

5. *The New York Times*, February 12, 1953, p. 11.

6. Dwight Eisenhower to author, January 7, 1954.

7. See Ezra Taft Benson, *Crossfire*, for numerous examples.

8. George Rothwell Brown, *San Antonio Light*, June 5, 1953.

9. Dwight Eisenhower, *Mandate for Change*, chap. 8.

10. *Congressional Record*, 83 Cong., 1 Sess., August 3, 1953.

11. John Garner to Sam Rayburn, January 4, 1954.

12. Herbert Parmet, *Eisenhower*, pp. 209–10.

13. Harry Truman to author, February 10, 1960.

14. Harry Truman to Sam Rayburn, January 11, 1957, SRL.

15. Edward Boyd, "Mr. Speaker," *American*, April 1955.

16. Ralph Yarborough to author, May 2, 1966.

17. Stewart Alsop, *Reader's Digest*, November 1958, p. 55.

18. *The New York Times*, October 24, 1954, p. 63.

19. Ibid., November 4, 1954, p. 25.
20. Ibid., October 30, 1954, p. 1.
21. Eisenhower, *Mandate for Change*, p. 437.
22. Sherman Adams, *Firsthand Report,* p. 168.
23. Robert Coughlin, "Proprietors of the House," *Life,* February 14, 1955.
24. *Washington Post,* January 14, 1955.
25. Eisenhower, *Mandate for Change*, p. 493.
26. Eisenhower, *Waging Peace*, p. 347.
27. Robert Donovan, *Eisenhower*, p. 109.
28. Eisenhower, *Mandate for Change*, p. 130.
29. Adams, op. cit., p. 25.
30. Gary Wills, *Nixon Agonistes*, p. 122.
31. Dwight Eisenhower to Sam Rayburn, November 3, 1959, SRL.
32. Dwight Eisenhower to Sam Rayburn, May 20, 1955, SRL.
33. Harry Truman to author, February 10, 1960.
34. Eisenhower Presidential News Conference, February 23, 1955.
35. Sidney Warren, *The President as World Leader*, p. 389.
36. Eisenhower, *Mandate for Change*, p. 608.
37. Eisenhower Presidential News Conference, February 23, 1955.
38. Eisenhower, *Mandate for Change*, p. 497.
39. Drew Pearson, "Washington Merry-Go-Round," March 15, 1955.
40. Richard Bolling, *Power in the House*, p. 191.

Chapter 26
RAYBURN AND JOHNSON

1. C. Dwight Dorough, *Mr. Sam*, p. 426.
2. *The New York Times*, December 5, 1954, p. 1.
3. George Smathers to author, October 10, 1967.
4. Robert Sherrill, *The Accidental President*, p. 97.
5. Adlai Stevenson to Sam Rayburn, September 30, 1955, SRL.
6. Adlai Stevenson to Sam Rayburn, January 10, 1956, SRL.
7. Adlai Stevenson to Sam Rayburn, January 23, 1956, SRL.
8. Allan Duckworth, *Dallas News*, April 2, 1956.
9. Sam Rayburn to Paul Butler, May 24, 1956.
10. Dorough, *Mr. Sam*, p. 495.
11. See O. D. Weeks, *One Party Government in 1956*.
12. Dwight Eisenhower, *Mandate for Change*, pp. 555–56.
13. Eisenhower, *Waging Peace*, p. 153.
14. Harry Truman to Sam Rayburn, October 1, 1954, SRL.
15. Carl Albert, Tape, SRL.
16. Arthur Schlesinger, *A Thousand Days*, p. 16.
17. Ibid., p. 17.
18. George Smathers to author, October 10, 1967.
19. Sam Rayburn to Frankie Randolph, August 24, 1956, SRL.
20. Sam Rayburn to Harry Truman, October 22, 1956, SRL.

Chapter 27
THE MISSION THAT FAILED

1. *The New York Times*, November 28, 1956, p. 1.
2. Robert Bendiner, *Obstacle Course on Capitol Hill,* p. 23.

3. *The New York Times*, July 27, 1956, p. 5.
4. Dwight Eisenhower, *Waging Peace*, p. 155.
5. Ibid., p. 159.
6. Ibid., p. 161.
7. *The New York Times*, January 5, 1959, p. 16.
8. Adlai Stevenson to Sam Rayburn, 1959, SRL.
9. Joseph Martin, *My First Fifty Years in Politics*, pp. 6–7.
10. Alla Clary, Tape, SRL.
11. Americans for Democratic Action Statement, October 15, 1959.
12. John Eisenhower, *Strictly Personal*, p. 225.
13. Dwight Eisenhower, *op. cit.*, p. 187.
14. Ibid., p. 180.
15. Ibid., p. 182.
16. Ibid., p. 272.
17. Ibid., p. 289.
18. Ibid., pp. 234–35.
19. John Eisenhower, op. cit., p. 225.
20. Dwight Eisenhower, op. cit., p. 557.
21. Bernard Schwartz, *The Professor and the Commissions*, pp. 223–24.
22. Dwight Eisenhower, op. cit., p. 385.
23. *Congressional Record*, 86th Cong., 1 sess., September 10, 1959, p. 18993.
24. *The New York Times*, July 7, 1959, p. 1.
25. Harry Truman to Sam Rayburn, July 8, 1959, SRL.
26. Robert Albright, *Washington Post*, July 25, 1959.
27. Eric Sevareid, "Face the Nation," CBS, March 31, 1958.
28. Theodore Sorensen, *Kennedy*, p. 92.
29. Ibid., p. 152.
30. *The New York Times*, June 4, 1961, VI, p. 32.
31. Ibid., January 3, 1960.
32. Sorensen, op. cit., p. 128.
33. Victor Riesel, in his syndicated column "Inside Labor," June 8, 1960.
34. Harry Truman to Sam Rayburn, January 11, 1957, SRL.
35. Harry Truman to Sam Rayburn, June 30, 1960, SRL.
36. Buck Henson, Tape, SRL.
37. Alla Clary, Tape, SRL.
38. Dwight Eisenhower to Sam Rayburn, May 14, 1960, SRL.
39. Buck Henson, Tape, SRL.
40. Dwight Dorough, *Mr. Sam*, p. 565.
41. Wright Patman to author, April 17, 1967.
42. *Fort Worth Star Telegram*, November 2, 1960.
43. Larry King, "My Hero," *Harper's*, October 1966.
44. Sorensen, op. cit., p. 193.
45. John F. Kennedy to Sam Rayburn, September 14, 1960.

Chapter 28
NOT A FUR PIECE FROM FLAG SPRINGS

1. Robert Albright, *Washington Post*, June 11, 1961.
2. *Texas*, American Guide Series, pp. 108–9.
3. *Readers' Digest*, "The Testing of a President," March 1962.

NOTES

4. Theodore Sorensen, *Kennedy*, p. 239.

5. Ibid., p. 340.

6. Carl Albert, Tape, SRL.

7. Robert S. Allen and Paul Scott in the syndicated column, "The Allen-Scott Report," January 9, 1961.

8. *The New York Times*, February 1, 1961, p. 1.

9. Robert Kennedy to author, September 22, 1966.

10. Sorenson, op. cit., p. 341.

11. Arthur Schlesinger, *A Thousand Days*, p. 651.

12. *Congressional Record*, 87 Cong., 1 Sess., May 3, 1961, pp. 7194–7195.

13. Albright, *Washington Post*, June 11, 1961.

14. Buck Henson, Tape, SRL.

15. Alla Clary, Tape, SRL.

16. Dwight Eisenhower to Sam Rayburn, February 23, 1961, SRL.

17. Dwight Eisenhower to Sam Rayburn, March 21, 1961, SRL.

18. Sam Rayburn, ABC "Face the Nation," July 16, 1961.

19. Sorensen, op cit., p. 341.

20. Edward Weintal and Charles Bartlett, *Facing the Brink*, p. 71.

21. *U.S. News and World Report*, October 9, 1961.

22. Leonard Baker, The Johnson Eclipse, pp. 69–70.

23. Sam Rayburn's bank checks for 1961, SRL.

24. *Summary of the Legislative Record*, 87th Cong., 1st sess., 1961, S. Doc. 62.

25. Richard Bolling to author, February 27, 1975.

26. Harry Truman to Kate Thomas and Medibell Bartley, SRL.

Bibliography

In addition to the sources listed in the Acknowledgments, there were also notes from previous visits to the F.D.R. Library at Hyde Park, New York, the Harry S. Truman Library at Independence, Missouri, plus the riches at the Library of Congress in Washington, D. C.

Besides correspondence, interviews, and records, such as wills and the Speaker's worksheet on the rostrum for the day, other primary source material included the Proceedings of the House of Representatives, Austin, Texas, Thirtieth, Thirty-first and Thirty-second Legislatures, 1907–1912- the *Congressional Record* from 1913 when Rayburn first came to Congress through the First Session of the Eighty-seventh Congress in 1961; and hearings and reports of the House Commerce Committee, on which he served from 1913 through 1936.

Alinsky, Sol D., *John L. Lewis*, New York, 1949
Acheson, Dean, *Present at the Creation*, New York, 1969
Acheson, Sam, *Joe Bailey: The Last Democrat*, New York, 1932
Adams, Samuel H., *Incredible Era: The Life and Times of Warren Gamaliel Harding*, New York, 1939
Adams, Sherman, *First-Hand Report*, New York, 1961
Albertson, Dean, ed., *Eisenhower as President*, New York, 1963
Alsop, Joseph, and Catledge, Turner, *The 168 Days*, New York, 1938
American Guide Series (Works Progress Administration)
    Tennessee, New York, 1940
    Texas, New York, 1940
    Virginia, New York, 1940

BIBLIOGRAPHY

Anderson, J. W., *Eisenhower, Brownell and the Congress: The Tangled Origins of the Civil Rights Bill of 1956–1957*, University, Alabama, 1964

Anderson, Jack and May, Ronald, *McCarthy: The Man, the Senator, and the "Ism,"* Boston, 1952

Bagby, Wesley, *Road to Normalcy*, Baltimore, 1962

Bailey, Thomas, *Woodrow Wilson and the Lost Peace*, New York, 1944

Baker, Leonard, *The Johnson Eclipse*, New York, 1966

Baker, Ray Stannard, *American Chronicle: Autobiography*, New York, 1945

—, *Woodrow Wilson: Life and Letters*, 8 vols., Garden City, 1927–1939

Barber, Hollis W., *The United States in World Affairs 1955*, New York, 1957

Barkley, Alben, *That Reminds Me*, New York, 1954

Bartley, Numan V., *The Rise of Massive Resistence: Race and Politics in the South during the 1950s*, Baton Rouge, 1969

Beal, John R., *John Foster Dulles*, New York, 1959

Beals, Carlton, *The Great Revolt and Its Leaders: History of Popular American Uprisings in the 1890s*, New York, 1968

Bell, Coral, *Negotiation from Strength*, New York, 1963

Bell, Jack, *The Johnson Treatment*, New York, 1965

—, *Splendid Misery*, New York, 1960

Bendiner, Robert, *Obstacle Course on Capitol Hill*, New York, 1964

—, *White House Fever*, New York, 1960

Benson, Ezra Taft, *Crossfire*, New York, 1962

Berding, Andrew, *Dulles on Diplomacy*, Princeton, 1965

Bledsoe, James M., *A History of Mayo and his College*, Commerce, Texas, 1946

Bloom, Sol, *Autobiography*, New York, 1948

Blum, John M., *From the Morgenthau Diaries, 1928–1938*, Boston, 1959

—, *Joe Tumulty and the Wilson Era*, Boston, 1951

Bolling, Richard, *House Out of Order*, New York, 1965

—, *Power in the House*, New York, 1968

Boorstin, Daniel J., *Genius of American Politics*, New York, 1953

Bowers, Claude, *My Life*, New York, 1962

Bowles, Chester, *Promises to Keep*, New York, 1971

Boykin, Edward, *The Wit and Wisdom of Congress*, New York, 1961

Brandeis, Louis D., *Other People's Money and How the Bankers Use It*, New York, 1914

—, *The Curse of Bigness*, New York, 1934

Brown, Stuart, *Adlai E. Stevenson*, New York, 1965

Brownlow, Louis, *A Passion for Anonymity*, Chicago, 1958

Bryan, William Jennings, *Memoirs*, New York, 1925

Burns, James M., *Roosevelt: The Lion and the Fox*, New York, 1956.

—. *Roosevelt: Soldier of Freedom*, New York, 1970.

—. *John Kennedy*, New York 1959.

Byrnes, James F., *All in One Lifetime*, New York, 1958

—, *Speaking Frankly*, New York, 1947

Caridi, Ronald, *The Korean War and American Politics*, Philadelphia, 1968

Carr, Robert K., *The House Committee on Un-American Activities, 1945–1950*, New York, 1952

Chalmers, David, *Hooded Americans*, New York, 1965

Chambers, Wittaker, *Witness*, New York, 1952

Chamberlain, Lawrence, *The President, Congress and Legislation*, New York, 1958

Childs, Marquis, *Eisenhower: Captive Hero*, New York, 1958
—, *I Write From Washington*, New York, 1942
Clark, Champ, *My Quarter Century of American Politics*, 2 vols, New York, 1921
Connally, Tom and Steinberg, Alfred, *My Name is Tom Connally*, New York, 1954
Cook, Fred J., *The Nightmare Decade: The Life and Times of Senator Joe McCarthy*, New York, 1971
Coolidge, Calvin, *Autobiography*, New York, 1929
Costello, William, *The Facts about Nixon*, New York, 1961
Cotner, Robert, *James Stephen Hogg*, Austin, 1959
Cox, James M., *Journey Through My Years*, New York, 1946
Cranston, Ruth, *The Story of Woodrow Wilson*, New York, 1945
Cuneo, Ernest, *Life with Fiorello*, New York, 1955
Coyle, David C., *Ordeal of the Presidency*, New York, 1960
Daniels, Jonathan Daniels, *Man of Independence*, New York, 1950
—, *End of Innocence*, New York, 1954
Daniels, Josephus, *Tarheel Editor*, New York, 1939
Daugherty, Harry, *Story of the Harding Tragedy*, New York, 1932
Davis, Kenneth, *Politics of Honor, A Biography of Adlai E. Stevenson*, New York, 1967
Dillon, Mary, *Wendell Willkie*, Philadelphia, 1952
Dixon, George, *Leaning on a Column*, Philadelphia, 1961
Donovan, Robert, *Eisenhower: The Inside Story*, New York, 1956
Dorough, C. Dwight, *Mr. Sam*, New York, 1962
Douglas, Paul, *In the Fullness of Time*, New York, 1971
Douglas, William O., *Democracy and Finance*, New York, 1940
—, *Go East, Young Man*, New York, 1974
Eisenhower, Dwight, *Mandate for Change*, New York, 1963
—, *Waging Peace*, New York, 1965
Eisenhower, John, *Strictly Personal*, New York, 1974
Evans, Rowland, and Novak, Robert, *Lyndon B. Johnson: Exercise of Power*, New York, 1966
Farley, James, *Behind the Ballots*, New York, 1939
—, *Jim Farley's Story*, New York, 1948
Feis, Herbert, *The China Tangle*, New York, 1953
Finer, Herman, *The Presidency*, New York, 1960
Flynn, John T., *The Roosevelt Myth*, New York, 1956
Flynn, Edward J., *You're the Boss*, New York, 1947
Forrestal, James, and Millis, Walter, *Forrestal Diaries*, New York, 1951
Friedel, Frank, *Franklin D. Roosevelt*, 4 vols., Boston, 1952, 1954, 1956, 1973
Galloway, George, *Congress at the Crossroads*, New York, 1946
—, *History of the House of Representatives*, New York, 1968
Garner, John N., *Behind the Ballots*, New York, 1938.
Garraty, John, *Henry Cabot Lodge*, New York, 1956
—, *Woodrow Wilson*, New York, 1968
Gompers, Samuel, *Seventy Years of Life and Labor: An Autobiography*, New York, 1925
Gray, Robert, *Eighteen Acres Under Glass*, New York, 1961
Gunther, John, *Inside USA*, New York, 1947
—, *Roosevelt in Retrospect*, New York, 1950
Halle, Louis, *The Cold War as History*, New York, 1967
Haynes, George, *The Senate of the United States*, 2 vols., Boston, 1938

BIBLIOGRAPHY

Henderson, Richard, *Maury Maverick*, Austin, 1970
Hicks, John, *The Populist Revolt*, Minneapolis, 1931
Hinshaw, David, *Herbert Hoover*, New York, 1950
Hofstadter, Richard, *Age of Reform*, New York, 1956
Hoover, Herbert, *Memoirs*, 3 vols., New York, 1951–1952
—, *Ordeal of Woodrow Wilson*, New York, 1958
Houston, David F., *Eight Years with Wilson's Cabinet*, 2 vols, Garden City, 1926
Hughes, Emmet J., *Ordeal of Power*, New York, 1963
Hull, Cordell, *Memoirs*, 2 vols., New York, 1948
Huthmacher, J. J., *Massachusetts People and Politics, 1919–1933*, Cambridge, 1959
Hyman, Sidney, *William Benton: The lives of*, Chicago, 1969
Ickes, Harold, *Secret Diary*, 3 vols., New York, 1953–1954
—, *Autobiography of a Curmudgeon*, New York, 1943
Inouye, Dan, *Journey to Washington*, Englewood Cliffs, New Jersey, 1967
James, Marquis, *Mr. Garner of Texas*, Indianapolis, 1939
Johnson, Walter, *1600 Pennsylvania Avenue*, Boston, 1960
—, *Papers of Adlai E. Stevenson*, Vol. 4, Boston, 1974
Jones, Jesse H., and Angly, Edward, *Fifty Billion Dollars*, New York, 1951
Koenig, Louis, *The Truman Administration*, New York, 1956
—, *Bryan*, New York, 1971
Kornitzer, Bela, *American Fathers and Sons*, New York, 1952
Krock, Arthur, *In the Nation, 1932–1966*, New York, 1966
—, *Memoirs: Sixty Years on the Firing Line*, New York, 1968
LaFeber, Walter, *America, Russia and the Cold War, 1945-1966*, New York, 1967
LaFollette, Belle and LaFollette, Fola, *Robert LaFollette*, 2 vols., New York, 1953
Lerner, Max, *Ideas Are Weapons*, New York, 1939
Lewis, Anthony, *Portrait of a Decade*, New York, 1964
Leuchtenburg, William E., *Franklin D. Roosevelt and the New Deal*, New York, 1963
Lief, Alfred, *Brandeis*, New York, 1936
Lindley, Ernest K., *Franklin D. Roosevelt: A Career in Progressive Democracy*, New York, 1932
Link, Arthur, *The New Freedom*, Princeton, 1956
—, *Woodrow Wilson and the Progressive Era*, New York, 1954
Longworth, Alice Roosevelt, *Crowded Hours*, New York, 1933
Lord, Russell, *Wallaces of Iowa*, Boston, 1947
Lyons, Eugene, *Herbert Hoover*, New York, 1964
MacNeil, Neil, *Forge of Democracy*, New York, 1963
Martin, Joe, *My First Fifty Years in Politics*, New York, 1960
Mason, Alpheus, *Brandeis*, New York, 1946
Maverick, Maury, *A Maverick American*, New York, 1937
Mazo, Earl, *Nixon*, New York, 1959
McAdoo, William G., *Crowded Years*, New York, 1931
McCall, Samuel W., *Life of Thomas B. Reed*, Boston, 1914
McCoy, Donald, *Calvin Coolidge: The Quiet President*, New York, 1967
McKay, Seth S., *Texas Politics, 1906–1944*, Lubbock, 1952
—, *Texas and the Fair Deal*, San Antonio, 1954
—, *W. Lee O'Daniel and Texas Politics, 1938–1942*, Lubbock, 1944
McKenna, Marian C., *Borah*, Ann Arbor, 1961
Michie, Allan A. and Rhylick, Frank, *Dixie Demagogues*, New York, 1939
Michelson, Charles, *The Ghost Talks*, New York, 1944

Millis, Harry A. and Brown, E. C., *From the Wagner Act to Taft-Hartley*, New York, 1950

Moley, Raymond, *After Seven Years*, New York, 1939

—, *27 Masters of Politics*, New York, 1949

Mooney, Booth, *Roosevelt and Rayburn*, Philadelphia, 1971

Mullen, Arthur, *A Western Democrat*, New York, 1946

Myers, W. S. and Newton, W. H., *The Hoover Administration*, New York, 1936

Nalle, Ouida Ferguson, *The Fergusons of Texas*, San Antonio, 1946

Neustadt, Richard E., *Presidential Power*, New York, 1960

Nixon, Richard, *Six Crises*, New York, 1962

Noggle, Burl, *Teapot Dome: Oil and Politics in the 1920s*, Baton Rouge, 1962

Norris, George W., *Fighting Liberal, An Autobiography*, New York, 1945

Pearson, Drew and Allen, Robert T., *Washington Merry-Go-Round*, New York, 1932

Pearson, Drew and Anderson, Jack, *The Case Against Congress*, New York, 1968

Phillips, Cabell, ed., *Dateline Washington*, New York, 1949

—, *The Truman Presidency*, New York, 1966

Pogue, Forest C., *George C. Marshall, Ordeal and Hope, 1939–1942*, New York, 1971

—, *Organizer of Victory, 1943–1945*, New York, 1973

Pringle, Henry F., *Alfred E. Smith*, New York, 1927

Randell, W. P., *The KKK*, Philadelphia, 1965

Robinson, William A., *Thomas B. Reed, Parliamentarian*, New York, 1930

Rogow, Arnold, *James Forrestal*, New York, 1963

Roosevelt, Franklin D., *His Personal Letters*, 4 vols., New York, 1947–1950

—, *On Our Way*, New York, 1934

Roper, Dan C., *Fifty Years of Public Life*, Durham, North Carolina, 1941

Rovere, Richard, *Affairs of State: The Eisenhower Years*, New York, 1956

Russell, Francis, *The Shadow of Blooming Grove: Warren G. Harding in his Times*, New York, 1968

Sawyer, Charles, *Concerns of a Conservative Democrat*, Carbondale, Illinois, 1968

Saloutos, Theodore, *Farmer Movements in the South, 1875–1933*, Berkeley, 1960

—, *Populism, Reaction or Reform*, New York, 1968

Schlesinger, Arthur, Jr., *A Thousand Days*, Boston, 1965

—, *Age of Roosevelt*, 3 vols., Boston, 1957, 1959, 1960

Schriftgiesser, Karl, *This Was Normalcy*, Boston, 1948

Schwartz, Bernard, *Professor and the Commissions*, New York, 1959

Sherwood, Robert, *Roosevelt and Hopkins, An Intimate History*, New York, 1948

Slosson, Preston W., *The Great Crusade and After, 1914–1928*, New York, 1930

Smith, Arthur D. H., *Mr. House of Texas*, New York, 1940

Smith, Merriman, *A President Is Many Men*, New York, 1948

Smith, Rixie and Beasley, Norman, *Carter Glass*, New York, 1939

Spanier, J. W., *The Truman-MacArthur Controversy*, Cambridge, 1959

Steinberg, Alfred, *Douglas MacArthur*, New York, 1961

—, *Dwight D. Eisenhower*, New York, 1968

—, *Herbert Hoover*, New York, 1967

—, *Man From Missouri: The Life and Times of Harry S. Truman*, New York, 1962

—, *Mrs. R.*, New York, 1958

—, *Sam Johnson's Boy: A Close-Up of the President from Texas*, New York, 1968

—, *The Bosses*, New York, 1973

— and Connally, Tom, *My Name Is Tom Connally*, New York, 1954

Stimson, Henry and Bundy, McGeorge, *On Active Service*, New York, 1948

Stokes, Thomas L., *Chips Off My Shoulder*, Princeton, 1940

BIBLIOGRAPHY

Sullivan, Mark, *Our Times, The United States, 1900–1925*, 6 vols., New York, 1926–1935
Taylor, Carl, *The Farmers' Movement, 1620–1920*, New York, 1953
Timmons, Bascom, *Garner of Texas*, New York, 1948
Texas State Historical Association, *The Handbook of Texas*, 2 vols., Chicago, 1952
Truman, Harry, *Years of Decision*, New York, 1955
—, *Years of Trial and Hope*, New York, 1956
Truman, Margaret, *Harry S. Truman*, New York, 1973
Tugwell, Rexford G., *The Democratic Roosevelt*, New York, 1957
Tully, Grace, *FDR, My Boss*, New York, 1949
Vandenberg, Arthur, Jr., ed., *The Private Papers of Senator Vandenberg*, Cambridge, 1952
Van Devander, Charles, *The Big Bosses*, New York, 1944
Voorhis, Jerry, *Confessions of a Congressman*, New York, 1947
Warren, Gaylord H., *Herbert Hoover and the Great Depression*, New York, 1959
Wechsler, James, *Labor Baron: A Portrait of John L. Lewis*, New York, 1944
Wecter, Dixon, *Age of the Great Depression*, New York, 1948
Weeks, O. D., *One Party Government in 1956*, Austin, 1957
—, *Texas in the 1960 Presidential Election*, Austin, 1961
—, *Texas Presidential Politics in 1952*, Austin, 1953
Weintal, Edward, and Bartlett, Charles, *Facing the Brink*, New York, 1967
Whalen, Richard, *The Founding Father*, New York, 1964
Wheeler, Burton K., *The Yankee From the West*, New York, 1962
White, William Allen, *Autobiography*, New York, 1946
—, *Puritan in Babylon*, New York, 1938
White, William S., *The Professional*, Boston, 1964
Willoughby, William, *The St. Lawrence Waterway*, Madison, Wisconsin, 1961
Wilson, Edith B., *My Memoirs*, Indianapolis, 1938
Woodward, C. Vann, *Tom Watson*, New York, 1938
—, *Origins of the New South, 1877–1913*, New York, 1951
Wyeth, John A., *That Devil Forrest*, New York, 1959
Young, Valton J., *The Speaker's Agent*, New York, 1956

Other written sources consulted included the following newspapers:
The *Austin Daily Tribune, Bonham Daily Favorite, Dallas Morning News, Denison Herald, Fort Worth Star-Telegram, Houston Chronicle, Houston Post, San Antonio Express* and *Sherman Democrat* in Texas; outside the state: *The New York Times, New York Herald Tribune, Washington Post, Washington Star* and *Washington Times-Herald.*

Of the magazines, those examined extensively were the *American Mercury, Atlantic Monthly, Business Week, Collier's, Fortune, Harper's Monthly, Life, Look, Nation, Newsweek, New Republic, Reader's Digest, Reporter, Saturday Evening Post, Southwest Review, Time* and *U.S. News and World Report.*

Index

INDEX

378

Federal Bureau of Investigation (FBI),
167
Federal Communications Act, 116, 130
Federal Communications Commission,
118–120, 182–183, 218, 284
Federal Crop Insurance Corporation, 53
Federal Deposit Insurance Corporation
(FDIC), 18, 115
Federal Emergency Relief Adminis-
tration (FERA), 109, 140
Federal Farm Board, 91
Federal Indian Claims Commission, 291
Federal Land Banks, 110
Federal Loan Agency, 149
Federal Power Commission, 267, 270
Federal Reserve Bank system, 49
Federal Reserve Bill, 49, 57
Federal Security Agency, 149
Federal Theater Project, 191
Federal Trade Commission, 45, 46, 48,
113, 117, 118, 125, 142, 165, 320
Ferdinand, Archduke Frances, 58
Finnegan, Jim, 307, 312
Fireside Chats, 175
Fletcher, Duncan U., 116, 117
Flynn, Ed, 219
Food, Drug and Cosmetic Bill, 154
Food Stamp Plan, 153–154
Forbes, Charles R., 69
Ford, Gerald, 317
Ford, Henry, 88
Fordney-McCumber Tariff Bill, 68
Formosa (Taiwan), 259, 281, 292, 293
Formosa Resolution, 292, 293, 294
Forrest, Nathan Bedford, 3
Forrestal, James V., 117, 242, 243
France, 310
World War II, 157, 161, 166, 210
Franco, Francisco, 156
Frankfurter, Felix, 112–113, 114, 129
Franklin, Benjamin, 299
Frazier-Lemke Act, 142
Fremont, John, 29
Frieze, E. K., 11
Fuel Bill, 137
Fulbright, William, 320

Gadsden, Philip H., 127
Galbraith, Bliven, 163
Gardner, Sam, 15–17
Garner, John Nance, 49, 55, 73, 83, 89,
94, 120, 124, 151, 191, 192, 195, 378

Connally and, 133
Hoover and, 93–95
Johnson and, 159
on labor, 149
Rayburn and, 32–35, 45, 84–86, 89–
103, 106–107, 132–133, 135–136,
158, 160–162, 178, 189, 247,
284–285, 344
Roosevelt and, 92, 96–103, 143–146,
149, 158, 160, 161
on tariffs, 40–41
Truman and, 196
Garner, Mrs. John Nance, 77, 124, 132,
133, 189, 247
"Garner's Pork Barrel Triplets," 95
Garrett, Finis J'., 73, 84
Gauntz, Roy, 206
General Accounting Office (GAO), 68
Germany, 256, 344
World War I, 58–59, 61
World War II, 156, 157, 160, 161,
166, 167, 169, 191, 194, 209–
212, 214, 231–232
GI insurance program, 59
Gillett, Frederick H., 63–64, 73, 85
Gilmer, Claude, 274
Gilmore, Clarence E., 20, 21
Glass, Carter, 49–50, 57
Glass-Steagall Banking Act, 115
Goldwater, Barry, 284
Gompers, Samuel, 54, 60, 64, 71
Goober, J. B., 26
Gore, Albert, 307, 308
Great Britain, 91, 113, 305–306, 310
World War I, 58
World War II, 157, 161, 164, 166,
167, 210, 212
Great Depression, 88–154
Greater Houston Ministerial
Association, 331
Greece, 238–239, 260
Greenville (Texas) *Banner*, 243
Greenville Herald, 221–222
Gregory, Thomas W., 56, 61
Grey, Edward, 57
Grundy, Joseph, 87
Guffey, Joseph F., 124–125, 137–138,
201
Guffey Bituminous Coal Commission
Act, 143, 146
Guffey Coal Bill, 138

INDEX